Transference and Countertransference Today

Why has Heinrich Racker's original work on transference and counter-transference proven so valuable?

With a passionate concern for the field created by the meeting of analyst and patient, and an abiding interest in the central importance of transference and countertransference in analytic practice, Robert Oelsner has brought together the thought and work of seventeen eminent analysts from Europe, the United States, and Latin America.

In new essays commissioned for this volume, the writers have set aside the lines that can often divide psychoanalytic groups and schools in order to examine in depth the variety of approaches and responses that characterize the best analytic practice today. The result is a collection of fresh, contemporary material centered on the two interrelated subjects – transference and countertransference – that make up the core of psychoanalytic work. Both in the clarity of their language and in moving clinical examples, the writers reveal in distinctively personal ways how Heinrich Racker's original thought, which brought the analyst's unconscious responses into the equation, has allowed them to evolve their own perspectives. Yet it is particularly interesting to find unexpected parallels among the chapters that point toward a shared vision. Clearly, whether in work with adults or children, transference and countertransference are now seen as encompassing a field that embraces both participants in the consulting room.

Making *Transference and Countertransference Today* still more valuable as a resource for teachers and students are several major contributions by authors whose work is not otherwise readily available in English. Psychoanalysts and others will find few books that present such a thoughtful picture of these crucial and fascinating analytic topics.

Robert Oelsner, a fellow of the Buenos Aires Psychoanalytic Association, is a training and supervising analyst and faculty at the Northwestern Psychoanalytic Society, Seattle. He is also a supervising analyst at PINC in San Francisco, and guest faculty at the Child and Adolescent Program of the San Francisco Center for Psychoanalysis. He teaches in both the United States and in Europe.

THE NEW LIBRARY OF PSYCHOANALYSIS
General Editor: Alessandra Lemma

The New Library of Psychoanalysis was launched in 1987 in association with the Institute of Psychoanalysis, London. It took over from the International Psychoanalytical Library which published many of the early translations of the works of Freud and the writings of most of the leading British and Continental psychoanalysts.

The purpose of the New Library of Psychoanalysis is to facilitate a greater and more widespread appreciation of psychoanalysis and to provide a forum for increasing mutual understanding between psychoanalysts and those working in other disciplines such as the social sciences, medicine, philosophy, history, linguistics, literature and the arts. It aims to represent different trends both in British psychoanalysis and in psychoanalysis generally. The New Library of Psychoanalysis is well placed to make available to the English-speaking world psychoanalytic writings from other European countries and to increase the interchange of ideas between British and American psychoanalysts. Through the *Teaching Series*, the New Library of Psychoanalysis now also publishes books that provide comprehensive, yet accessible, overviews of selected subject areas aimed at those studying psychoanalysis and related fields such as the social sciences, philosophy, literature and the arts.

The Institute, together with the British Psychoanalytical Society, runs a low-fee psychoanalytic clinic, organizes lectures and scientific events concerned with psychoanalysis and publishes the *International Journal of Psychoanalysis*. It runs a training course in psychoanalysis which leads to membership of the International Psychoanalytical Association – the body which preserves internationally agreed standards of training, of professional entry, and of professional ethics and practice for psychoanalysis as initiated and developed by Sigmund Freud. Distinguished members of the Institute have included Michael Balint, Wilfred Bion, Ronald Fairbairn, Anna Freud, Ernest Jones, Melanie Klein, John Rickman and Donald Winnicott.

Previous general editors have included David Tuckett, who played a very active role in the establishment of the New Library. He was followed as general editor by Elizabeth Bott Spillius, who was in turn followed by Susan Budd and then by Dana Birksted-Breen.

Current members of the Advisory Board include Liz Allison, Giovanna Di Ceglie, Rosemary Davies and Richard Rusbridger.

Previous Members of the Advisory Board include Christopher Bollas, Ronald Britton, Catalina Bronstein, Donald Campbell, Sara Flanders, Stephen Grosz, John Keene, Eglé Laufer, Alessandra Lemma, Juliet Mitchell, Michael Parsons, Rosine Jozef Perelberg, Mary Target and David Taylor.

ALSO IN THIS SERIES

Impasse and Interpretation Herbert Rosenfeld
Psychoanalysis and Discourse Patrick Mahony
The Suppressed Madness of Sane Men Marion Milner
The Riddle of Freud Estelle Roith
Thinking, Feeling, and Being Ignacio Matte Blanco
The Theatre of the Dream Salomon Resnik
Melanie Klein Today: Volume 1, Mainly Theory Edited by Elizabeth Bott Spillius
Melanie Klein Today: Volume 2, Mainly Practice Edited by Elizabeth Bott Spillius
Psychic Equilibrium and Psychic Change: Selected Papers of Betty Joseph Edited by Michael Feldman and Elizabeth Bott Spillius
About Children and Children-No-Longer: Collected Papers 1942–80 Paula Heimann. Edited by Margret Tonnesmann
The Freud–Klein Controversies 1941–45 Edited by Pearl King and Riccardo Steiner
Dream, Phantasy and Art Hanna Segal
Psychic Experience and Problems of Technique Harold Stewart
Clinical Lectures on Klein and Bion Edited by Robin Anderson
From Fetus to Child Alessandra Piontelli
A Psychoanalytic Theory of Infantile Experience: Conceptual and Clinical Reflections Eugenio Gaddini. Edited by Adam Limentani
The Dream Discourse Today Edited and introduced by Sara Flanders
The Gender Conundrum: Contemporary Psychoanalytic Perspectives on Femininity and Masculinity Edited and introduced by Dana Breen
Psychic Retreats John Steiner
The Taming of Solitude: Separation Anxiety in Psychoanalysis Jean-Michel Quinodoz
Unconscious Logic: An Introduction to Matte-Blanco's Bi-logic and Its Uses Eric Rayner
Understanding Mental Objects Meir Perlow
Life, Sex and Death: Selected Writings of William Gillespie Edited and introduced by Michael Sinason
What Do Psychoanalysts Want?: The Problem of Aims in Psychoanalytic Therapy Joseph Sandler and Anna Ursula Dreher
Michael Balint: Object Relations, Pure and Applied Harold Stewart
Hope: A Shield in the Economy of Borderline States Anna Potamianou
Psychoanalysis, Literature and War: Papers 1972–1995 Hanna Segal
Emotional Vertigo: Between Anxiety and Pleasure Danielle Quinodoz
Early Freud and Late Freud Ilse Grubrich-Simitis
A History of Child Psychoanalysis Claudine and Pierre Geissmann
Belief and Imagination: Explorations in Psychoanalysis Ronald Britton
A Mind of One's Own: A Psychoanalytic View of Self and Object Robert A. Caper

Psychoanalytic Understanding of Violence and Suicide Edited by Rosine Jozef Perelberg

On Bearing Unbearable States of Mind Ruth Riesenberg-Malcolm

Psychoanalysis on the Move: The Work of Joseph Sandler Edited by Peter Fonagy, Arnold M. Cooper and Robert S. Wallerstein

The Dead Mother: The Work of André Green Edited by Gregorio Kohon

The Fabric of Affect in the Psychoanalytic Discourse André Green

The Bi-Personal Field: Experiences of Child Analysis Antonino Ferro

The Dove that Returns, the Dove that Vanishes: Paradox and Creativity in Psychoanalysis Michael Parsons

Ordinary People, Extra-ordinary Protections: A Post Kleinian Approach to the Treatment of Primitive Mental States Judith Mitrani

The Violence of Interpretation: From Pictogram to Statement Piera Aulagnier

The Importance of Fathers: A Psychoanalytic Re-Evaluation Judith Trowell and Alicia Etchegoyen

Dreams That Turn Over a Page: Paradoxical Dreams in Psychoanalysis Jean-Michel Quinodoz

The Couch and the Silver Screen: Psychoanalytic Reflections on European Cinema Andrea Sabbadini

In Pursuit of Psychic Change: The Betty Joseph Workshop Edited by Edith Hargreaves and Arturo Varchevker

The Quiet Revolution in American Psychoanalysis: Selected Papers of Arnold M. Cooper Arnold M. Cooper, Edited and Introduced by Elizabeth L. Auchincloss

Seeds of Illness and Seeds of Recovery: The genesis of suffering and the role of psychoanalysis Antonino Ferro

The Work of Psychic Figurability: Mental States without Representation César Botella and Sára Botella

Key Ideas for a Contemporary Psychoanalysis: Misrecognition and Recognition of the Unconscious André Green

The Telescoping of Generations: Listening to the Narcissistic Links Between Generations Haydée Faimberg

Glacial Times: A Journey through the World of Madness Salomon Resnik

This Art of Psychoanalysis: Dreaming Undreamt Dreams and Interrupted Cries Thomas H. Ogden

Psychoanalysis and Religion in the 21st Century: Competitors or Collaborators? David M. Black

Recovery of the Lost Good Object Eric Brenman

The Many Voices of Psychoanalysis Roger Kennedy

Feeling the Words: Neuropsychoanalytic Understanding of Memory and the Unconscious Mauro Mancia

Constructions and the Analytic Field: History, Scenes and Destiny Domenico Chianese

Projected Shadows: Psychoanalytic Reflections on the Representation of Loss in European Cinema Edited by Andrea Sabbadini

Encounters with Melanie Klein: Selected Papers of Elizabeth Spillius Elizabeth Spillius

Yesterday, Today and Tomorrow Hanna Segal

Psychoanalysis Comparable and Incomparable: The Evolution of a Method to Describe and Compare Psychoanalytic Approaches David Tuckett, Roberto Basile, Dana Birksted-Breen, Tomas Böhm, Paul Denis, Antonino Ferro, Helmut Hinz, Arne Jemstedt, Paola Mariotti and Johan Schubert

Time, Space and Phantasy Rosine Jozef Perelberg

Rediscovering Psychoanalysis: Thinking and Dreaming, Learning and Forgetting Thomas H. Ogden

Mind Works: Techniques and Creativity in Psychoanalysis Antonino Ferro

Doubt, Conviction and the Analytic Process: Selected Papers of Michael Feldman Michael Feldman

Melanie Klein in Berlin: Her First Psychoanalyses of Children Claudia Frank

The Psychotic Wavelength: A Psychoanalytic Perspective for Psychiatry Richard Lucas

Betweenity: A Discussion of the Concept of Borderline Judy Gammelgaard

The Intimate Room: Theory and Technique of the Analytic Field Giuseppe Civitarese

Bion Today Edited by Chris Mawson

Secret Passages: The Theory and Technique of Interpsychic Relations Stefano Bolognini

Intersubjective Processes and the Unconscious: An Integration of Freudian, Kleinian and Bionian Perspectives Lawrence J. Brown

Seeing and Being Seen: Emerging from a Psychic Retreat John Steiner

Avoiding Emotions, Living Emotions Antonio Ferro

Projective Identification: The Fate of a Concept Edited by Elizabeth Spillius and Edna O'Shaughnessy

Creative Readings: Essays on Seminal Analytic Works Thomas H. Ogden

The Maternal Lineage Edited by Paola Mariotti

Donald Winnicott Today Edited by Jan Abram

Symbiosis and Ambiguity: A Psychoanalytic Study Edited by John Churcher, José Bleger and Leopoldo Bleger

Psychotic Temptation Liliane Abensour

Supervision in Psychoanalysis: The Sao Paulo Seminars Antonino Ferro

Transference and Countertransference Today Edited by Robert Oelsner

TITLES IN THE NEW LIBRARY OF
PSYCHOANALYSIS TEACHING SERIES

Reading Freud: A Chronological Exploration of Freud's Writings Jean-Michel
  Quinodoz
Listening to Hanna Segal: Her Contribution to Psychoanalysis Jean-Michel
  Quinodoz
Reading French Psychoanalysis Edited by Dana Birksted-Breen, Sara Flanders
  and Alain Gibeault
Reading Winnicott Lesley Caldwell and Angela Joyce
Initiating Psychoanalysis: Perspectives Bernard Reith, Sven Lagerlöf, Penelope
  Crick, Mette Møller and Elisabeth Skale
Infant Observation Frances Salo
Reading Anna Freud Nick Midgley

TITLES IN THE NEW LIBRARY OF
PSYCHOANALYSIS 'BEYOND THE COUCH' SERIES

Under the Skin: A Psychoanalytic Study of Body Modification Alessandra Lemma
Engaging with Climate Change: Psychoanalytic and Interdisciplinary Perspectives
  Edited by Sally Weintrobe
*Research on the Couch: Single Case Studies, Subjectivity, and Psychoanalytic
  Knowledge* R. D. Hinshelwood
Psychoanalysis in the Technoculture Era Edited by Alessandra Lemma and
  Luigi Caparrotta

THE NEW LIBRARY OF PSYCHOANALYSIS

General Editor: Alessandra Lemma

Transference and Countertransference Today

Edited by Robert Oelsner

Routledge
Taylor & Francis Group

LONDON AND NEW YORK

First published 2013
by Routledge
27 Church Road, Hove, East Sussex BN3 2FA

Simultaneously published in the USA and Canada
by Routledge
711 Third Avenue, New York, NY 10017

Routledge is an imprint of the Taylor & Francis Group, an Informa business

British Library Cataloguing in Publication Data
A catalogue record for this book is available from the British Library

Library of Congress Cataloging in Publication Data
Transference and countertransference today / edited by Robert Oelsner.
pages cm
Includes bibliographical references and index.
1. Transference (Psychology) 2. Countertransference (Psychology) I. Oelsner, Robert, editor of compilation.
RC489.T73T7273 2013
616.89--dc23
2012048872

ISBN: 978-0-415-83070-6 (hbk)
ISBN: 978-0-415-83071-3 (pbk)
ISBN: 978-0-203-49467-7 (ebk)

Typeset in Bembo
by Saxon Graphics Ltd, Derby

Contents

Contributors   xi

Foreword   xvii
CLÁUDIO LAKS EIZIRIK

Acknowledgments   xxi

Introduction   1
ROBERT OELSNER

1   Observations on countertransference as a technical
instrument: Preliminary communication   18
HEINRICH RACKER

2   Transference-countertransference: A testimony   30
R. HORACIO ETCHEGOYEN

3   "Well, you'd better ask them": The countertransference
position at the crossroads   49
HAYDÉE FAIMBERG

4   Countertransference: A contemporary approach from
the River Plate region   68
ABEL FAINSTEIN

5   Freud's countertransference? Reviewing the case histories
with modern ideas of transference and countertransference   88
R. D. HINSHELWOOD

Contents

6 Misconceptions, enactment, and interpretation   106
HEINZ WEISS

7 Transference on the couch   127
ALESSANDRA LEMMA

8 Some reflections on transference and countertransference:
The effects of social political violence in children, in the
analyst, and in the psychoanalytic process   150
YOLANDA GAMPEL

9 Transference and countertransference in child analysis   177
MIRTA BERMAN-OELSNER

10 The psychoanalytic covenant: "Human sacrifice" as the
hidden order of transference ↔ countertransference   196
JAMES S. GROTSTEIN

11 Transference – or caesura?   215
ARNALDO CHUSTER

12 Transference minute to minute: Analysis of an analysis   236
ROBERT OELSNER

13 Nonverbal cues in transference-countertransference
interactions: Reflections on their role in the analytic
process   256
THEODORE J. JACOBS

14 The analyst's self-reflective participation and the
transference-countertransference matrix   269
STEVEN COOPER

15 Role-reversal and the dissociation of the self:
An exploration of a somewhat neglected transference-
countertransference dynamic   289
FRANCO BORGOGNO AND MASSIMO VIGNA-TAGLIANTI

16 Psychoanalysis and the influencing machine:
Psychoanalysis as the influencing machine   314
ADRIENNE HARRIS

17 Transference and countertransference with somatic patients   333
MARILIA AISENSTEIN

Index   354

Contributors

Marilia Aisenstein is a training and supervising analyst of the Paris Psychoanalytical Society and the Hellenic Society. She is a past president of the Paris Psychosomatic Institute and is coeditor of the *Revue Française de Psychosomatique*. She now teaches in the Paris Psychosomatic Institute IPSO-MARTY and is in private practice, and has written articles and books in the field of psychoanalytical psychosomatics. She is presently the European representative to the Executive Committee of the International Psychoanalytic Association.

Mirta Berman-Oelsner is a fellow of the Buenos Aires Psychoanalytic Association and the Northwestern Psychoanalytic Society in Seattle. She is a training analyst and supervisor as well as an IPA Certified Child and Adolescent Psychoanalyst. She is faculty at the Northwestern Psychoanalytic Society Institute and guest faculty of the Child and Adolescent Psychoanalytic Program at the San Francisco Center for Psychoanalysis.

Franco Borgogno, PhD, is a training and supervising analyst of the Italian Psychoanalytical Society, and full professor of clinical psychology at the University of Turin, Italy. He is associate editor and on the editorial board of many European, North American, and South American psychoanalytic journals and the author of numerous books, including *Psychoanalysis as a Journey*, *The Vancouver Interview*, and *The Young Lady Who Committed Hara-Kiri and Other Clinical and Historical Essays* (Karnac, 2013). In 2010 he was chosen to receive the Mary S. Sigourney Award for outstanding contributions to psychoanalysis.

Arnaldo Chuster, MD, is a doctor in psychiatry and medical psychology, a member of the Brazilian Psychiatric Association, and a psychoanalyst and training and teaching analyst at the Rio de Janeiro Psychoanalytic Society, Brazil. An honorary member and professor at the Wilfred Bion Institute in Porto Alegre, he coordinates study groups on the work of Wilfred Bion in Rio de Janeiro, Porto Alegre, and Ribeirão Preto, and has published 150 papers and seven books. His most recent book is *O Objeto de Psicanálise: mudar o paradigma em psicanálise* (The Psychoanalytic Object: Changing the Paradigm in Psychoanalysis).

Steven Cooper is a training and supervising analyst at the Boston Psychoanalytic Institute; supervising analyst and faculty, Massachusetts Institute for Psychoanalysis; clinical associate professor, Harvard Medical School; and joint editor-in-chief of *Psychoanalytic Dialogues*. He is the author of two books, *Objects of Hope: Exploring Possibility and Limit in Psychoanalysis* (2000), and *A Disturbance in the Field: Essays in Transference–Countertransference Engagement* (2010).

Cláudio Laks Eizirik, MD, PhD, is associate professor in the Department of Psychiatry at the Federal University of Rio Grande do Sul, in Brazil, and the former dean of the medical school. A training and supervising analyst in the Porto Alegre Psychoanalytic Society, he is a former president of the International Psychoanalytic Association and of FEPAL (Federación Psicoanalitica de América Latina). In his many writings he is particularly interested in analytic technique and training, the human life cycle and aging, and the interrelation of psychoanalysis and culture.

R. Horacio Etchegoyen obtained his MD from the Universidad Nacional de La Plata. He is a training and supervising psychoanalyst of the Buenos Aires Psychoanalytic Association, and honorary professor of the University of Buenos Aires. A past president of APdeBA, the Argentine Psychoanalytic Association, he was president of the International Psychoanalytical Association from 1993 to 1997, and since 2010 has been the honorary vice president of the IPA. A recipient of the Mary S. Sigourney Award in 1999, in 2011 he received the IPA's award for Outstanding Scientific Achievement. His book *Fundamentals of Psychoanalytical Technique* (Fundamentos de la técnica psicoanalítica) is now available in English, Portuguese, Italian, and French, with German and Romanian editions in preparation.

Haydée Faimberg, MD, is a training and supervising analyst with the Société psychanalytique de Paris and the Asociación Psicoanalítica Argentina, and a former vice-president of the IPA. She is in private practice in Paris. Using a concept she initially coined for listening in the session, she created what came to be called the Haydée Faimberg "listening to listening" method for clinical group discussions. A recipient of the Haskell Norman Award in 2005, she has written on transmission of trauma between generations, the psychic consequences of Nazism in psychoanalytic patients, Lewis Carroll and Italo Calvino, and is a contributing author to fifteen books; her best-known book is *The Telescoping of Generations: Listening to the Narcissistic Links between Generations* (Routledge, 2005).

Abel Fainstein is a full member, training analyst, and former president of the Argentine Psychoanalytical Association, Buenos Aires (2000–2004), where he directed the H. Racker Clinic during the same years. He has served as chair of the Chicago IPA Congress program committee, and regional co-chair of the Rio de Janeiro IPA Congress program committee. He is a member of the Education Section of the *International Journal of Psychoanalysis*; board member of the Masters Degree Program in Psychoanalysis, USAL-APA; and professor of the Masters Degree Program in Psychoanalysis at La Matanza University, AEAPG, in Argentina.

Yolanda Gampel is a training and supervising analyst and a professor in the faculty of Social Sciences, Department of Psychology and the Program of Advanced Psychotherapy, Sackler Medical School, Tel-Aviv University. She is past president of the Israel Psychoanalytic Society; vice-president, European Federation of Psychoanalysis; and the Representative for Europe, on the board of the International Psychoanalytic Association. She is a recipient of the Hayman International Prize for Published Work Pertaining to Traumatized Children and Adults (2001), and the Mary S. Sigourney Award (2006). She works as a researcher and psychoanalyst in the field of the impact of sociopolitical violence on children and adolescents, and is the author of books and articles on this theme.

James S. Grotstein is a clinical professor of psychiatry at the David Geffen School of Medicine, UCLA, and training and supervising analyst at the Psychoanalytic Center of California and the New

Center for Psychoanalysis. He is the author of numerous papers and books that have mainly emphasized the works of Melanie Klein, Wilfred Bion, and W. R. D. Fairbairn. His most recent works are *A Beam of Intense Darkness: Wilfred Bion's Legacy to Psychoanalysis* (2007), and *… But at the Same Time and on Another Level … Psychoanalytic Technique in the Kleinian/Bionian Mode*, Volumes I and II (Karnac, 2009). Two recent papers include "Dreaming as a Curtain of Illusion: Revisiting the Royal Road with Bion as Our Guide" (2009), and "Envy and Gratitude Revisited," currently in press.

Adrienne Harris, PhD, is faculty and supervising analyst at the New York University Postdoctoral Program in Psychoanalysis and Psychotherapy, and at the Psychoanalytic Institute of Northern California. She is the author of *Gender as Soft Assembly* (2005), and with Steven Botticelli the coeditor of *First Do No Harm: The Paradoxical Encounters of Psychoanalysis, Warmaking, and Resistance* (Routledge, 2010). She and Lewis Aron edit the Routledge Relational Book Series, including most recently *Innovation and Expansion* (2005) and *Evolution of Process* (2011).

R. D. Hinshelwood is a fellow of the British Psychoanalytical Society, and has worked for many years in the National Health Service as a consultant psychotherapist with a special interest in therapeutic communities, as well as in private psychoanalytic practice. He has written on Kleinian psychoanalytic theory and technique, as well as the application of psychoanalysis to social science; currently he is interested in developing methods of using clinical material as research data. For a bibliography and more on his work in clinical psychoanalysis, psychotherapy, and the history of psychoanalysis, see his website, www.RDHinshelwood.net.

Theodore J. Jacobs is a training and supervising analyst of the New York Psychoanalytic Institute and the Institute for Psychoanalytic Education, and clinical professor of psychiatry, Albert Einstein College of Medicine. He is the author of *The Use of the Self: Countertransference and Communication in the Analytic Situation*, and coeditor of *On Beginning an Analysis*.

Alessandra Lemma is a fellow of the British Psychoanalytical Society. She is director of the Psychological Therapies Development

Unit, Tavistock and Portman NHS Foundation Trust, and clinical lead of the Psychological Interventions Research Centre at University College, London. She is Honorary Professor of Psychological Therapies in the School of Health and Human Sciences at Essex University, and visiting professor in the Psychoanalysis Unit, University College, London. She is the editor-in-chief of the journal *Psychoanalytic Psychotherapy: Applications, Theory and Research* (Routledge), and the editor of the *New Library of Psychoanalysis* book series (Routledge).

Robert Oelsner is a fellow of the Buenos Aires Psychoanalytic Association, a training and supervising analyst at the Northwestern Psychoanalytic Society in Seattle, a member and supervising analyst at the Psychoanalytic Institute of Northern California, and is also guest faculty at the Child and Adolescent Program of the San Francisco Center for Psychoanalysis. He is co-author of *Bion Conocido/Desconocido* (Bion: The Unknown/Known), and *Melanie Klein en Buenos Aires*, and author of numerous articles on theory, psychopathology, and technique. He teaches regularly in America where he relocated in 2003, and in Europe. He has a private practice in Seattle.

Heinrich Racker (1910–1961) was a training analyst and the former director of the Psychoanalytic Institute of the Argentine Psychoanalytic Association. His pioneering works on countertransference include among many others the articles "A Contribution to the Problem of Countertransference" (1952), "The Meanings and Uses of Counter-transference" (1953), and the book *Übertragung und Gegenübertragung: Studien zur psychoanalytischen Technik*, his most widely known work, which was published in English as *Transference and Countertransference* in 1968.

Massimo Vigna-Taglianti is a child neuropsychiatrist and full member of the Italian Psychoanalytic Society. He has served as the chief of the Psychiatric Day Hospital of the Child Neuropsychiatry Division, Turin University, and adjunct professor of Child Neuropsychiatry in Aosta University, Val d'Aosta, Italy. In his private practice he works with children, adolescents, and adults. In his clinical work and in his writings he is particularly interested in transference-countertransference dynamics, and above all in role-reversal phenomena, as well as in the meaning of actions and play in psychoanalysis.

Heinz Weiss, MD, is a psychoanalyst and member of the Deutsche Psychoanalytische Vereinigung and the DGPT; a guest member of the British Psychoanalytical Society, he is the director of the Department of Psychosomatic Medicine, Robert-Bosch-Krankenhaus, Stuttgart, Germany. He teaches at the University of Tübingen and is a member of the editorial board of *Psychoanalytic Psychotherapy*, and the Education Section of the *International Journal of Psychoanalysis*. Among his other publications he edited a Festschrift for Hanna Segal (1999) and is coeditor of the series *Perspektiven Kleinianischer Psychoanalyse* (Perspectives of Kleinian Psychoanalysis). His most recent book is *Das Labyrinth der Borderline-Kommunikation. Klinische Zugänge zum Erleben von Raum und Zeit* (The Labyrinth of Borderline Communication: Clinical Explorations into the Experience of Time and Space), from Klett-Cotta, Stuttgart, 2009.

Foreword

Cláudio Laks Eizirik

"The almost inexhaustible topic of transference ... " (p. 99) was the way Freud chose to begin his classical paper of 1912 on transference and its dynamics; today we could easily add countertransference to this description, and perhaps this quality of abundance can give us a first glimpse into the remarkable work of Robert Oelsner, who has put together seventeen essays from as many authors–analysts from a wide range of different theoretical persuasions who share their approaches to these fascinating issues whose extent, even today, remains almost inexhaustible.

When we approach each one of the book's chapters and attempt to get in touch with each author's perspective on these issues, it is impossible to avoid at least two different questions. First, what has this chapter to do with the others? And, second, is there anything in common among these papers aside from the fact that they deal with two similar words and their related concepts?

It seems to me that apart from the central concepts of the unconscious and the role of dreams, no other notions are as relevant for psychoanalysis as transference and countertransference today. So let me try to address these two questions.

Apart from dealing with the meaning of the two related words themselves, each of these chapters tells a story, and each of these stories reveals something similar. It is the story of how each author followed his or her way, first in the personal work of understanding these qualities of the mind, and then through their transformation in the field of analytic practice, and in doing so making use of a notion that was not fully understood by Freud. Here we can observe how transference and countertransference have challenged our most creative authors to develop and give a deeper meaning to something that was only partially perceived in those pioneering days. Moreover this meaning is not fixed, as we can see in this book, and it is still a work in progress, with space for different paths and as a consequence for different approaches in analytic practice.

Another relevant issue is the fact that the authors are from different regions and different analytic cultures. This could be seen as a weakness or as a strength. It would be a weakness if we were to consider that the book does not present a homogeneous view, or that it fails to follow the thought of a specific analytic school. However it would show the book's strength if we consider that the very notion of the existence of some kind of homogeneous view or central analytic school is currently a sort of a myth, since what we see in our time is an active search for dialogue among analysts of the same region and especially between analysts from different regions, regardless of their theoretical influences. A leading trend of our analytic community these days is an active search for opportunities to listen to the other and to try to understand the logic of views different from ours. One of the pioneers of psychoanalysis in Brazil, Mario Alvarez Martins, once said that he saw the analytic movement as a kind of international foundation that has the aim of developing not only continuous research but also mutual conversations on the main analytic concepts. In this he was not referring to an institution but to an intellectual enterprise without borders. In my view, what we have here corresponds exactly to what he had in mind, and I believe this is one of the main strengths of this book.

In each analyst's development it is also possible that the discovery of these two concepts repeats the sequence of their historical appearance; first one learns to understand the meaning of transference and its different forms, then countertransference is slowly understood and takes its relevant role in the analytic process – or, to be more precise, from a modern view, in the analytic field, as originally described by Willy and Madeleine Baranger, and further developed by other authors. However, Robert Oelsner did something different here: he decided to begin with Heinrich Racker's preliminary communication on countertransference – published here for the first time in English – as a way of introducing a different approach. This made me think about Winnicott's notion that there is no such thing as a baby, in the sense that we cannot understand a baby without his mother. And in fact what can be seen as something relevant for our current view is that we are also dealing with two simultaneous or inseparable phenomena; we owe a lot to Racker, an analyst whose writings brought about a paradigm change. In general, both Racker and Paula Heimann are considered the two authors who first offered this new perspective and opened a new path; but in my view, despite their almost simultaneous initial proposals for considering the central role of countertransference, it was Racker who mainly devoted his creative efforts, by way of a group of papers, to examining, deepening, and clarifying the full extent of this concept for our analytic practice.

So we have here an astute selection of authors who deal with transference and countertransference from distinct theoretical perspectives, and who also address the relevance of these experiences in adult and child patients, their social implications, and some of their specific configurations, as for example in psychosomatic patients, and ways of dealing with nonverbal clues, as well as some specific contemporary developments according to some of our more creative authors from Europe, Latin America, and North America.

Another major strength of the book is its clinical material. In these chapters we can follow how each of the authors not only conveys to us his or her way of conceptualizing transference and counter-transference, but also tells us how he or she deals with them in clinical practice. The more detailed the clinical accounts are, the more useful they are in clarifying the approach, as we are invited to take part in these lively analytic encounters and try to put ourselves in the author's mind and to feel and think or at least to imagine the way he or she was feeling or thinking in these important analytic moments.

Sometimes we hear or read that there is a crisis in psychoanalysis, and that it is no longer as relevant as in earlier years, or no longer an effective method to deal with emotional suffering, while others assert that its main foundations are no longer part of the main theoretical ideas of our time. It is even argued that psychoanalysis is old-fashioned, outdated, and does not fit into the contemporary zeitgeist. As I have been repeatedly stating, I cannot see this crisis in any of the realms of psychoanalysis. Nevertheless, when I have the opportunity of reading a book like *Transference and Countertransference Today* I feel reassured that our discipline is far from being in any state of crisis. What we can find here is precisely a careful and detailed study of what have proven to be, from their first introduction, two of the most relevant analytic concepts. We have the privilege of observing how each continues to follow its ongoing evolution according to different theoretical views, while having the benefit of learning more about the different ways they can be understood and used in the consulting room. In my view, we are all indebted to Robert Oelsner and his colleagues for this remarkable achievement, one that beautifully illustrates the way that psychoanalysis is and continues to be a lively and creative work in progress.

Acknowledgments

I would like to express my debt of gratitude to all the co-authors of this volume for the excellence of their contributions and for their willingness to work with me as a team to bring this book to fruition. Additional thanks go to my copyeditor, Sigrid Asmus, who brought her care for analytic thought and language to the authors and their writing, and whose professional expertise and advice were invaluable, and to Kate Hawes, Kirsten Buchanan, and Susannah Frearson at Routledge, and proofreaders Sarah Fish and Martin Barr for their patience and expertise. Finally, a special acknowledgment must go to Alessandra Lemma for her support and encouragement from the first day I discussed my project with her.

We are also grateful for permission to reprint the following material:

Heinrich Racker

We thank the *Revista de Psicoanálisis* of the Argentine Psychoanalytic Association for their kind permission to translate and publish Racker's "Observations on Countertransference as a Technical Instrument: Preliminary Communication" in Chapter 1. The article was first published in Spanish as "Observaciones sobre la contratransferencia como instrumento técnico: Comunicación preliminar," in *Revista de Psicoanálisis*, 9(3), 1952: 342–354.

We also wish to thank Valeria Muscio and Robert Oelsner for their translation of the original Spanish text.

Haydée Faimberg

Portions of Chapter 3 were first published in "A Plea for a Broader Concept of Nachträglichkeit" in © *Psychoanalytic Quarterly*, 76(4), 2007: 1221–1240.

Judith Filc

For Chapter 4, we thank Judith Filc for her translation of Abel Fainstein's original Spanish text.

Heinz Weiss

Portions of Chapter 6 were first published in Chapter 7 of the author's book, *Das Labyrinth der Borderline-Kommunikation. Klinische Zugänge zum Erleben von Raum und Zeit* (The Labyrinth of Borderline Communication: Clinical Explorations into the Experience of Time and Space), pp. 133–150. © Klett-Cotta (Stuttgart, 2009).

Ursula Haug

For Chapter 6, we thank Ursula Haug for her translation of Heinz Weiss's original German text.

Yolanda Gampel

Portions of Chapter 8 appeared in the author's book *Ces parents qui vivent à travers moi: Les enfants des guerres* © La librairie Arthème Fayard (Paris, 2005). We thank the publisher for their kind permission to publish this chapter in English.

Steven Cooper

Portions of Chapter 14 appeared earlier in *A Disturbance in the Field: Essays in Transference-Countertransference Engagement* (Routledge, 2010).

INTRODUCTION

Robert Oelsner

When two personalities meet, an emotional storm is created.
W. R. Bion, 1979

It must have been Buenos Aires 1976 when as a second-year candidate I presented a case to the clinical seminar[1] in my institute. It was a patient who came to me referred by someone I had never heard of, and I reported to the group that when I opened the door to him I immediately thought he was a robber who would break into my office and from there to my home, a floor below. After two meetings I decided to take him in for analysis but changed my fee policy just for him, asking him to pay in advance. In the seminar, Professor Evelson – who had been analyzed by Heinrich Racker – said we needed to look at the meaning of my distrust, which had caused my policy change, in order to understand what it told us about the patient. For one month the patient came dutifully to all of his appointments but each time he came he claimed he had forgotten to bring the payment. At the end of that month I decided to interrupt his treatment, since he had not paid – and I thought he never would. My initial view of him as a robber certainly weighed strongly in my decision. It took me some years to see that this is what countertransference is about, and that my intuition, which did prove to be correct, led me to perform the role of an object – like many people in his life – that had treated him poorly and then dropped him. I am certain that that is what my teacher, in line with Racker's thought, had tried to say to me.

1

Three years later, as a young graduate, I presented my first analytic paper, entitled "The countertransference of the analyst to the patient who cannot dream" (Oelsner, 1979). Now I described my experience with an adolescent who had a schizophrenic breakdown, toward whom I experienced strong murderous impulses. It took me a while to realize that my feelings were provoked by his way of crushing with his fingers the buds of a fern in my office, one that I grew with great care, and that his destructive behavior reflected his attack on his and my own inchoate thoughts, a process that was at the core of his psychotic disorder. Soon he started to bring in a passport photo of his that he carefully placed on the couch each session while he and I were sitting in chairs at the side, now observing the flattened, inanimate him. This illuminated my understanding of his tragic illness: in my reaction I must have embodied his own murderous superego – Bion's "super" ego proper of schizophrenia.[2] Some years later I was able to see that not only does the analyst have countertransference fantasies toward the patient, but that the patient often responds to these unspoken messages.

Somewhere between these two analyses I treated an adult patient with a severe borderline condition who became my first control case. This man, very odd in both his behavior and appearance, would lie on the couch in a dissociative state and not speak for long periods while my own mind wandered away. Or so it seemed. When he managed to say something – every now and then – he would only report visual images he was having, as if he lived in an ongoing dream state. One day before his hour I found myself considering painting the ceiling above the staircase that led to the floor of my office. That day the patient came in and lay down inertly as he customarily did and said nothing while the time went on. In my distraction I thought again about the staircase and tried to imagine how a painter would manage to place a ladder there and then climb it to whitewash the ceiling. I was stunned when my distraction was interrupted by the patient's voice reciting mechanically: "I can see a painter on the top of a ladder with a can of white paint painting a ceiling." While I could explain the first two experiences by resorting to what I had learned about countertransference, this last one was beyond my intellect. Twenty years later I am aware that two papers on intuitive reception and analytic work were the result of my interest in these matters (Oelsner, 1993, 1995). The interest in the mysteries of communication between patient and analyst has never left me. This volume in fact embodies my interest in its most recent form.

2

It is to be noted that Freud's German word for transference is *Übertragung*, which, when used in conjunction with the prefix *Gedanken*, thus *Gedankenübertragung*, means extrasensorial communication or telepathy. In three little-known articles he elaborates on these matters (Freud, 1921, 1922, 1933), and concludes by stating to his audience:

> There is, for instance, the phenomenon of thought-transference, which is so close to telepathy and can indeed without much violence be regarded as the same thing. It claims that mental processes in one person—ideas, emotional states, conative impulses—can be transferred to another person through empty space without employing the familiar methods of communication by means of words and signs.
>
> (1933, p. 39)

Both Marilia Aisenstein and Adrienne Harris in their chapters touch on these matters, relating them to unconscious communications from mind to mind in regressive states – transference and countertransference in a double-arrow relationship. James S. Grotstein writes about the hidden order of transference and countertransference and analytic work as a form of exorcism, here exorcism of the destructive spirits that haunt the patient's mind. Theodore Jacobs describes the nonverbal bodily clues through which analysts and patients alike pick up unconscious thoughts (*Gedanken*) from each other. R. D. Hinshelwood has managed to capture and define three subtle steps by which he considers transference to produce countertransference enactments in the analyst in response to the patient. Like Jacobs, Aisenstein, and others in this volume, he also sees the two-way communication in which patients pick up unconscious clues relating to the analyst, just as the analyst picks up theirs. There seems to be an agreement among most of us that transference and countertransference are unconscious emissions – and receptions – but a difference may be noted in whether we believe that these are based on nonverbal or paraverbal signs that we may pick up in unconscious ways, or whether we entertain the possibility of some direct communication between one unconscious and another.

Horacio Etchegoyen points out that transference of the very early stages of the mind can only emerge in paraverbal or preverbal modes, and thus demands changes both in the mode of observation and in the recollection of the corresponding clinical material (see also Oelsner, this volume). However, it is not only those transferences belonging to the early strata of the mind that are pre- or paraverbally transmitted. What is repressed will also circumvent the censorship of the superego, resorting to nonverbal codifications or encoded communications to free itself from the prison of the unconscious and then revealing its meaning to the analyst. Freud's analysis of hysteric conversions is an eloquent example of this kind of encoded language. What remains to be differentiated, however, in order to further understand the level of ego function, is whether and to what extent the language of an unconscious content has reached a symbolic representation.

The clinical illustration Jacobs offers in his chapter reveals that not only does the patient communicate in nonverbal codes, but that the analyst also communicates in this way to the patient, just as Balint and Balint (1939) suggested when they described all the circumstances through which analysts may reveal themselves and their personalities, usually far more and more often than they are aware of. I recall here a new patient who, on seeing the box of tissues on the couch, exclaimed, "Oh, so you are expecting patients to cry, I see!"[3] The conceptions I have brought in so far consider transference and countertransference as a link, a channel of communication between patient and analyst, thus making them two parts of the same phenomenon (see also Chuster, this volume).

Transference

Having just discussed transference and countertransference as a mode of communication I now want to explore what is and what is not transference according to its content, as information that circulates between patient and analyst. Melanie Klein (1952) and Betty Joseph (1985) speak of transference as a total situation. This does not mean that everything that the patient brings to analysis is transference, but rather that the transference of the patient's total situation from the infantile past to the present needs to be teased out from the totality of the material in the session. Etchegoyen adds to this that not everything that a patient brings from the past is transference. It can sometimes belong to the realm of his experience, which enhances understanding rather than hinders it. He also goes on to say that what is new in an analysis − that is, the psychic change that occurs along with the

experience of understanding and being understood – is not transference, and we certainly all hope that this newness will come about.
Etchegoyen, Grotstein, Aisenstein, and Mirta Berman-Oelsner use
the term transference to indicate the manifestation in the session of the
clinical neurosis coming from the infantile neurosis. I take it that the
same is true with regard to perversion, psychosis, somatosis, and other
states. Berman-Oelsner agrees with the British Kleinians that
transference is the externalization of patients' internal object relations
and their psychic reality, which includes its historical roots, while
Alessandra Lemma makes a slightly different point, suggesting that our
view of the present is filtered through the lens of our internal world
and its ongoing internal dramas (see also Oelsner [2011] where I argue
a similar view). So we can see different conceptions, the one broadly
speaking, where a cluster of unconscious phantasies from the infantile
past or its present version in the internal world get actualized in the
analytic process, the other in which internal infantile situations make
up the viewpoint from which a patient observes and understands what
is going on in the analytic relation. I believe that these two conceptions
are not mutually exclusive but may be different gradients of the
manifestation of the unconscious.

Berman-Oelsner sees that children actively bring their transferences
in the form of the mechanism we know as projective identification.
This explains itself due to the fact that young children are closer to the
state in which verbal representation in the preconscious is yet
incompletely achieved. They transfer not only onto the analyst but
also onto their toys in the analytic playroom in very creative ways.
What a child does with his toys and with his analyst is revealing of the
transference if the analyst is trained to understand this prevailing
nonverbal encodification. She elaborates further by remarking that
parents of children make their own transferences onto the treatment,
although the analyst is not in a position to interpret to them. The
immaturity of a child allows us to have a vantage point from which to
observe transference almost in its pure culture, but of course transference
via projective identification occurs in adult treatments as well.

An additional range of transference contents is noted by Harris,
Gampel, and Faimberg, who extend the scope of transference from
the classically accepted view to the intergenerational past, which is
implied in Grotstein's chapter as well. For Harris and Gampel the
sociohistorical past that speaks through the transference is particularly
that which has been unassimilated – traumatic – in past generations.

When it is impossible for traumatic events to be comprehended in their time, they cannot be restored to the generational history and therefore cannot become history to the patient. Such events remain like foreign bodies; they are conveyed in their unmetabolized form to the next generations, who receive them in their unconscious minds. The unspoken trauma then results in a range of clinical phenomena, one of which is the transference situation. Gampel speaks of the presence of such events as radioactive, referring to the dangerous toxicity of the generational traumas that the psyche is unable to see or understand. Harris sees the influencing machine as the similarly invisible impingement of the violence of the industrial revolution on minds unable to metabolize it.

These latter contributions, moreover, extend the conception of transference to the unmetabolized past in which the transference relation becomes an opportunity to relive, make sense of, and assimilate into the self its history as history for the first time.

In addition these conceptions both Harris and Gampel include as content of the transference current traumatic events that affect analyst and patient alike and that may exert an influence on the analytic process but remain unrecognized by both participants. This consideration extends Freud's "blind spot" (1912) from its origin in a conflict in the analyst between internal structures to include a conflict with external reality, Freud's third master served by the ego. This raises the question of whether present external reality may remain a continuing trauma – and hence unmetabolized by the analyst – or so anxiety ridden that it is denied, leaving the analyst paralyzed to help his patient. In instances of this kind transference and countertransference merge concordantly, leaving both patient and analyst in the lurch.

I would like to illustrate this through my work with a patient during the military dictatorship in Argentina when analysts and patients alike lived in danger from the terrorism of the state. While we were hearing unofficially that people were being kidnapped by the paramilitary forces and disappeared, the patient, who indeed belonged to the resistance, began to bring nightmares about friends of his being violently pulled out of their homes by some shadowy figures. While both he and I were in actual danger, which must have terrified us, we were unwilling to face the reality that either of us might no longer be there the next session, which we denied by saying "till tomorrow" at the end of each hour. It took my supervisor – one of whose family members had in those days actually disappeared – to help me to recognize my denial. Only then I could help the patient to wake up from his nightmares and be able to face the traumatic social reality we were both living in. This constitutes an example of unrecognized transference phenomena due to the counter-resistance of the analyst, for whom the external reality and the patient's transference manifestation coalesced and paralyzed his insight.

Several of the chapters in this volume address another important question, namely whether transference is or is not "created" in the analytic setting. Chuster considers transference as that which lies in between patient and analyst, calling this in-between area the 'caesura', a term he takes from Bion. How one answers this question depends on what one means by transference. Bion's statement that "when two personalities meet, an emotional storm is created" (1979, p. 321) may suggest that the encounter creates a new product. From a different perspective also relational analysts agree with a new product being formed, like a co-creation of an infantile drama emanating from the internal worlds of analyst and analysand. Several contributors (Chuster, Harris, Fainstein, Cooper, Oelsner) refer to the analytic field created by the passionate meeting of analyst and patient. By passionate I refer to Bion's emotional links of Love, Hate, and Knowledge suffusing the analytic relationship. From Chuster's and Bion's point of view, transference is in itself an evolution (or an attempt to move, I would say) from the infinite unknown into the analytic situation. It is neither a facsimile nor simply a shift from the past to the present, but rather a transformation from the unknown toward or into something apprehendable, or what Bion calls a transformation from O to K.[4] This evolution, if we call it transference, would regularly have an effect of surprise when met by the analytic couple if both are open to the new knowledge coming from the past unknown.

Another fairly new development comes from a wider acceptance of the psyche or some rudimentary mind existing already before birth (Bion, 1991b). According to this view it should not seem strange to us that even prenatal vestiges might emerge and evolve in the transference into more mature thoughts. Chuster's patient W, whose mother was in a coma between his sixth and eighth month of gestation, showed in the transference evidence of this intrauterine experience, while the analyst in his countertransference identified with the comatose mother.

In psychosis the transformation of experience into thoughts is reversed. What we may observe instead in the transference is the result of the struggle of the mind "against" its ability to know and think, a form of counter-intelligence. In this respect Chuster reminds us of Bion's transformation in hallucinosis – that is, the ability of the psyche to make narcissistic substitutions so that a self-created product takes the place of knowledge of reality. Weiss, drawing on Money-Kyrle's concept of "misconceptions," gives an account of a patient's delusional transference at a time in her analysis where she could not bear a painful experience of loss. Situations of this kind then force us to recognize that while we would hope transference to be the royal road to the understanding of the unconscious, it sometimes sadly becomes only the muddy alley in which analysts can get caught. Even so, having different vertices will allow one to look into these complex transference situations with some hope to help patients get out of these difficult places. While Weiss and Chuster take the view that this dysfunction – the psychotic or the delusional transference – is an attack on knowledge of the truth that needs to be faced, others like Borgogno, Vigna-Taglianti, and Grotstein seem to be inclined toward the idea that these transferences are searching for the analyst to contain them, sometimes for long periods of time. Borgogno and Vigna-Taglianti see in role reversal, that is, the process in which the patient submits the analyst to his own pains while himself taking the upper hand, a sign of hope. In their view the "terrorism of suffering" in the reversal of patient and analyst roles can allow unspoken trauma to be brought into the transference. In any case, what is being highlighted here is that not only do contents from the conflicted infantile past or the internal world arise in the transference but that defenses against their awareness may also strongly suffuse the transference situation. Transference may thus be the emergence of what has been otherwise resisted, and also the resistance itself. Weiss's and Chuster's cases illustrate the latter. Variations and combinations of these two positions – transference as a need to be contained, and as the manifestation of a clinical neurosis or psychosis – appear in every chapter in this book.

All analysts agree that transference happens whether we like it or not. We can say that there is within the psyche a compulsion to transfer, as Aisenstein puts it. I see this compulsion originating in the need of the mind to give itself shape and to represent its internal dramas in order to make them thinkable. Piera Aulagnier (1986) holds the position that we are "condemned to cathect" our objects for the same reasons that Aisenstein states that we are compelled from within to transfer. Grotstein, in his terms, says that we transfer so that we can come to represent – as in a play – the political situation between the self and its objects. Similarly one could argue that Freud's view of the ego and its relations to its three masters (1923) describes the politics going on between ego, id, superego, and the external world.

The theatrical model seems to be present in the thinking of many analysts. Berman-Oelsner shows that in child analysis this playing theater that includes the analyst is manifest, as she describes how children often ask their analysts to be this or that character in the analytic hour. We could say that the patient and his inner objects are in the situation of the players in Pirandello's *Six Characters in Search of an Author* as they irrupt through the transference into the analytic session again and again.[5] The analyst is to become one or many supporting actors as well as the designer of the (analytic) setting so that the play can take place, hopefully in the theater of the office, although the urge of the inner characters to go on acting makes acting-out a possibility. Even in narcissism the analyst is cast into a role: that of the excluded, ignored, or diminished helpless self.

With regard to the roles analysts may be invited to play, some may be more or less tolerable depending on the analyst's personality and personal equation. A note of caution is given by Etchegoyen, who identifies the risk for the analyst who is too happy in his maternal containing function and so may miss the interpretation of the sexual impulses that are a part of the oedipal conflict, which may be less comfortable to face and name.

In accord with the discussions by the authors and chapters we have mentioned above, the content emanating as transference includes repressed infantile neurosis or illness (or any of its elements); early preverbal phantasies, conflicts, and defenses; the prenatal past or vestiges of it; unmetabolized generational trauma; and social trauma.

Countertransference

While countertransference and transference are dealt with by many as both the communicative channel as well as its two stations, countertransference as a technical instrument for the understanding of the transference is a different matter. This is Racker's signature contribution, which he devoted himself to understanding in his all too short life. His interest is grounded in seeing the countertransference as a receptive organ that captures unnoticed and oftentimes silent transferences. The fact that analysts' psyches are not really different from those of their patients contributes to the sensitivity of the analyst in perceiving what is going on in the mind of the patient. Negative countertransference feelings, for instance, may come from the patient frustrating the analyst's desire to cure, thus being an indicator of a subtle negative transference, rivalry, guilt, or envy that may halt the cure.

For some, as was the case for Racker, countertransference – like transference – is both an obstacle and a source of information about what is going in an analysis. Freud's dictum (1912) that countertransference has to be overcome holds true only when we confine the concept to the analyst's unanalyzed neurosis.[6] But the broader view of countertransference as encompassing many other elements obliged analysts to develop the new technical tools that Racker and Paula Heimann (1950) initiated. Faimberg, Fainstein, Weiss, and some others including myself, following Racker, now see countertransference as a development that, when well understood in relation to the transference, offers us a way to transform a potential vice into a virtue: we make use of it rather than being used by it.[7] Enactments in this respect are, as Hinshelwood points out, the end result of unnoticed countertransferences. Sometimes – perhaps more often than we would like to admit – we are enacting the countertransference, although if noticed this can still offer us a good opportunity for analytic understanding.

A different and perhaps more mysterious view of countertransference links it to the function of intuition, *un oeil en trop*, as André Green (cited by Bion, 1991b, p. 537) says. Harris, Gampel, and Aisenstein seem to maintain this position and illustrate from their experience situations in which intuition allowed them to capture "things invisible to mortal sight," a Miltonian way of saying that transference is not visible or even audible or touchable and can only be intuited. A note of caution is also needed in this respect, however. In Bion's *Memoir of the Future* (1991a, p. 37)[8] an enigmatic character called S.F. emerges. S.F. seems to stand alternatively for selected fact,[9] shadowy figures, science fiction, scientific fact, or silly fool. We need to be aware that our countertransference, when used as a tool for intuition, may lead to any of the above, from employing a scientific method to unveil the shadowy transference objects of the patient to foreseeing what is yet to evolve – like Jules Verne's submarine or Leonardo's flying machine. Countertransference intuition may also play tricks on us – silly fools – if we omnipotently believe we can know the unknown. Britton and Steiner (1994) discussed the risks of intuition going astray, yet I think many of us would agree that we need it in our toolbox and use it with caution. In this respect Racker makes a useful distinction between empathy – which I relate to intuition – and countertransference, noting that the understanding we gain through empathy may be interfered with by countertransference. That is, he considers countertransference to be a source of resistance on the analyst's part, while also showing that the "understanding" of one's countertransference may clear the road for the analyst to further understand his patient. This is a point I deal with when describing the usefulness of supervision as a means to help the analyst remove the obstacles to his understanding.

While for Racker countertransference is an instrument that assists in an understanding of the transference others consider it to be a container for the patient's transferences, much as the mother's mind is for the baby's projected anxieties. From this perspective, countertransference in the analytic process is part of a natural history in which the analyst offers himself as an object for relieving the baby-patient's anxieties and impulses as well as an understanding object to be internalized into the patient's psyche. Grotstein's sacrificial mother-analyst is an expression of this position. Borgogno and Vigna-Taglianti, advocating for the analyst to become the "interpreter" of the role of the patient in pain, rather than returning it in the form of interpretation of the transference, seem to align themselves with this position, as do Lemma and Gampel.

To sum up, I would like to again highlight the two positions. One is countertransference as an instrument for understanding – much as if we were listening to a radio or telephone message – which is Racker's original observation, while the other views counter-transference as a therapeutic device that may make it possible to contain the projected pain of the patient, a view mainly expressed by the authors inspired by Bion and also Winnicott.

The personal elements that influence the analysts' work are another extension of countertransference. Faimberg's concept of "counter-transference position" and Cooper's concept of "countertransference surround" speak to that which an analyst brings with him before he meets the patient, and which affect the way he listens. Both include the analyst's filiation, that is the presence in his work of the fidelity to or love for his role models, the analyst of the analyst, the supervisors, the teachers, and the institute where the analyst trained, to which I would add the experiences that have accrued over time in his clinical work, what was successful and what failed. Cooper alerts us that the "countertransference surround" may surround the analyst's understanding, creating a form of counter-resistance. Faimberg suggests that in order to overcome that counter-resistance, we should be able to listen to the way we listen from a decentered position, reconcilable with Lemma's description of the "aerial view," which she contrasts with the "pedestrian view" in which both analyst and patient are immersed in the analytic field. The countertransference surround or position, coming neither from the patient nor the analyst's neurosis but from the analyst's history, sometimes even an intergenerational one, could also fairly be called "pre-formed countertransference," parallel to Meltzer's pre-formed transference (1967). In support of this view Fainstein illustrates the influences of iconic analytic figures on analysts in the River Plate region, which for Faimberg and myself as Argentinean émigrés have contributed to the position we listen from.

Other factors too play an important role in the analyst's countertransference. His present conflicts and personal concerns constitute an inescapable part of what he brings to the analytic encounter and do not go unnoticed by patients. Aisenstein and Jacobs refer to situations where a current personal concern had a dramatic impact on the transference of their patients, which they noticed once they could examine the transference-countertransference from a decentered position. This extension of the term is quite different from the two positions mentioned above for it is neither a response to the patient's transference (Freud) nor a technical instrument (Racker) but rather the personal ingredients analysts bring to their work and that may sensitize them to better capture certain aspects of their patients but also blind them to others. This is a potent reminder of the importance of peer clinical discussions and supervision.

Transference, countertransference, and technique

Not only our listening but also our technical choices are informed, explicitly as well as implicitly, by our filiations, both positive and negative. The feelings we have toward diverse psychoanalytic theories constitute our transference to the entire area of analytic work. The present book, with contributions by analysts from different geographies and analytic cultures, will, I hope, both open new prospects and create new interests in where we stand and what we can comprehend – and also acknowledge what we inevitably leave out – and indeed may miss out on – as a result of the theoretical and technical choices we have made.

Freud, for instance, could not see the transference that Little Hans made to his father, as Hinshelwood shows. Freud's technical limitations at that time, along with his belief that children could not be analyzed as adults could, might well have been the cause of his skepticism. Similarly, the absence of a theory of technique that allowed him to use the countertransference rendered him unable to see his enactments with both the Rat Man and the Wolf Man and other patients as Hinshelwood and Faimberg suggest – although these lacks take nothing away from his groundbreaking discoveries and lifetime of invaluable work.

The diversity of current ideas on transference and counter-transference carries implications for technique. Racker's classical view of countertransference, which is also that of Heimann, Joseph, and of most contemporary Kleinians, inclines those who support it toward investigating the transference in the light of the emotional responses in the analyst. It is the analyst who is, as Fainstein notes in quoting Racker, both subject and interpreter of the transference, and who acts as a mirror only in that he speaks to the patient about what belongs to the patient and deals privately with his personal matters. The implication is that both the close monitoring of the transference and countertransference and the interpretive work are effective in releasing the fixations that caused the patient's infantile and clinical neurosis. The choice to interpret the transference sooner rather than later is based on the view that in this way the patient can be spared much suffering.[10] Countertransference is, in this case, used as an instrument to achieve the goal of understanding – and ultimately making conscious the unconscious through the analyst's interpretations of what he has understood.

Bion's containing function and the theory of the container $\longleftrightarrow$ contained relation, as well as Winnicott's concept of holding have helped analysts to realize that while they were doing their work they were also functioning as a maternal thinking breast and not just

13

as a feeding-interpreting one, and in addition that they were also holding their patients' illusion of being whole and self-sufficient in the analyst's presence. These views are evident in several of the chapters in this book. Like Molière's *Le Bourgeois Gentilhomme* who did not realize that he had been speaking prose all along, we did not notice that we have been performing functions beyond those we were aware of. Faimberg's concept of the "missing concept" addresses this point. Having become aware of the function of holding and of the model for thinking we convey to our patients, we nowadays, I believe, give more importance to this aspect of our work. Interpreting, walking along, witnessing without shaming, sustaining role reversals, dreaming the session, spontaneous occurrences – all are varieties of actions and functions that take place while we are "speaking prose."

The matter of the timing of transference interpretation is a key technical question explored in several chapters. Borgogno and Vigna-Taglianti support the idea that the analyst need not rush to make transference interpretations on the ground that waiting until the patient has had the experience of having his terror modulated puts him in a better position to reintroject it albeit as a more tolerable feeling. That is, they are privileging the experience of patients being held and contained as a therapeutic action. Lemma also subscribes to this idea, and Gampel finds it crucial, especially when working with patients experiencing current or intergenerational traumas. Berman-Oelsner sees that the acceptance of roles and of playing them out in child analysis is just what it is, not a choice, and that you work from there. Chuster waits until some new shadowy figure – Bion's S.F. – takes off its mask and then calls it by its name. Weiss finds himself caught by a patient who has masked the analyst, as it were, and struggles to remove it so as to be present again as analyst. Etchegoyen has to try to wear a female mask, that of a mother, which he does not feel naturally comfortable with, in order to address his female patient's unconscious homosexual phantasies. Racker shows how the analyst needed to look at himself in the mirror of his dressing room – perhaps in his supervision – to notice what mask he had on. Supervision provides an essential space within which we can recognize the characters and identify the nature of the plot of the patient's inner world and the role the analyst has come to play in it (see Oelsner, this volume). And so we all keep trying to titrate that point when a patient is ready to hear and make use of an interpretation.

14

My warmest hope is that reading the voices gathered here will contribute to a deeper illumination of our minds, and to a better understanding of our work with patients, but first and foremost to a better understanding of each other's language and thinking to the benefit of all. As for myself, coming from a Jewish family from Germany, having been born and raised in Argentina, educated in a British school in Buenos Aires, and having relocated to the United States a decade ago, I find that a wider understanding of our work is unequivocally part of the multi-filiation that led me to edit this book.

Notes

1 Conducted by an extraordinary teacher, Professor Elena Evelson, in the Institute of the Buenos Aires Psychoanalytic Association.

2 Although this treatment lasted only a few months it was one of those experiences that taught me the most in my professional life. Forty years later, strikingly, the patient traced me to my new country and called me. He and I were deeply moved to talk with each other. He remembered, he said, that he was then so ill that he could not really get to know me and felt he now had a chance, over Skype, to see and recognize me and to express his gratitude. It was useful for us both to realize that we had survived each other's murderousness.

3 But what a patient does then with those communications belongs to the patient's transference.

4 K being Bion's symbol for knowledge as a link with an object; that is, the link whose foundation is the desire of the mind to know an object. O is Bion's sign for the ultimate unknown or Kant's Thing-in-itself.

5 *Six Characters in Search of an Author* recounts the fate of a family of characters left unrealized by their author. Desperate to come to life, the characters interrupt the rehearsal of another Pirandello play and demand that the director and cast stage their story.

6 This motivated Freud to recommend what became the training analysis for the analyst.

7 Hannah Segal often said that countertransference is the best of servants but the worst of masters.

8 This book is a trilogy, presented as a theater play with many characters who stage much of Bion's theoretical thought, now brought to life.

9 Bion borrowed the expression "selected fact" from the French mathematician Henri Poincaré, using it to refer to the element that makes it possible to give coherence to a field of scattered data.

10 I make a distinction between making a transference interpretation and interpreting the transference. The latter comes naturally once the analyst understands where the patient is and is in touch with the patient's deepest anxieties. With the former, one runs the risk of imposing oneself on the patient.

Bibliography

Aulagnier, P (1986) Condamné à investir. In *Un interprète en quête de sens* (pp. 239–264). Paris: Ramsey.

Balint, A. and Balint, M. (1939) On transference and counter-transference. *International Journal of Psychoanalysis*, 20: 223–230.

Bion, W. R. (1979) Making the best of a bad job. In *Clinical Seminars and Four Papers* (pp. 321–331). Abingdon, UK: Fleetwood, 1987.

Bion, W. R. (1991a) Book I: *The Dream*. In *A Memoir of the Future* (pp. 1–217). London: Karnac.

Bion, W. R. (1991b) Book III: *The Dawn of Oblivion*. In *A Memoir of the Future* (pp. 427–580). London: Karnac.

Britton, R. and Steiner, J. (1994) Interpretation: Selected fact or overvalued idea? *International Journal of Psychoanalysis*, 75: 1069–1078.

Freud, S. (1912). Recommendations to physicians practicing psycho-analysis. *The Standard Edition of the Complete Psychological Works of Sigmund Freud*, J. Strachey (ed., trans.), vol. XII: 109–120.

Freud, S. (1921) Psycho-analysis and telepathy. *SE* 18: 173–194. London: Hogarth Press.

Freud, S. (1922) Dreams and telepathy. *SE* 18: 195–220.

Freud, S. (1923) The ego and the id. *SE* 19: 1–66

Freud, S. (1933) Lecture 30: Dreams and occultism. In *New Introductory Lectures on Psycho-Analysis*. *SE* 22: 31–56.

Heimann, P. (1950) On counter-transference. *International Journal of Psychoanalysis*, 31: 81–84.

Joseph, B. (1985) Transference: The total situation. *International Journal of Psychoanalysis*, 66: 447–454.

Klein, M. (1952) The origins of transference. In *The Writings of Melanie Klein*, vol. 3 (pp. 48–56). London: Hogarth, 1975.

Meltzer, D. (1967) *The Psychoanalytical Process*. London: Heinemann.

Oelsner, R. (1979) La Contratransferencia del Analista frente al Paciente que no puede Soñar (The countertransference of the analyst to the patient who cannot dream). Paper presented at the II Symposium and Annual Conference, Buenos Aires Psychoanalytical Association, October 1979.

Oelsner, R. (1993) Olfato, Captación intuitiva y Trabajo Analítico (Smell, intuitive perception, and psychoanalytic working-through). Paper presented at the XV Symposium and Annual Conference, Buenos Aires Psychoanalytical Association, October 1993.

Oelsner, R. (1995) Transferencia, Captación Intuitiva y Trabajo Psicoanalítico (Transference, intuitive perception, and psychoanalytic working-through). Paper presented at II Argentine Conference of Psychoanalysis, Mendoza, Argentina, May 1995.

Oelsner, R. (2011) Über die Deutung der Realität – die Wechselseitigkeit von psychischer und äusserer Realität (On the interpretation of reality: The reciprocity between psychic reality and the external world). Paper presented to the Deutsche Psychoanalytische Gesellschaft, Robert Bosch Krankenhaus, Stuttgart, Germany, March 2011.

1

OBSERVATIONS ON COUNTERTRANSFERENCE AS A TECHNICAL INSTRUMENT
Preliminary communication

Heinrich Racker

In a previous paper about a number of problems concerning countertransference (Racker, 1948),[1] I also made reference to the fact that *countertransference reactions can provide evidence to the analyst of what is going on in the analysand.*

In a subsequent study (Racker, 1950),[2] I briefly returned to this issue and made a first attempt at phrasing the "objective" and general meaning of a certain countertransference reaction that is both frequent and important. That is, I first attempted to establish a rule that would enable us to deduce from countertransference the psychological state of the analysand. Shortly afterward, in the *International Journal of Psychoanalysis*, I found a recent paper by Paula Heimann (1950) on the same subject that was in agreement with the perspectives and conclusions put forward in the aforementioned papers.[3] Indeed, Heimann's essay has encouraged me to communicate some of the observations I have made with regard to this subject since the first communication.

However, before I do so, I would like to recapitulate the ideas on countertransference that I have already put forward. In the first paper, while addressing paranoid countertransference reactions, I analyzed the anger sometimes felt by the analyst when he is faced with the analysand's resistances, and I pointed out that this reaction stems from the internal states of both the analysand and the analyst. In particular, I stated that countertransferential hate points toward the existence of aggressiveness and anxiety in the analysand, which originate, in turn, in certain relationships with the analysand's introjected objects.[4] In the second paper I summarized these ideas as follows:

> The analyst's perception of his own countertransference states could prove *an important instrument for the understanding of the analysand's transference states.* If the analyst can use his negative countertransference reactions in favor of the treatment, he is usually able to overcome them. When does negative countertransference appear? In general terms, it could be said that it is the result of the analyst feeling that the analysand has frustrated him. In this sense, we could claim, although it may only be partly accurate, that whenever the analyst is angry, the analysand has a feeling of guilt about his transference aggressiveness. To put this in the terms of the present paper: whenever the analyst experiences anger, the analysand is defending himself from the basic paranoid situation, which is being transferred in a latent fashion by means of the identification with the "bad object" (that is, the frustrating object). Deep down, what has been projected onto the analyst is a persecutor; on the surface, it is the superego that reproaches him for his tendencies, or behavior, that correspond to the aforementioned identification.[5]
>
> (Racker, 1950, p. 37)

Before I make my observations – in a series of examples that illustrate my thesis – I would like to emphasize that I am merely trying to point out that countertransference, which is frequently experienced as a hindrance to [our] work, and is associated with feelings of guilt, could also be used to advance the analytic treatment. The key to understanding our patients continues to be, as always, the capacity to pick up unconscious phenomena by means of the analyst's own unconscious. However, both this understanding as well as the working-through of what has been understood are more or less frequently interfered with by countertransference reactions;[6] it is in cases such as these that the approach adopted in this paper provides important advantages.

I will now present an *example* of a countertransference reaction that revealed to the analyst an analysand's transference situation and, thus, the way to interpret the main resistance and its underlying fears.[7]

19

Bertha, the analysand (whom the analyst described as a very intelligent and friendly young woman), one day told him of a conversation she had had with the analyst's daughter, who was 5 years old, and whom she had met at the door of the house. The conversation was amusing and Bertha laughed warmly while she recounted it; against his better judgment the analyst soon joined in laughing. Bertha continued to describe, one after the other, the little girl's amusing remarks, and they both continued to laugh. However, at some point, the analyst was assailed by a doubt: "Could Bertha be making fun of me – he wondered – making up witticisms and pretending they are my daughter's? Could she be playing with my paternal pride, making me believe that the wit displayed by my daughter is in fact hers?"

This paranoid fear, on the one hand, and on the other, the hypomanic state manifested by both the analysand and the analyst, led the latter to commit a serious breach in technique: he interrupted the analysand and asked her whether her last remark was actually her daughter's, or rather her own. Bertha took offense at the analyst's distrust and, judging from the way she reacted, the analyst clearly perceived that Bertha's account had been faithful. He felt guilty and wondered how he could have made such a blunder. He told himself that, in truth, he seldom distrusted his analysands, and neither did he fear being made fun of by any of them. However, this had been the case with Bertha, therefore he could suppose that his paranoid reaction, albeit wrong as to the point when it occurred, was nevertheless not wholly arbitrary; rather, it constituted a countertransference response, which in a sense was appropriate to one of the analysand's transference states. He immediately remembered that he had every reason to distrust Bertha, because during the first stage of analysis (for six months) she had deliberately concealed a very important aspect of her life from him. At the same time, the analyst felt that there was also a current motive: his paranoid distrust was a reaction to Bertha's strong tendency to despise, dominate, and make fun of him, a tendency he had previously perceived and that he considered to be a defense against a basic situation of dependence through the inversion of this situation (by means of "manic defenses" against paranoid anxieties through identification with the persecutors). The analyst's paranoid reaction showed him how strong Bertha's "manic defenses" must have been, and subsequent analysis confirmed this.

It could also be supposed that the analyst's question had affected her so deeply because she reproached herself for having been somewhat insincere or something equivalent to that. Bertha confirmed this interpretation by saying that she had concealed something important in the previous session: she was no longer interested in Roberto, her latest "flirt."[8] She later added that she had decided to withdraw her affection from Roberto when she realized how little understanding she received from him. While Bertha was speaking, the analyst perceived that he continued to feel guilty about his technical blunder, or, rather, at his aggression toward Bertha. And it was precisely this perception that led him to listen with closer attention to the kind of mood she was in that day, which led him to feel that, beneath her accusation, apparently so truthful, of Roberto, there was a depressive state that (in view of what Bertha said next) the analyst considered to be a consequence of the aggression he himself had shown toward her. However, he had a reason to connect his own aggression with that of Bertha's superego, because if Bertha had not cruelly accused herself of insincerity the analyst's words would hardly have hurt her so much. In other words, Bertha's latent depression was due to the aggression of her own superego, and the analyst perceived the magnitude of this aggression through the magnitude of his own feelings of guilt over his aggressive behavior. On then leading Bertha to analyze her depression, it was seen that the accusation directed at Roberto was concealing the wish to find an excuse to stop seeing him. However, it was this behavior, which had led her to "pass from one man to the next," that meant she unconsciously felt like a prostitute; and thus her superego and – through projection – her analyst as well, were felt to condemn and despise her.

It can be seen how the two most conspicuous countertransference reactions in this session pointed toward Bertha's most significant transference situations, and to the resistances connected to them. The danger of falling into a frustrating affective and libidinal dependence was Bertha's worst fear, a fear that led her to adopt the opposite behavior both within and outside analysis: she was haughty so as not to feel inferior to others; she faked independence and coldness to avoid depending on others; she laughed at people in order to prevent becoming the butt of everyone's jokes, and so forth. The analyst had reacted with distrust to these defensive tendencies and it was the awareness of his own reaction that led him to analyze Bertha's manic defenses and their underlying paranoid fears.

On the other hand, Bertha's neurotic independence and repression of affects – which had led her to "pass from one man to the next," and which included all her hatred toward the seductive and frustrating objects of her basic dependence – made her feel intensely guilty. Her behavior in analysis was also determined by this manic defense, and for this reason Bertha unconsciously felt accused and hated by her analyst. The analyst felt an enormous sense of guilt when he was actually aggressive toward Bertha; that is, when a real occasion to be aggressive presented itself. Thus, the analyst's feelings of guilt – which on the one hand were inappropriate to the aggression committed, but, on the other, were appropriate to Bertha's depression – became a guide to an analysis of the aggression of Bertha's moral superego against her ego, where she had introjected the seductive and frustrating primary objects (the "primary persecutors"). These feelings also proved useful in analyzing her "secondary paranoid anxieties," that is, the counter-aggression (retaliation) of the (internal) objects that she frustrated with her hypomanic behavior.

In reality, the analyst had already perceived this aspect of the transference situation on previous occasions through his countertransference reactions. His annoyance at Bertha's apparent lack of libidinal and affective bonds (owing to the repression of her profound fixation to the primary objects, which she *only appeared* to transfer to the analyst without actually doing so) had taught him to understand the transference situation. The analyst's annoyance was, roughly, the mirror of Bertha's superego criticizing her behavior, while her aggression and pseudo-independence were the defensive (and retaliatory) responses to the frustrations she had borne in her libidinal relationship with her primary objects.

To sum up, (1) the analyst's *paranoid anxiety* (distrust) drew his attention to Bertha's *manic defenses*; that is, it showed him Bertha's identification with the persecutors through which she had inverted the basic (paranoid) situation, placing the analyst in the position of the one being *persecuted*. And (2), the analyst's feeling of *annoyance* (aggression) as a reaction to his own anxiety pointed out to him the aggression of Bertha's superego against her "bad" ego; that is, it showed him Bertha's *feelings of guilt* about her manic behavior.

This example shows, above all, that the content of the countertransference reaction can teach us about the content of the transference situation. In addition, the countertransference situation can enlighten us on another important technical issue: what should be interpreted from all the material provided by the analysand. The answer to this question is usually found in the analyst's understanding of the analytic material, and in his knowledge of the therapeutic and pathological mechanisms, from which the interpretation needed by the analysand is derived. It is empathy that ought to indicate this need by directing the analyst toward the core of the situation and its affective tone. However, empathy is sometimes interfered with by countertransference reactions, which overlap with the former; that is, with the analyst's identification with the ego and the id of the analysand. In situations such as these, paying attention not only to the nature but also to the *intensity* of certain countertransference reactions could prove helpful. For example: a young university student who sought analysis due to an obsessional neurosis one day told his analyst that he was reading the works of Freud and was in doubt as to whether this was right or wrong. A year before, shortly after he had begun analysis, the analyst had suggested that he interrupt his psychoanalytic reading for a while. With the purpose of clarifying the present situation, the analyst told him he no longer needed to follow his suggestion, to which the analysand replied: "Thank you so much." This phrase made the analyst feel intensely guilty, in particular due to the note of "self pity" in the analysand's voice. The analyst felt that he had always been an extraordinarily cruel tyrant toward the analysand. This feeling, which was a far cry from what was actually going on in the analytic situation, clearly showed the amount of sadism present in the objects (either real or fantasized) that the analysand transferred to the analyst. The great *intensity* of the countertransference reaction showed the analyst what was important and needed to be analyzed.

Likewise, countertransference feelings frequently indicate whether the analysand is "moving on," that is, if he is overcoming resistances or not. For instance, when the analyst actually feels the aggressions of an analysand whose aggressiveness had been blocked until then, and if, perhaps, he is feeling offended, or guilty over what the analysand reproaches him with, he can quite rightly conclude that the analysand has begun to fear him less and, therefore, that he is making progress, whereas boredom in the analyst is, most of the time, a sure sign of the resistance of the analysand. It goes without saying that each of these countertransference reactions is never completely "objective": both the subject and the object play a part in them. Complementary series should not be overlooked when considering this issue. For instance, the stronger the analyst's disposition toward paranoid reactions, the more irritated he will be by the analysand's resistance or sadomasochism.

On the other hand, the analyst will rarely feel annoyed by chance; rather, he will sense, albeit distortedly, part of the unconscious reality of the analysand.[9] However, while the *subjective* factor was the main focus of my previous paper (on the countertransference, its pathological mechanisms, and their *negative* consequences), in this one the focus is on what countertransference can tell us about the *object* and the analysand; that is, I am emphasizing the *positive* contribution that countertransference could make to the treatment.[10]

I will now present another example, which illustrates how a countertransference reaction showed the analyst the direction he needed to take in the treatment. Pedro, a young man, sought analysis due to impotence and, despite the fact that he was already free of symptoms, continued analysis owing to the remaining difficulties he had with women. In the days before the session in question he had, for the very first time, started going out with an obviously better object. Until then, he had unconsciously sought, and found, women who attracted and frustrated him, but this girl he was seeing was far healthier and more caring. In the session we are discussing, Pedro told the analyst he had taken the girl to a fancy restaurant and he complained of the cost: "But women – he said – like expensive restaurants." Later he mentioned that the girl had asked him if he knew what the possibility of establishing an intimate relationship with her would entail. He replied with a long speech: he knew he was not supposed to see other women, and he was willing to accept that. He pursued certain activities (study group meetings), but only once a week. In addition, he said he knew he was not expected to leave her soon after the start of their romance, but, on the other hand, that it would be too early to consider marriage. And on he went in the same vein.

As the analyst had known the analysand for quite some time, he knew what had happened: everything Pedro told the girl was in fact directed at the imago of the "mother-moloch" he had projected onto her.[11] There was every indication that the girl had little in common with the features of that imago. In contrast, the analysand's mother was very domineering and controlled his social life – who he went out with and how often – and was jealous if he met new people, girls in particular. The serious libidinal and affective frustrations he had suffered in his childhood made him experience eroticism as highly dangerous, in the sense of his becoming absorbed, emptied, castrated, and so on. He defended himself from this danger

24

mainly through his identification with the bad object and, therefore, he too wanted to take advantage of women, to seduce them, and to be unfaithful and indifferent to them. These were the tendencies that triggered his usual feelings of guilt which, in turn, he sought to temper by subjecting himself to the object and seeking frustration. In this way secondary masochism developed and protected him from the consequences of sadism (in "taking advantage of" or "emptying" others). This is why he hastened to assure the girl that he would not be unfaithful to her and that he would go out without her only once a week, and this was also why he had taken her to a restaurant he could hardly afford; however, he had also felt the urgent need to add that he did not want to marry her. Pedro's behavior was a transaction between the "sadistic" defense derived from his identification with the frustrating object, and the cancellation of this sadism through his submissiveness.

However, between the situation described by the analysand and the interpretation offered by the analyst something else happened which, incidentally, is the reason why we are including this episode here: a countertransference reaction. While the analyst was listening to the analysand, and was attempting to understand his behavior, he realized that he was feeling annoyed with Pedro and an insult equivalent to "spineless" kept coming into his mind. The analyst understood that his annoyance was a neurotic reaction to his own anxiety, which originated, in turn, in the risk of therapeutic failure Pedro's behavior presented. In other words, the analyst perceived that Pedro had hardly changed with regard to this aspect, and that – given the interrelation between the transference situation and the situation with the girl – the analyst continued to be, deep down, as bad an object to the analysand as his primary objects had been. The perception of his countertransference reaction was in this case also an indication of the line that should be followed in the session. There could be no doubt about the importance of analyzing not only Pedro's submissiveness toward the girl, but also *the transference situation that was included in this behavior*. We have already discussed Pedro's behavior toward the girl. With regard to the transferential meaning of his behavior, analysis demonstrated several facets. The analyst's *in mente* [silent] aggressive reaction was, on the one hand, a response to Pedro's sadomasochism, which he had apparently transferred from his ambivalent relationship with his father. In Pedro's unconscious the girl represented the analyst's wife (Pedro's mother), and his relationship with her had to end both in order to avoid castration and to not lose his analyst. At the same time, by his suffering, by his submissiveness toward his analyst and his acceptance of symbolic castration, he redeemed himself from his guilt within the analytic situation, which allowed him to fulfill his sexual desire "later on" ("in the future"). In addition, by making the analyst fail (by castrating him) Pedro unconsciously triumphed over him. This aggressive tendency, embodied in Pedro's masochistic behavior, was what made the analyst anxious, hence the countertransference annoyance. On a deeper level, the analyst represented Pedro's mother, and the aggressive countertransference reaction was the analyst's emotional response to Pedro's sadomasochism in his relationship with the imago of his mother, which he had transferred to him. On this level, the stratification of his relationship with the analyst was similar to the one in his relationship with the girl, a representative of the "mother-moloch." The countertransference reaction (the analyst's anger at Pedro's submissiveness) clearly showed him both what Pedro thought about himself when he behaved in a submissive fashion, and, at the same time, his anger toward his castrating and domineering objects, both internal and external.

Lastly, I will mention an example where a countertransference reaction, a feeling of slightly malicious glee, guided the analyst toward interpretation. The analysand, an attorney, described what happened to him when he was leaving after the last session. He had been flirting for some time with the janitor of the analyst's building, a middle-aged, relatively well-preserved woman. Their conversations referred in particular to the appealing aromas coming from her kitchen. For the purpose of this paper it is not necessary to analyze in detail the analysand's conduct. Suffice it to say that, on the one hand, the transference situation impelled him to act out and to adopt the attitude of a Don Juan toward the janitor, and on the other, that his problem with "people of the working classes," toward whom he consciously felt hatred and revulsion, and, in turn, guilt for harboring these feelings, played a part. That evening, then, as he was leaving after his session, the janitor asked him to stay for dinner, something he found deeply annoying. He had tried to escape from this situation but she had insisted that he stay. The analysand was forced to take first a snack, then a dish, followed by another dish, and another, and another, ad infinitum, while he languished there, desperate to recover his lost freedom. The analyst found this situation highly amusing and it was then that he became aware of the feeling of malicious glee. Where did it come from? What could it tell him about the analysand? The first thing that came to the analyst's mind was the way children feel when the bad characters in their stories, the "bad wolf" for instance, fall into a trap; it was also similar to the feeling of glee one has at the "trickster tricked." Moreover, since the analyst reacted in that way it was because he identified with the objects the analysand persecuted. Therefore, it was very likely that the analysand was also identifying the analyst with the objects he intended to persecute and to deceive. Subsequent analysis showed that this was true, and that the countertransference reaction was appropriate to the central neurotic position of the analysand. In fact, in order to defend himself from paranoid anxieties, the patient had behaved like a "wolf" (that is, like the object that persecuted him),[12] while at the same time he sought punishment for this behavior in those situations where he himself fell victim to others, or else felt he might.

Translated from the Spanish by Valeria Muscio and Robert Oelsner.

Italics below reproduce those in the original publication. – ed.

Summary

Observations on counter-transference as a technical instrument

When empathy or identification with the analysand – that is, the principal mechanism for understanding him – is being interfered with by *countertransference reactions*, these can constitute an *important guide for analytic treatment*. On the one hand, they can be a *key for the comprehension* of what is happening in the analysand, i.e., of the *content* of his psychological situations, and on the other hand they can be a measure of the *intensity* of his processes. Thus they help the analyst to perceive *what is to be interpreted* and explored and when it is *time* to do so.

It is evident that when this kind of use is made of counter-transference reactions, the sources of subjective errors, i.e., the analyst's *personal equation*, must be taken carefully into account.

These affirmations are illustrated by a series of examples.

Notes

The paper in this chapter was first presented at the Argentine Psychoanalytic Association in 1951.

Where the text of Racker's original publication of this paper included words or phrases in italics, they are shown in italics here. Most works shown in Racker's original footnotes now appear in endnotes, and have been edited in the style of this book. The original English summary of the paper is also reproduced. – ed.

1   Heinrich Racker, "A contribution to the problem of countertransference" (Contribución al problema de la contratransferencia), paper presented to the Argentine Psychoanalytic Association, Buenos Aires, Argentina, 1948.

2   Heinrich Racker, "A contribution to the psychoanalysis of transference neurosis" (Aportación al psicoanálisis de la neurosis de transferencia), paper presented to the Argentine Psychoanalytic Association, Buenos Aires, Argentina, September 1950.

3   Paula Heimann, "On countertransference," *International Journal of Psychoanalysis*, 31: 81–84, 1950. [Heimann's paper appeared in September of that year. – ed.]

4   See Racker, "A contribution to the problem of countertransference" (1948): 20–22, 24, later published in the *International Review of Psychoanalysis*, 34: 313–324, 1953.

5   Racker, "Aportación al psicoanálisis de la neurosis de transferencia" (1950): 37. In order to clarify the preceding ideas I must add a few words. In the aforementioned paper I tried to put forward, with the example of the transference neurosis, the psychopathological stratification I have encountered in all the clinical cases I was able to examine. In the first place, I found that *in each of the libidinal levels* there is a paranoid situation, which is a consequence of the frustrations encountered: the subject is libidinally fixated to frustrating objects and thus experiences any libidinal bond as presenting a constant danger of being attacked or destroyed (primary persecution). The predominant defense mechanism of the subject is to identify with the "bad object" (the persecuting object), and that is why he reverses the earlier situation, now becoming the persecutor and placing the object in the position of the one persecuted. The main fears of retaliation and the main feelings of guilt refer to this bad ego and the tendencies it represents.

6   This understanding is not always interfered with by countertransference. Sometimes the analyst understands correctly (through empathy, that is, by way of identification with the wishes, defenses, and imagos of the analysand's object). However, both the reactions to what he has grasped (the working-through of them) and the corresponding interpretative

capacity are disrupted by the analyst's neurosis (see Racker, "Contribución al problema de la contratransferencia," 1948: 1–24).

7 With this *preliminary communication* I only intend to put forward the main thesis and to illustrate it with some examples. I will later on present a longer paper where I will elaborate on "Countertransference as a technical instrument," in connection with other problems of countertransference from a broader theoretical and case perspective. In addition, the examples will be presented in a systematic way, that is, in an order that follows the emergence of different aspects inherent to countertransference and "countertransference neurosis."

8 [The word "flirt" (crush) is in English in the original. – ed.]

9 See Freud (1922).

10 The complex problem presented here – the "subjectivity" and "objectivity" of countertransference reactions – will be addressed in more detail in the forthcoming paper I have earlier made reference to.

11 [Moloch, a male deity mentioned in the Bible, was offered child sacrifices. – ed.]

12 I am making reference to his behavior as a Don Juan, since in English slang such a person is called a *wolf*.

Bibliography

Freud, S. (1922) Some neurotic mechanisms in Jealousy, Paranoia and Homosexuality. In *The Standard Edition of the Complete Psychological Works of Sigmund Freud*, J. Strachey (ed., trans.), vol. 18, pp. 221–232. London: Hogarth Press, 1955.

Heimann, P. (1950) On countertransference. *International Journal of Psychoanalysis*, 31: 81–84.

Racker, H. (1948) A contribution to the problem of countertransference. Paper presented to the Argentine Psychoanalytic Association, Buenos Aires, Argentina, 1948.

Racker, H. (1950) A contribution to the psychoanalysis of transference neurosis. Paper presented to the Argentine Psychoanalytic Association, Buenos Aires, Argentina, September 1950.

TRANSFERENCE-COUNTERTRANSFERENCE

A testimony

R. Horacio Etchegoyen

Much has been written about the subject of transference and countertransference, as I have as well on many occasions. It is only because Robert Oelsner asked me that I decided to contribute to this book. Later, on second thought, I considered that this would give me an opportunity to speak my mind without having to be constrained by the legitimate, balanced views that one has to represent when speaking in the name of various authors. This is, then, my own personal testimony and not a scholarly essay that takes into account the view of others, and therefore I omit citations, quotations, and bibliographic references.

Freud introduced the concept of *transference* in chapter IV of *Studies on Hysteria*, that is, "The Psychotherapy of Hysteria" (1912), and he used the same word in chapter VII in the book on dreams to offer there a concept more linguistic than clinical, and more meta-psychological in terms of cathexis and countercathexis, than of transference of meaning. What perhaps most differentiates Klein from Lacan is that she thought Freud introduced the idea in 1895 whereas he places it in 1900. The difference is the same as that which obtains between object relation and signifier. Both of them nevertheless think, as do all analysts, that with the discovery of transference Freud changed forever the concept of interpersonal relations and showed us how much of the unconscious is present in human interaction. It is really a pity that the Swedish Academy did not realize in the first 30 years of the last century that Freud deserved the Nobel Prize, which was justly gained in 1906 by Ramón y Cajal for his discovery of the neuron. Freud could have been awarded the Nobel in 1900, or 1905, and in other subsequent years.

Transference (and its counterpoint, countertransference, as was understood by Racker and Heimann in the middle of the twentieth century) is a phenomenon that is there for all to see, and yet it easily goes unperceived. Only Freud, with his insuperable genius, was able to discover it. The transference is always surprising and often difficult to access. It frequently happens that each theory (and each analyst) conceives of it in his own fashion and maintains that his outlook is the only one possible. There are many ways to understand transference, and this paper is intended to show how I see it, without pretending to be original or believing my view to be the right one. My aim is to encourage others to think, reflect, disagree, or to even agree with what I say.

It is quite clear that in 1895 Freud stresses the importance of the physician and his relationship with the analysand. We all remember the famous example of that woman who, at the end of a session, had the wish that Freud would kiss her, and then, in the following session, felt disturbed and unable to cooperate. When she finally managed to communicate this to Freud he not only discovered the transference, but also linked her wish to a similar episode that had taken place with another man in the past. Freud realized the transference of the wish from the man to himself and also realized that he was in the presence of a regular and frequent phenomenon. From here onward he applied this experience to inform his ordinary daily tasks. At this stage Freud explained the situation with his idea of false connections; later on, in new editions of his works, he would understand the dynamics of transference within the dialectic of remembering and repeating.

Nevertheless I believe Freud never fully understood the negative transference, in contrast to Wilhelm Reich and Melanie Klein who, coming from different paths, managed to do so in the 1920s. Freud always saw the negative transference as a resistance and not as a legitimate component of the psychoanalytical process. In 1912 Freud affirmed that the transference is unavoidable and necessary to carry out analytic work, but he conceived of it only as erotic, perhaps driven by a wish to not agree with Adler, who had given aggression an important role in life and in neuroses.

Freud had early realized that sexuality exerted an enormous pressure on the transference, and, after Little Hans, he described the importance of castration anxiety as related to the Oedipus complex, particularly in men. These discoveries allowed Freud to explain the etiology and development of neurotic illnesses in a way that psychiatry could never have imagined. During these fertile years Freud could understand the Rat Man and the Wolf Man, but he did not completely understand Dora, I would say, even though with her he more fully rounded out his theory of transference, no longer as a false connection but as a reproduction of the past. Lacan believes that in this famous case Freud made a mistake when he did not reverse the third dialectic problem, which would have made Dora face her homosexuality. Freud, to a degree, would seem to agree with Lacan here as he reproaches himself about not having paid enough attention to his patients' homosexuality in their analysis. He failed to interpret Dora's homosexual love for Mrs K because he could not accept that she loved Mrs K and not Mr K. According to Lacan, Freud was identified with Mr K in feeling betrayed. This unconscious countertransference conflict prevented Freud from addressing Dora's homosexuality. I believe, nevertheless, that Freud could not properly have resolved Dora's case, not only because he had not read "Fragment of an Analysis of a Case of Hysteria" (!) and Dora took him by surprise, but also because he was not able to distinguish between the positive transference and the working alliance (as introduced, much later on, by the ego psychologists), and because he did not fully understood women. In his genius, Freud clearly saw women's penis envy – an envy of such intensity at times that it does not cease to surprise and frighten me in the consulting room – but neither Little Hans nor I share Freud's horror of the female genital, which he always saw as a wound and as a lack of a penis, a conception adhered to by Lacan. Karen Horney, Melanie Klein, and without a doubt Ernest Jones, realized that the female genital is an authentic and autonomous organ and that it does not necessarily have to be uncanny. Little Hans is delighted to see it in his younger sister Hanna and he expresses his view with candid clarity, but Freud does not listen to him. Many years later Janine Chasseguet-Smirgel and Joyce McDougall would agree with Jones's view on this matter.

When Freud wrote his two later papers on female sexuality he had to conclude that the Oedipus complex can only be properly applied to men; but in Wiesbaden (1932) Jones declared himself "*plus royalist que le Roi,*" and affirmed that the Oedipus complex applies to both sexes and that women have a particular organ, one that is not the result of Adam's rib, as Freud, the nonbeliever and atheist, and most of his disciples thought. Freud completely believed that the clitoris was a failed penis, taking refuge in the fact that both organs develop from the same embryological site; but this is an ideological kind of reasoning that has nothing to do with psychology. Most modern biological thinking, if I do not misunderstand it (and I am not a specialist), sustains the view that we are all initially XX and what evolution has done is to cut out a segment of one of the X chromosomes; I realize that I might be here naively geometric! But I do not think it is advisable to extrapolate from the capricious detours of evolution to psychological or sociological theories.

In this respect I think Freud could not overcome the prejudices of his time. He felt too "macho" to be able to operate with the maternal transference. He always placed himself in the position of the father; and, therefore, he could only interpret to men their castration anxiety and their homosexuality, just as he interpreted to women their transference love and their penis envy. This is not, of course, all there is to it. Klein realized this early on and found that the maternal transference could be interpreted. However, in a similar way, if too much emphasis is put on the containing function of the analyst (holding, reverie) only one part, although no doubt an important one, of the maternal transference is interpreted, sometimes at the expense of leaving out the interpretation of the sexual impulses.

I am not, of course, the first analyst to think that the sex of the analyst might have an influence on the analytic process, but I would like to highlight, at this point, that the maternal or paternal transferences *do not* depend on the (real) sex of the analyst, but rather on the analysand's unconscious phantasies. It is because we tend to be excessively attached to reality and because it is easier for a man to operate with the paternal transference and for a woman with the maternal one that we might not be aware that very often the man is seen as a woman, by both sexes, and vice versa.

Nevertheless, if the transference is what it is, the analysand would see us a father or mother (or sibling or uncle) according to his or her need. A woman was able to fall madly in love with Spitz's blond hair, even though he had had white hair for years.

The great mistake that all analysts may make is to believe that they are interpreting the transference when what we are interpreting is the current conflict or the infantile conflict.

33

I do not find it difficult to interpret to women their transference love or their penis envy, as for example to my "penetrating" interpretation. I do not find it hard either to interpret to both men and women their relationship with the breast in Melanie Klein's terms; but I do find it very difficult to interpret their homosexuality to women in the transference, because reality obliterates my role as a woman or mother, even though it would be exclusively from this position that I would be interpreting the transference strictly. When I tell a woman patient that she is in love with a female friend or with her mother in childhood, I am interpreting the homosexual impulse in the current conflict with the friend or the infantile conflict with the mother but not in the transference. Male analysts find it difficult to place themselves in the position of the female and visa versa, partly due to cultural usages; but we really have to be able to occupy both places. In general, male analysts tend to interpret to women their homosexuality with other women and not with us. I do not mean to say that this type of interpretation might not be relevant or enough, but sometimes it is not. I am also trying to say here that I interpret not only the transference but also the current and the infantile conflicts.

I am reminded now of a case in which I was able to interpret, reasonably well to my mind, to a woman patient her homosexual transference with me as a woman. I shall now present her material as it shows how this problem can be solved and also because it shows my way of working, oscillating from one role to the other.

A woman approaching her fortieth birthday and the end of her analysis consulted a gynecologist on account of repeated bleeding. The experienced doctor made a diagnosis of multiple fibroids (myomas) and recommended a hysterectomy. In that opportunity I limited myself to just telling her that she was talking not only about her uterus but also about her sexuality. The patient's associations were with the possible termination of her analysis and with the fact that some things would not be resolved in her love and sexual life.

On the Friday preceding the week I am going to report, and after the session, she had again gone to the gynecologist, who had confirmed the diagnosis and his therapeutic indication, and they again discussed a further planned second-opinion consultation with an eminent professor in the field. During the course of her visit the specialist tried to remove her intrauterine coil, but he could not find the strings to pull it out. This setback affected the patient greatly and she felt an enormous depression that lasted until Sunday.

Monday

On Friday night she dreamt that *she was on the eighth floor of a building where she* [an architect] *had built many small pink houses. The odd thing was that from the eighth floor one could see the sky* [as in that other dream when she had wanted to open up the ceiling of her bedroom]. *The flat was completely empty, and there were marks on the floor of demolished construction. The building extended upward, from the empty eighth floor.* Later, she dreamt that *she was going to leave for the movies when they tell her that her father, nearing his death, wanted to bid farewell. She went to the place where her father was. He was sitting on the bed surrounded by many people. She felt very anxious and could not stay still, while he was saying his good-byes to the people in the room before dying; when her turn arrived she felt such a profound pain that she did not want to listen to him.* She awoke from the dream crying. (I thought she could not bear the depressive anxiety.)

The analysand associated the eighth floor with the length of her analysis and remembered that a few weeks earlier I had interpreted that, for her, to end the analysis meant to have a baby with me. She was a mother of boys, yet the babies (small houses) in the dream were pink, the color generally associated with girls, at least in our culture. The patient also connected the dream with the Friday consultation with the gynecologist when he could not extract the IUD and also with the dream about the bedroom with the open sky. She remembered in passing how angry she had been with my interpretation then. (Identical disagreements had occurred several times, which I had never been able to properly solve.)

I interpreted the dream, initially, from the perspective of the ending of an analysis that could fail. Similarly to the gynecologist, I would be unable to find the strings that would allow me to extract something that she feels is bad (in the sense of preventing internal babies coming to life) that is lodged in her sexuality. (I thought about homosexuality but I did not mention it to her since I am not much in favor of interpreting more than one thing at a time and I try not to interpret from my knowledge and my theories; homosexuality is also not mentioned in the material nor is it implied in her associations.)

I also told her that, according to the dream, the end of the analysis appeared as a sad experience in which I die and she loses her uterus, the counterpart of having a baby with me.

35

Tuesday

We continued with the analysis of the dream, now more in terms of success and professional rivalry between us. There had been a recent positive development in her professional life that she attributed to progress in her analysis. Her personal abilities and her sense of beauty had been applied to her work, which resulted in her gaining professional prestige and clientele. She had just been chosen to be in charge of a big enterprise, a fact that had made her feel very happy. The situation gave rise to conflicts related to rivalry, guilt, and envy. In this sense, the death of her father in the dream was not only an expression of pain and mourning, but also the expression of her professional triumph vis-à-vis him, old and ill, when she was about to go to the movies. The aged father in the dream obviously represented her analyst. But I again preferred not to say this, on two counts: firstly, because this would appear obvious to her, and secondly because it could reinforce her rivalry in this context.

Wednesday

After the consultation with the professor she came to her session sincerely moved. The doctor confirmed the diagnosis but he only advised the removal of the tumors and did not recommend a hysterectomy. He added that his long experience had taught him to respect not only women but also the uterus itself. He only indicated radical surgery when life was at risk. He sustained that point of view over and above the fact that she was almost 40 years old and that she did not intend to have any more children. He would have told her the same thing even if she were 30 or 50. The patient felt very impressed by the wisdom of that man, who confessed to her of only once having made a mistake in a similar case. A young woman insisted in having her uterus removed and he agreed with her wish; only later on did he find out that the patient was a lesbian.

She had mentioned to the doctor the failed attempt to extract the coil and he had said that it should be attempted again.

The incident with the coil had allowed me to interpret to her on Monday that she considered that I had been unable to extract something she feels odd and encrusted in her sexuality. Now, after the consultation with the professor, she could admit that at times she found me unskillful. She thought again that there was something bad in her sexuality that I was unable to solve. (With her associations to the professor and his lesbian patient a new path opened for the interpretation of her homosexuality. Furthermore, we must not lose sight of the fact that her distrust was well-founded: one had to be very skillful to extract that IUD [homosexuality] lost in her unconscious. So I did not jump to her unconscious homosexuality, but kept on paying attention to her associations and to my countertransference.)

Suddenly, the transference turned from the father to the mother. It was not just that her penis envy (coil) showed my impotence to eliminate a bad introjected penis. There was, in addition, a conflict with the mother of my patient, who had suffered a radical hysterectomy when she herself was 30 years old, soon after the birth of her second daughter. She remembered this fact when the professor told her that he would not take away her womb even were she were 30 or 50. Her next associations (which I shall not detail here) depicted me as a woman unable to avoid receiving a bad fecal penis inside her (negative maternal transference).

She recognized then, that, for a moment, she had thought that the admired professor was wrong and that the hysterectomy proposed by her own gynecologist was the correct treatment. After surmounting a countertransference resistance (i.e., my initial resistance about mentioning homosexuality), I told her that she thought that I, like the professor, could be wrong and would not discover her to be a lesbian.

This interpretation produced a certain impact. The session was coming to an end as I was thinking how difficult I find it to interpret homosexuality in women in the context of the maternal transference, which is the best place where, I think, it can be validly solved.

It was easy for Freud (and for me!) to interpret penis envy from the paternal transference and deduce from it the resulting homosexuality. It is harder, however, to interpret female homosexuality in the frame of the maternal transference. In order to do so it is not enough to operate with the theory of penis envy: one has to deal with the relationship between the mother and her daughter in the preoedipal phase or, as I would prefer to do, within the early oedipal complex, at the feminine phase and through the theory of primary envy, that is, the envy of the penis that gives pleasure and babies. This Melanie Klein could do. But, of course, she was a woman!

Thursday

The patient announced that she was going away, on holiday, along with her family for a week. She explained the (reasonable) motives for this decision and added that she would bring the money to pay me at the next session, the last one of the month. Her announcement surprised me and alerted my countertransference. They had planned, she reminded me, a short holiday in Punta del Este (a well-known Uruguayan beach resort, not too far away from Buenos Aires), but the travel agency had to change it to an earlier date. She then had an association with her sister Emily, who had to have a study of her ovaries. She remembered again the consultation where the IUD could not be extracted the previous Friday.

When she would be back from her short holiday on the beach – she continued – they would all go to the country house to spend the summer vacation. After giving it much thought she had decided not to come to the January sessions, as she would normally do. Things had become very complicated as, at this precise time, they had only one car. My countertransference was by now on red alert. As she did not want to inconvenience me – she went on – she was willing to pay for those sessions and she would like to know what I thought in with regard to this. I told her that the payment was not the most important factor for me but rather what all this might mean for her.

She pointed out that this time things had changed and that she had to be in Buenos Aires in February, during my own summer holidays, to deal with her new commitments. She could not leave her family in the country house with no car, nor could she leave her business unattended for so long. She had plenty of work to do – the new enterprise under her own name was very important and this had complicated matters enormously. Now that she felt much better thanks to the analysis she was no longer willing to make the effort she had made in the past. (Here the risk of error was very high and I remained silent for the time being, so as to avoid both complaisance – that is, accepting her reasons – or authoritarianism, through an interpretation of her resistances and/or her acting out. I never interpret, or at least I try not to, when my countertransference advises me that I may be misunderstood.)

The patient went on to say that other things might be involved, but that frankly she did not feel willing to spoil her holidays to come in for her sessions. She did not know if her decision could alter the progress of her treatment, but she felt that she was somewhat afraid of raising this issue, because I could take it as a slight. (The intensity of the projection rendered it unadvisable to return it back to her.) She then said that something had come into her mind, she did not know if it might be related with what she was talking about, however she wanted to tell me about it.

Yesterday she had gone to her mother's and had found her sister crying desperately because of her boyfriend, Alfred, who did not want to give her a lift back when they left a conference they had both attended. Alfred said there was no room in his car for her. My patient added that it was pouring, there was a terrible storm going on, but he (Alfred) had already committed himself to giving a ride back to other colleagues and the car was full. Emily cried and unsuccessfully tried to get a taxi for her ride home. She then went back to Alfred, begged him, and he finally consented to drive her back along with the others. When Emily told her about this episode my patient felt preoccupied and furious. What does this girl (her sister) have in her head? What model of womanhood has our mother given us? The moment Alfred bought himself the car he has became unbearable, she exclaimed.

The situation became clear to me, and my countertransference anxiety abated. I told the patient that she was talking about her "*auto-analysis*" (auto = car). She became thoughtful and said that the "auto-analysis" made her think of separating from me and that it made her sad; but she could not see what the "auto-analysis" had to do with her sister and Alfred. "That you might use the 'auto-analysis' as Alfred uses his car" (*auto* means "car" in Spanish) I responded.

Patient: No! This is very painful. Do you mean to say that I am like Alfred, that I abandon you? [Silence] Alfred is a very disturbed guy. He is not a good guy. I worry that my sister chooses men like that. [Brief pause] I misunderstood what you said about the "auto-analysis." When you say that I am Alfred this is very far from what I think about "auto-analysis." [Long silence] It makes me very anxious to think that ... Now I get the wish to say no, if that is the case, I will come in January. [I actually worked the first fortnight of January.]

Analyst: This would only be a case of your becoming Emily and I Alfred.

P: But you insist in something I cannot accept. You are wrong. "The donkey returns to the hay!" as my grandmother would say. We are in the same situation as always. I do not believe that I want to abandon you. There are

39

many ways of abandoning. I think in Alfred's case it would be in the area of contempt, lack of love, and lack of manhood. A man cannot do that to a woman. He just cannot say, I do not have room in the car. I do not want you to say that I am slighting you. Because I love you very much [with sincere emphasis].

A: As you said yourself this is a theme that recurs. I do not know if my interpretations are right. They might be and you might not be able to accept them because you find it very painful; it might be that they are incorrect and that I place myself in a very intransigent position, as you have pointed out to me more than once.

P: It is a very conflictive point in our relationship. I feel very anxious that you might think so, that I might do such a thing. [Silence] [I perceived the analysand's conflict: the anxiety that *I* should think such a thing (projection); the anxiety that *she* could do such a thing (insight, depressive anxieties.)]]

A: It is a problem which defines clearly two irreconcilable positions: that I am stubborn, or that you can be bad.

P: But there is another option, which I do not like at all, and that is, when I accept all that you say, I am stupid and your word is the word of God.

A: Certainly! If I am God, you will be the donkey that goes back to the hay. [Repetition.]

P: This is very complex. I cannot take on board the other extreme either. I think, nevertheless, that *you* are the donkey, that you get stuck and do not move, a Basque beast. [She is referring here to the stubbornness generally attributed to Basques.][1]

A: Yes, there are two meanings to "donkey" as you say very well: you are a donkey because you do not understand and I am a donkey because I am stubborn.

P: I can see that more clearly now. But when you say that I am Alfred you cause me great pain; furthermore you offend me.

A: Yes. There is no doubt that what I told you is for you an offense, not an interpretation. [Here lies a fundamental point in my technique or, better put, in the way I understand psychoanalytic technique: separating interpretation from opinion. Interpretation is something that I suppose that the patient unconsciously thinks; opinion is something that I (and not the patient) think.]

P: I feel offended because when I have the car I give lifts to people backward and forward, all the time.

A: That's why I started off by telling you that the car (*auto* in Spanish) is the *auto*-analysis: it all centers around the issue of how you are going to implement your auto-analysis in the future, your autonomy.

P: If you think that I would use my improvement to slight you, you are very wrong.

A: I am wrong, in your view, when I tell you that you might use your improvement (auto-analysis, autonomy) as Alfred uses his car. [This is a cautious and neutral interpretation which only aspires to delineate positions, to clearly show the point of disagreement without in any way attempting to make a case, just to avoid being misunderstood, and here I think of the admirable Money-Kyrle.]

P: [With insight] This hurts my soul. But I will not avoid thinking that it might just be like that. Sometimes I find it easy to realize what is going on. I do not know if I am going to be left with an empty car or a full car ...

She then returns with some humor to the dream of the empty flat, and when the session ends I am left with the impression that we are on a good path. I wondered if we could untie this Gordian knot in the only remaining session of the term without having to cut it through in one blow like Alexander the Great, that is, to accept her going away or, on the contrary, to reject her doing so. As far as possible, I tried to avoid misunderstandings that the patient could use as indications that I approved or disapproved her decisions. I thought that the fact that the analysand had been able to use her sense of humor and to symbolize by the end of the session were favorable signs.

Friday

She returned feeling well disposed to carry on with the themes of the previous session. To put it briefly, there is something about which we cannot agree. I say that she does not want to come because she is full of work, that her car is full like Alfred's; and she considers that such a view is another instance of my stubbornness, because I do not want to recognize that she has other obligations apart from her analysis. She herself does not want to be stubborn, but it causes her

41

unbearable pain to see herself as contemptuous and ungrateful. She also thinks, nevertheless, that if she finds it so unbearable, there must be a reason for it. She feels rebellious as a woman for what Alfred did. A man who does something like that has no balls. He is not a man.

A: I think that, at the moment, you see me as a woman who is not capable of defending her feminine position: If you are Alfred then I am Emily.

P: What I am worried about is really, what does all this mean? Could it be then that I use the auto-analysis to keep a masculine part? I am telling you that Alfred makes me feel enormously rebellious *as a woman*. I cannot understand why Emily carries on crying and does not get angry or indignant. I cannot accept her response, because when a man does such a thing, in my eyes, his balls fall off.

A: I have told you that you feel like Alfred, that you despise me with your full car, let me add now that you have problems with your masculinity.

P: Then, if I tell you that I am not going to come because I have other professional commitments, I am telling you this *as a man*, a man without balls? But, if I tell you that I would come so that you do not get angry, then I am a submissive woman?

A: That's right. I think you see me as a woman who is not capable of defending her female condition in front of this Alfred with his full car who despises her.

P: This would be using my auto-analysis to keep a masculine part of myself.

A: I think so. From this point of view, the car *is* the penis. [Here I am appropriately interpreting, I believe, her rivalry and her penis envy "à la Freud."]

P: I am always alert, as a woman, to any denigrating attitude of men toward women, but you are telling me that I do this as a man and not as a woman. The truth is that when I hear a man calling me "poor you" I feel a veritable indignation. Poor *what*? Poor woman, poor devil? I feel it as "auto-defense" [self-defense]. Again the car! [She laughs] There is nothing "poor" about me. No man is going to "poor" me. I feel that I defend myself as a woman but you say I do it as a man. I must believe that I am wrong. What image of womanhood has our mother given us? I recognize that this has been a difficulty of mine and I have to conclude that, in this case, you are trustworthier than I, because you are the analyst and I the patient. [Brief silence] I prefer to continue analyzing this issue. [It is evident to me that there is at this point a moment of insight; nevertheless I think it convenient to keep on listening.]

A: This conflict does exist regardless of what you decide to do. In some way you want to push me in the wrong direction of solving it via a false alternative between submissiveness or rebellion.

P: I do not know if I want to push you or if I want you to say what would be better. But I do know that I have a good analysis and that you are not going to say that. [That is, to advise her, to give her an opinion. I take note that here she recognizes me in my capacity as analyst.]

A: The problem we are discussing here is what kind of a woman am I when I have to confront Alfred.

P: But then I would have to accept that you are a better woman than I. You would let Alfred stew in his own sauce. You do not cry to Alfred, you do not beg to Alfred, you do not tell Alfred what he has to do …

A: I am trying to rescue my femininity because this is an issue between women. [I try to make her conscious of the maternal transference.]

P: You are a better woman than I to confront this situation. This makes me very angry. Your feminine capacities make me feel envious. In these circumstances, you do better than I. When I want to defend my femininity, my womb, my place as a woman, it seems as if I appeal to masculine resources. Yes, I think so, I feel more convinced. [Now that she has accepted me as an analyst–woman–mother it becomes possible to analyze the homosexual conflict in the framework of the maternal transference. And I do this cautiously, coming back to the subject of the professor.]

A: You were recalling earlier the consultation with the professor, the hysterectomy, and your uterus.

P: I think that the professor is a man who recognizes and respects the place of women. In any case, either he or you could find or use femininity better than I can. It sounds very odd that when you play your female role I do not know whether I get angry or envious. You seem able to do something that I cannot do. Both you and the professor do it better than I. [It is interesting that she talks in the plural form, as this implies that she feels that this is a conflict she has with others, not only of mine with her.]

A: To put it in perhaps somewhat sophisticated terms, you are now thinking that I am a better woman-architect than you are. In fact, we are dealing with that precise issue at this very moment. If I manage, I would be a good analyst (woman = architect = mother), I would be giving you a good model to be one yourself; if, on the contrary, I did not, you would say sometime in the future, and with reason, what did my analyst do that did not give me the resources that I need? – much in the same way as you are wondering about the model of womanhood that your mother provided for Emily and yourself.

P: As you were talking it occurred to me to ask you if there would be any chance, should I come these two weeks, of altering my times slightly, so that I could return to the country house earlier. I realized that if I changed my commitments with the partners of the company for the new enterprise a bit, I could still have my holidays and come to analysis.

A: This question might have many interpretations (submission, condescension), but I am inclined to think that it is a recognition of my capacity as an analyst in this session. [I try to help her to accept her homosexuality and her envy; I say "in this session" so as not to give the interpretation a general and apodictic character. The interpretation aims to assist her in accepting her homosexuality and her envy of the mother's womb/breast, a difficult task indeed.]

P: It would be a recognition that makes me angry. [She laughs]

A: It makes you angry but also makes you feel better. You said that, in the last resort, you have to trust me more than yourself because I am the analyst. If I am really the analyst and you the analysand, it would be only too logical to think that I would be less involved than yourself with this conflict. It would not be so much my merit but …

P: … a condition of your role. [Thoughtful] [After this acknowledgment I am in a position, I believe, of referring to the patient's infantile behavior with her mother.]

A: What happens is that you sometimes question my role. I do not know how things actually were in your infancy; but I do know what is happening in the session. It may have been that your mother did not always give you a model of womanhood; but we have also got to admit that you might have reacted with envy when she did. [This is a moment in which the transference situation has been dealt with and the patient recognizes me as her analyst. I believe that at this juncture one should reduce the transference situation, as Reich would say, and remit the conflict to infancy. I answer in this way her repeated question about the model of womanhood that her mother provided for her.]

44

P: Sure! ... I had never before experienced so acutely the envy, I do not know if this is the correct word, that a clear and defined attitude gives rise in me. I always imagined it to be different.

A: That is, the attitude of that lesbian patient to the professor.

P: Yes, she was looking at him with contempt because he took care of her womb.

A: Exactly. The professor said that his mistake consisted in not having realized that the patient was a lesbian and that, for her, the womb was not important. The professor did not realize that that woman did not want to defend her womb but rather to dispose of it. Thus, he was pushed into a homosexual game with her by agreeing to the surgery. This is precisely what you attempted to do in your role as Alfred, a woman who intends to seduce me and make me submit to her imaginary penis. [A rather long interpretation but well focused to my mind. I try also to help in her working through.]

I had kept this material for a few years and I was about to throw it away when I received Robert's kind invitation and I thought I could use it to illustrate my way of working. I always interpret in accordance with what I understand the material dictates at that particular point. I interpret the positive and the negative transference impartially, and I believe, as the old master Pichon-Rivière used to say, that an interpretation must be *complete*, that is here and now with me, as there, far away and long ago with the original objects. A complete interpretation must include the transference, the current conflict, and the infantile conflict. To this I would add the early conflict, which, by definition, is preverbal, but that can be recovered in the infinite vicissitudes of the transference-countertransference. When we are dealing with the early conflict, the data provided by our countertransference are vital, as they reach us from the preverbal and from the paraverbal (as David Liberman used to say). I still prefer to talk about the early transference rather than the now popular "enactment" that for me could be used to disguise acting out or acting in. The early transference, "memories in feelings," as Klein called them, is a communication and not a special form of acting out. Acting out, as I understand it, does not have the intention to communicate. The early transference is communicated, even though it obviously will not be through words; of course this does not rule out that it might be enlisted in acting out.

There is an almost unanimous agreement among analysts that the transference is what is essential in our work, and this material also confirms this view. However, I may possibly give more of a place to the current conflict, the infantile conflict, and the early conflict. Sometimes, and it can be a beautiful experience, I interpret *all* the conflicts in the same material, as I did in Helsinki. When this is possible the beauty of the method (Meltzer) and its epistemological validity (Klimovsky) come to the fore.

I have already said that there are many – almost infinite – ways of understanding the concept of transference. The form that I support is the most classic, the most conservative: that of Freud.

I would also like to mention that I do differentiate the total relationship with the patient from the transference relationship. I only call transference something that belongs to the past and is actualized at that particular moment. It is a restricted use of the concept, but it is the one that Freud proposed and that Strachey pointed out. I think it is not advisable to extend it, as the concept would lose in specificity. It is also true that Freud said that what is established between the patient and the analyst is a dialogue; but he did not mean to say (or so I understand it) just any dialogue. A dialogue is psychoanalytic when it develops within the norms of reserve and asymmetry that he established (albeit that Freud himself as an analyst did not always practice them), and when it implies repetition and the past. Something new that comes up in a session might be to the point and useful, but in my view it is not transference.

In the material just presented the early conflict does not figure specifically, but the positive and negative maternal and paternal transferences do. It's not every day that a male psychoanalyst (as I believe I am!) has the chance to interpret to a woman the homosexual transference, as in this case.

The analytic dialogue always has the past as a background. Some analysts believe that their task consists in (and ends with) the analysis of the transference, but I do not believe this. If one were to do so one would run the risk of splitting the present and the past that in general takes the form of idealizing the present (the analyst) and denigrating the past (the bad parents, frustrating, castrating, or abandoning). In this way a very important area of working through is left out. The process of working through consists in the analysand's realization that what happens to him with me also happens to him at home, at work, and as a child in the house of his parents.

It is possibly clear from my way of working that I consider the therapeutic (or working) alliance to be an integral part of my task. I learnt this from the ego psychologists. I have already said that Freud sometimes confused the positive transference and the working alliance, and I think that the idea of a sublimated positive transference is in itself contradictory.

I would also like to add that, to my mind, not all that comes from the past is transference. It is sometimes *experience*, and this then could help me (or the patient) to use the past, not to misunderstand it. When I am facing a difficult task and I think of Zulema Briasco, Arminda Bolano de Casteran, and other of my teachers, and even more so, my mother, I am using the past to understand the present and not to misunderstand it.

Klein, who was as much a genius as Freud, discovered the mental life of the baby, which, for Robert Wälder and Freud was only reflex or neurological. Klein gave back to the act of breast-feeding its psychological nature and understood it as a complex human relationship (without primary narcissism), suffused with early or psychotic anxieties, and thus demonstrated the enormously complex relationship between the baby and the breast. In my opinion, Klein did not totally grasp that the act of taking the breast's milk belongs not only to the area of conflict but also to the carrying out of a *task*. Great thinkers are not always faithful to their own discoveries.

I would like to establish a bridge between the early conflicts and the working (or therapeutic) alliance, with the latter understood as a joint task of the baby and the breast (or the mother). The baby not only sucks at the breast to satisfy his need and express his love but also to awaken the mother's love and to stimulate, in this joint task, lactogenesis. I would very much like to stress how much of a psychological task the act of breast-feeding really is.

The psychotic anxieties that Klein discovered and described go hand in hand with the accomplishment of a joint task between the baby and the breast, without which life would not be possible. These are some of the wonders of evolution. I think Melanie Klein perceived this, but, possibly for reasons more personal than theoretical, she did not stress this aspect of working or the therapeutic alliance that would later on be underlined by the ego psychologists, who, in turn, for personal reasons, could not tune in to her work.

When Elizabeth Zetzel takes support from Heinz Hartmann's terms (conflict-free area, secondary autonomy) to sustain her concept of therapeutic alliance, she finally ends up relying on the relationship between the baby and his mother.

I would like to finish by saying what I have said in many other occasions: there is transference in everything but not everything is transference. The art and the science of psychoanalysis consist in being able to discriminate the two.

Our profession is very difficult, but not impossible.

Note

1   Etchegoyen is a Basque family name. – ed.

3

"WELL, YOU'D BETTER ASK THEM"

The countertransference position at the crossroads

Haydée Faimberg

Introduction

Countertransference took a long time to be accepted as a valid concept in the analytical experience. As a concept, it was not understood or defined in just one way, given that any definition hinges on the underlying theory involved.

Through the concept of the countertransference position, I attempt to incorporate from my own theoretical and clinical perspective questions that were arising on the basis of the acceptance and also rejection of the concept of countertransference.

I shall try to put in a nutshell the questions arising from a debate on countertransference. *What is important in an analysis: the actual person of the analyst, the neutrality of the analyst, the psychic work of the analyst, the analyst as a subject?* The concept of "subject" presupposes in turn a complex theoretical field, as does the concept of "object relation." The questions that form part of this debate include: the importance given to neurotic and psychotic functioning; an oedipal and/or narcissistic functioning; and the place occupied by the concepts of projection and projective identification (according to various authors). Last but not least, we need to consider the importance of the unconscious dimension in the analytical experience. These are some of the parameters I have chosen to indicate the complexity of the problem.[1]

The expression "countertransference position" is used in certain contexts, and was used on occasion by Heinrich Racker.

In some passages (relating in particular to training analyses), Racker uses the expression "countertransference position" to designate aspects of the transference that the analyst had not analyzed in his own analysis and that may therefore have been transmitted without being noticed. He gives the name of "countertransferential occurrences" to unexpected ideas, apparently unrelated to the patient's discourse, that may anticipate what emerges in the same or another session. It should be noted that in France the expression "countertransference position" is used not as a concept such as I define it, but rather as essentially a way of denoting the response – frequently the affective (conscious and unconscious) response – of the analyst.

As far as I can see I believe that I am contributing a new conceptual definition that does not necessarily contradict others but broadens them. In particular, I do not think that it is in contradiction with Racker's understanding of the term "countertransference position."

What has led me to redefine the question is the desire to include in the very definition parameters chosen in the light of the debates in which the concept of countertransference has been accepted or rejected. In other words, this redefinition raises in its very structure issues that from my perspective are essential for our psychoanalytical experience.[2]

I am writing this paper against the backdrop of what I owe to the work of Racker, while realizing that his ideas have been transformed by my own particular way of thinking. We may consider that his concepts were transmitted, whether directly or through the agency of oral tradition, in more than one way. I did not have the privilege of knowing him personally. (Racker died at the early age of 50 in 1961.) From my chosen perspective, recognizing this filiation means that the analyst structures his thinking from and around the basic idea that *his psychic functioning affects the way he listens to his patient and his conscious or unconscious way of interpreting or remaining silent.*

Filiation means that Racker's ideas are implicitly or explicitly present there. We discover with surprise that we agree with them: we thought that we were inventing them until we discovered that he had already thought of them, or else, without knowing exactly when, we realize that we had been approaching the problem from some other angle (even without having ourselves posed the problem). In Argentina, where I received my training before migrating to France in 1976, the filiation with the work of Racker was inevitable because, over and above our readings of his work, his ideas were transmitted orally, often without it being realized, by way of seminars, supervisions, and discussions among colleagues.

It may usefully be recalled that Racker defines countertransference as the totality of the analyst's response to what occurs in the session.

The countertransference position

Let us define the countertransference position (Faimberg, 1989) as all the psychical activity of the analyst, including of course its unconscious dimension, intended to *restore what corresponds to the history of the transference*. It is a clinical concept; it develops further the approach initiated by Racker from a perspective that shall be set out in this chapter.

I speak of *position* because I am referring to the way the analyst places himself in relation to his psychic functioning. I spoke first of the *countertransference* position (and not just of a listening position) to make it clear that the purpose of analyzing the analyst's listening position is to identify what kind of *transference* (not yet recognized as such) is involved in it. This position may be modified by various factors that are interlinked in a nonlinear, dialectical causality.

The countertransference position can be detected by the analyst by listening, in a way that I like to call *de-centered*, to his own psychic functioning. He thereby seeks to maintain a dissymmetrical position in order to listen to his patient. I do not say "asymmetrical" because that would imply that the position has no form, and it does have one. *Dissymmetrical in this context means that the psychic functioning of the analyst offers a means of discovering – with* the patient – the *patient's* unconscious conflicts.

The basic assumption of the countertransference position is then that the analyst silently analyzes in turn his own psychic functioning in such a way as to overcome the obstacles that he discovers in the oscillations of that position in order to *restore* what corresponds to the *history of the transference*.

When we discover as analysts that we occupy a *symmetrical* position, we come face to face with the need to analyze the type of *impact* that this is having on our psychic functioning in regard both to what the patient says and to that which he cannot yet say.

51

Given that every analyst has an unconscious way of functioning, from my perspective it can be decided only *retroactively* whether there has been a neurotic response. For example, when the analyst has *repeated* difficulties in listening to certain aspects of what the patient says and cannot say and he cannot overcome those difficulties, it seems right to infer the involvement of a *neurotic resistance from within his own psyche*.

Let us just mention a particular aspect: the *analyst's narcissistic resistance* (Faimberg, 2001) to listening to something new or unexpected, which could make him lose his bearings, and in particular what happens when his theory (as he conceives it at that point) is no longer in resonance with what he is listening to in the session.

Among the factors that impinge on the analyst's psychic functioning let us mention the following:

a) Aspects of the patient's transference exist, though not yet recognized as such, which have not been restored to him by way of interpretation.

b) The analyst's personal background and the history of the transference with his own analyst (plus the relation to supervisions and teachers) form part of the way in which the analyst listens to his patient and decides to interpret or not.

c) The *theoretical* position of the analyst forms an inescapable part of the definition of the countertransference position that I am proposing. The theoretical options are linked to what has been implicitly transmitted by his own analyst in the course of his analysis, by his supervisions (implicitly and explicitly), and by the psychoanalytic institution to which they all belong.

d) Moreover, the analyst may prefer one theoretical option in part because it is more in resonance with his own mode of psychic functioning.

e) We could also endeavor to discover the *origin of the ideas that are transmitted in psychoanalytic institutions*. The fate of these ideas is frequently linked to the way in which concepts and clinical approaches were carried through the migration of analysts and to how the new psychoanalytic culture received, transformed, rejected, or disregarded them.

f) In addition, the analyst's readings, his life experience, cultural interests, and so on, form part of his psychic functioning and determine his countertransferential listening position. It will be recalled that culture in general and literature in particular had an important place in Freud's thinking.

In the proposed definition theory forms part of the components of the countertransference position. In my own analytic work, my listening position includes the concept of "complementary identification" – which I shall now go on to explore.

Complementary identification

> The complementary identifications are produced by the fact that the patient treats the analyst as an internal (projected) object, and in consequence the analyst feels treated as such; that is, he identifies himself with this object.
>
> (Racker, 1957, p. 135)

I came to realize that while the concept of complementary identification is an irreplaceable one for me, I am using Racker's concept in a slightly different way inasmuch as the *theoretical assumptions on which I base my clinical work* differ in many respects from those of Racker.[3]

In this context I prefer to say that in the complementary identification, the analyst identifies himself – unconsciously – *with the object with which the patient identifies him*. The analysis of the countertransference position reveals the object with which the analyst has identified himself: thus we know, *retroactively*, what the transference object was with which the patient had identified him. In other words, it reveals the transference that had been contained in the countertransference position.

It should be noted that the complementary and the concordant identifications that Racker defines separately are not separable for him in clinical reality. He says this explicitly in his texts and his clinical examples. However, what particularly interests me in his thinking is the concept of complementary identification. I shall refer exclusively to how I understand the term. Furthermore, although Racker speaks of a *failure* in concordant identification, I believe that he would have agreed that, while there is a tendency for the analyst to have this type of identification (in his words), this cannot be taken for granted but is also an outcome of his own analytic activity. It would be interesting to study concordant identification and countertransference in relation to contemporary writings on the concept of "empathy." By the way, the concept of counter-resistance proposed by León Grinberg may be considered as *a particular case* of complementary identification (as defined by Racker).

The psychic presence of the analyst and his countertransference position

The psychic presence or absence of the analyst should be seen as a key indicator of his countertransference position.

The acceptance of the concept of countertransference as a valid concept in clinical psychoanalysis has been, at times, jeopardized for certain historical reasons. Let us consider an example: the criticism that Jacques Lacan leveled at Michael Balint's idea of a "basic fault"[4] addresses Balint's concept from the perspective of Lacan's concept of "lack" (*manque*).[5] On the one hand, we have the problem that the object is ill-suited to fully satisfy the drive – hence the concept of a lack – and, on the other, we have to take account of the analyst's psychic presence. Although I share the idea that the object cannot fully satisfy the drive, in my view this does not compromise the idea that the analyst is psychically present to listen to what the analysand is trying to communicate: psychic presence and suitability of the object do not have the same theoretical status.

The oscillation between psychic presence and psychic absence of the analyst forms part of his *shifting listening position*.

Here, the debate around the concept of countertransference includes the view that countertransference is "the analyst's resistance" (as it was called by Lacan). Although this is not the place to examine the status of the analyst's desire (an essential concept in the thinking of Lacan and in psychoanalysis) or to link it to the concepts of countertransference and the countertransference position, let us try to retrace the origins of the idea of equating "countertransference" and "the analyst's resistance."

We may think that, in regarding countertransference as the analyst's resistance, Lacan referred to one of the many perspectives opened up by the following statement by Freud:

Other innovations in technique relate to the physician himself. We have become aware of the "countertransference" which arises in him *as a result of the patient's influence on his unconscious feelings* and we are almost inclined to insist that he shall recognize this counter-transference in himself and overcome it. Now that a considerable number of people are practising psycho-analysis and exchanging their observations with one another, we have noticed that *no psychoanalyst goes further than his own complexes and internal resistances permit*; and we consequently require that he shall begin his activity with self-analysis.

(Freud, 1910, p. 144, emphasis added)

In his translation of this passage, Jean Laplanche notes that *Selbstanalyse* may designate both one's analysis by an analyst and "self-analysis."

In this context, Freud would be speaking of the analysis of the future analyst, which came to be called "training analysis." He thus acknowledged that there is an obstacle that must be overcome and that this is only possible through personal analysis. The history of countertransference for Freud remains linked to the history of training analysis by way of the concept of resistance.

Owing to this link established to the training analysis, one current of analytical thought was able to maintain that a successful analysis should not lead to a countertransference situation. Paula Heimann (1950) was the first who through her work gave full recognition to the concept of countertransference as not being synonymous with the analyst's neurosis on the basis that countertransference is triggered by the patient. This is not the place to go into the similarities and dissimilarities between the ideas that I am proposing here and those that she set out in her seminal work, although traces of her ideas may be detected in the present essay.

For my part, as a starting point for defining the countertransference position, I find that I have also followed other paths, some of which are also present in the Freud quotation.

Let us begin by noting that for Freud the countertransference is the analyst's *unconscious response* to what is triggered by his patient; this response is linked both to the *unconscious affects* of the analyst and to a broader network created by the analyst's own *psychic configuration* – and, in addition, but *not exclusively, to his own resistances.*

I wish to recall another of Freud's deep and rather sobering insights: "*Unfortunately, we can only turn neurotic misery into ordinary human suffering, which lies beyond our reach*" (quoted by Laforgue in 1956). If we consider the unconscious dimension that exists in all "ordinary human suffering," *even for Freud "unconscious" would not necessarily be synonymous with "neurotic."*

From this perspective, I do not think that it is possible to presuppose that the countertransference position has a neurotic character simply by virtue of the fact that there is an *inevitable* unconscious dimension in the functioning of the analyst: if there is a neurotic reaction in the countertransference response, this will be recognized *retroactively*.

The analyst's transference on to the patient and his countertransference position

In a letter to his brother, John Keats writes that what he admires in Shakespeare is his "negative capability." Marion Milner drew attention to this expression in 1934 and, in 1967, Bion took it up in his celebrated recommendation to listen to the patient "with neither memory nor desire." In line with Bion and with Theodor Reik, let us consider surprise to be an indicator of the discovery of an unconscious register.

"Negative capability" is a psychic activity whereby the analyst places himself *actively*, let us say it once again, in the countertransference position of "not knowing." It is an important condition for gaining access to what is not known; the surprise shared by analyst and patient denotes this discovery.

All this presupposes on the part of the analyst the capacity to contain the anxiety of not knowing (including not knowing that he does not know) and to take his bearings in relation to what cannot yet be expressed in words. Put in another way, the analyst places himself in *the countertransference position of containing the anxiety* generated both by what the patient rejects from himself because it provokes displeasure, and by what provokes displeasure in the analyst insofar as he cannot give a meaning to what is still an enigma. Here the expression "*countertransference* position" reminds us that these are features of that part of the transference that has *not yet* been analyzed.

What happens when the analyst cannot contain the anxiety that derives both from the patient's psychic functioning and from his own? If the analyst does not contain the anxiety in this case it is the analyst himself who *transfers* to the *patient's* psyche the conflicts that have been reactivated in him in the session.

Heinrich Racker began his investigation of countertransference on the very basis of the problem arising from what the analyst transfers to the patient. He accordingly wrote about various oedipal conflicts that are reactivated in the analyst and interfere with his capacity to interpret. Racker read this study, entitled "The Neurosis of Countertransference," in 1948 before the Argentine Psychoanalytic Association. He withheld it from publication until 1953 under the pressure of his colleagues, who considered that it was not proper for an analyst to show in his own clinical cases neurotic aspects of countertransference. In Racker's words, speaking about Margaret Little on the subject of the myth of the impersonal analyst, "without the concept of countertransference the analytic situation consists in the coming together of a healthy person, the analyst, and a sick person, the patient." In his subsequent work, Racker studied the analyst's countertransference without using the concept of neurosis. It is likely that the work of Paula Heimann, in 1950, may have influenced the acceptance by the psychoanalytic institution of Racker's published work precisely from 1952.

The "missing concept[s]"

In a dialogue with colleagues from various cultures, many of whom had not been familiar with the ideas of Racker, I became aware of the need for the concepts developed by him of complementary unconscious identification and complementary countertransference. Up to that point in the analytic milieu in Argentina Racker's concepts were so omnipresent that we might have thought that they formed part of a kind of "natural" analytical listening. At the same time, we were well aware that the analyst's implicit basic assumptions partake of what Bion (following Poincaré) called the "selected fact." *Accordingly, let us say, there is no such thing as natural analytical listening.*

Thus, recognizing that the concept of complementary identification was not present in the clinical work of analysts belonging to other psychoanalytic traditions, I was paradoxically able to identify this concept as *necessary* and as *not* being there.

It is always quite interesting to identify a *gap* between what we listen to in the session and what a particular theoretical conception might lead us to conceive; or what an author explicitly tells us in the text and what our reading leads us to reinterpret on the basis of another conceptualization. Let us say that the cause of this gap should be regarded as an *as-yet-unformulated* concept: a "missing concept."

When one does not use a concept, one does not miss it. In order to point to a "missing concept" we must justify the fact that its inclusion *adds a dimension which is not recognizable in its absence.*

Let us consider that a psychoanalytic concept has been "missing" when its inclusion (once it has been possible to formulate it) *changes the perspective* of listening to the patient or of reading a psychoanalytic text; something is thereby *added that it would not be possible to understand without this concept.*

In the case to which we were referring, "complementary identification" was such a "missing concept" (for analysts belonging to a different background than mine). This realization made it easier for me, at that time, to recognize that I was using it from my own theoretical perspective.

Moreover we may wonder about the possible consequences, for theory and for the analytic experience, of *the absence of the concept of the countertransference position.*

Freud and the accounts of Maryse Choisy and Abraham Kardiner in the light of the concept of the countertransference position

I shall now look at two testimonies to the clinical work of Freud in the years 1921–1925. Abraham Kardiner described his analysis with Freud in 1921–1922 in his book *My Analysis with Freud* (1977); and Maryse Choisy had three sessions with Freud in 1925 when she was 22 years old.[6]

Let us study in these two texts the way in which *Freud's theory is reactivated* by what the patient says, how does he say it, and what are the unconscious conflicts that form the context in which he says it.

Why am I interested in the theoretical standpoint while considering the problems concerning the concept of the analyst's listening position?

Insofar as Freud's unconscious way of functioning *cannot* be determined, let us choose to focus on *one* of the components of his countertransference position (and that form part, as I wrote, of my definition), which I consider can to some extent be explored: the level of his theorization reached at that time, which can indeed be compared when we consider these two clinical cases. For obvious reasons, the relationship with his own analyst, supervisions, and the relationship with the psychoanalytical institution (some of the components of the countertransference position) cannot be taken into account in this case! I have forgone the temptation of inferring other dimensions in Freud's psychical functioning ...

Let us specially explore *whether the concept of the countertransference position here proposed does or does not throw new light on what already could be said* without *this concept.*

In 1956 Maryse Choisy devoted a special issue of *Psyché*, the journal she founded and directed, to a commemoration of Freud's 100th birthday.

On that occasion she gave an account of her experience with Freud without recounting a dream that she had recounted to him, adding that she might reveal it in her memoirs. In the chapter "Memories of My Visits with Freud" (the English version of the same text that appeared in the compilation *Freud as We Knew Him* [1973]), she includes the text of the dream, saying that she does so in the belief that no living analyst would have the genius of Freud in discovering what he was able to discover. She also writes that her analysis was a failure – "like the analysis of Dora."

Of course to develop a technique distinguished guinea pigs are necessary. Only a genius is able to build up a magnificent success out of two failures. [...]

My analysis [...] went *too* well. It was interrupted in the third session. I told of a dream which seemed quite incomprehensible. [...]

It all happened in the big somewhat old-fashioned kitchen of our family castle near Saint Jean de Luz. I was a pretty Siamese cat with a very long pedigree. Since I was the youngest kitten, despite my ancestry I had to wait for my food until all the alley cats without any pedigrees had finished their plate on the flag-stone. I felt humiliated and hungry. Then I began to scratch everybody. I woke up with a start and remained anxious for awhile. Associations. It was the castle where I was born and raised. I was not allowed in the kitchen. Good little girls weren't in those days. I sometimes slipped unnoticed into the kitchen because it was forbidden fruit. This was a plot between the cook and me. I once stole some pudding and got indigestion.

I always had Siamese cats. I love them. I have one now.

Freud pondered for a few minutes over my dream, then uttered without warning, "Such and such an event happened in your family when you were still in the cradle." [...]

Many a good family has a skeleton in the closet. Closets are quite useful for that purpose. Still it was a shock. I did not believe Freud. I even became indignant.

"What you say is quite impossible, I would have known it. Such things are simply not done in *my* family. It's against their principles."

Though I could not see him behind me, I knew he was smiling. He just gave me the following advice, "Well, you'd better ask them."

I jumped on the first plane back to Paris. I ran to my aunt's house. I spoke to her the moment I got there. Believe it or not, Freud's extravagant story of an event which I had never suspected (at least consciously) turned out to be true. [...]

Freud did then what he later warned all his pupils to avoid: he interpreted too early, when the analysand was still unable to accept what he was. This Freud called *wild psychoanalysis.* [...]

(Choisy, 1973, p. 471)

Reading her account, the idea came to my mind that Freud may have told her that by her dream she revealed the *unconscious fantasy* of being adopted or of being illegitimate; or that she *was* in fact that kind of child. Being something or having the unconscious fantasy of being something are different levels of truth.

In Maryse Choisy's narrative, we do not know in what style Freud formulated the construction and we realize that this is of considerable importance. We do know, however, the style *in which she responded to the interpretation/construction, and what interests us first and foremost is the style in which Freud answered her.*

Maryse replies: "What you say is quite impossible, I would have known it. Such things are simply not done in *my* family. It's against their principles."

Maryse Choisy responds with what I consider to be narcissistic resistances to the wound caused to her by the interpretation, a wound that might be inferred from her words: "Still it was a shock" and "when the analysand was still unable to accept what [she] was." I shall come back to this point.

If this hypothesis is acceptable (that she responds to Freud's perspicacious construction by a narcissistic resistance) then we may go on to analyze the *impact of Maryse's response on Freud.*

Freud answers in the *language of action, with an injunction, which leads Maryse Choisy to check in external material reality that Freud's interpretation/ construction corresponded to the material facts as they had occurred in the past.*

Freud obtains by the analytic method the key to interpreting the dream, but he does not use the analytic method to work through with Maryse Choisy "the conviction of the truth of the construction" (Freud, 1937). As a consequence, Maryse Choisy decided not to return to Freud and for years she avoided contact with analysts.

We could object that Freud's article on construction where he theorizes about truth and construction was written by him in 1937 and that we have no evidence that what he maintains in that article was already theorized by him at the time of that session.

It is here that Kardiner's account is essential to see what method was used by Freud at *that* time to validate his construction. As we shall see, the work with Kardiner is in line with what he says in the 1937 article. On the question of dates, it is to be noted that clinical experience preceded the publication of his theoretical work.

Having written elsewhere from another perspective about Abraham Kardiner's analysis (Faimberg, 2006) I shall confine myself here to showing in what way Freud's interventions with Kardiner and with Maryse Choisy *differ*.

Kardiner writes:

> I had a dream about a mask, from which I awoke with great apprehension. The dream stimulated very important associations which led to the discovery of a childhood phobia that I had had, namely, the fear of masks and clothed wax figures. Freud asked, "What was there about the mask that frightened you so?" My first response was that it was the facial immobility, the lack of expression, the fact that it neither smiled nor laughed, and that the face was immobile. I myself had had several dreams in which I could see myself in the mirror, and the face would not reflect my emotional expression; that is, I would smile or I would frown, but the expression in the mirror did not change.
>
> Freud drew the conclusion that the possibility was that "*the first mask you saw was your dead mother's face.*" Now, this idea sent shivers through me when I first thought about it, but the circumstantial evidence from this dream and the associations led to the striking possibility that I had discovered my mother dead, while I was alone with her in the house.
>
> (Kardiner, 1977, p. 61)

Kardiner does not immediately accept the possibility that he had seen the face of his dead mother ("this idea sent shivers through me when I first thought about it"). In the analytic process, he then goes through a latency period, following which he begins to accept the "*circumstantial evidence from this dream and the associations* [that] led to the *striking possibility* that I had discovered my mother dead" [emphasis added].

Unlike what happens with Maryse Choisy, Freud does not ask for this evidence to be confirmed from external sources.

Obviously, the analysis takes place in Vienna. When later Kardiner travels to New York, his sister confirms to him that he had stayed alone with his chronically sick mother. "Apparently, I wanted something and I shook her. She did not respond or answer, and I was frightened. When my sister came home for lunch, she discovered that my mother was dead and that I was alone in the room crying" (1977, p. 62). At the time Kardiner was 3 years old and his sister was 11.

Back in Vienna, Kardiner tells Freud this story, which confirms the construction, and receives the following reply: " 'Well', said Freud, 'it's *obvious from your associations* that the mask represented your mother's dead face. Therefore, all masks or wax figures were associated with death, and brought back the old terror' " (Kardiner, 1977, pp. 61–62, emphasis added).

In other words, *Kardiner's associations within the analytic framework, respecting the analytic method, serve Freud as a way of validating his construction*: "It's obvious." We note that the construction is cast in the hypothetical form.

Considering the very different ways in which these two analysands received a construction, we might explore in turn whether these provide keys to understanding Freud's different responses.

In Kardiner, after his initial emotion ("shivers"), a working through occurs that leads to the *conviction that the construction proposed by Freud is true* ("but the circumstantial evidence from this dream and the associations led to the striking possibility ... ").

Maryse says in her account that when she heard Freud's revelation, "it was a shock," thus referring to a commotion in *her being*, in the person she always believed herself to be ("when the analysand was still unable to accept what [she] was"): in short, a threat to the narcissistic core of her being. It is indeed in response to this narcissistic wound that Maryse Choisy rejects the construction with peremptory, narcissistic assertions ("What you say is quite impossible, I would have known it. Such things are simply not done in *my* family. It's against their principles").

As we might read this, she says that she belongs to a type of French aristocratic family: could it be that Freud's interpretations do not mean anything to her because Freud and she have different family lineages? (Whatever may be Maryse Choisy's conception of her family.)

Moreover, might we imagine that Freud would have heard something equivalent to "You don't belong to this elite"? (Whatever the different levels of significance that "not belonging to" might have had *for Freud*.) There is no way of knowing.

From the chosen perspective, there is a *narcissistic struggle about who is right*: Maryse Choisy who does not accept the validity of the construction, or Freud who *then responds by the injunction, which Maryse Choisy imagines ("knows") is accompanied by a smile*:

"Well, you'd better ask them." (The "smile," whether it existed or not, would confirm that, at least from her side, there was such a narcissistic struggle.)

We do not know Freud's unconscious emotional response but, whatever it may have been, it is *not* possible to infer that there was *a point-for-point response* to what Maryse Choisy unconsciously experiences. At the conscious level, Maryse Choisy gives us an indication from her standpoint: "I even became indignant." If we consider, as I am doing, that Maryse Choisy *triggers a response* from Freud that is also emotional, this unconscious emotional response is filtered through Freud's *own* psychic characteristics.

"I would have known." These words of Maryse call into question the basic assumption of the analysis: *the unconscious knowledge that every patient may have, which remains unknown*. The enigma of the analysis is that it is the patient who communicates what she "does not know that she knows" (in this case by means of a dream), and it is the analyst who listens to what as an analyst he did not know. And from this encounter between two not-knowings a conviction emerges that the construction speaks the truth.

So it happens with Kardiner, who responds with shivers. We might imagine that Freud's response is influenced by what Kardiner describes as "shivers" – that I take to mean his helplessness. We do not know what this triggers in Freud (maybe related to his helplessness?). But we *do know that it allows him to use his own theory and to respect the analytic method*.

In contrast with the narcissistic struggle that we have postulated in the face of Choisy's response, Freud's response to Kardiner brings him into consonance with his ideas. *It is not a matter of who is right, it is a matter of analyzing what type of unconscious truth is at stake.*

My hypothetical conclusion is that the enigma presented by the two analyses could be addressed on the basis of the concept of the countertransference position.

Let us imagine that Freud's countertransference position was different with Maryse Choisy and with Abraham Kardiner and that *his listening position impinges on the way in which he could have used the theoretical resources already at his disposal, as we saw in Kardiner's account.*

If what I have been talking about as being likely has any cogency, *the concept of the countertransference position would add a new understanding to this clinical enigma.*

In this case, could we say that the concept of countertransference position would prove to be a *necessary* concept?

Conclusion to mark an opening

Edward Glover (1931) wondered how analysts worked before a particular concept had been formulated. His work on the inexact interpretation had considerable repercussions in psychoanalytical institutes. I think that, in addition to its intrinsic value, it was this central question that interested us all.

The concept of countertransference was not defined in just one way. Starting from my theoretical position, which underpins this entire essay, I have proposed a conceptualization of the countertransference position which, as far as I know, is new. The expression "*countertransference* position" highlights the dissymmetrical nature of the analyst's listening, with the aim of restoring the patient's unconscious conflicts revealed by the transference but not yet recognized as such. Once this issue is clear the concept as proposed in this essay can be expressed by "countertransference position" *or* "the analyst's listening position." But let me emphasize that I consider these two expressions (the "countertransference position" and the "analyst's listening position") to be equivalent.

With this concept I hope also to contribute to a contextualization of the concept of countertransference so that it becomes possible to listen to a *new* dimension.

I emphasize the unconscious dimension and differentiate it from neurosis; I include the analyst's theoretical position and I link it to all of his psychical functioning. I likewise assign considerable importance to the institutional context in which concepts and clinical approaches are transmitted down through the generations – from our own historical and cultural context.

Just as there is no such thing as a natural psychoanalytic listening, so *is there no such thing as "a kind of patient" without reference to the way in which an analyst may place himself in a given listening position.* To say this in no way calls into question the scope of psychoanalysis.

In this chapter I have set myself the goal of developing the reasons that have led me to regard the concept of the countertransference position or the analyst's listening position as essential in my psychoanalytic experience and thinking. We know that when we do not use a concept, we do not miss it.

A definition of the countertransference position (or, let us add, the analyst's listening position) is presented together with the requirements to be met by this concept in order for it to be considered a "missing concept." Of course other concepts may also be subject to the same requirement.

I wished to propose a concept that may add a supplementary dimension to psychoanalytic listening and to our theoretical thinking. If I have been able to convey the reasons for my proposing such a concept, shall we be able to assign to it, retroactively, the status of a "previously-missing concept"?

As in every analysis, the discovery of a new dimension has a paradoxical function: at the same time as we discover that something was missing we have a tendency to include it in what it seems that we have always naturally known.

Could it be that the condition for accepting a new concept is that, when it is placed before us, we have the uncanny feeling *that it had always been there*?

I am very grateful to Michael Fineberg for his invaluable assistance in editing the English text of this paper.

Notes

1   For an explicit statement of the theoretical assumptions of this article I refer the reader to my book *The Telescoping of Generations* (2005) where in chapter 4 (1989), pp. 42–49, this topic was addressed for the first time in the frame of the clinical theoretical position set out in the other chapters.

2   This redefinition – inasmuch as it could relaunch the polemics triggered by the concept of countertransference – might seem redundant to some readers, and insufficient to others.

3   This is not the place to define these (implicit and explicit) theoretical assumptions.

4   Jacques Lacan (1953) "The Function and Field of Speech and Language in Psychoanalysis," in *Écrits: A Selection*, A. Sheridan (trans.) (London: Tavistock, 1977); see also Jacques Lacan, *Écrits* (Paris: Seuil, 1966).

5   This is not the place to examine Balint's or Lacan's concepts more extensively.

6   Both in the cases of Maryse Choisy and Abraham Kardiner the quotations are faithfully taken from the published English texts.

Bibliography

Bion, W. R. (1967) Notes on memory and desire. *Psycho-Analytic Forum*, 2: 272–280.

Choisy, M. (1956) 'Qu'est-ce qu'ils en feront?': Souvenir de mes visites à Freud. *Psyché* 107–108, Numéro spécial: Freud.

Choisy, M. (1973) Memories of my visits with Freud, in H. R. Ruitenbeek (ed.), *Freud as We Knew Him* (pp. 291–295). Detroit, MI: Wayne State University Press.

Faimberg, H. (1989) The countertransference position and the countertransference. In *The Telescoping of Generations* (pp. 42–49). London: Routledge, 2005.

Faimberg, H. (2001) Narcissistic discourse as a resistance to psychoanalytic listening. In *The Telescoping of Generations* (pp. 101–104). London: Routledge, 2005.

Faimberg, H. (2005) *The Telescoping of Generations: Listening to the Narcissistic Links between Generations*. London: Routledge, 2005.

Faimberg, H. (2006) Plea for a broader concept of *Nachträglichkeit*. *Psychoanalytic Quarterly*, 76(4): 1221–1240, 2007. (Joint Anniversary issue of the *Quarterly* and the *Revue Française*.)

Freud, S. (1910) The future prospects of psycho-analytic therapy. *The Standard Edition of the Complete Psychological Works of Sigmund Freud*, J. Strachey (ed., trans.), vol. 11: 144–145.

Freud, S. (1937) Constructions in analysis. *SE* 23: 255–269.

Glover, E. (1931) The therapeutic effect of the inexact interpretation. *International Journal of Psychoanalysis*, 12(4): 397–411.

Heimann, P. (1950) On countertransference. *International Journal of Psychoanalysis*, 31: 81–84.

Kardiner, A. (1977) *My Analysis with Freud: Reminiscences*. New York: Norton.

Lacan, J. (1953) The function and field of speech and language in psychoanalysis. In *Écrits: A Selection*, A. Sheridan (trans.). London: Tavistock, 1977.

Lacan, J. (1966) *Écrits*. Paris: Seuil.

Laforgue, R. (1956) Freud et son génie. *Psyché*, 107–108, *Numéro spécial*: Freud, 1956.

Racker, H. (1948) La neurosis de contratransferencia. Paper presented to the Argentine Psychoanalytic Association, Buenos Aires, Argentina, September.

Racker, H. (1953) The countertransference neurosis. *International Journal of Psychoanalysis*, 34(4): 313–324. In *Transference and Countertransference* (105–126). New York, International Universities Press, 1968.

Racker, H. (1957) *Estudios sobre técnica psicoanalítica*, Buenos Aires: Paidós. English translation in *Transference and Countertransference*. New York: International Universities Press, 1968.

4

COUNTERTRANSFERENCE

A contemporary approach
from the River Plate region

Abel Fainstein

Countertransference, a concept defined by Freud (1910) in Nuremberg in his essay "The Future Prospects of Psychoanalytic Theory," ought to be revisited and discussed in light of current psychoanalytic practice in the River Plate region. Why?

1 Because of the relevance of countertransference to clinical work in Argentina and Uruguay.
2 Because, following pioneering developments by Heinrich Racker first, and León Grinberg later, Willy and Madeleine Baranger's (1961) ideas on the analytic field constitute a major input toward the understanding of this notion.
3 Due to the significant reformulation of its clinical implementation based on Lacan's contributions, which have circulated in the region during the last 30 years. It is in this context that the concept of countertransference must be articulated with the concepts of the desire of the analyst and of the analyst's subjective engagement in the cure.[1]
4 Because of the need to account for its wide use in clinical practice. In this sense, I agree with Freud's suggestion that the use of countertransference must be adjusted to the patient's psychopathological structure.

Building on my own experience, I intend to (1) identify some controversial issues regarding the clinical implementation of the countertransference based on the writings of Freud and mainly of Racker; (2) further its conceptualization by articulating it with other ideas generated in this region of the world, particularly W. and M. Baranger's field theory, and with the concepts of subjective engagement and the desire of the analyst; and (3) drawing from Laplanche and Pontalis (1973), link countertransference to evenly suspended attention, one of the components of the analytic method, in connection with Sandler's (1976) notion of "free-floating responsiveness."

On clinical implementation

Freud already viewed countertransference as a "practical" issue. In 1910 he wrote that "we have become aware of the 'counter-transference' which arises in him [the physician] as a result of the patient's influence on his unconscious feelings, and we are almost inclined to insist that he shall recognize this counter-transference in himself and overcome it" (Freud, 1910, pp. 144–145). As we can see, the countertransference is the influence brought to bear by the patient, and not only by his transference, on the analyst's unconscious feelings – and I stress unconscious. Freud suggests that we elucidate and master the countertransference insofar as it constitutes an obstacle to the cure.

However, we may add to this perspective the one that appears in his "Recommendations to Physicians." Freud states there that the physician "is to be in a position to use his unconscious in this way as an instrument in the analysis" (Freud, 1912, pp. 115–116). Racker's (1951) view is also pertinent here. According to this author, "the analyst's perceptions of his own countertransference states could prove an important instrument for the understanding of the analysand's transference states" (Racker, this volume). I thus put forth the use of the countertransference as a tool and highlight its unconscious condition. Let us recall that in stating that it emerges "as a result of the patient's influence on [the physician's] unconscious feelings," Freud does not specify that the countertransference is unconscious. Rather, he asserts that it is a product of the patient's influence on the analyst's unconscious feelings.

Racker (this volume) claims that Freud's notion of counter-transference encompasses the totality of the analyst's psychological response, and proposes to call it total countertransference. The latter comprises what the analyst transfers – infantile or primordial as well as current, especially analytic, experiences. It is worth noting that to the patient's material and its effects on the analyst's unconscious feelings we may add the latter's theories, built on the basis of his readings and of his exchanges with other practitioners. I will come back to this issue later on.

In short, we are faced with a concrete problem, namely, the ways in which we conduct our practice. Let us go back to Freud's 1910 text, where he claims that

> [N]o psycho-analyst goes further than his own complexes and internal resistances permit; and we consequently require that he shall begin his activity with a self-analysis and continually carry it deeper while he is making his observations on his patients. Anyone who fails to produce results in a self-analysis of this kind may at once give up any idea of being able to treat patients by analysis.
>
> (Freud, 1910, p. 145)

Moreover, that same year Freud writes to Ferenczi:

> Why didn't I scold you and in so doing open the way to an understanding? Quite right, it was a weakness on my part; I am also not that ψα superman whom we have constructed, and I also haven't overcome the countertransference. I couldn't do it, just as I can't do it with my three sons, because I like them and I feel sorry for them in the process.
>
> (Freud and Ferenczi, 1910, p. 221)

In 1912, by contrast, he favors personal analysis over self-analysis.

We may, therefore, ask ourselves:

1   What does Freud mean by "the patient's influence over [the physician's] unconscious feelings"? What is the relationship between such influence and the concept of countertransference?
2   How do we articulate the latter with the evenly suspended attention advanced by the psychoanalytic method?

In later years the debate continued to hinge on these issues. Racker (1968) prioritized the analyst's perception of his own counter-transference states as the way to understand the patient's transference states. To illustrate this perspective, he claimed that when the analyst feels anger, the analysant[2] feels guilty because of his transference aggressiveness. Luisa de Urtubey (1994) believed instead that countertransference appears in consciousness as signs that must be deciphered. In other words, the conscious affective manifestation must be analyzed. Affects, associations, fantasies, images, slips of the tongue, comparisons or metaphors, interventions, and so on are either the offspring of the unconscious or direct manifestations of it in the case of invading affects. The countertransference is hence dynamically unconscious despite its conscious and preconscious aspects, and the analyst must address it. The same is true for manifest signs of transference.

Based on Freud's letter to Ferenczi, should we become aware of the fact that we are identifying our patients with our children and avoid doing so? And in that case, how should we go about it? Is it only a matter of exerting our will once we have become aware of our feelings? Or is this identification manifest, so that it must be analyzed? In the quoted paragraph Freud saw his behavior as a weakness; he wanted to scold Ferenczi but could not do so. We know that at times we are unable to acknowledge our feelings.

Given that awareness alone does not seem to solve our feelings, I think that the so-called work of de-identification is the proper strategy to pursue (to tackle) this challenge, and that such work can only be the product of self-analysis or personal analysis. If according to Freud the countertransference is necessary to the internal progress of psychoanalysis from a technical point of view, I believe that its poor utilization by analysts, and the ethical problems ensuing from these deficiencies, have been responsible to a great extent for the decline in the social and professional recognition of our work. The analysis of analysts is, therefore, called into question.

Freud did not return to this topic, and the notion of countertransference was not developed further until the 1950s. Etchegoyen (1991), however, mentions Reik, who in the 1930s pointed out the significance of intuition – the analyst's need to let himself be surprised by his unconscious. It is my contention that Reik should be incorporated into this discussion because he was the analyst of Angel Garma, a leading figure in the evolution of Argentine and Latin American psychoanalysis. For Reik, countertransference constituted a resistance on the part of the analyst that must be overcome through self-analysis. He thus distinguished it from intuition.

Countertransference as a tool

Paula Heimann and Racker were the ones who, to all appearances independently from each other, described countertransference as an instrument through which the analyst may understand the analysant's psychological processes, from which it stems to a certain extent. They did so in 1950 and 1953, respectively, and published their findings in the *International Journal of Psychoanalysis*. In these essays they link the thoughts that come to the analyst's mind during the session to the countertransference. Racker presented his paper on countertransference neurosis at the Asociación Psicoanalítica Argentina (Argentine Psychoanalytic Association) (APA) in September 1948. This essay was published in the *International Journal of Psychoanalysis* in 1953, and an abridged version of it appeared in the APA's journal in 1955. This was its first Spanish publication.

Racker (1968) points out that while Freud urges analysts to eschew compassion and adopt the internal attitude of a surgeon, thus favoring an objective position, compassion aroused by the analysant may actually serve to assist the analyst in understanding the underlying transference. In the same way, analysts' feeling of failure may be stirred by patients' projection of their own failure and impotence. The analysant thus dissociates and projects part of his ego onto the analyst, and the latter must return it to the patient after subtracting his own personal elements.

Thanks to these contributions the countertransference has ceased to be merely an obstacle. Like the transference, it can be an obstacle, an instrument, and a space for the unfolding of the cure by changing the fate of an old object relation. For Racker, the analyst's perception of countertransference feelings serves as an indicator of the progress of the analysis – of whether patients are overcoming their resistances. In this sense, feeling bored would be a sign of resistance, while perceiving a patient's aggression, despite the latter's blocked aggressiveness and offense, or taking the blame the patient is pinning on us, may be understood as progress insofar as the patient is less afraid of us.

Racker also pointed out the need to differentiate what comes to the analyst's mind during the session from what he called countertransference positions. Thoughts, free associations, or fantasies do not carry great emotional intensity and are slightly foreign to the ego. Anger toward a patient, by contrast, is an example of a countertransference position and entails greater engagement on the part of the ego. Adopting Racker's emphasis on the analyst's experiences during the analytic situation, some prefer to talk about "experiences" rather than "listening." The latter term, although more common, has a more limited meaning.

Countertransference as an obstacle

In this context it is worth mentioning Cabral's (2009) specification concerning Freud's use of the word indifference (*Indifferenz*) in 1915. According to Freud, analysts can attain indifference by keeping countertransference in check (*Niederhaltung*). Cabral stresses that Freud insists on countertransference as an obstacle that is destined to be kept in check. This fate is different from that of repression and points to a non-neurotic subjectivity in the analyst that is oblivious to oedipal clichés and open to the novelty of the encounter with the analysant – with his true being. It is the analysant who, through his actual presence, exposes, or, rather, predisposes the analyst to his own passions.

Cabral (2009) recalls Lacan's (1961) observation that the longer an analyst has been in analysis, the more likely it is that he will truly love or hate his patient. These feelings correspond to the ones that Winnicott (1960) defined as the analyst's responses and distinguished from the countertransference. Strictly speaking, the counter-transference is the product of the analyst's residual neurosis – of repressed identifications. A stronger desire in the analyst – the desire to analyze – would be at the heart of this harnessing, which does not exclude the analyst's passions. On the contrary, it distinguishes them both from the repressed and from the lack of repression.

Racker himself (Racker, this volume) suggests that the countertransference may hinder direct unconscious-to-unconscious communication, empathy, and identification, as well as the working-through of what may be grasped by these means. The countertransference would thus disturb the analyst's interpretive ability.

How do we explain the countertransference?

The analyst is both object and interpreter of the transference. The debate about whether it is the patient's transference that triggers the process and induces the countertransference response, or the analyst's

73

transference that acts as a counterpoint to the analysant's, is still active. I believe that the analyst's subjectivity is part of the analytic situation. That is why, as I understand it, Winnicott's (1949) description of an objective countertransference (more precisely, of an objective hate experienced by any analyst toward some patients) is hard to uphold unless we think, along with Racker, that analysts' objectivity requires that they detach themselves from the obsessive isolation of their subjectivity and avoid plunging into the countertransference. As Racker put it, "true objectivity is based on a form of internal splitting that enables the analyst to take himself – his own subjectivity or countertransference – as an object of continual observation and analysis" (Racker, 1968, p. 231). I will come back to this issue with regard to Grinberg's (1956, 1957) notion of projective counter-identification.

The analyst's subjectivity – his real person – thus takes center stage through its role as an obstacle and/or a tool. Far from the idea of a mirror-analyst, what is at play in the analytic situation is not one but two, albeit symmetrical, subjectivities. Gabbard (1990) refers to this question in terms of the interpenetration of subjectivities; for him the countertransference is a joint production by means of projective identification. Ogden (1994), in turn, states that projective identification creates an analytic third, the subject of projective identification, which is unconscious and intersubjective. These authors' ideas, therefore, are close to W. and M. Baranger's notion of the analytic field.

The metapsychology of countertransference

Freud described the countertransference early on as a clinical phenomenon but did not deal with its metapsychology. Racker, conversely, did concern himself with it. Based on the second topography and on the notions of the ego and of internal objects, Racker studied the countertransference from the perspective of identifications. His conceptualizations were later enriched through the addition of projective identification, and acquired their highest expression in Grinberg's (1956) work on projective counter-identification. This concept refers to the real effects on the object of the peculiar use of projective identification by regressive personalities. Even though he downplayed this view in his last article (1982) on the topic, Grinberg considered that projective counter-identification

74

only operates in the analysant. The violence of the analysant's projective identification forces the analyst to play a role, regardless of his unconscious conflicts. The countertransference is not at play here; the same patient may lead different analysts to enact what he projectively identifies in them. As I pointed out earlier, the concept of projective counter-identification is, in this sense, close to Winnicott's idea of objective hate.

But is this at all possible? Not according to Etchegoyen (1991), who agrees with Grinberg and Money-Kyrle (1956) regarding the use of projective identification to understand countertransference, but who also challenges Grinberg's ideas. What would make the analyst surrender to projective counter-identification other than his psychic structure, his unconscious conflicts, his particular form of mental functioning? Etchegoyen claims that the difference between projective counter-identification and Racker's complementary countertransference is only a matter of degree. Furthermore, he adds that Grinberg himself wrote, years later, that projective counter-identification need not necessarily be the final link in this process, thus making room for the analyst's subjectivity.

We should recall here that Racker described two types of countertransference. *Concordant* countertransference stems from a sublimated positive countertransference and from the analyst's identification with the analysant's ego and id. *Complementary* countertransference, in turn, is the product of the analyst's identification with the analysant's internal objects. Along the same lines more recently, Borensztejn (2009) highlights the differences between Grinberg's notion of projective counter-identification and the concept of enactment. While the former involves a foreign body forced into the analyst by the patient that generates the same response in every analyst, enactment entails a personal, idiosyncratic reaction on the part of the analyst that depends on his own mode of internal object relations. Borensztejn believes that the notion of enactment subsumes the contributions of Racker, Grinberg, and W. and M. Baranger. She stresses the close connection between Racker's concept of complementary countertransference, based on the analyst's identification with the patient's internal objects, and that of enactment.

Field theory, in turn, offers a metapsychological alternative for the understanding of the countertransference. We have already mentioned that the transference-countertransference dynamic is a product of the analytic field, of the analytic situation. This perspective avoids a causalistic view of the transference-countertransference axis in either direction. Both the concept of unconscious field fantasy, which is bipersonal and constructed on the basis of projective identifications between both members of the patient–analyst couple, and the idea that any interpretation is a field interpretation tacitly include, claims Borensztejn, the notion of enactment, which was formulated many years later. According to W. and M. Baranger, the analyst needs a second look to rescue himself from this intersubjective construction. Personal analysis, self-analysis, and supervisions play a key role in this process.

In de Urtubey's (1994) view, the latent dimension of the countertransference includes the internal objects of analyst and patient and may range from a fusion-type unity to a plurality of objects. Furthermore, it also encompasses the analyst's ego, superego, and ego-ideal identifications. Such complexity requires that analysts perform countertransference work – a working-through that aims to disassemble the countertransference and that is guided by the desire to know and to analyze. In this sense, Cabral asserts that analysts must transcend their ideals to reach a subjective repositioning that will facilitate the progress of the analytic process.

Concerning clinical practice

I would like to reflect now on the clinical dimension of the countertransference. To do so, I will start from Freud's suggestion that psychoanalytic technique must "be modified in certain ways according to the nature of the disease and the dominant instinctual trends in the patient" and his question concerning "how far the instincts which the patient is combating are to be allowed some satisfaction during the treatment, and what difference it makes whether these impulses are active (sadistic) or passive (masochistic) in their nature" (Freud, 1912, p. 145). Even though Freud is referring specifically to neurosis, we should take his suggestion into account in the treatment of patients with narcissistic, borderline, and depressive pathology, as well as with somatosis.

How do we make use of the countertransference today? While it is an instrument by which to approach the unconscious, it may also become an obstacle. Its use varies according to the theoretical-clinical perspective of individual practitioners and the pathologies they face.

We may start from the idea that the analyst's negativization of himself, in order to benefit both his desire to know and to analyze, is necessary for the typical cure of neurotic patients, and that de-identification is at the heart of this process. Yet as Cabral (2009) makes clear in his reading of Lacan, negativization does not exclude the analyst's passions or the effectiveness of the encounters between analyst and patient in the analytic situation. So-called calculated vacillations of neutrality may be worth more than any interpretation. Analysts thus engage in the transference in the first person, resorting to the singularity of their own being, independently of their identifications.

Yet neutrality is hard to sustain in the analysis of non–neurotic patients, and more particularly so in that of patients with a narcissistic or borderline functioning. For this reason, the technical implementation of the countertransference is more common in the treatment of patients with narcissistic pathologies, especially in regressive states and in cases where there is a symbolization deficit. These cases require that analysts make themselves present even further, even to the point of satisfying the patient's drive demands to a certain extent by way of a calculated vacillation in neutrality.

Racker (this volume) already advanced the idea that instead of demanding or forbidding, analysts who are experienced in the handling of countertransference may sometimes very fleetingly play the role induced by their analysants and later analyze what happened and what was acted out. Racker suggests this strategy – as only a transitory prop – in situations with patients who take advantage of the fact that analysts do nothing but interpret in order to disable the analyst's performance.

Concerning the role of the analyst in the cure, I would like to turn, albeit with some differences, to the description offered by Szpilka (1973). This author describes two initial moments in every analysis, which he calls the *evacuative* and the *illusional*, when the analyst occupies a defined, entirely positive place. Then there is a third, *elaborative* moment when the analyst negativizes himself so that his analyzing function may fully emerge. Instead of considering only this third state as the one truly psychoanalytic moment, I think it would be more useful, in view of the expansion of our practice, to think of the three moments as part of a psychoanalytic process that will require a greater or lesser presence of the analyst, and hence of his countertransference, depending on the patient's pathology and on the stage of the process. I would save Szpilka's description for patients with a more neurotic functioning.

As far as I am concerned, I use the countertransference as a guide to understand the patient's psychic production. I set aside the debate about whether it expresses what is repressed or what was never repressed. Instead, I view it – insofar as it represents the coming into contact with intersubjectivity – as a valuable tool for the analytic process. This is particularly true when a more primitive functioning of the psyche prevails in the patient and when the symbolization of perceptive traces and their first inscriptions has been halted. In these cases the historicizing of these traces, which may be detected through the countertransference, favors their symbolization. This is what we call *symbolizing historicization*.

Analysts' impotence, helplessness, frustration, eroticization, or aggressiveness may be revealed by way of self-analysis or by the analysis of the countertransference, which sometimes takes the guise of bodily discomfort. I only resort to the satisfaction of demands for attention, care, and security for those patients undergoing regressive states who may be unable to tolerate unyielding neutrality. My behavior is a conscious decision, but I am also alert to the possibility of satisfying this type of demand independently of my will or as a result of projective counter-identification. Timely verbalization during the treatment tends to rechannel the cure. In this sense, I think that Racker's abovementioned description of a total countertransference, or – as it is depicted today, an expanded countertransference that includes the analyst's theorizations – is still valuable.

The analyst's theories and their effects on his practice

Dennis Duncan (1983) writes that, after van Gogh, anyone painting sunflowers will have to respond to the sunflower and to van Gogh. I remembered this quote when I recently supervised a case of a 15-year-old young woman. The patient had sought help because she claimed she was possessed by seven demons since the Devil had entered her. The possession was due to the weakness she had shown after a séance with a cousin who was considered a pervert by a family with incestuous features. Freud's question to Fliess rapidly came to mind: "Do you remember that I have always said that the theory of the Middle Ages and of the ecclesiastical courts concerning possession was identical to our theory of the foreign body and the splitting of consciousness?" (Freud and Fliess, 1897). How could one avoid answering Freud's question when hearing this clinical narrative?

According to Duncan, analysts direct their interpretations based on their speculations, and a living dialogue between theory and intuition is a facet of these conjectures. Duncan thus suggests that we engage in a "dim dialogue with theorists" (1983, p. 250) instead of subjecting ourselves to them. I believe that the disjunction between theory and practice is both structural and a source of creativity. We must maintain our ability to be surprised (and only then ask ourselves which theory we have in mind), to accept the fact that we do not understand, and to listen to the unknown and the enigmatic, which theory tries to represent, while being always traversed by the analyst's unconscious.

Concordant and complementary countertransference

As I mentioned earlier, Racker (1951, this volume) described a *concordant* and a *complementary* countertransference. For him, the countertransference points both to the analysant's central conflict in his transference object relations and to the reactions of his internal objects, especially those of the imago placed in the analyst and then introjected. Nevertheless, for this to happen the analyst must acknowledge and master the countertransference by overcoming its negative and sexual modes. These are inevitable spontaneous reactions due to identification with the transferred object, but they must also be transitory.

Racker's concordant countertransference is indispensable, in my view, in the first stages of the treatment. Although it is not easy to achieve, let alone to impose on oneself, much of the continuity of the treatment rests on it. I agree with Etchegoyen (1991) that the problem is that concordant countertransference in itself entails a narcissistic bond. Here Etchegoyen concurs with Racker (this volume), who asserted that this type of countertransference cancels the object relation that should be attained in every analytic process. Moreover, it constitutes a narcissistic identification on the part of the analyst with the ego or with other structures of the patient, and expresses the analyst's ability to understand, which he has achieved with his sublimated positive countertransference.

We see here that Racker includes understanding in the counter-transference, more specifically in concordant countertransference, and understanding is narcissistic. For this reason, many authors nowadays question the function of understanding as a strictly

79

psychoanalytic tool. What seems to be necessary at first may become an obstacle later if not overcome. Cabral (2009) quotes Lacan's *Seminar XII, Crucial Problems for Psychoanalysis* (1974–1975), where the French theorist states that no analyst may be exempt from the suspicion of participating in an improper identification. Lacan is referring here to the manifestations of the analyst's residual neurosis, which he must clear away if he is to act in a more effective way with the patient. This is what some analysts specifically designate as countertransference.

Racker (this volume) considers that the analyst's empathy is essential in order to achieve an adequate understanding of the patient. I agree with him that the fate of the treatment depends to a great extent on analysts' ability to maintain their positive countertransference. We must, therefore, avoid both the impossible, intolerable lack of empathy stemming from the lack of identification with the patient's ego, and a full empathetic identification, which hinders analysis. Racker asserts that Freud's suggestion that the analyst be like a mirror means that analysts must speak to their analysants only about the latter, and should not talk about themselves unless it is indispensable. He clarifies, however, that such behavior does not mean that one must "stop being flesh and bone and become glass covered with silver nitrate" (Racker, 1958, p. 31), and says that analysts' interest in and affection for their analysants should not be negated or impeded.

The challenge, therefore, is to find a way to favor the object relation as much as possible, a step that is also essential for the evolution of the analytic treatment. In this sense, the appearance of a complementary countertransference under the guise of hate or eroticization, even if more conflicting, could be a sign of progress, because such an appearance implies the patient's having left behind the concordant countertransference and its narcissistic features. Now the patient treats the analyst as an internal object, and the analyst identifies with this object and feels that he is it. We thus see the difference between this approach and the one that considers complementary and concordant countertransferences as mere obstacles that result from the analyst's counter-resistance.

I highlight here the relevance of the initial symbiotic interaction between analyst and analysant for the treatment of patients with serious pathologies – those for whom their psychic life is at stake. This is the context for concordant countertransference, which supports understanding and empathy. Yet this type of countertransference does not always arise. If it does, furthermore, it requires a subsequent de-identification with the patient that the latter cannot always tolerate. At other times, the analyst's own complementary responses insist on this identification and prevent its disassembly. We know that resistances to hate and eroticization in both participants in the analytic field are part of this problem. For this reason, the narcissistic bond often persists and gives rise to bastions or episodes of acting out.

I have already pointed out that the analyst's timely awareness of erotic or aggressive feelings in the countertransference is often a sign of an important shift in the process. Such an awareness enables the disassembly of the narcissistic identification typical of concordant countertransference. In the context of the object relation, and once the analyst has overcome the more narcissistic bond, these affects may denote repressed or dissociated aspects of the patient's primary relationships that may now be retrieved and historicized.

Clinical vignettes

The following vignettes are offered to illustrate some of the ways I use countertransference in clinical practice.

Over a long period I once treated a teenager with serious acting-out and self-destructive behavior. The basic countertransference feeling was of care and concern for her. She and her father had been estranged from each other by mutual agreement for several years. Guided by my countertransference affects, I decided to call him in for a series of interviews. We were able to discuss his difficulties concerning the relationship with his daughter, which stemmed from scarcely conscious fears of it becoming eroticized. After a few interviews he resumed the relationship and rescued his daughter from a mother who claimed she did not expect anything from her.

In other opportunities, two female patients whose lives were at risk for different reasons were referred to me, the first by an acquaintance, due to the effects of the latest of many suicide attempts, and the second owing to an extremely serious illness. The initial countertransference was guided by my desire to take care of them and that they survive, a desire that one of the families had apparently long since lost. This concordant countertransference gave way later to other, more complementary ones. These, which were erotic and aggressive, changed over the course of the treatment, helping it to overcome an initial symbiotization that might have been necessary. During this symbiotization I contributed my own mental functioning to process intense death feelings in one instance, and in the other the patient's attacks on the immediate surroundings as well as her identification with them, which discouraged her from staying alive.

Countertransference and the psychoanalytic method: suspended attention and enactment

Since evenly suspended attention is part of the analytic treatment – especially with neurotic patients who are capable of engaging in free association – I think it is important finally to dwell on the articulation between the countertransference and free-floating attention, as well as between the countertransference and enactment. According to Steiner (2006), such articulation only occurs in relation to the rule of abstinence and to neutrality.

Freud (1912) considered that communication between patient and analyst must be a communication between one unconscious and another, in the manner of the connection between the telephone receiver and its handset. This is what Reik (1948) described as listening with the third ear. Every analyst has in his own unconscious an instrument with which he can interpret the manifestations of the patient's unconscious without their passing through consciousness (although a more thorough investigation should be conducted as to the participation of the preconscious). Independently of its function as an analytic tool, the countertransference may also hinder the perception or working-through of this resonance between the unconscious of the patient and that of the analyst (Racker, 1968).

Nonetheless, given that in the case of free association the suspension of conscious purposive ideas results in the primacy of unconscious ones, how can we achieve an evenly suspended attention? We have already mentioned that Cabral (2009) points out that *Indifferenz*, which Strachey rendered as neutrality and Ballesteros as *neutralidad*, is better translated into Spanish as *indiferencia*, as Etcheverry did.[3] Indifference, which stems from keeping countertransference in check, is for Canestri (1993) a condition of evenly suspended attention. In other words, suspended attention must be evenly distributed among the totality of the material contributed by the patient. Personal and self-analysis would help to achieve this harnessing, but Laplanche and Pontalis (1973) warn that evenly suspended attention is an ideal that in practice clashes with certain incompatible requirements. Just as analysants associate more freely as they progress in their analysis, so the analysis of their counter-transference may render analysts aware of the instances where evenly suspended attention is lost and thus make possible its resumption.

Although Freud did not describe this mode of attention in the context of the second topography, Laplanche and Pontalis (1973) describe three trends in the reflections on this topic by present-day psychoanalysts:

1   Some authors follow Reik and consider that communication between one unconscious and another constitutes a form of mainly subverbal empathy. The countertransference attests to the depth of this communication and corresponds to Racker's concordant countertransference.
2   For other thinkers, even though the main facet of psychoanalytic dialogue takes place between egos, evenly suspended attention demands the relaxation of this agency's inhibitory and selective functions. Analysts should be open to the exhortations of their own psychic apparatuses in order to prevent the interference of defensive compulsions.
3   Finally, for other authors the goal is to give as free a play as possible to the structural similarity between language and unconscious phenomena, as described by Lacan (1955–56). As we all know, to do so analysts must strictly observe neutrality and the fundamental rule, although such observance is not always indicated or feasible.

Unlike the third mode, which applies more specifically to the analysis of neurotic patients, the first two options, in my view, are indispensable for the treatment of patients with serious narcissistic pathologies. Enactment, in turn, refers to acting-out episodes within the analytic situation and implies the pressure of primordial object relations through the transference. It is particularly useful both for the evolution of the analytic process, and for its therapeutic role in clinical practice with narcissistic patients. The analyst perceives through the counter-transference, and expresses it as an act. In this sense, Borensztejn (2009) quotes Sandler (1976) regarding the need for analysts to add "free-floating responsiveness" to their evenly suspended attention.

Conclusion

I have reviewed the history of the notion of countertransference in psychoanalytic theory and practice in the River Plate region. I started with Freud's 1910 writings and Racker's pioneering 1950s texts, and moved on to the current influence of intersubjective approaches. In particular, I discussed W. and M. Baranger's developments about the analytic field and Lacan's teachings. My discussion was based on a broad view of the countertransference as both obstacle and instrument, and included theorizations about the analyst's total response to the patient or to the analytic situation. Some brief vignettes of mine served the purpose of illustrating the discussion of the role of theory and of concepts such as concordant and complementary countertransference in clinical practice, specifically in the case of patients with borderline functioning or serious psychic helplessness.

Translation from the Spanish by Judith Filc.

Notes

1   *Implication subjective* (in French) has been translated into English alternately as "subjective implication" and "subjective engagement." I consider the latter a better choice. – J. F.
2   The author has chosen to use *analizante* instead of the more common term *analizando* in order to stress the active nature of the patient's role. For this reason, I have translated it as *analysant* instead of *analysand*. – J. F.
3   Luis López Ballesteros was the first Spanish translator of Freud's *Complete Works*. This work was done between 1922 and 1934 and was published by Biblioteca Nueva in Madrid. Later José Luis Etcheverry translated Freud's *Complete Works* for Amorrortu Editores in Buenos Aires, 1974–1985.

Bibliography

Baranger, W. and Baranger, M. (1961) The analytic situation as a dynamic field. *International Journal of Psychoanalysis*, 89: 795–826, 2008 (La situación analítica como campo dinámico). Also in *Problemas del campo psicoanalítico*, Buenos Aires: Kargieman, 1993.

Borensztejn, C. (2009) El enactment como concepto teórico convergente de teorías divergentes (Enactment as a converging theoretical concept for diverging theories). *Revista de Psicoanálisis*, 66(1), *El Psicoanálisis en Estados Unidos* (Psychoanalysis in the United States).

Cabral, A. (2009) *Lacan y el debate sobre la contratransferencia* (Lacan and the countertransference debate). Buenos Aires: Letra Viva.

Canestri, J. (1993) A cry of fire: Some considerations on transference-love. In E. Spector, A. Hagelin and P. Fonagy (eds.), *On Freud's "Observations on Transference Love"* (pp. 146–164). New Haven, CT: Yale University Press. (Un grito de fuego. Algunas consideraciones sobre el amor de transferencia, in *En torno a Freud. Acerca del amor de transferencia.* Madrid: IPA-Biblioteca Nueva, 1998.)

de Urtubey, L. (1994) Sobre el trabajo de contratransferencia (On countertransference work). *Revista de Psicoanálisis*, 51(4): 719–727.

Duncan, D. (1983) Theory in vivo. *International Journal of Psychoanalysis*, 74: 25–32. (Las teorías en vivo. *Revista de Psicoanálisis*, 49(2): 239–251, 1987).

Etchegoyen, R. H. (1991) *Fundamentals of Psychoanalytic Technique*. London: Karnac. (*Los fundamentos de la técnica psicoanalítica.* Buenos Aires: Amorrortu Editores, 1986.)

Freud, S. and Ferenczi, S. (1910) Letter from Sigmund Freud to Sándor Ferenczi, 6 October. In E. Brabant, E. Falzeder, P. Giampieri-Deutsch (eds.), P. T. Hoffer (trans.), *The Correspondence of Sigmund Freud and Sándor Ferenczi* (pp. 221–223). Cambridge, MA: Harvard University Press, 1993. Vol. 1, 1908–1914.

Freud, S. and Fliess, W. (1897) Letter to Fliess, 17 January. In S. Freud and W. Fliess (1985) *The Complete Letters of Sigmund Freud to Wilhelm Fliess 1887–1904.* J. M. Masson (trans.). Cambridge, MA: Belknap Press of Harvard University Press.

Freud, S. (1910) The future prospects of psychoanalytic therapy. *The Standard Edition of the Complete Psychological Works of Sigmund Freud*, J. Strachey (ed., trans.). London: Hogarth. Vol. 11, 144–145. (Las perspectivas futuras de la terapia psicoanalítica, *OC*, Vol. XI.)

Freud, S. (1912) Recommendations to physicians practicing psycho-analysis. *SE* 12: 109–120. (Consejos al médico en el tratamiento psicoanalítico. *OC* XII.)

Gabbard, G. (1990) *Psychodynamic Psychiatry in Clinical Practice*. Washington, DC: American Psychiatric Press. (*Psiquiatría psicodinámica en la práctica clínica.* Buenos Aires: Editorial Panamericana, 2000.)

Grinberg, L. (1956) Sobre algunos problemas de técnica psicoanalítica determinados por la identificación y la contraidentificación proyectiva (On some problems of psychoanalytic technique posed by projective identification and counter-identification). *Revista de Psicoanálisis*, 13(4): 507–511.

Grinberg, L. (1957) Perturbaciones en la interpretación por la contraidentificación proyectiva (Disturbances in interpretation caused by projective counter-identification). *Revista de Psicoanálisis*, 14(1–2): 23–30.

Grinberg, L. (1982) Más allá de la contraidentificación proyectiva. Introducción al panel Los afectos en la contratransferencia. XIV Congreso Latinoamericano de Psicoanálisis, FEPAL, Garamond, Actas, 205–209. In Spanish: L. Grinberg, M. Langer, and E. Rodrigué (eds.), *Psicoanálisis en las Américas* (pp. 93–106). Buenos Aires: Paidós, 1962.

Heimann, P. (1950) On countertransference. *International Journal of Psychoanalysis*, 31: 81–84.

Lacan, J. (1955–56) *The Seminar. Book III, The Psychoses*, J.-A. Miller and R. Grigg (trans.). London. Routledge, 1993.

Lacan, J. (1961) La transferencia. In *Seminario 8* (pp. 213–215). Buenos Aires: Paidós, 1993.

Lacan, J. (1974–75) *Seminar XXII. Ornicar?*, R.S.I., 2, 3, 4, 5.

Laplanche, J. and Pontalis, J. B. (1973) *The Language of Psycho-Analysis* D. Nicholson-Smith (trans.). London: Hogarth. (*Vocabulaire de la psychanalyse*. Paris: Presses universitaires de France, 1967; *Diccionario de Psicoanálisis*. Barcelona: Labor, 1973.)

Money-Kyrle, R. E. (1956) Normal counter-transference and some of its deviations. *International Journal of Psychoanalysis*, 37: 360–366.

Ogden, T. H. (1994) The analytic third: Working with intersubjective clinical facts. *International Journal of Psychoanalysis*, 75: 3–20.

Racker, H. (1948) La neurosis de contratransferencia. In *Estudios sobre técnica psicoanalitica*. Buenos Aires: Paidós, 1964.

Racker, H. (1951) Observations on countertransference as a technical instrument: Preliminary communication (V. Muscio and R. Oelsner, trans.) (this volume). In Spanish: Observaciones sobre la contratransferencia como instrumento técnico. Comunicación preliminar. *Revista de Psicoanálisis de la Asociación Psicoanalítica Argentina*, 9(3): 344–607, 1952.

Racker, H. (1953) A contribution to the problem of countertransference. *International Journal of Psychoanalysis*, 34: 313–324.

Racker, H. (1958) Classical and present techniques in psycho-analysis. In *Transference and Counter-transference* (pp. 22–70). New York: International Universities Press, 1968.

Racker, H. (1968) *Transference and Counter-transference*. New York: International Universities Press.

Reik, T. (1948) *Listening with the Third Ear: The Inner Experience of a Psychoanalyst*. New York: Grove Press.

Sandler, J. (1976) Countertransference and role responsiveness. *International Journal of Psychoanalysis*, 3: 43–47.

Steiner, J. (2006) Interpretative enactments and the analytic setting. *International Journal of Psychoanalysis*, 87: 315–320.

Szpilka, J. (1973) *Bases para una psicopatología psicoanalítica* (Bases for a psychoanalytic psychopathology). Buenos Aires: Kargieman.

Winnicott, D. W. (1949) Hate in the counter-transference. *International Journal of Psychoanalysis*, 30: 69–74. Also in *Through Pediatrics to Psycho-Analysis* (pp. 194–203). New York: Basic Books, 1975. (Odio en la contratransferencia. In *El proceso de maduración en el niño*. Barcelona: Laia, 1975.)

Winnicott, D. W. (1960) Counter-transference. *British Journal of Medical Psychology*. 33: 17–21. Also in *The Maturational Processes and the Facilitating Environment* (pp. 158–165). Madison, CT: International Universities Press, 1965. (Contratransferencia. In *El proceso de maduración en el niño* (pp. 188–199). Barcelona: Laia, 1975.)

5

FREUD'S COUNTERTRANSFERENCE?

Reviewing the case histories with modern ideas of transference and countertransference

R. D. Hinshelwood

Since Freud's death the theory and practice of psychoanalysis has evolved very considerably. Around 1950, a change occurred that resembles a paradigm shift conforming to Kuhn's classic description. Anomalous facts, particularly concerning the psychoanalyst's experiences and feelings, had accumulated – see, for instance, Ferenczi (1919), Glover (1927), Balint and Balint (1939), Racker (1948),[1] and Winnicott (1949) – resulting eventually in a shift in the *clinical use* of countertransference. This was articulated most concisely by Heimann (1950). New ideas of the here-and-now transference, countertransference, and enactment rapidly developed and have been increasingly employed since then.[2]

The emotional experience of the transference-countertransference process is now considered essential for understanding the problems and progress of the treatment and the patient. If these newly understood features of the psychoanalytic process are genuine, they cannot have been absent from the work prior to 1950. We might expect traces of them to be left in the records we have from the past, which may function as a retrospective verification. Much of Freud's detailed clinical work in his classic cases remains available – notably Little Hans and the Rat Man – and can be investigated for traces of the processes not then recognized. If such emotional traces exist, then it is likely that the modern conception is not just an artifact of theory, nor of our contemporary assumptions, but is deeply inherent in the psychoanalytic process itself.

Previously, I used the published account of the Little Hans case to show traces of the existence of a "transference" as it might be understood today (Hinshelwood, 1989). Little Hans related to his father with anger at feeling intruded into, and exposed. Such a conclusion is significant in the debate about whether children *can* have a transference to a parent. But that is not the point here. Rather, the unsuspecting past can still yield evidence for questions in the present. Can more recent conceptualizations of countertransference therefore also be discerned in Freud's case material?

In this chapter, three of Freud's case reports (the Wolf Man, the Rat Man, and Little Hans) are reexamined from this point of view. In each it is possible to show elements of our contemporary understanding of transference, countertransference, and enactment. Reviews of these phenomena occurring in Freud's case material have been occasionally reported (Blum, 2007; Etchegoyen, 1988; Gottlieb, 1989; Hinshelwood, 1989; Mahoney, 1984, 1986; Matthis, 1994; Rudnytsky, 1999) – but countertransference has been discussed only rarely.

Characteristics of countertransference

In order to spot moments where countertransference appears, I shall use a set of three characteristics that must each be present to define a countertransference moment. These criteria are: (1) the patient's transference; (2) indications of the psychoanalyst's emotional responses expressed indirectly; (3) some untoward action of the analyst appropriate to his or her linked emotional state.

These are perhaps well captured in Bion's ironic description:

> The analyst feels he is being manipulated so as to be playing a part, no matter how difficult to recognize, in somebody else's phantasy – or he would do if it were not for what in recollection I can only call a temporary loss of insight, a sense of experiencing strong feelings and at the same time a belief that their existence is quite adequately justified by the objective situation …
>
> (Bion, 1961, p. 149)

I shall now attempt to use these three criteria systematically in three of Freud's case histories.

The Wolf Man

The importance of Freud's Wolf Man case was, in part, that it allowed him to report and demonstrate theoretical advances. The Wolf Man (Sergei Pankejeff) was treated in 1913–1914. At the time, Freud was writing his comprehensive papers on metapsychology. However, the case was not published until 1918. In it Freud revealed the childhood phantasy of the *primal scene*, and the identifications of the child, in imagination, with *both* parents.

The patient's transference

The patient remained passively in a chronic positive transference. Freud wrote:

> The patient with whom I am here concerned remained for a long time unassailably entrenched behind an attitude of obliging apathy.
>
> (1918, p. 11)

Freud was impressed, more or less from beginning to end, with the Wolf Man's passivity. However Freud's language suggests something more as well.

The analyst's emotional state

When Freud wrote, "unassailably entrenched" and "obliging apathy," he conveyed a quite strongly affective response to the patient. He is not complimentary. It appears Freud was exasperated by the passivity. He continued:

> His shrinking from a self-sufficient existence was so great as to outweigh all the vexations of his illness.
>
> (1918, p. 11)

These emotive expressions are not an artifact of translation.[3] Freud's frustration explains some of his subsequent actions.

Some untoward action of the analyst
appropriate to the linked emotional states

Freud was provoked to take action on the basis of the emotional state of frustration. Referring to the Wolf Man's shrinking from self-sufficiency, he wrote

> Only one way was to be found of overcoming it. I was obliged to wait until his attachment to myself had become strong enough to counter-balance this shrinking, and then played off this one factor against the other.

> (1918, p. 11)

What was Freud overcoming? Explicitly, it was the Wolf Man's "shrinking" behind his unassailable apathy. Having been provoked, Freud's irritation and impatience led him to become correspondingly active. One could say Freud was overcoming something else, his own frustration, which played some part, as Bion depicted, in relation to the patient's transference.

We know too that subsequently he was also active on the Wolf Man's behalf by finding money for him (even asking friends on the patient's behalf [Jones, 1955]). Freud's action – setting a termination date – enacted their two states of mind, the patient passive, and the analyst active. Freud was not, of course, in a position to recognize the link between the primal scene theory he evolved and the emotive role-enactments and drama he was helping the patient to act out. Interestingly, instead, Freud wrote about his patient's *active* and *passive* identifications in the primal scene. In a way, the theorizing could be seen as his own defense. But there is more here than just a defensive retreat into theorizing: he played a specific part in a relationship with the Wolf Man; Freud became the active partner to the Wolf Man's passive one.

The match between the countertransference enactment and the new theorizing is a striking engagement; Freud could not of course recognize or interpret the enactment, because psychoanalytic technique had not advanced enough for that. He developed his theoretical formulations instead of his technique.

The next instance is a much shorter moment of micro-process from a treatment that progressed more satisfactorily.

The Rat Man

Much as with the Wolf Man case, Freud's analysis of Ernst Lanzer, the "Rat Man" (Freud 1909a), was written up for the purpose of extending analytic theory. Earlier, Freud (1894) had postulated intense unmodified aggression and sadism in obsessional patients. The Rat Man gave him a chance to demonstrate in considerable clinical detail what he had previously understood. The Rat Man felt in great pain because of the pain he intruded into others, via alarming and cruel phantasy rituals. He was also bothered by word-insertion into ritualistic sentences, prayers, and so on, that turned benign thoughts into malign ones as repressed infantile anal-sadistic impulses returned in the form of these rejected thoughts and images.

Whereas hysterics repress the precise meaning of their symptoms while retaining the emotions, the obsessional does the reverse; the patient retains a conscious knowledge of the wishes while repressing the sadistic pleasure. With the Rat Man case, Freud confirmed these ideas and added further ones. In particular, symptoms frequently seemed to be one version or another of *undoing* a previous action, invariably an aggressive one. And in addition, with the Rat Man, Freud found he was impressed by the way that the obsessional's imagination seemed to have real consequences – "the omnipotence of phantasy" (Freud, 1909a, p. 233).

Freud left process notes of the case, which were published by Strachey in the *Standard Edition*. I propose to take a single instance from the Notes (1909a, pp. 280–282; also referred to in the text of the paper, pp. 166–167) to illustrate Freud's possible "countertransference" and its aptness to the dynamic contents of the case.

The patient's transference

Freud described the patient's free associations as a "confession" (Freud, 1909a, p. 282), and thought the patient needed help to confess his painful guilt. The Notes tell us Freud felt it was like a forty-minute struggle to reveal

> the element of revenge against me and [I] had shown him that by refusing to tell me and by giving up the treatment he would be taking a more outright revenge on me than by telling me.
>
> (p. 281)

Freud was describing the rather cruel intention the patient had toward him. By this date, Freud was aware of the negative transference and its anal–sadistic roots. Moreover, the Rat Man felt in great pain because of the pain his mind inflicted on others.

> At all the more important moments while he was telling his story his face took on a very strange, composite expression. I could only interpret it as one of horror at pleasure of his own of which he himself was unaware.
>
> (pp. 166–167)

So in his transference there was a compromise formation between his revenge and his exquisitely regretful confession. Both – the revenge and the confession/regret – can be seen in the struggle.

The analyst's emotional state

In reaction to this transference, Freud felt some sympathy, and was moved by the patient's anguish:

> He proceeded with the greatest difficulty: "At that moment the idea flashed through my mind that this was happening to a person who was very dear to me."
>
> (1909a, p. 167)

And in the Notes about this moment,

> only after this did he give me to understand that it concerned my daughter. With this, the session came to an end.
>
> (p. 281)

Although the torture referred to the Rat Man's fiancée, there is now a threat to Freud's daughter. Freud's reaction is conveyed by the Notes, but put in the form of the patient's observation:

> After a struggle and assertions by him that my undertaking to show that all the material concerned only himself looked like anxiety on my part, he surrendered the first of his ideas.
>
> (p. 281)

93

The patient observed Freud as anxious, but in reality it is unlikely that Freud would not have reacted with anxiety to the Rat Man's fantasy about Freud's own daughter. So the Rat Man's supposition that Freud was anxious may well have been an accurate observation. However, this arousal of anxiety in Freud is also a version of a sadistic intrusion, in this case a psychological intrusion into Freud's peace of mind.

Freud was, like the Rat Man, set to struggle with opposing feelings – his sympathy for the Rat Man, and an alarm for his daughter. Perhaps it is a fundamental principle that there is no neurotic conflict in the patient without there being a countertransference conflict in the psychoanalyst. But in this instance the intrusion of sympathy and alarm is no doubt also an enactment of the sadistic phantasy in the transference-countertransference, at a profoundly unconscious level.

Some untoward action of the analyst appropriate to the linked emotional states

Freud did not interpret the conflict – as manifested in the material, and in the character of the countertransference. It is instead obvious that Freud contributed to the enactment. His sympathy took the form of helpful interjections. In the published text:

> I went on to say that I would do all I could, nevertheless, to guess the full meaning of any hints he gave me. Was he perhaps thinking of impalement? – "No, not that; ... the criminal was tied up ..." – he expressed himself so indistinctly that I could not immediately guess in what position – " ... a pot was turned upside down on his buttocks ... some rats were put into it ... and they ... " – he had again got up, and was showing every sign of horror and resistance – " ... bored their way in ...." – Into his anus, I helped him out.
>
> (p. 166)

Freud was impelled by his anxious countertransference, pushing the patient to divulge his secrets. Thus it became dramatized as an actual struggle between them – Freud's probing enquiring, both helpful and intruding, and the Rat Man's confessional hesitation and provocation of alarm. Of course, overcoming resistance was the conventional view of analytic work at the time. However, with the circumspection deriving from a modern understanding, we can see this process being turned unconsciously into a representation of the symptom itself.

In the two cases of the Wolf Man and the Rat Man, evidence appears of a transference-countertransference interaction conforming to the contemporary understanding of countertransference enactments. I have described them systematically with the help of the three criteria given at the outset. We can therefore seriously claim a retrospective verification of our current understanding of countertransference.

Response to countertransference

Interestingly, the Rat Man case also points to an aspect of countertransference that is still not as studied as it might be even today. The Rat Man interpreted that Freud's "undertaking to show that all the material concerned only himself looked like [Freud's] anxiety" (see quote above). The Notes indicated, in that extract, that the Rat Man was telling Freud that he (the psychoanalyst) was anxious; they do not tell us if Freud actually *did* feel anxious. It was the Rat Man's construction that Freud's peace of mind *had* been "harmed." Should we accept, however, the Rat Man's construction? And is it significant that the Rat Man was aware of his impact on the analyst?

When the psychoanalyst does react to the patient it may be completely understandable! Understandable to both, actually. In indicating Freud's anxiety about the potential danger to Freud's daughter, the Rat Man conveyed a response to the countertransference – the guilt about his secret intrusiveness, including his intrusion of anxiety into Freud. The significance was not apparent to Freud. Freud was simply on another track. Only 30 years later did Balint (in the wake of Ferenczi's wild experiments) conclude that

> the analytical situation is the result of an interplay between the patient's transference and the analyst's counter-transference, complicated by the reactions released *in each by the other's transference* on to him.
>
> (Balint and Balint, 1939, p. 228; italics added)

This was reiterated more than a decade later by Margaret Little (1951), in the joint effort with Winnicott to understand the interactive aspects of "transitional space," the in-between of the interpersonal in a two-person psychology.

95

[T]ransference and counter-transference are not only syntheses by the patient and analyst acting separately, but, like the analytic work as a whole, are the result of a joint effort. We often hear of the mirror which the analyst holds up to the patient, but the patient holds one up to the analyst too.

(Little, 1951, p. 37)

The Winnicott-defined paradox of "me" and "not-me" was formulated a little differently by Money-Kyrle (1956) in his writing about "normal countertransference" (some years before Bion [1959] described normal "projective identification"). Money-Kyrle said there are *three* things to work out: (1) the transference, (2) the psychoanalyst's reactive countertransference, and (3) the patient's reaction to the analyst's countertransference:

If the analyst is in fact disturbed, it is also likely that the patient has unconsciously contributed to this result, and is in turn disturbed by it. So we have three factors to consider: first, the analyst's emotional disturbance, for he may have to deal with this silently in himself before he can disengage himself sufficiently to understand the other two; then the patient's part in bringing it about; and finally its effect on him.

(Money-Kyrle, 1956, p. 361)

This third element has not yet been followed up very extensively. However, in a paper treading similar territory to Money-Kyrle's, Irma Brenman-Pick (1985) saw the mobilization of the psychoanalyst's mentation as a kind of "mating" between the two:

If there is a mouth that seeks a breast as an inborn potential, there is, I believe, a psychological equivalent, i.e. a state of mind which seeks another state of mind.

(Brenman-Pick, 1985, p. 157)

Thus, the patient seeks a *state of mind* in the analyst; and Brenman-Pick exemplified this with a patient who sought out a "sympathetic" analyst:

[T]his supposes the transference on to the analyst of a more understanding maternal figure. I believe though, that this 'mates' with some part of the analyst that may wish to 'mother' the patient in such a situation.

(Brenman-Pick, 1985, p. 159)

This *analyst-centered* focus of the patient (Steiner, 1993) needs to be recognized in order to keep close to the patient's actual preoccupations and experiences.

Money-Kyrle also notes that, having reached the point of reacting to the countertransference, the analysis has to go on from there; it cannot go back to the *status quo ante*; "it was useless to try to pick up the thread where I had first dropped it. A new situation had arisen which had affected us both" (Money-Kyrle, 1956, p. 363).

Traces of that engagement between the two subjects are hinted at in Freud's case histories, while unrecognized by him. The Rat Man spotted his very personal impact on Freud, and responded to it with guilt. Another example of the same process may perhaps be seen with Little Hans, who reacted to his Father's "countertransference" intentions and desires.

Little Hans

The 5-year-old boy, Herbert Graf, known as Little Hans, was not in treatment – although eventually Freud thought therapeutic effects resulted, apparently relieving the boy's phobia of horses (Freud, 1909b). Instead, the boy's father had regular "conversations" with his son that he noted down and took to Freud for instruction and interpretation. Hans's father (Max Graf) was part of Freud's inner circle in the very early days and his wife had an analysis with Freud. The purpose of the conversations was to confirm Freud's developmental theory of the libido. The material (Father's Notes) is quite comprehensive. There is potential therefore for examining it for the equivalent of "countertransference." In an earlier publication (Hinshelwood, 1989), I used the material to show that Little Hans had his own unconscious transference. If that is the case, was there then a corresponding "countertransference" in the observer?

The patient's transference

First, the transference; see my 1989 paper mentioned above. The child did have angry feelings about being intruded into. This is shown in material about a piece of paper that Hans crumpled up, although it emerged initially as an oedipal phantasy concerned with separating the parents, represented in his fantasies as two giraffes. One night, Hans awoke and insisted on sleeping with his parents, saying he would explain it in the morning. Queried by father in the morning, Hans spoke of having had a vivid phantasy. Three months into their conversations, the Notes state:

> During the night of 27th–28th Hans surprised us by getting out of bed whilst it was quite dark and coming into our bed. His room is separated from our bedroom by another small room. We asked him why; whether he had been afraid, perhaps. 'No', he said; 'I'll tell you tomorrow'. He went to sleep in our bed and was then carried back to his own.
>
> Next day I questioned him closely to discover why he had come to us during the night; and after some reluctance the following dialogue took place, which I immediately took down in shorthand:
>
> He: 'In the night there was a big giraffe in the room and a crumpled one; and the big one called out because I took the crumpled one away from it. Then it stopped calling out; and then I sat down on top of the crumpled one'.
>
> I (puzzled): 'What? A crumpled giraffe? How?'
>
> He: 'Yes'. (He quickly fetched a piece of paper, crumpled it up, and said:) 'It was crumpled like that'.
>
> (1909b, p. 37)

Hans had produced one of his characteristically vivid phantasies. This material appears initially as an oedipal phantasy concerned with separating the parents. However, there is a very suggestive element. Hans demonstrated the crumpled giraffe by crumpling up some paper. This equation of the giraffe with the paper he crumpled suggests that Hans's dream of crumpled-up paper appears to be a destructive response to the notes, and that he had been disturbed by Father taking their conversations down in shorthand. (In effect, the crumpling of the paper represented Father's Notes.)

The observer's emotional state

What now about residues of *countertransference*, that is, Father's reactions as observer to Hans's own unconscious transference? Father seemed anxious in the face of Hans's unconscious efforts to communicate something they did not understand – Why sit on a crumpled giraffe? Why come into the parental bedroom? Was it a dream or phantasy? (1909b, p. 37). Father appeared to be lost and groping in the dark. He pressed Hans,

> I: 'And you sat down on the crumpled giraffe? How?' He again showed me by sitting down on the ground.
>
> I: 'Why did you come into our room?'
>
> He: 'I didn't know myself.'
>
> I: 'Were you afraid?'
>
> He: 'No, of course not'.
>
> I: 'Did you dream about the giraffe?'
>
> He: 'No. I didn't dream it. I thought it all. I'd woken earlier'.
>
> I: 'What can it mean; a crumpled giraffe? You know you can't squash a giraffe together like a piece of paper'.
>
> (p. 37)

in a more and more urgent way, leaving Hans increasingly anxious. Father asked concrete questions in the hope that something would give him a clue about Hans's phantasy or dream. Hans denied it was a dream – perhaps to emphasize the reality the phantasy had for him.

Some untoward action of the analyst appropriate to the linked emotional states

Father's questioning implies his anxious wish to clarify, perhaps with an eye on his supervisor (Freud). But this is already an active reaction to Hans, both the conversations and their purposes. Father's very concrete questions led Freud to insert a footnote that "Hans was saying quite definitely that it was a phantasy," and he later remarked:

At this point I must put in a few words. Hans's Father is asking too many questions, and was pressing the enquiry along his own lines instead of allowing the little boy to express his own thoughts. For this reason the analysis began to be obscure and uncertain. Hans went his own way.

(1909b, p. 64)

There is here an active response by Father. His countertransference state of mind became a frank "enactment" as the next exchange between them vividly makes clear:

He: 'Of course I know. I just thought it. Of course there aren't any really and truly. The crumpled one was lying on the floor, and I took it away – took hold of it with my hands'.

I: 'What? Can you take hold of a big giraffe like that with your hands?'

He: 'I took hold of the crumpled one with my hand'.

I: 'Where was the big one meanwhile?'

He: 'The big one just stood further off'.

I: 'What did you do with the crumpled one?'

He: 'Held it in my hand for a bit till the big one had stopped calling out. And when the big one had stopped calling out, I sat down on top of it'.

I: 'Why did the big one call out?'

He: 'Because I'd taken away the little one from it'. (He noticed that I was taking everything down, and asked) 'Why are you writing that down?'

(pp. 37–38)

Finally, Hans has noted, now quite consciously, Father's note-taking. This whole passage is very significant for the interactive nature of the conversations at the unconscious level.

Response to the countertransference

This *enactment* became very explicit. Despite Hans's castration anxieties, which they were both negotiating, Hans did have the courage to react to Father's reactions – that is, to make a response to the countertransference. Hans's challenge was put in the form of someone else being stripped and shown to the Professor. Continuing the last quotation, Father responded factually to Hans's question about why the conversation was being written down:

> I: 'Because I shall send it to a Professor, who can take away your "nonsense" for you'.
>
> He: 'Oho! So you've written down as well that Mummy took off her chemise, and you'll give that to the Professor too?'
>
> I: 'Yes, but he won't understand how you think that a giraffe can be crumpled up'.
>
> (1909b, p. 38)

Hans is now aware of Father's wish to open up Hans's inner world to view (Father's and Freud's view). He has observed the here–and–now situation, and is reacting to Father's intentions, with a characteristic way of experiencing the conversations. He experienced an exposure, probably outrageous, like being rendered naked in public. Father's factual explanation seemed to assume that since he was making notes with good intentions, therefore Hans would take this as well intentioned. However, Hans did not take it as well intentioned, and crumpled the giraffe/paper in what seemed an aggressive way. It is hard not to see this as an enactment of a potential castration scene between father and son. Hans was responding to Father's countertransference reactions, and both were seemingly unconscious of the deep castration significance, although as Freud worked out with the Notes that was the core of the case.[4]

Further issues in the countertransference debate

The evidence, dredged almost archaeologically from the past, speaks to current issues about the nature of countertransference. It also points to the need for more precision about the nature of interpretation and its effects. It would be important now to find ways of discriminating between such reactions to countertransference, and a *response to interpretation* in the therapeutic sense. Without clearly discriminating between a response to the enlightenment of an interpretation and a response to the psychoanalyst's emotional reactions, it is not possible to gauge a patient's real progress. Indeed the detailed unraveling of

101

these mutual interactions at the unconscious level is probably the way to achieve that necessary discrimination. Further investigation of the relation between countertransference and interpretation is therefore needed (and a further publication is in preparation).

Finally, this present work does not comment on the current debate about whether countertransference, in part, arises from the intention of the patient to provoke it (as the Rat Man case implies) or accidentally from being set off, as it were, by the patient's becoming snagged on an unconscious problem of the analyst's, or from a mixture of both in varying possible proportions.

Conclusions

I have attempted a systematic presentation of clinical material from long ago. It demonstrates the transference relationship in three separate cases, together with the reactive state of mind of the psychoanalyst (his countertransference), and an enactment arising from those unconscious active elements. A countertransference, as seen in the current wider view, does appear to occur even within the technique acceptable at the time of Freud's work. These phenomena could not have been conceptualized until later theoretical developments, long after the treatments had taken place. A retrospective verification of contemporary conceptions in the work of unsuspecting forerunners is strong evidence of the validity of the modern view of countertransference.

The pressure of the Wolf Man's passivity on Freud goaded him into a reluctantly active mode, thus enacting the infantile phantasy of intercourse. Just as clearly, the psychological intrusion by the Rat Man into Freud's mind enacted the physical intrusion of rats into a victim's anus that comprised the Rat Man's ghastly phantasy. Finding these occurrences depends on the emotional transparency of well-written case reports, and Freud, in line with so much of his writing, was particularly perspicacious in this respect. The psychoanalyst's struggles are revealed as surely as the patient's, and the convergence of the two is an indication of considerable significance.

In addition, I have been able to point to illustrations of the rather neglected but surely important response to countertransference. Clearly these kinds of occurrences between patients and their analysts have been going on since Freud's earliest cases.

So, this paper is a plea for the wider reviewing of already published clinical material, especially perhaps that which is used to introduce and justify new theoretical developments. Such secondary analysis of data, in turn, requires us to develop more systematic methods for reading clinical material, which in turn again will help develop more systematic writing of clinical material in key cases.

Notes

1   Racker originally gave a lecture in 1948 entitled "The Counter-transference Neurosis"; it was later included in English as a chapter in his posthumously published *Transference and Counter-transference* (Racker, 1968, pp. 104–126).

2   Currently, this wider notion of countertransference has become a more general discussion of "intersubjectivity," within which I distinguished two main forms, the intrapsychic and the interpersonal (Hinshelwood, 2012). The present chapter lies within the intrapsychic variant in which the analytic couple is seen as two separate subjective systems open to each other.

3   Strachey's translation was accurate. A German scholar, Ian Runnacles, noted about my assessment of the passages I quote:

> The sentences you quote, as published in German read: "*Der Patient, mit dem ich mich hier beschäftige, blieb lange Zeit hinter einer Einstellung von gefügiger Teilnahmslosigkeit unangreifbar verschanzt. … Seine Scheu vor einer selbständigen Existenz war so groß, daß sie alle Beschwerden des Krankseins aufwog. Es fand sich ein einziger Weg, um sie zu überwinden. Ich mußte warten, bis die Bindung an meine Person stark genug geworden war, um ihr das Gleichgewicht zu halten, dann spielte ich diesen einen Faktor gegen den anderen aus.*" I think I might translate "*einer Einstellung von gefügiger Teinahmslosigkeit*" as "a stance of compliant indifference." However it is translated, it confirms your feeling about Wolf man's passivity as contrasted with Freud's own active emotionality. I do not sense there is any softening by translating "*unangreifbar verschanzt*" as "unassailably entrenched." "*Angreifen*" (the verb) means to attack and "*Schanze*" means a trench and has (and had in 1918) definite militaristic connotations.
>
> Wolf man's "*Scheu*" (related to the English "to shy away from") might be better rendered as "timidity" or perhaps stronger as "dread" – there is a definite affect-content of this word. "*Ich mußte warten*" is simply "I had to wait" – "was obliged to" does add a tone of impatience

which the German can sometimes express, but if he wished to emphasise the compulsion he might have used other words such as *"gezwungen"* which have more countertransference strength, if it can be so called. (Ian Runnacles, 1999, personal communication)

4   This unconscious negotiation between them may have been a significant factor (perhaps *the* factor) in Hans's resolving the horse phobia. After all, sons and fathers do mostly negotiate this level of their relationship unconsciously.

Bibliography

Balint, A. and Balint, M. (1939) On transference and counter-transference. *International Journal of Psychoanalysis*, 20: 223–230.

Bion, W. R. (1959) Attacks on linking. *International Journal of Psychoanalysis*, 40: 308–315. Republished in W. R. Bion, *Second Thoughts* (pp. 93–109). London: Heinemann, 1967; and in E. B. Spillius (ed.), *Melanie Klein Today, Volume 1*. London: Routledge, 1988.

Bion, W. R. (1961) *Experiences in Groups*. London: Tavistock.

Blum, H. (2007) Little Hans. *Psychoanalytic Study of the Child*, 62: 44–60.

Brenman-Pick, I. (1985) Working through in the countertransference. *International Journal of Psychoanalysis*, 66: 157–166. Republished in E. Spillius (ed.), *Melanie Klein Today, Volume 1* (pp. 34–47). London: Routledge, 1988.

Etchegoyen, H. (1988) The analysis of Little Hans and the theory of sexuality. *International Review of Psychoanalysis*, 15: 37–43.

Ferenczi, S. (1919) On the technique of psychoanalysis. In *Further Contributions to the Theory and Technique of Psychoanalysis* (pp. 198–217). New York: Basic Books, 1952.

Freud, S. (1894) Obsessions and phobias. *The Standard Edition of the Complete Psychological Works of Sigmund Freud*, J. Strachey (ed., trans.), vol. 3: 69–82. London: Hogarth.

Freud, S. (1909a) *Notes upon a case of obsessional neurosis*. SE 10: 153–249. London: Hogarth.

Freud, S. (1909b) *Analysis of a phobia in a five-year-old boy*. SE 10: 3–149. London: Hogarth.

Freud, S. (1918) From the history of an infantile neurosis. SE 18: 3–122. London: Hogarth.

Glover, E. (1927) Lectures on technique in psycho-analysis. *International Journal of Psychoanalysis*, 8: 503–551.

Gottlieb, R. (1989) Technique and countertransference in Freud's analysis of the Rat Man. *Psychoanalytic Quarterly*, 58: 29–62.

Heimann, P. (1950) On counter-transference. *International Journal of Psycho-Analysis*, 31: 81–84. Republished in P. Heimann, *About Children and Children-No-Longer*. London: Routledge, 1989.

Hinshelwood, R. D. (1989) Little Hans' transference. *Journal of Child Psychotherapy*, 15: 63–78.

Hinshelwood, R. D. (2012) On being objective about the subjective: Clinical aspects of intersubjectivity in contemporary psychoanalysis. *International Forum for Psychoanalysis*, 21: 136–145.

Jones, E. (1955) *The Life and Work of Sigmund Freud, Volume 2*. London: Hogarth.

Little, M. (1951) Counter-transference and the patient's response to it. *International Journal of Psychoanalysis*, 32: 32–40.

Mahony, P. (1984) *Cries of the Wolf Man*. New York: International Universities Press.

Mahony, P. (1986) *Freud and the Rat Man*. New Haven, CT: Yale University Press.

Matthis, I. (ed.). (1994) *On Freud's Divan: Freud's Case Stories in Seven New Interpretations*. Stockholm: Natur och Kultur.

Money-Kyrle, R. (1956) Normal counter-transference and some of its deviations. *International Journal of Psychoanalysis*, 37: 360–366. Republished in D. Meltzer and E. O'Shaughnessy (eds.), *The Collected Papers of Roger Money-Kyrle*. Perthshire: Clunie Press, 1978, and in E. Spillius (ed.), *Melanie Klein Today, Volume 2*. London: Routledge, 1988.

Racker, H. (1948) La neurosis de contratransferencia. Paper presented to the Argentine Psychoanalytic Association, Buenos Aires, Argentina, September. In English: Racker, H. (1968) The countertransference neurosis. In *Transference and Countertransference* (pp. 105–126). London: Hogarth.

Racker, H. (1968) *Transference and Counter-transference*. London: Hogarth.

Rudnytsky, P. (1999) "Does the Professor Talk to God?": Countertransference and Jewish identity in the case of Little Hans. *Psychoanalysis and History*, 1: 175–194.

Steiner, J. (1993) *Psychic Retreats*. London: Routledge.

Winnicott, D. W. (1949) Hate in the countertransference. *International Journal of Psychoanalysis*, 30: 69-74. Republished in *Through Paediatrics to Psychoanalysis*, pp. 194–203. London: Tavistock, 1958.

6

MISCONCEPTIONS, ENACTMENT, AND INTERPRETATION

Heinz Weiss

Introduction

In his paper "Cognitive Development" (1968), Roger Money-Kyrle defines the aim of psychoanalytic treatment as enabling the patient to gain access to a knowledge he innately already knows, but for various reasons has warped or twisted. For instance, even in the analysis of apparently normal individuals he had observed that many possible versions of the parental intercourse may occur in dream material, "*except the right one*" (p. 417). In his view, the misrepresentation of the primal scene is only *one* example of the more general conflict between the human predisposition to discover the truth and the will to distort it. Therefore, for him the task of psychoanalysis is to help the patient to understand and overcome those emotional barriers that stand in the way of acknowledging psychic reality (see Money-Kyrle, 1971, p. 442).

In his 1968 paper Money-Kyrle gave descriptive examples of the complicated mechanisms and constructions that underlie the misrepresentation of psychic reality. He spoke of "misconceptions" and showed how they serve to artfully avoid anxiety and psychic pain at the cost of contact and development. Later on he argued that the evasive maneuvers are directed against certain aspects of reality that are especially difficult to bear and of which he thought three to be of central significance: the dependency on the breast as an external source of goodness; the recognition of the parental intercourse as a "supremely creative act," from which the child is excluded because of its smallness and immaturity; and finally the recognition of the "inevitability of time and ultimately death" (Money-Kyrle, 1971, p. 443).

It is these three "innate preconceptions" or "facts of life" (Money-Kyrle, 1968, p. 420) that often give rise to distortions and misunderstandings. Although Money-Kyrle did not explicitly refer to the impact that misconceptions have on the transference situation, it seems clear that the analyst often becomes involved in the subtle mechanisms by which the misconception is construed and perpetuated in order to maintain the patient's psychic equilibrium (see Joseph, 1989). This is often the case when the status quo is threatened, be it by a new insight, emerging guilt feelings, or fears of loss, as with an impending break.

From very early on Money-Kyrle (1956) made it clear that the analyst's task is thus to take in the patient's projections, to transform and differentiate them from his own internal objects, and finally to "re-project" them in a symbolic form via his interpretations. In his model of countertransference as a transformation (Frank and Weiss, 2003), which was influenced by Paula Heimann's (1950) writing on this theme and by Melanie Klein's (1946) investigation of the processes of projective and introjective identification, Money-Kyrle not only anticipated Bion's theory of container–contained (Bion, 1962), but also examined the different factors that might interfere with the analyst's capacity to understand (e.g., the role of his superego or the quality of the anxieties that are evoked in his counter-transference). In this way Money-Kyrle's work links up with the outstanding contributions made by Heinrich Racker (1948, 1951, 1958), Paula Heimann (1950), and other pioneers (Little, 1951; Reich, 1951) at around the same time in this field.

I will argue that some of these early thoughts on the role of countertransference can be seen as precursors of important developments in psychoanalytic technique, as they have been intro-duced some 30 years later by the understanding of the transference as a "total situation" (Joseph, 1985), the examination of the analyst's "involvement" (Feldman, 1997), the description of subtle "enactments" between patient and analyst (Gabbard, 1995; Jacobs, 1986, 1993, 2001; Joseph 1971, 1975; McLaughlin 1987, 1991), or the use of "analyst-centered" interpretations (Steiner, 1993).

To illustrate this, I want to present clinical material from a border-line patient. I will attempt to explore how such "misconceptions" are introduced into the analytic relationship especially at times of loss, where they may lead to impasse or dead ends. This is especially the case when the analyst unwittingly becomes part of this process and finds it difficult to disentangle from the various pressures the patient exerts on him.

Following the clinical material I will describe a psychotic misrepresentation in the first year of the analysis that was based on omnipotent, delusional beliefs, which ended up in confusion and paranoid anxiety. I will try to show how the patient, in the course of analysis, no longer reacted psychotically, but mainly resorted to narcissistic and perverse mechanisms to cope with separation anxiety. Although this gave rise to various distortions and twists, reflecting a borderline organization of her personality, it did not result in a complete denial of psychic reality. Finally, two sessions from the fifth year of her analysis are presented, when the patient – under the impression of the impending ending – seemed partially to fall back onto such mechanisms, but now appeared in a better position to manage her sadness and anxiety. To conclude, I will discuss some of the technical problems that arise from this situation, referring to Money-Kyrle's early papers and connecting them to some more contemporaneous ideas.

Clinical material

Mrs H, a lawyer in her mid-thirties, came to analysis when her marriage was in a severe crisis and she was close to a psychological breakdown. In her biographical details, her vulnerability regarding situations of separation and loss was marked. Such moments could trigger catastrophic anxiety and had in the past repeatedly led to severe psychological crises – such as a brief psychotic breakdown at age 18 when a student of theology had rejected her intense love feelings.

The failure of her marriage confronted her with similar anxieties when her husband, a successful manager, spent less and less time with her and eventually demanded that she tolerate his relationship with his girlfriend. The separation forced her to confront the failure of her wish to start her own family. In a painful way she was reminded of her anxiety about never having her own child. There was some medical condition indicating that she might have had difficulties getting pregnant due to an illness earlier in her life.

Although she felt partly threatened by such experiences of loss, Mrs H tended to rapidly establish a feeling of special trust in relationships with men, which quickly turned into erotized closeness. There was evidence that this tendency reflected her relationship with her father, whose favorite daughter she felt she was. Her helplessness and despair in the face of separation seemed, however, more closely related to her futile efforts to access her mother's emotional world; even as a child she had experienced her mother's gaze as rejecting, impervious, and threatening.

At the start of the analysis, Mrs H created an enthusiastic and excited mood, but was repeatedly in distress when shorter or longer breaks caused panic and anxiety. When these anxieties became unbearable, the transference developed in such a way that the emotional experiences related to the separation were misrepresented. The patient introduced misconceptions into the relationship that protected her from acute anxiety, but also put her in a state of mind in which she lost contact with her own feelings, so that her relation to external reality could only be maintained at the cost of distorting and twisting her inner reality. These misconceptions could be constructed in different ways and had the effect of blocking the psychic development of the patient. At times they seemed to lead to a state of confusion.

In the following material I would like to investigate the different forms of misconceptions that developed during the course of treatment. I will try to examine their impact on the transference situation, and how they encased me in the countertransference so that it was difficult to get an idea of what was going on. To begin with, I will describe the emergence of psychotic elements in the transference.

The development of a psychotic misrepresentation in the first year of treatment

The despair and anger with which the patient had begun therapy dissipated after only a few weeks to be replaced by an excited mood. She dreamt that we would have an "exemplary therapy" with each other, which would lead to fundamentally new discoveries, and she experienced the analysis like a journey of discovery into a fascinating and (to her) unknown world, which she compared to the exotic areas of the Pacific. I felt encouraged to speculate and interpret, and after only a short time she evoked the feeling in me that our research had indeed led to some remarkable discoveries. The patient reinforced this feeling by swamping me with dream material and numerous associations; these seemed to confirm my interpretations but led me to overlook her fragmented inner state.

The sessions were dominated by a dreamlike, erotized atmosphere, which made time seem to fly by. The mood in these sessions was illustrated by a postcard of a Gauguin painting that the patient brought in, and by a novel by W. Somerset Maugham, *Rain*, that she was reminded of. This story, set on a South Pacific island, dealt with a desperate struggle between a missionary and a prostitute: *While the missionary is attempting to convert the prostitute to Christianity, the prostitute is intent on seducing the missionary. The story ends with the missionary being found dead on the island's beach with his throat cut.*

I was obviously so blinded by the wealth of the material that the significance of this story occurred to me only afterward. In the transference, which had become increasingly delusional before the first long break, the patient had become convinced that I had fallen in love with her, while I was trying – like the missionary – to "convert" her with my interpretations about her separation anxiety. She ignored these interpretations, or lightly dismissed them – or even seemed to take them in on occasion as a confirmation that *I* and not *she* had difficulties with this separation. I learned later that on leaving the last session she had noticed a pram in a car parked next to the consulting room, and that this observation had irritated her.

During the subsequent two-week break she joined a religious sect in her hometown and initially felt seduced by its leader, who quickly pursued and manipulated her as he showed brief sequences of films and spoke about religious themes. She returned after two weeks in a state of acute paranoid anxiety, feeling like a puppet on a string, and believing that her capacity to think was being destroyed.

In the first session after this break, filled with psychotic anxiety, she needed nearly half the session time to feel her way along the walls of the consulting room to the couch, on which she finally sat. From there, she looked at me full of mistrust and horror, her hands over her ears, shouting at me, "Don't say a word!" She obviously feared that I would project sequences of speech into her, treat her like a puppet, and manipulate her thinking.

Although I attempted to interpret her anxiety about how desperate she had felt during the break, and now felt that something horrible of mine was going to come back to her, it was difficult to establish a meaningful contact. She said that she could not feel and think anymore and no longer knew who she was. Toward the end of the session she could express her despair that she had lost her capacity to dream, and her hope that she could with my help find a way out of the films of the religious man. In the subsequent sessions her psychotic anxiety gradually subsided. She now reported dreams in which the treatment situation was represented as an alchemist's dangerous kitchen. The work on this material enabled her to partly work through her anxieties and to take back the projections bit by bit. However, although she did not react psychotically again, subsequent breaks in the therapy remained a big problem for the patient.

I think that the delusional transference-love, which she projected into the sect during the break, contained a misconception of the experience of separation and loss, and particularly of Money-Kyrle's second "fact of life," the recognition of the parents' intercourse as a "supremely creative act." Evidently, the patient was reminded of her own childlessness and her separation from me and my family by seeing the pram after the last session before the break. This led to a collapse of her denial, which confronted her with such anxieties of fragmentation that she could not think about this experience, but had to ward it off by omnipotent means in a delusional way by escaping into a psychotic organization, represented by the sect and its leader. She did not find any security there, however, and returned to treatment full of confusion and paranoia. I think the leader of the sect stood for the "missionary," who responded to her attempts to seduce him by powerful and delusional "conversions" that made her feel she was his puppet.

The question whether this psychotic episode could have been avoided if I had managed to address the delusional elements in her transference early enough before the break remains open. Nevertheless, the patient reproached me for this on several occasions later in the analysis. Instead we had got into a dead end, where I had unwittingly assumed the role of the "missionary" – that is, a psychotic object relation. As long as this misconception was maintained, the break was "no problem" for the patient, until this construction collapsed and she felt overwhelmed by catastrophic anxiety.

Borderline organizations and perverse misrepresentations

In describing the further course of treatment, I would like to illustrate how the patient, who no longer reacted psychotically, now used

111

various borderline mechanisms to deal with the experience of separation and loss. These too led to misconceptions and entanglements, but they were easier to recognize and interpret and therefore did not lead to another catastrophic breakdown.

A second break only a few months later led to a similar experience for her. The patient again erotized in a near-delusional way a relationship with a South American acquaintance, although without quite losing sight of her panic-like anxiety of loss.

In the penultimate session before the break she reported a dream *in which a little girl was hit by a car and was dying. She herself called the emergency doctor and attempted to keep the girl alive by mouth-to-mouth resuscitation until his arrival. The girl needed artificial respiration. Then a passing boy put his penis in the girl's mouth. She recognized the danger, pulled the penis out, and continued with mouth-to-mouth resuscitation until the emergency doctor arrived.*

I imagine that this dream expressed the dreadful anxiety the patient felt exposed to in the face of the forthcoming break. The penis in the girl's mouth indicated that the patient was looking for a possibility of managing the anxiety of loss, as she had done when the transference was dominated by an idealized, sexualized mood and she experienced my interpretations as if they were a penis in her mouth. But now she recognized the danger and resuscitated the girl by keeping her airways free until the doctor arrived. In this way she could separate herself from the sexualized scene and assume an understanding, maternal position toward a desperate needy part of her self.

At that time, the patient still had the feeling that she could only survive the breaks in a mechanical state by functioning in a robot-like and rigid way, like an artificial respiration machine, as she lost contact with projected parts of herself, which then became inaccessible to her. In this phase of therapy she used her dreams less to communicate her inner state, and more to draw me into particular dream sequences in order to eliminate the experience of separateness. For instance, she would start a session with a comment such as: "I have brought three dreams today. No. 1, No. 2, and No. 3. You can choose which one you want to hear!" I have given a detailed account of this in another paper (Weiss, 2002). This way of using her dreams was particularly apparent before therapy breaks and represented a desperate effort to get into me and to make me enact various forms of togetherness with her. Such enactments can assume complex forms of misconceptions, which are not always easily recognized as such by the analyst.

112

In other situations, the patient got into agoraphobic and claustrophobic anxieties, such as before one Christmas break when she initially reacted with massive agoraphobic anxiety to her feeling of abandonment, but then, right before the first session after the break, got into a panic because she feared that the central locking system of her car would not open from the inside and that she would not be able to come to her session.

Clinical material of two sessions
in the fifth year of analysis

I would like to go on to present two sessions from the fifth year of analysis in greater detail. The patient had made noticeable progress in therapy despite some stressful external life changes. She had not only been able to mourn the death of her father, but had also lovingly cared for her increasingly dementing mother without getting too confused herself, as she had feared she might. After three years she had met a man of the same age and had set up house with him after some initial difficulties. Her partner's close relationship to his family was a problem for her, as was the fact that she remained childless in this relationship too, despite various efforts to have this investigated. As mentioned earlier, there was some indication that there were medical problems that made it difficult for her to get pregnant. She was jealous of his mother and his sister, found it difficult to bear that he spent so much time with them, and tried in turn to get even with him by mocking him and making him jealous of her analysis.

A few months prior to the sessions I will present, I had informed the patient that I would move to another town due to a career change. Because of the long distance this would make a continuation of the analysis fairly unrealistic if not completely impossible. Initially she curtly answered that she could end the analysis at any time she liked, but then decided to stay to the end. It remained unclear whether or not she would continue her analysis with a female colleague I had recommended and to whom I could refer her. In the preceding session, the patient had reported a dream.

In this dream the patient, together with other young people, emptied the contents of a bag into a swimming pool, but then feared that this could produce a poisonous mixture. A 6-year-old girl, standing on the edge of the pool, who was missing her parents, fainted. The patient resuscitated this girl, but had to take in some of the poison in the process. Eventually, the little girl stabilized. The patient tried to control her breathing, heartbeat, and the reaction of her pupils. When the emergency doctor arrived he told her that she had done well and he did not have to do anything further ...

This dream was related to earlier dreams in which a small child was threatened. In this case, I interpreted the dream in the context of her fear that her arrogant, destructive feelings could poison her relationship and threaten the small child in her, who feared that she might fall in the water and lose the analysis. Most likely, however, the patient had also experienced me as a part of the "young people," seeing the end of the analysis as a manic-destructive attack on my part. Then it was I who "poisoned" the water, leaving her to "take out the poison" and "resuscitate" herself on her own.

First session

The patient arrived in tears to the following session and thought that this might be sadness about the forthcoming end. Maybe she would have to separate from her boyfriend, Mario, as well. He had told her that he wanted to check the electrical supply in his sister's house on Sunday morning together with an acquaintance. That would keep them busy all morning. After that they would all go to a restaurant to eat and he would like her to join them there. At that moment she had felt desperate again and felt a "thorn."

I related this "thorn" to her feelings of rancor and resentment, feeling abandoned by me.

But she continued with her complaints and grew more and more angry. Mario had betrayed her. Instead of sleeping with her on Sunday morning, he preferred the house of his sister. In April he was planning to go climbing on his own, while she was desperately longing for a baby. She angrily attacked him, cried, and mentioned a dream.

When I asked her for the dream, she described *that she was in discussion with a woman, a sociologist, who was superior to her. Then her mother joined and said that in the past she had had a lesbian relationship with a nurse. She herself imagined how fascinating it would be to be this nurse.*

In the context of this dream she remembered having seen a pram in the stairwell when she left the previous session. When a woman carrying a small child came down the stairs, she had wondered whether this was my wife.

I was reminded of her noticing a pram before her psychotic breakdown in the first year of her analysis and interpreted that the end of therapy made her feel left out by me and my family just as she felt left out by Mario and his family. This sadness made her react with despair and rage.

She did not want to relate these feelings to me and continued with her accusations about Mario. She talked about her wish to have children and went on to mention a client in her office who had left her lover and had returned to her husband. Now she was missing her lover and wished her husband dead. Then she added; "I cannot accept that my womb will remain empty … I just cannot accept this!" My patient said her client then went on to mention suicidal thoughts, such as cutting her throat or cutting into her belly, much to the horror of her colleagues.

I was struck by the cruelty of this and noted how much she discriminated between the idealized lover and the hated husband. I voiced the assumption that her hatred was related to the reality of her loss here, and that the urgent wish to have a baby was, at least in part, an attempt not to acknowledge this loss.

After this she attacked me. I probably did not want to understand her at all. On the contrary, I just wanted to mock her and not admit to her she was right in her criticism of Mario.

I was affected by her reproach and explained that while I could see the difficulties with her partner, I believed that her own strong feelings of hatred and jealousy were contributing to the difficulties. I brought in the analogy in the dream from the last session, where a poisonous mixture was produced by emptying the bag and the girl at the side of the pool needed to be resuscitated.

She cried and said reproachfully that she felt like someone who had worked for nothing and was now standing alone at the station with her few possessions.

I commented that she withdrew further and further into hatred and despair, to which she replied that I seemed to see her as a puppet.

Toward the end of the session, however, she said: "I cannot take it that you are leaving. It is so hard!" She mentioned her anxiety that she might do something mad, and this seemed to express her actual concern much more realistically.

Discussion

As illustrated in the clinical material, in this moving session the patient had been dealing with the necessity of acknowledging reality while struggling with her hatred of reality. She attacked her friend Mario because he preferred his sister's house, and attempted to protect me although she knew that I was going to leave. This attempt to not attack or to not blame me was reflected in the memory of the client in her office who had split off the hated husband from the missed lover.

My attempt to interpret this split resulted in her attack on me and her reproach toward me that I did not understand her at all. Like Mario, I now became someone who only thought of his own plans, had no consideration for the needs of others, and even mocked her. She had to protect herself from such a person and get into a close relationship with an idealized figure. Her dream indicated a possibility of such a solution by way of a lesbian union with the nurse/mother/wife, now united in hatred of the abandoning father.

It was not clear from this whether the patient hated *me* or just *what I did to her*. At the beginning of the session I had not addressed her obvious despair, but had concentrated on her anger about Mario. I had thus possibly acted out a part of this cruelty. She now attempted to fill her inner void with her desperate wish to have a baby. I think that in this moment she felt herself to have something like an "empty bag" inside her, which she desperately sought to fill with jealousy, rage, sexuality, or a baby from me.

In this way, the idea of a baby contained a misconception of the reality of separation and loss. Some elements were reminiscent of her first year in analysis: the bag with the poisonous mixture, the resuscitation of the girl, the cutting of the throat – as in the novel by Somerset Maugham – as well as her reproach that I treated her like a puppet (as the leader of the sect had once done). By the end of the session, however, the patient was in a better state to acknowledge reality. Her disappointment and rage now gave way to (surprised) concern. The scene at the station conveyed an impression of sadness, maybe even a wish to follow me on the train. Now she no longer talked about a mad client, but about her own fear of possibly doing something mad.

Second session

Using material from the following session I would like to further investigate the development of the misconception.

The following day the patient appeared to be in a hurt and angry mood. After the session of the previous day she had had fantasies regarding Mario, such as "Competition will liven up things!" and she thought about meeting other men and buying herself elegant clothes in order to make him jealous. She had really enjoyed these fantasies, had gone to dinner on her own, and watched television far into the night. At three o'clock in the morning she awoke from a dream *in which she was chased by a police car although she was innocent. Her only hope was to get away from the police car.*

On awakening from this dream she was drenched in sweat and full of anxiety. She had had many thoughts but then it all turned into hatred of me. She imagined that I had said in the previous session *that the reason she could not get pregnant was that she was incapable of loving Mario.* That meant I thought she was inferior, I was in a superior position, and wanted her to accept that she could not have a baby and a family, while I had both – and on top of that I was mocking her.

I commented that the police car in her dream probably represented the way she had experienced my interpretations of the previous day, as though I chased her and accused her although she was not guilty, like a superior power who mocked her and from whom she could only take flight.

She seemed to calm down following this intervention and returned to talking about Mario and his family, but now in a less accusatory and more mournful and regretful manner. We could now investigate her anger toward me in more detail. In this context she began to talk about some childhood memories and mentioned that her mother had worked very hard during the pregnancy with her and as a consequence she had been born prematurely in the eighth month. She completed primary school in three rather than the customary four years and everybody had been very proud of her … While she talked about this she cried.

I responded that she seemed to have the feeling that she had to end her analysis prematurely because of my career change. Part of her felt obliged to show me how well she had done and what progress she had made, perhaps to make me proud of her. Another part of her, however, felt terribly lonely, abandoned, and in need of support.

She responded that her parents had always taught her "to accept fate." You had to get through things, you had to "pull yourself together."

I said that she seemed to think that I demanded the same from her.

She then went on to think of continuing the analysis with someone else in case she needed further help. However, she feared that Mario would hold her in contempt for that and mock her.

I suggested that the problem might be that a part of herself (not just Mario) would be contemptuous if she needed to avail herself of more analysis. I added the question of whether it was possible that what she was demanding from herself was to not need further analysis.

She confirmed this and went on to ask about the possibility of continuing with the colleague I had mentioned. A warmer mood developed and I felt less guilty about my leaving than I had previously.

I took her back to the dream of the session before last about the bag with the poisonous contents and attempted to take it up as an expression of her situation in the analysis. She had possibly feared that she could only evacuate, but not tolerate, the poisonous feelings about reality, which took away the air the little girl needed to breathe. And she was not sure whether she would be able to deal with this situation on her own or whether she would need the help of an emergency doctor.

She responded that this poison came up particularly strongly when she experienced me as empathic and understanding. This especially incensed her and angered her.

The patient remained in treatment with me for the final two months and subsequently continued her analysis with the colleague to whom I had referred her.

Discussion

Looking at the course of the session, it seemed that the patient had returned to the excited, superior position of the previous day. She let me know that she enjoyed her fantasies, whose aim it was to make Mario, and presumably me, jealous. In this way, she attempted to deny her feelings of exclusion and abandonment and projected them into another person.

She had then watched TV late into the night, as if it had been difficult for her to stay with her internal reality and she had to distract herself somehow. In her dream, which possibly was a continuation of a TV program in her internal world, she was pursued by a police car, although she was innocent, and had to take flight. I suspect she had good reason to feel guilty. She had projected her feelings of jealousy into Mario. While thinking about the dream, her feelings of persecution flipped into hatred of me, as she imagined that *I* had said *the reason* for her not having any children was that she was unable to love Mario.

This idea obviously contained a misrepresentation of my interpretation that her wish for a baby was a manifestation of her denial and her hatred of reality regarding the forthcoming end of therapy. We had got into a dead end at exactly this place. From her point of view I had pushed the guilt back into her and had assumed the role of prosecutor. Nevertheless, she did not seem *entirely* convinced that I had put it *exactly* like this. However, the thought that the urgent wish to have a baby might contain a denial of the reality of separation and loss seemed unbearable to her.

She calmed down when I was subsequently able to acknowledge her subjective reality, conceding that she seemed to have experienced my interpretation like a persecuting superego, which accused her for no reason. Evidently she had experienced my intervention in such a way that I had not *actually* persecuted her and triumphed over her with my interpretations, by way of projecting my own guilt feelings (because of my leaving) into her. Only now was she able to retract some of her projections, as the subsequent material about her premature birth, along with the skipping of a year of primary school and the parents' pride about this clearly indicated how difficult it was for her to deal with her own needs in the face of the end of the analysis.

In the further course of the session, the patient did not return to a persecutory version of the separation scenario, but could go on to acknowledge at the end of the session that she could feel a readiness to respond to destructive impulses, particularly at times when she experienced me as more sympathetic or understanding. In that way, she saw me as less cruel and heartless and enabled me, in turn, to feel less cruel and guilty about my leaving.

Some further thoughts

The sequence of the two sessions gives an impression of the patient's reemerging need to resort to psychotic and borderline mechanisms when confronted with the end of her analysis. The use of these mechanisms allowed her to evade frightening and painful feelings at the cost of a misrepresentation of reality.

Psychotic anxiety could be seen in the dream material as well as in the distorted perception of certain interpretations, while borderline mechanisms seemed active in the way Mrs H dealt with feelings of isolation between the sessions by turning them into something exciting, for example, the fantasy of making her boyfriend jealous by attracting the attention of other men. The idea of a lesbian union held together by hatred of the abandoning father contained elements of such a misconception.

By way of such thoughts, the reality of separation and loss is acknowledged to a certain degree, but at the same time disavowed and secretly negated. Steiner (1993, p. 129) described this process as "turning a blind eye," that is, to take a position in which certain aspects of reality are seemingly accepted, but at the same time are twisted and distorted to cover up the truth.

By simultaneously accepting and disavowing reality, its painful contradictions cannot be fully acknowledged and worked through. Instead a split is being introduced that leads to a *slicing* of reality that makes the contradictions almost unrecognizable. To render the cracks between these slices imperceptible, misconceptions are introduced, which often take the form of complex arguments by treating the disparities as if they didn't exist. Mrs H achieved this, for example, by turning the separation into a wish fulfillment. The corresponding arguments then went as follows: it was not the analyst who convinced her with his interpretations, but *she* has led him to exciting new discoveries … a penis is as good as mouth-to-mouth respiration for resuscitation … or she could accept the separation if only she could get pregnant, and so on.

It is the skillful bridging of these contradictions, rather than an acceptance of them, which leads to the construction of misconceptions. As long as the argument is convincing, the painful contradictions do not have to be acknowledged and some form of denial can be maintained. The structure of such arguments can be seen for instance in Mrs H's conviction that I had said the only reason she could not get pregnant was *because* she was unable to love her boyfriend, or her belief that *if* only she could get pregnant I would not leave her.

This bridging process poses a technical problem in that the analyst often becomes integrated as part of the misconception and subsequently may unwittingly be drawn into various forms of enactment – a concept that has been formulated under the headings of "counter-resistance" (Racker, 1958), "projective counter-identification" (Grinberg, 1962, 1985), "acting-in" (Joseph, 1971), "role-responsiveness" (Sandler, 1976), or "actualization" of an object relationship (Sandler and Sandler, 1978), and has since then been extended and deepened by analysts from different psychoanalytic schools (Feldman, 1994, 1997, 2009; Gabbard, 1995; Jacobs, 1986, 1993, 2001; McLaughlin, 1987, 1991; O'Shaughnessy, 1992; Steiner, 2006). However, as early as 1956 Money-Kyrle had described an entanglement of this kind when a patient, by contemptuously rejecting all his interpretations, made him feel useless and bemused. It was only when he realized that his state of mind was very similar to that of the patient at the beginning of the session that he gradually felt able to interpret what was going on. He described this as a "*slow motion*" sequence in which he had first to accept the state of "mental impotence" the patient had evoked in him (Money-Kyrle, 1956, p. 336).

In the case of my patient such a situation arose when I said in the first session that her wish for a baby was an expression of her hatred of the reality of the loss here, which she experienced as an attack on her by me, to which she had to retaliate by attacking me in return. Such *patient-centered* interpretations (Steiner, 1993, p. 131), given prematurely, contain the risk of being experienced as counter-projections by the analyst, a risk that Money-Kyrle had already pointed out in his 1958 paper "The Process of Psycho-Analytical Inference" long before this subject was taken up and further developed by his followers (see Feldman, 1997; Joseph, 1971, 1975, 1989; O'Shaughnessy, 1981, 1992; Steiner, 1993). According to Money-Kyrle (1958), the patient may then have the feeling that the analyst is robbing her or him of the only protective measure she or he has, that is, the ability to project, and to use it against the other. He continues by suggesting that what has to be analyzed in such a situation "is a specific form of persecutory fear – the patient's fear of becoming victim of projective identification emanating from the analyst – of the analyst's 'blowing first', and so of being overwhelmed with confusion, illness, failure and death." And he adds: "If this is brought into the open, it may be possible to show that the fear itself is the result of a projection" (p. 351).

What Money-Kyrle clearly realized was not only that powerful projections "can affect a recipient" (1958, p. 347), but also that the analyst may defensively re-project into the patient and therefore create a dilemma that can only be resolved by turning to analyst–centered interpretations.

When I made use of an analyst-centered interpretation in the following session, acknowledging the patient's subjective reality by saying that she seemed to experience my interpretations like the pursuit of a police car, she felt relief and could retract her projections. However, the outcome is not always guaranteed to be that positive. Sometimes the patient experiences an analyst-centered interpretation not as an interpretation but simply as a confirmation of his projections (see Steiner, 1993, p. 145). This can result in a situation that I have called a "second-degree dilemma" (Weiss, 2007), in which *patient-centered interpretations are experienced by the patient as re-projections by the analyst, while analyst-centered interpretations are experienced as confirmation of the patient's own projections.*

I cannot pursue the technical issues that ensue from this dead-end situation in more detail here. Suffice it to say that in the first years of her analysis Mrs H seemed to depend on the use of misconceptions to cope with catastrophic anxieties centered on loss. When the analysis was going to be terminated prematurely for external reasons, she regressed temporarily to these means. However, she now seemed to be in a better position to work through her depressive anxieties, which she had not been able to do in this way at the beginning of her treatment. This allowed her to recognize the symbolic meaning of the material, as well as her own neediness, so that she could decide to overcome her grievance and defensive pride and continue her analysis with a colleague a few months later.

As a strategy for interpreting, looking more closely at misconceptions is presumably not just relevant in phases of separation. It allows analyst and patient to register the almost unnoticeable distortions of what Money-Kyrle came to call the basic "facts of life." At times, it is the mood of the session, a vague feeling in the countertransference, or talking at cross purposes (Feldman, 2009) that gives an indication of the presence of a misconception. If one manages to identify such misunderstandings, one can at times observe the development of misconceptions in the making. Using the fine grain of the session, these observations can be transformed into transference interpretations, and subsequently the analyst may go on to examine the patient's reaction to his interpretation. These reactions in turn form the basis for further interpretations, which deepen the understanding of the relationship. On the other hand, if misconceptions remain unnoticed, an "escalating misunderstanding" (Weiss, 2003) may develop and the patient can incorporate the "undigested interpretations" into his defensive organization (Mitrani, 2009).

In his paper "Cognitive Development," Money-Kyrle (1968) described the complex structure and functions of what he called "misconceptions" of psychic reality. Therefore, in his view, one aim of psychoanalysis is "to help the patient understand, and so overcome, emotional impediments to his discovering what he innately already knows" (Money-Kyrle, 1971, p. 442). This can be done by unraveling the structure of "perverse arguments" (Steiner, 1993, pp. 88–102), which are introduced to evade reality and to cover up the truth. As seen in the example of Mrs H, the resulting misconceptions can be constructed in different ways and serve different purposes. The first year of her analysis was thus dominated by psychotic mechanisms, which went hand in hand with the development of a delusional transference. In the further course of analysis narcissistic and perverse mechanisms were brought into play, which enabled the patient to create parallel versions of reality without fully acknowledging their painful implications and disparities. She temporally returned to these measures when, toward the end of her analysis, she felt confronted with another basic "fact of life," the acknowledgment of time and loss, although she now seemed able to deal in a more human way with the sadness and anxieties that came along with them.

Translated from the German by Ursula Haug.

Note

Portions of this clinical material have also been published in Weiss (2009).

Bibliography

Bion, W. R. (1962) *Learning from Experience*. London: Heinemann.

Feldman, M. (1994) Projective identification in phantasy and enactment. *Psychoanalytic Inquiry*, 14: 423–440.

Feldman, M. (1997) Projective identification: The analyst's involvement. *International Journal of Psychoanalysis*, 78: 227–241.

Feldman, M. (2009) *Doubt, Conviction and the Analytic Process: Selected Papers of Michael Feldman*, B. Joseph (ed.). London: Routledge.

Frank, C. and Weiss, H. (eds.). (2003) *Normale Gegenübertragung und mögliche Abweichungen. Zur Aktualität von R. Money-Kyrles Verständnis des Gegenübertragungsprozesses* (Normal countertransference and some of its deviations: On the actuality of R. Money-Kyrle's understanding of the process of countertransference). Tübingen: edition discord.

Gabbard, G. (1995) Countertransference: The emerging common ground. *International Journal of Psychoanalysis*, 76: 475–485.

Grinberg, L. (1962) On a specific aspect of counter-transference due to the patient's projective identification. *International Journal of Psychoanalysis*, 43: 436–440.

Grinberg, L. (1985) *Téoria de la Identificación*. Madrid: Tecnipublicaciones.

Heimann, P. (1950) On counter-transference. *International Journal of Psychoanalysis*, 31: 81–84.

Jacobs, T. J. (1986) On counter-transference enactments. *Journal of the American Psychoanalytic Association*, 34: 289–307.

Jacobs, T. J. (1993) The inner experiences of the analyst: Their contribution to the analytic process. *International Journal of Psychoanalysis*, 74: 7–14.

Jacobs, T. J. (2001) On misreading and misleading patients: Some reflections on communications, miscommunications and counter-transference enactments. *International Journal of Psychoanalysis*, 82: 653–669.

Joseph, B. (1971) A clinical contribution to the analysis of a perversion. *International Journal of Psychoanalysis*, 52: 441–449.

Joseph, B. (1975) The patient who is difficult to reach. In P. L. Giovacchini (ed.), *Tactics and Techniques in Psychoanalytic Therapy. Volume 2, Countertransference* (pp. 205–210). New York: Jason Aronson.

Joseph, B. (1985) Transference: The total situation. *International Journal of Psychoanalysis*, 66: 447–454.

Joseph, B. (1989) *Psychic Equilibrium and Psychic Change: Selected Papers of Betty Joseph*, M. Feldman and E. B. Spillius (eds.). London: Routledge.

Klein, M. (1946) Notes on some schizoid mechanisms. *International Journal of Psychoanalysis*, 27: 99–110. Reprinted in *The Writings of Melanie Klein*, vol. 1 (pp. 1–24). London: Hogarth Press, 1975.

Little, M. (1951) Counter-transference and the patient's response to it. *International Journal of Psychoanalysis*, 32: 32–40.

McLaughlin, J. T. (1987) The play of transference: Some reflections on enactment in the psychoanalytic situation. *Journal of the American Psychoanalytic Association*, 35: 557–582.

McLaughlin, J. T. (1991) Clinical and theoretical aspects of enactment. *Journal of the American Psychoanalytic Association*, 39: 595–614.

Mitrani, J. (2009) Excogitating Bion's *Cogitations*: Further Implications on Psychoanalytic Technique. Paper presented at the Bion in Boston conference, Boston, Massachusetts, July 25.

124

Money-Kyrle, R. (1956) Normal counter-transference and some of its deviations. In D. Meltzer and E. O'Shaughnessy (eds.), *The Collected Papers of Roger Money-Kyrle* (pp. 330–342). Strath Tay, Perthshire: Clunie Press, 1978.

Money-Kyrle, R. (1958) The process of psycho-analytical inference. In D. Meltzer and E. O'Shaughnessy, (eds.), *The Collected Papers of Roger Money-Kyrle* (pp. 343–352). Strath Tay, Perthshire: Clunie Press, 1978.

Money-Kyrle, R. (1968) Cognitive development. In D. Meltzer and E. O'Shaughnessy (eds.), *The Collected Papers of Roger Money-Kyrle* (pp. 416–433). Strath Tay, Perthshire: Clunie Press, 1978.

Money-Kyrle, R. (1971) The aim of psycho-analysis. In D. Meltzer and E. O'Shaughnessy (eds.), *The Collected Papers of Roger Money-Kyrle* (pp. 442–449). Strath Tay, Perthshire: Clunie Press, 1978.

O'Shaughnessy, E. (1981) A clinical study of a defensive organisation. *International Journal of Psychoanalysis*, 52: 359–369.

O'Shaughnessy, E. (1992) Enclaves and excursions. *International Journal of Psychoanalysis*, 73: 603–611.

Racker, H. (1948) A contribution to the problem of counter-transference. *International Journal of Psychoanalysis*, 34: 313–324.

Racker, H. (1951) Observations on counter-transference as a technical instrument: Preliminary communication (this volume).

Racker, H. (1958) Counter-resistance and interpretation. *Journal of the American Psychoanalytic Association*, 6: 215–221.

Reich, A. (1951) On counter-transference. *International Journal of Psychoanalysis*, 32: 25–31.

Sandler, J. (1976) Countertransference and role-responsiveness. *International Review of Psychoanalysis*, 3: 43–47.

Sandler, A.-M., and Sandler, J. (1978) On the development of object relationships and affects. *International Journal of Psychoanalysis*, 59: 285–296.

Steiner, J. (1993) *Psychic Retreats: Pathological Organizations in Psychotic, Neurotic, and Borderline Patients.* London: Routledge.

Steiner, J. (2006) Interpretative enactments and the analytic setting. *International Journal of Psychoanalysis*, 87: 315–320.

Weiss, H. (2002) Reporting a dream accompanying an enactment in the transference situation. *International Journal of Psychoanalysis*, 83: 633–645.

Weiss, H. (2003) Verstehen als Wiedergutmachung – Deutung als Reprojektion. Zur Aktualität von R. Money-Kyrle's Verständnis der Gegenübertragung als Transformationsprozeß (Understanding as reparation: Interpretation as re-projection. On the actuality of R. Money-Kyrle's concept of countertransference as a transformation). In C. Frank and H. Weiss (eds.), *Normale Gegenübertragung und mögliche*

Abweichungen. Zur Aktualität von R. Money-Kyrle's Verständnis des Gegenübertragungsprozesses (pp. 158–173). Tübingen: edition diskord.

Weiss, H. (2007) Ein mehrphasiges Modell der projektiven Identifizierung [A multiphasic model of projective identification]. *Psyche – Zeitschrift für Psychoanalyse*, 61: 153–171.

Weiss, H. (2009) *Das Labyrinth der Borderline-Kommunikation. Klinische Zugänge zum Erleben von Raum und Zeit* (The labyrinth of borderline-communication: Clinical explorations into the experience of time and space). Stuttgart: Klett-Cotta.

7

TRANSFERENCE ON THE COUCH

Alessandra Lemma

> Experience brings it home to you that you can give what we call
> 'answers' but they are really space stoppers. It is a way of putting
> an end to curiosity – especially if you succeed in believing the
> answer is *the* answer.
>
> Bion, 1976, p. 22, italics in original

"The peculiarity of a psycho-analytic session, that aspect of it which
establishes that it is psycho-analysis and could be nothing else," writes
Bion, "lies *in the use by the analyst of all material to illuminate a K
relationship*" (1963, p. 69, my italics), where K represents a link
between the analytic couple in which the analyst is in the process of
getting to know the analysand, and in which the analysand desires
getting to know the mindful object. This aim, articulated so clearly
by Bion, is entirely consonant with what I consider to be the primary
aim of the analytic process.

In his next sentence Bion moves on to the importance of the
transference: "The transference interpretation is peculiar in that it
refers to all material without discrimination, but is highly selective in
appraising its significance" (1963, p. 69). As is the case in many
psychoanalytic writings, as soon as Bion has stated the aim of analytic
work – in his words to "illuminate a K relationship" – he alights now
on the transference interpretation as a core technique that supports it.
I am broadly in agreement with this position, but I want to retain the
focus on the first of Bion's two statements, because it is here that he
separates the aim that defines the work as psychoanalytic from the

specificity of the technique. It is in this spirit that I want to revisit the *verbal* interpretation of the here-and-now transference, that is, against a background that prioritizes the analytic process we are hoping to facilitate through our interventions in order to achieve our aim(s) (Lear, 2009). In this chapter I thus want to consider not only the importance of the interpretation of the transference, but also its potential overvaluation, which can contribute to a rote – even fetishized – use of this central and powerful technique, eclipsing along the way more subtle uses of the analyst's understanding of the transference that underpin other kinds of interventions, not least *not* interpreting the transference, and which may also facilitate the analytic process.

Transference today

What is and what is not psychoanalytic work is a question that engages us passionately and divides us most obviously at the level of technique (Busch, 2010; Kächele, 2010; Widlöcher, 2010). Although we would probably all agree that "working in the transference" is a sine qua non of psychoanalytic practice, we encounter important differences over how this activity is defined and whether there is a so-called "real" relationship that is not transference. It is beyond the scope of this chapter to engage with this important debate. Rather, I will delimit the range of my exploration to the notion of working in the here-and-now of the transference that underpins contemporary British object relational approaches influenced by Kleinian thinking, which is the framework that informs my work conceptually and, to a large extent, technically.

Significant advances in technique have been made possible by object relational approaches. These developments arise from the appreciation of a vitally important fact: the most valuable insights into the patient's difficulties are found in examining how the patient *currently* relates to his objects, and not least to the analyst in the session. Careful observation of the patient's relationship with the analyst reveals the idiosyncratic reading of the present as it is filtered through an internal world of object relations. This is not a reading of the present in terms of the past, but rather I am referring to the transference as a process in which *current* emotions, phantasies, and parts of the self are externalized in the relationship with the analyst. This allows the analyst to *experience* the relational implications of internalized early developmental models that are to some degree modified through projective processes. In this sense working in the transference enables us to appreciate that the present moment is pregnant with meaning and its analysis provides a "royal road" toward psychic change.

For many analysts the interpretation of the here-and-now transference is at the epicenter of technique. It is a way of conceptualizing the "movement and activity" (Joseph, 1985, p. 447) in the exchanges between patient and analyst. Accordingly, the analyst's attention is primarily concentrated on tracking the minute shifts in the patient's state of mind and the use he makes of his internal and external objects to construct a world that he can safely inhabit, albeit one that sometimes may also be severely restricted and restricting of development (Steiner, 1993). This work takes place at multiple "levels" (Roth, 2001) and requires careful monitoring of the inevitable enactments by the analyst that may ensue (Steiner, 2000).

The earlier trend toward caricatured, excessive interpretation of the "you mean me" variety has given way to an increasingly sophisticated and differentiated approach. Nowadays careful attention is paid to the importance of the timing and frequency of interpretations, of the moment-by-moment assessment of the patient's tolerance for a transference focus (Rosenfeld, 1983), and of the way transference dynamics may be most helpfully approached in an interpretation (e.g., the use of therapist-centered or analyst-centered interpretations (Steiner, 1993).

Notwithstanding this more considered approach to working in the transference, we nevertheless accord it a privileged position in our conceptualizations of what promotes change, and hence what we think we should be doing with a patient, with the attendant risk that when we are *not* taking up the transference the analyst may feel that he is not working psychoanalytically. In turn, this can make it harder to examine the value of other interventions in an unprejudiced way.

In putting the interpretation of the here-and-now transference "on the couch," as it were, I am extending an invitation to examine what we can learn from the interventions we use *in addition to the verbal interpretation of the transference*,[1] not as a replacement of it or in order to downgrade its importance. In my experience interpreting the transference is the most mutative intervention with some patients much of the time, with many patients *some* of the time, and with a minority it needs to be used very sparingly, if at all. In other words, it is not the only effective route to psychic change for all patients.

Indeed the range of what we actually do in our consulting rooms is much broader than that found in "official" clinical theory (Jiménez, 2009; Tuckett, 2008). While some analysts undoubtedly privilege and deftly use a greater focus on the transference, if we cast our mind back to our own analyses, and to our daily practice, I am sure we will recognize that we all say and do a range of helpful things that would not be defined as "interpreting the transference." For example, over the course of an analysis we make observations about patterns apparent in the patient's external relationships, we ask questions to clarify meaning or to encourage further elaboration of associations, we remain silent, we may laugh with the patient, we interpret dreams.

The apparent disjunction between official theory and practice is a fact worthy of our attention. It often proves easier, however, to debate how we might "adapt" technique – as Eissler (1953) did through introducing the notion of "parameters" – to meet the needs of particular patients than to ask why the verbal interpretation of the transference (be it of the here-and-now Kleinian variety or of a more reconstructive kind) sits at the top of a more or less implicit hierarchy of interventions assumed to be mutative. Such a hierarchy, unless it is revisited in our conceptual formulations of what we are aiming to do, gives rise to three closely interconnected problems that I would like to explore in more detail. First, it feeds into a fantasy of what transpires in an analytic session in which the "proper" analyst is taking up the transference much, if not all, of the time. This obscures the range of interventions that analysts actually draw on, and hence precludes a richer elaboration of our understanding of therapeutic action (Tuckett, 2008). Second, it can lead us to take up "moralistic" positions in relation to each other – and within oneself – about what is and what is not psychoanalysis (Denis, 2008; Schafer, 1994). Thirdly, it can have an insidious effect on psychoanalytic education, which at its best should operate in the spirit of unprejudiced enquiry rather than make us pursue "overvalued ideas" (Britton and Steiner, 1994).

The analyst's transference to working in the transference

In my role as a supervisor I am repeatedly struck by how my colleagues often appear to have internalized a view that "proper" psychoanalytic work is defined by a focus on the interpretation of transference, especially of the here-and-now kind, which is sometimes pursued irrespective of the patient's response to it. "Making the interpretation" can become imperative in the clinician's mind, with the patient's response to it almost incidental to the process. This could be explained as bad practice, but the examples I have in mind are of colleagues who are conscientious and talented in many respects, yet who have fallen prey to the idealization of technique, often to avoid the disorienting experience of being immersed in an analysis or psychotherapy and not quite knowing which way to turn. Moreover they have not necessarily been helped in their psychoanalytic education to conceptualize their model of working. One consequence of this is that those techniques that are most influential in the analytic institute where they have trained are adopted wholesale, while not yet being fully integrated into their analytic skin (Lemma, 2012) so as to allow the flexibility that is required for any technique to be implemented effectively.

For example, a talented colleague began one of our supervision sessions with an apology: "I'm afraid that what I said to the patient was really quite pedestrian. I know I should have taken up the transference, but instead I asked the patient a question. I know this was wrong." Even before I could question this assumed "wrong," she went on: "I have been thinking about what made me do this. I think this patient finds it hard to think and I get caught up in this and end up asking inane questions."

When I hear this kind of statement – and it is not that uncommon in my experience as a supervisor – I am curious both about what may have indeed been going on between the patient and the analyst (was this an enactment, for example) *and/or* about what may be going on between the analyst and psychoanalysis as an object in her mind, that is, her transference to the concept of working in the transference, which inevitably becomes the transference to me as supervisor/ analytic superego. There is often significant anxiety and guilt in the analyst over apparent departures from "proper" analytic technique and this inevitably interferes with a capacity to think critically and hence creatively about the aim(s) of a psychoanalytic process and what can effectively support it.

The "moralistic stance" that we may all adopt in defense of our own preferred techniques as we listen to colleagues describing work that differs from our own is perhaps an inevitable symptom of the struggle with anxiety that analytic work produces (Schafer, 1994). The demands made on the analyst by the very nature of our work may help us to understand the fierce attachments we can develop to ideas. We feel the need for an organizing structure in the face of a patient's pain or indeed madness. Under this kind of pressure, and needing to manage the challenge of "not knowing," we can find ourselves relating to our theoretical ideas and techniques not as guiding principles but as fetishes (Denis, 2008; Ferro, 2009). But, as we all learn within the reality of the consulting room, analytic work requires the relinquishment of a magical investment in any one technique at our disposal.

To return to the supervision session I mentioned earlier: as my colleague and I reflected on her intervention it became clear that her anxiety about not "doing the right thing" had interfered with her capacity to listen to the patient's response. Her confessed sin[2] was a simple but well-timed clarificatory question in the context of the patient's report of a difficult exchange with a work colleague, which promoted a deepening of this patient's exploration of the event. It actually helped this patient to stop and take notice of what was happening in the "here-and-now" of his affective experience as he was relating this event. It was not a transference interpretation, which may also have aided this process, but it was nevertheless an intervention that allowed for an important elaboration of the patient's experience that was emotionally alive and furthered the work. I am not suggesting that asking a question as opposed to interpreting the transference is always helpful, but it can be and was so in this instance.

On the merits of being a bit pedestrian

When my colleague apologized for her intervention she mobilized in me a number of thoughts, prompted in particular by her choice of a word to capture her anticipation of how I would view her intervention: "pedestrian." From the Latin *pedester*,[3] meaning prosaic or plain, being pedestrian is the mark of something, de facto, unremarkable. In Latin it is contrasted with *equester*, meaning "on horseback" – a presence that is noticeable: one even has to look up to see the rider. Moreover, the rider benefits from an aerial view (a view, quite literally, from above) that cannot be appreciated from the busy street through which the pedestrian travels or in which he dwells.

For me, the contrast between the pedestrian view and the equestrian view captures an important feature of analytic work. As analysts, we need to strike the right balance between immersion in the analytic field – where both patient and analyst are working together, "on the street," as it were – while also retaining an "aerial" view so that we can think with the patient about what is happening on the street without, of course, depriving him of an opportunity to approach at his own pace the landscape that is opening up before him, or that is being defaced by him, in his mind. The aerial view is indispensable, but it also requires us to monitor that the view it affords us is not shared with the patient from an "on-high," superior position.

I imagine I am not entirely alone in finding myself, sometimes for extended periods of time, silently walking on the street with the patient, or getting lost, or misreading the signposts or, at best, making pithy interventions that function a bit like punctuations of the journey along the way. These interventions might serve, for example, to invite the patient to attend to a particular feature of the psychic landscape we are traveling through or getting stuck in, as the case may be, or they may simply be the emotionally present, if silent, accompaniment of the patient's own process. The feature they share in common is that they are "unremarkable" in one sense; that is, they do not offer to the patient the analyst's more saturated – noticeable, if you like – processing of what is being revealed in the psychic landscape (the aerial view), which would be more of a "this is what I think is happening in your mind now" type of interpretation.

It is interesting to consider what can be gained if one is simply a pedestrian, walking along the street with the patient. By this I mean using our interventions to accompany the patient along the sidewalk of his associations, or to create crossings to the possibility of representing experience, or making the kind of "behind the bar" observations that Bolognini (2005) has so evocatively written about.

There is a reticence, however, to share our more pedestrian comments for fear of what our colleagues will think (Bolognini, 2005). I have in mind here the questions, clarificatory statements, and descriptions of the patient's state of mind that address preconscious experience (i.e., they do not address unconscious phantasy). Yet when I have had the opportunity to reflect on such interventions in my own practice, as well as in the work of colleagues I supervise, and whose audio-recordings of sessions I sometimes listen to,[4] I have been struck not only by how common such interventions are, but also by how helpful patients find them insofar as they generate a rich elaboration of the patient's experience. Importantly, these interventions are informed by the analyst's more or less implicit understanding of the transference-countertransference dynamics, which at times can be merely an intuition. When such interventions are legitimized in supervision through a conceptual formulation of what the analyst was trying to do and why, this then creates the possibility for a disciplined use of the analyst's understanding of the transference to inform a variety of interventions.

I would now like to share some clinical material of my own to illustrate the kind of internal work the analyst engages in, which is informed by my understanding of the transference but does not only involve taking it up in the form of an interpretation.

A clinical case

Mr F – a successful businessman in his late thirties – canceled his Monday and Tuesday sessions due to being ill. Such cancellations were a common part of his relational repertoire: he inched closer to his objects only to then withdraw. With only a string of carefully choreographed long-distance relationships in his life, Mr F found himself seeking analysis because he was preoccupied with death and suffered terrible nightmares, which led to a fear of going to sleep.

The most immediate trigger for seeking help had been the death of his mother, who had raised him alone after the father's death when he was 7. Theirs had been a close relationship, and he had relied on his mother extensively, but he also experienced her as intrusive, demanding, and suffocating. The death of his mother destabilized him – he felt suddenly alone and lost, revisiting the early loss of his father too.

Mr F had always struggled to form intimate relationships, fearing a repeat of the seductive yet claustrophobic experience with his mother. Despite these profound anxieties Mr F nevertheless also longed to have a relationship – a longing that was colored by his memory of a father who had been quietly present and whose loss had been devastating for him, exposing Mr F to a mother who needed him at all costs to assuage her own pervasive anxiety. Eighteen months into our work he had nevertheless managed to settle into a more stable relationship with a woman he was now contemplating living with, though this prospect had thrown him, once again, into crisis.

In the session in question, the third of the week, Mr F began by saying he was feeling overwhelmed by the "long list" of decisions he had to make. He was considering buying a bigger property so as to move in with his partner, but this raised the question of starting a family, which he simply did not want to think about. He accused his partner of putting pressure on him to face his procrastination. All he wanted, he said emphatically and irritably, was some "peace of mind." He said that his partner reminded him on these occasions of his mother and how she had "kept him on a leash" – an expression that he had used before to describe how he felt his mother had always kept him in line, telling him what to do, interfering in his personal affairs.

As I listened I sensed that he was warning me I should not get him to think about this external situation or his missed sessions, that I should instead simply listen and not add to his already "long list." This was a not unfamiliar instruction: Mr F was very controlling of his objects and this was a prominent experience in the transference.

Mr F went on to say that he felt there was no space for him in his life and then he mentioned that the one thing he had enjoyed doing – in fact the only thing that had made him feel better in himself over the past few days (which straddled the days of his absence from the sessions, and to which he made no conscious reference) – had been a "workstation" he had been building at home. After months of indecision he had finally got round to creating his own office space. Now that he had achieved this he felt resentful at the thought of leaving it all behind in order to set up a new home with his partner. He then detailed how he had sourced all the materials for the workstation, designed it himself, and created what he tellingly described as "something out of nothing." He was very pleased with the result. His closest friend had called round when he was "in the thick of it," and he had felt irritated by this interruption, but his friend had in fact made "a small observation" that he now realized had "some relevance" to the design he had in mind. His friend was "understated," which he liked. He sometimes wished he could be like that but he feared that unless he imposed himself on others, as he recognized he often did, he was at risk of being "taken over."

As I listened I was mindful of the transferential implications in what he had been saying. I felt powerfully that he needed to impress on me that he had created his safe work enclave as an alternative to his analysis (and to the prospect of cohabiting with his partner) and that this is where he needed to retreat to – a "station" no less, conjuring up in my mind the image of a superior, more substantial structure than our analytic work space. Significantly he had built it himself by himself and for himself – a space from which he could control the object/me, not least through canceling his sessions.

I was mindful too that Mr F had also seemingly lied about his reason for canceling his sessions, since he had evidently been well enough to build his workstation. Lying was a feature in many of his relationships, a strategy he used to titrate closeness. I was aware also of another communication: of a "nothing" state of mind that he had got into, which as I knew by now captured Mr F's experience of feeling lost, "without spine," as he had put it on other occasions, and the meticulous care that had gone into the creation of a workstation – a "something-out-of-nothing" – that held him together in his mind. I felt I needed to approach this carefully, respecting the construction while not ignoring the plight of its architect. In other words, I considered that I needed to intervene, but I did not think that a here-and-now transference interpretation would help. On the contrary, at this juncture, I thought that a transference interpretation would simply play into a rather predictable dynamic: I would impose on him the demand to work with me and build something together and he would simply pull away insisting that he did not need my help and that he could do the work of analysis much better by himself.

If I took up the meaning of the missed sessions this would have been "correct" in one sense – his not coming was significant, and the way he related to me now in the session was yet another instance of how he kept me "on a leash" in his mind. But I doubt any of this would have helped him: I felt as if it would have simply been read as my "long list" of things he had to attend to.

At the same time not intervening did not feel appropriate either. This is a common dilemma for the analyst: silence can be helpful, and often necessary, but it can also abandon the patient who needs to be accompanied, not led. Here I was guided by Mr F's account of how his friend had in fact "made a small observation" that he now realized had "some relevance" to the design of his workstation. I took this as an indication that he could take something in from his object even though he could only do so if he felt in control and superior (after all he refers to the friend's observation as "small" and it is only granted "some relevance" to his grander design, so he is not giving the friend that much credit, but he does at least acknowledge him). I felt that I needed to find a way to communicate that I was present, walking on the street with him, and that I could make a small contribution rather than riding in with my interpretations.

Informed by my internal processing of the transference, I made a simple, descriptive observation aimed at capturing Mr F's state of mind when building his workstation (i.e., the concentrated solo effort to build a safe refuge without any help from the other) and which I felt was also live in the here-and-now: "You carefully built this workstation for yourself, by yourself, from scratch, and you feel better and safer in the space it gives you." My aim was simply to begin to engage with Mr F's "something-out-of nothing" experience and its function in his psychic economy.

Mr F replied, irritated, that *of course* he had built it from scratch because he preferred to do things himself, that not even money could buy "quality" these days. I immediately felt the brunt of his contempt, as my carefully chosen words appeared to intrude into his safe enclave, imposing on him the demand to acknowledge my presence, which he had immediately to quash.

And yet in the long silence that ensued I did not feel irritation or anger toward him, as I had done on other occasions when I felt he "kept me on the leash." Instead I felt connected to him and sensed that Mr F was perhaps beginning to work with me. When he resumed speaking he told me about a nightmare he'd had a few days earlier in which his favorite nanny (who had looked after him for many years when he was a child) was singing to him a "simple yet soothing lullaby." In the dream he desperately wanted to sleep, but something inside him – "like a sore tooth pulsating in anger" – had kept him awake. His thoughts were incoherent in the dream and he feared he was going mad. He woke up in a sweat reaching out for his partner, only to realize she was not there. He then said that sometimes he worried that his procrastination might lead his partner to leave him. She was a good woman, but there were times when she was indistinguishable in his mind from his mother, and then he felt trapped. He recognized that sometimes he longed for her presence, felt he needed her, but if she was there he could just as easily find himself wishing her away, recoiling from her embrace. This pattern tormented him as he could not see a way out.

I did not say anything although there was a great deal that could have been said, but I did not think there was any need to intervene because Mr F now appeared to be representing through his recounting of the nightmare, and hence processing, his assault on me as well as his objects, and on his own mind. At a not-yet-conscious level I thought that he recognized my "simple yet soothing" attempt to reach him, just like the nanny in the dream, and how in response he had bitten me with his angry tooth. Having attacked me he was left on his own. Importantly, this biting-him also disturbed him: he knew this was the path to a kind of madness and that it left him bereft of the comfort of the other (as he wakes from his nightmare, he reaches out for his partner, but she is not there, which I also took to be a reference to the other side of his experience of the missed sessions: he knows he needs the analysis but he has deprived himself of what he needs).

There was the risk that by not intervening at this stage I would be experienced by him as not being there when he reached out. In the moment I was guided by the intangibles of the live affective experience in the room – by my countertransference – which in this instance inclined me to trust that Mr F was able to continue without my active intervention and, moreover, that he was not yet ready to take in what I might have to offer: he both wanted to reach out but also warned me that he might recoil away from me.

Mr F paused some more and then said that his girlfriend had been upset the previous day because they had agreed to prepare supper together, but in the event he had started to cook without her in order to "surprise" her. He observed, bemused, that this had really upset her: "I could not understand why she was upset that I spared her the trouble of cooking! And then she walked out in a huff and I ended up eating alone." He added that she missed out on a "jolly good meal." His tone edged on his characteristic contempt, but his use of the past tense ("I could not understand why" as opposed to "I cannot understand why") intrigued me, as it suggested the possibility – however tenuous – that he was perhaps now not entirely seduced by his own construction of the event. At this juncture I asked a question informed by my experience in the transference of him needing the analysis to be his own creation without any interference from me, mindful too, however, that he was worried that this did "upset" me. Playing on the concrete and symbolic registers, I asked: "Who were you cooking for?"

After a silence Mr F interestingly replied that my question had brought to his mind an advertisement for meals-for-one at the local supermarket, which he now never bought because he thought the food was full of preservatives. Nowadays he was buying only organic food from a local health-food store, but this meant he could not rely on them having what he wanted when he wanted it. He thought it was best to stick to this new regime.

After another long silence he said, now in a more reflective tone, that he could see that he had left his partner out, that he had reneged on their agreement to cook dinner together, and that she probably read into this his inability to share his life with her, which is why she must have been upset. He added: "And she's right in one way … just like my *work bench* [my emphasis] is for me, made by me, and no one can interfere with this … I do this here all the time too … If you tell me something I often feel this impulse to just tell you to shut up and my voice … the voice in my head as I imagine myself saying this to you sounds horrible … It sounds … well, I can't think of how else to put it, but it's like a guttural sound, savage almost, like it's a matter of life and death."

He then vividly relayed a story about a wildlife documentary he had seen some weeks previously where they had showed, "in slow-frame motion," how a crocodile had "set upon" a buffalo drinking by the water's edge. It had bitten right into him. Mr F said that he had found himself strangely very affected by this scene because it was such a calm, beautiful "everyday scene" – the buffalo "only taking what he needed to survive" – which was then defaced by the brutality of the attack.

Mr F then became tearful. I now felt very moved by the road Mr F had traveled on in the session and the intersection of thoughts he had reached. I was struck by two details that marked, in my view, how his state of mind had progressively evolved toward a more depressive level of functioning without much active intervention from me. First, his grand "workstation," which at the beginning of the session was felt to be safer and superior to the work space of his analysis, is now referred to as a more modest "work bench." Second, Mr F mentions the wildlife scene that evidently moved him and is shown "in slow-frame motion" – a detail which I took to refer to how he was now able to replay and watch, in slow motion (i.e., attentively), the scene of his own attack: how at some level he recognized that he defaced everyday exchanges, with me in the analysis, and importantly with his partner, whom he feared would leave him because of this.

At this point I thought the timing was ripe for a transference interpretation because Mr F had elaborated sufficiently in his own way his experience without much interference from me: all the pieces were there for us to share an aerial view of what he was struggling with. And yet I also had to ask myself why I would make this interpretation given how the session had evolved. Why not, instead, let him know I am following him and let him continue to work over the meaning of what is forming in his own mind. In deciding not to interpret more fully I was informed by my countertransference, because not interpreting could well have resulted from a wish on my part not to be identified with the maternal object he needed to "keep on a leash" in his own mind. However, that is not how I felt. In the event I thus only said: "You are both the crocodile and the buffalo."

Mr F replied that he was not sure what I meant – why was he both? He could see how he was the crocodile toward others, "biting the hand that feeds me." He said: "I can be aggressive to others especially when I feel under threat ... if they try to tell me what to do ... but no ... this is not just about that ... it is something about the 'hand that feeds me' ... like not accepting your help, not letting you in." Mr F went on in this vein for a few minutes and then said, "but I cannot understand how I can be the buffalo ... I'm intrigued ... all I can see is his face lowered into the water bank and he is drinking peacefully ... I am never peaceful."

Now I thought that Mr F was actively inviting me to "cook together": he needed my help and I took this as a cue for intervening in a more extensive way: "You have a clear view in your mind from the river looking out at the unsuspecting buffalo, who is doing the most ordinary thing: he drinks the water he needs to survive as he is set upon. I think that you recognize how you set upon the very people you need because you fear they will take you over – so you come here to your analysis with your prepared meal-for-one on which you have been feeding yourself since we met last week."

Mr F was silent at first and then went on to say that he was aware that we had not discussed the missed sessions and that he was surprised I had not raised this as he had "expected" me to. He now felt guilty about having missed them because he had not, in fact, been unwell: he had simply not wanted to come as he was so wrapped up in building and did not want to abandon this. He could now see that he had retreated into his DIY as a way of avoiding having to think about what sharing space with his partner brought up for him. He then said, with sadness in his voice, "I guess I am not good at cooking with someone."

Mr F's state of mind was now palpably mournful, but also desolate, and I considered that he needed my very active presence to stay with this experience, so I took this as a cue to intervene: "What seems so painful is that you know meals-for-one are not good for you, that simple things may have their value but you cannot provide them for yourself by yourself – you have to rely on others. So in a way you are also the victim of your own bite: you are the buffalo who is set upon by a part of your mind that warns you against the dangers of allowing yourself to long for what you need in order to survive emotionally, and to take comfort from 'everyday' moments, like working together here with me or cooking with your partner."

I will not go further into this session. I share this excerpt because it is, in one sense, a rather mundane one insofar as the transferential implications are clear at the start of the session. It is also not unrepresentative as there are many intersections in an analytic session, just as in this one, when we could take something up in the transference directly. I can appreciate that this could have been a way of proceeding with this patient in the session. But what this excerpt also illustrates, I hope, is that the patient was able to arrive at an important and moving insight without the transference interpretation being made, but through four other interventions. Over their course the patient gradually represented his experience through recounting the nightmare and then through a series of associations that led him to the moving and harrowing scene of the crocodile and the buffalo.

The first type of intervention, I refer to as "active-in-passive," and the other three interventions are explicitly "active" in the sense that despite their relative under-saturation they nevertheless "interfere" with the patient's own process because they explicitly present the analyst's mind to the patient's attention. The "active-in-passive" intervention – which is the one I especially want to draw attention to – is the internal formulation in the analyst's mind (i.e., the analytic "work") that informs the decision *not* to make a fulsome transference interpretation. This is then followed by the more active interventions in the form of transference-informed observations ("*You carefully built this work station for yourself, by yourself, from scratch, and you feel better and safer in the space it gives you*" and later "*You are both the crocodile and the buffalo*"), and of a transference-informed question ("*Who were you cooking for?*"). All these interventions support the aim of drawing the patient's attention obliquely to the object relationship dominant in his mind in relation to his partner and to the analyst in the transference. This way the path is laid for the patient to arrive at his own interpretation when he realizes *emotionally* that he cooks-for-one in his life, including in the session, and is led to the scene of the crime against his objects and himself in the form of the attack on the buffalo by the crocodile.

Of course, not all patients have Mr F's capacity, but the point here is only to illustrate that there are varied ways of "working in the transference" that do not involve its direct interpretation. I am not suggesting that this way of working will be of equal help to all patients.

Using the transference and interpreting the transference

Our skill as analysts lies in being able to digest a great deal of information and many sensations (for example, in deciphering one's own somatic countertransference) and to find meaning in them. This process often requires us to walk alongside the patient, sometimes even *behind* him, so as to ensure we don't overtake him with our understanding of what he does not yet know, and/or may fear knowing, and that we too may not yet know enough about. We have to be careful not to rise to the invitation in the transference to seduce, control, compete with, or triumph over the patient through our interpretations. All the time we have to make a distinction between using the transference to inform our work and actively interpreting it, recognizing when the latter may deprive the patient of the opportunity of arriving at his own interpretation. *Not* interpreting (Bonaminio, 1993, 2008; Gabbard, 1989), as well as intervening in the kind of pedestrian way I have been describing, are much underrated analytic techniques that aid the analytic process.

Both Winnicott (1969) and Bion (1976), each in their distinctive ways, have brought to our attention the importance of facilitating the patient's discovery of himself, noting how easy it is to interfere with this. Interpretations can be too saturated with the analyst's need to know. Indeed Bion evocatively referred to the way the analyst's interventions can become "space stoppers ... putting an end to curiosity" (1976, p. 22). In a similar vein, Winnicott wisely observed:

It is only in recent years that I have become able to wait and wait for the natural evolution of the transference arising out of the patient's growing trust in the psychoanalytic technique and setting, and to avoid breaking up this natural process by making interpretations. It will be noticed that I am talking about the making of interpretations and not about interpretations as such. It appalls me to think how much deep change I have prevented or delayed ... by my personal need to interpret.

(Winnicott, 1969, p. 711)

I would like to now briefly turn to some research that is relevant to the thrust of this discussion. In an interesting series of empirical studies, Per Høglend and colleagues (2008, 2010) have put to the test the widely accepted notion that the interpretation of transference leads to greater insight over time (see also Kuutmann and Hilsenroth, 2011). They did this by comparing two groups of patients randomly allocated to psychodynamic therapy with and without a focus on the transference. They found that those patients with lifelong patterns of "low quality of object relations" and personality disorder pathology benefited more from therapy with a focus on the transference. The even more interesting finding, which is pertinent to this discussion, is that for those patients who scored highly on quality of object relationships the focus on the transference did *not* predict outcome. The authors make an interesting observation about this finding: "One may speculate that healthier patients present more subtle transference cues, thus *forcing therapists to base transference interpretations more on inference than concrete evidence*" (Høglend et al., 2010, p. 445, my italics).

This study is interesting on many levels, not least because it provides empirical evidence to support a transference focus, and because it also alerts us to the fact that when the transference is more "obvious" (Glover, 1955), as it often is with more disturbed patients for whom anxieties about rejection or dependency are more clearly in evidence, then our interpretation of the transference can be tested against the live evidence in the room. It is therefore less inferential, and I would add, possibly more necessary.

When the patient is not as disturbed then the risk is that the analyst may overextend himself in the direction of speculation and interpret because this is what he thinks he should be doing rather than interpreting because the patient will be helped by it. Of course, this tendency may be present in the analyst irrespective of the type of patient, as I have been suggesting. Either way, this is an instance of "interpreting-in-minus-K" where "being a proper analyst" takes precedence in the analyst's mind over listening to the patient.

143

Working in the here-and-now transference becomes a default position that inhibits the analyst in responding to what is happening in the here-and-now of the patient's experience.

As Bion (1962) articulated, K as a "getting to know" (Ogden, 2004) can readily become an internal imperative to know *the* answer. The function of interpretation in the service of enlivening curiosity, of opening up a dialogue, becomes hijacked by "knowing that," rather than being used in the service of engaging the patient in a "process of knowing" about his mind (Bell, 2011; Busch, 2010).[5]

At its best an interpretation should be an expression of a K relationship with the patient in order to support the patient's capacity to experience and know himself as someone who has a mind. A fundamental aim of analysis is to provide the patient with an experience of being with another person who is interested in thinking with him about what distresses or is disturbing to him, as well as what may give him pleasure or excite him, in order to stimulate the patient's own curiosity about his mind and that of others. This process supports the internalization of a capacity to reflect on his own experience.

A variety of interventions can support the aim of "illuminating a K relationship." Asking the patient a question that deepens an exploration of a feeling or a phantasy or the associative linkages in a dream (Boesky, 1989; Sousa et al., 2003) may also engage the patient in a process of knowing about his mind as effectively as a transference interpretation. I am suggesting therefore that technique should be informed by this aim, that is, the helpfulness of the interpretation of transference needs to be evaluated against the criterion of whether it helps stimulate the patient's capacity to represent his own subjective experience in relation to others. For example, we need to repeatedly evaluate the extent to which the unconscious phantasies that are active in the patient's mind can be explored in a more emotionally "persuasive" way by a here-and-now transference focus as opposed to a focus on what is happening in the patient's relationships outside analysis.[6]

A fundamental task for the analyst is to create and safeguard the conditions in which the patient's curiosity can flourish and also to examine how his interventions support or inhibit this aim. The analyst's "safeguarding" activity emphasizes the importance of both the external setting within which the analytic process unfolds, and which has to be managed by the analyst, *and* the analyst's internal setting, so as to minimize impingements on this space. It is this internal setting, that is, the *analytic attitude*, which I am suggesting is the constant that allows the analyst to orient himself toward his work and that sustains him internally such that he can "interpret-in-K."

The analytic attitude, as I define it here, refers to the analyst's state of mind (i.e., his intentional state, that is, his beliefs, desires, feelings)[7] in relation to the patient and to the work of psychoanalysis. I conceptualize the latter as the "objectivation" of subjectivity (Green, 2000) through careful attunement and receptivity to unconscious mentation in both patient and analyst. As Green is careful to note, this "objectivation" should not be confused with objectivity. Rather we are invariably speaking about an approximation of what the analyst believes to be going on in the patient's mind *and* in his own mind, as grasped through the experience of the transference as the "total situation" (Joseph, 1985). This experience-led understanding informs the basis for the analyst's interventions, which may be declarative (e.g., verbal interpretation) or implicit, arising out of the unverbalized yet active process that unfolds over the course of analysis. From this perspective representational work or supportive work is no less "analytic" than transference-focused work (Gorman, 2002, 2008; Lecours, 2007; Ogden, 1982; Poland, 2002).

Conclusion

In this chapter I have been concerned with finding a way of conceptualizing the central importance of interpreting the transference without eclipsing the value of other interventions that we probably all use to varying degrees and which are supported by the analyst's understanding of the transference. The interventions that support the patient's curiosity about his own mind are those that grow out of a K state of mind in the analyst – a state of mind that is in practice very hard to sustain.

The distinctiveness of psychoanalytic work, in my view, lies in the analyst's *systematic use* of the transference, which involves maintaining an analytic stance rooted in the analyst's experience of the transference in order to inform his understanding of the patient's state of mind and how to intervene most productively. We should always "use" the transference in this sense, while being curious about the different ways we can engage and support the patient's curiosity about his own mind, not least, but not only, through the verbal interpretation of the transference.

Notes

1   When I refer to working in the transference I am using the term in a Kleinian sense: the transference is more than just a repetition of the patient's patterns of relating to significant figures in the past; rather, it is primarily about the patient's internal world – his world of unconscious phantasy – as it becomes manifest in his total attitude to the therapist and to the analytic setting.

2   Confession may not be a healthy state of affairs, but it is at least preferable to not even openly acknowledging the so-called deviation, because then there is no opportunity for thinking about what is and is not helpful. For example, some years ago when I carried out a small survey about whether psychoanalytic therapists/analysts used humor in their work, the vast majority "admitted" to doing so, but also mentioned that they would not discuss this in supervision or with other colleagues for fear that this would be construed as "not analytic" (Lemma, 2000).

3   Douglas Harper, Online Etymology Dictionary (www.etymonline.com), accessed 6/20/2010.

4   This is regularly done as part of research studies.

5   The distinction between "knowing that" and the "process of knowing" is directly attributable to Busch (2012), but Bell (2011) also makes a similar point.

6   With some patients, for example those who have few actual relationships, the transference relationship becomes a primary entry point into the patient's affective experience and into his imaginative life. For others, however, their report of current relationships outside of analysis may be affectively charged and provide sufficient immediacy for the analyst to be able to engage the patient in a live exploration of what troubles him in his mind. Always bringing everything back to the here-and-now transference may not "add" anything, but how we determine when this applies or not can only be guided by our understanding of the transference.

7   I am informed here by Modell's (2003) definition of intention as the interest directed toward a future aim, which is invariably affectively laden.

Bibliography

Bell, D. (2011) Knowledge as fact and knowledge as experience: Freud's 'Constructions in Analysis.' *Bulletin of the British Psycho-analytical Society*, 47(1): 9–21.

Bion, W. R. (1962) *Learning from Experience*. London: Tavistock.

Bion, W. R. (1963) *Elements of Psycho-Analysis*. London: Heinemann.

Bion, W. R. (1976) *Four Discussions with W. R. Bion*. Strath Tay, Perthshire: Clunie Press.

Boesky, D. (1989) The questions and curiosity of the psychoanalyst. *Journal of the American Psychoanalytic Association*, 37: 579-603.

Bolognini, S. (2005) Il bar nel deserto. Simmetria e asimmetria nel trattamento di adolescenti. *Rivista Psicoanalisi*, 51: 33–44.

Bonaminio, V. (1993) Del non interpretare: alcuni spunti per una rivisitazione del contribuito di M. Balint e due frammenti clinici. *Rivista di Psicoanalisi*, 39: 453–477.

Bonaminio, V. (2008) The person of the analyst: Interpreting, not interpreting, and countertransference. *Psychoanalytic Quarterly*, 77: 1105–1146.

Britton, R., and Steiner, J. (1994) Interpretation: Selected fact or overvalued idea? *International Journal of Psychoanalysis*, 75: 1069–1078.

Busch, F. (2010) Distinguishing psychoanalysis from psychotherapy. *International Journal of Psychoanalysis*, 91: 23–34.

Denis, P. (2008) In praise of empiricism. In D. Tuckett et al. (eds.), *Psychoanalysis Comparable and Incomparable*, 38–49. London: Routledge.

Eissler, K. R. (1953) The effect of the structure of the ego on psychoanalytic technique. *Journal of the American Psychoanalytic Association*, 1: 104–143.

Ferro, A. (2009) *Mind Works*. London: Routledge.

Gabbard, G. O. (1989) On "doing nothing" in the psychoanalytic treatment of the refractory borderline patient. *International Journal of Psychoanalysis*, 70: 527–534.

Glover, E. (1955) *The Technique of Psychoanalysis*. New York: International Universities Press.

Gorman, H. E. (2002) Growing psychoanalysis: Rethinking psychoanalytic attitude. *Canadian Journal of Psychoanalysis*, 10: 45–69.

Gorman, H. E. (2008) An intention-based definition of psychoanalytic attitude. *Psychoanalytic Review*, 95: 751–776.

Green, A. (2000) Commentary. *Journal of the American Psychoanalytic Association*, 48: 57–66.

Høglend, P., Bøgwald, K., Amlo, S., Marble, A., Ulberg, R., Sjaastad, M. Sørbye, O., Heyerdahl, O., and Johansson, P. (2008) Transference interpretations in dynamic psychotherapy: Do they really yield sustained affects? *American Journal of Psychiatry*, 165: 763–771.

Høglend, P., Bøgwald, K., Amlo, S., Marble, A., Ulberg, R., Sjaastad, M., Sørbye, O., Heyerdahl, O., and Johansson, P. (2010) The mediating role of insight in long-term improvements in psychodynamic therapy. *Journal of Consulting and Clinical Psychology*, 78(3): 438–448.

Jiménez, J. P. (2009) Grasping psychoanalysts' practice in its own merits. *International Journal of Psychoanalysis*, 90: 231–248.

Joseph, B. (1985) Transference: The total situation. *International Journal of Psychoanalysis*, 66: 447–454.

Kächele, H. (2010) Distinguishing psychoanalysis from psychotherapy. *International Journal of Psychoanalysis*, 91: 35–43.

Kuutmann, K., and Hilsenroth, M. (2011) Exploring in-session focus on the patient–therapist relationship: Patient characteristics, process and outcome. *Clinical Psychology and Psychotherapy*, 18 (March 2: e-pub ahead of print).

Lear, J. (2009) Technique and final cause in psychoanalysis: Four ways of looking at one moment. *International Journal of Psychoanalysis*, 90: 1299–1317.

Lecours, S. (2007) Supportive interventions and non-symbolic mental functioning. *International Journal of Psychoanalysis*, 88: 895–915.

Lemma, A. (2000) *Humour on the Couch*. London: Whurr.

Lemma, A. (2012) Some reflections on the 'teaching attitude' and its application to teaching about the use of the transference: A British view. *British Journal of Psychotherapy,* 28(4): 454–473.

Modell, A. (2003) *Imagination and the Meaningful Brain*. Cambridge, MA: MIT Press.

Ogden, T. H. (1982) *Projective Identification and the Psychotherapeutic Technique*. New York: Jason Aronson; London: Karnac, 1992.

Ogden, T. (2004) An introduction to the reading of Bion. *International Journal of Psychoanalysis*, 85: 285–300.

Poland, W. S. (2002) The interpretive attitude. *Journal of the American Psychoanalytic Association*, 50: 807–826.

Rosenfeld, H. (1983) *Impasse and Interpretation*. London: Routledge.

Roth, P. (2001) Mapping the landscape: Levels of transference interpretation. *International Journal of Psychoanalysis*, 82: 533–543.

Schafer, R. (1994) A classic revisited: Kurt Eissler's "The Effect of the Structure of the Ego on Psychoanalytic Technique." *International Journal of Psychoanalysis*, 75: 721–728.

Sousa, P. L., Pinheiro, R. T. and Silva, R. A. (2003) Questions about questions. *International Journal of Psychoanalysis*, 84: 865–878.

Steiner, J. (1993) *Psychic Retreats*. London: Routledge.

Steiner, J. (2000) Containment, enactment and communication. *International Journal of Psychoanalysis*, 81: 245–255.

Tuckett, D. (2008) On difference, discussing differences and comparison: An introduction. In D. Tuckett et al. (eds.), *Psychoanalysis Comparable and Incomparable*, 5–37. London: Routledge, 2008.

Widlöcher, D. (2010) Distinguishing psychoanalysis from psychotherapy. *International Journal of Psychoanalysis*, 91: 45–50.

Winnicott, D. W. (1969) The use of an object. *International Journal of Psychoanalysis*, 50: 711–716. Also in Winnicott, D. W., *Playing and Reality*, pp. 115–127. London: Routledge, 2005.

8

SOME REFLECTIONS
ON TRANSFERENCE AND
COUNTERTRANSFERENCE

The effects of social political violence
in children, in the analyst,
and in the psychoanalytic process

Yolanda Gampel

Psychoanalysis uses language and words, words that operate on
memory, through memory. The process of remembering that
develops during treatment in the transferential space allows the
regaining of the active traces, which have been forgotten, deformed,
or transformed through the effects of history, time, imagination, and
narration. The words we pronounce, the speech that we deliver to
tell our story, to talk about our subjective state of mind, make each
of us what we are. We can view the psychoanalytical enterprise as a
historiographical anamnesis, within the movement of interpretation
and appropriation. It weaves and remodels the envelope of memory
that assures the feeling of the continuity of the self in time, of the
sense of identity, and permits feeling the difference while projecting
ourselves into the future.

Analysis deals with the most secret passions, the "craziest" sexual
fantasies, and fantasies about aggression and sadism. The psychoanalyst's
demand for truth requires him to hear everything – both what troubles
him and what pleases him. He is not supposed to enter the narcissistic

game but to retain a listening function. He should neither flee the transference neurosis nor give in to the patient's demands for satisfaction.

We know that psychoanalytic space enables adaptive regression in both the patient and the analyst (Bion, 1970; Freud, 1912; Heimann, 1950; Little, 1951, 1986; McDougall, 1990; Money-Kyrle, 1956; Racker, 1951, 1957; Sandler, 1976; Searles, 1979; Winnicott, 1947, 1960). The analyst who works along with and not against countertransference must be prepared, "on occasion, to become situationally ill" (Bollas, 1987, p. 204). In a similar vein, Michel de M'uzan (1976) used the term "paradoxical thought" or "paradoxical system" to describe certain experiences through which the psychic apparatus of the analyst becomes changed literally into that of the analysand.

Where within this razor-edge position does the impact of chronic, massive social violence or social violence that occurs in actuality enter the clinical material?

When terror and social violence exist in the patient's and analyst's environment, should the analyst introduce this external reality into the session if the patient does not make any associations that connect with what is going on outside? How does the analyst deal with transference and countertransference? How is it for the analyst to hear what is happening outside more than what is going on within the patient's inner world? Conversely, if the analyst refrains from bringing in the social violence that is taking place in the present, is that an act of participation in the patient's denial? Is it some sort of ethical breach? (Danieli, 1982, 1984; Gampel, 1992a, 1998).

Auschwitz and Hiroshima have shown us that death and violence belong to the most intimate and concealed parts of our identity. The monstrous and painful memories they left behind overload or destroy the perceptual and representational systems of their victims and bystanders. These memories create a legacy that gives rise to cruel and violent forms of identification both in those affected and their children. While the children of survivors do not have their own personal memories of the Shoah,[1] the internal reality of their family's past loss, suffering, and humiliation has been deposited in them by intergenerational transmission (Faimberg, 1988, 2005; Gampel, 1982, 1986, 1992b; Spero, 1992a, 1992b).

This at once raises the issue of experiences that cannot in any way be assimilated into the individual's range of inner representations. People who, as children, experience a trauma as huge as the Shoah are faced with an astounding, unbelievable, and unreal reality that cannot fit in with everything or anything they have known before the war. The extreme violence they have witnessed, we might speculate, has permeated them like radioactivity. Their external reality, and in some cases their psychic reality, has been penetrated by terrible, violent, destructive human forces capable of causing death or madness. Many survivors have to live with terrible wounds that can only partially heal. Moreover, this sociopolitical radioactivity is invisible, formless, odorless, and soundless. The contaminated survivors have none of the usual clues to rely on to tell them what is happening. The "radiation" penetrates unknown, to become the sole silent constructor of social subjectivity. Another important point is that the radiation leaves its wounds, contamination, and traces in different spaces and layers of the psyche and body. Nor is the "radioactive deposit" the effect of a single concern or event, but of many separate events. When this "deposit" eventually makes its presence known, it will do so in combination with some aspect or element of the survivor's drives, and will affect different functions and systems of the psychic apparatus.

These radioactive elements lie scattered about – hidden in images, nightmares, and symptoms – through which, however, they are detectable. And one of the primary ways these radioactive phenomena turn up during treatment is within the transference-countertransference dynamics (Gampel, 1998, 2005).

Thus it is that we must locate accurate and adequate internal space within ourselves to accommodate the survivor's transference. How can we let the survivor be free to use us as an object (Winnicott, 1968, 1971a) to more fully symbolize his emotional pain? In order to allow such processes to occur the analyst must heighten his countertransference readiness, and listen more carefully to the way the patient is using him.

For survivors' children, the trauma assumes demonic forms, fantasies of imagined scenes of primal terror, transmitted to them by the parents. For those who have themselves undergone the horrors of the camps these images reflect actual reality. That is, the images belong to specific feelings, to visual perception, to physical experience. This is the difference between imagined traumatic reality and trauma sprung from reality.

But how is the traumatic material transmitted by the parents? As we shall see in the case history presented here, the radioactivity that has infiltrated the parent and that lies in their unconscious is deposited into the child by some means of nonlinear, transgenerational transmission in intersubjective space. Perhaps the parents are unconsciously calling on the child to share their burden of suffering and in doing so pushing the child to enter their world. The consequence is unwitting radioactive identification. The analyst who enters this world and encounters what is deposited there through transference and countertransference movement should work through these deposits. In this way he can enable the children to articulate and differentiate the internal from the external reality, their parents' traumatic reality from their own reality, and thus to gain some control over their lives (Kestenberg, 1982a, 1982b).

We now come to the clinical illustration regarding transference and countertransference dynamics that arise in psychoanalytic work with a child whose grandparents were themselves adolescents during the time of the Shoah.

Leah – a 9-year-old girl

I shall present the case of Leah, which forced me to tackle the issues of transference, countertransference, and interpretation in my own psychoanalytic work. In this paper, I shall discuss these issues as they occurred over a period of five years (Gampel, 2005).

Leah, a 9-year-old, was afraid of being alone; when her mother and brother were not close by, she was afraid that something bad would happen to them. Leah was the elder child, followed by a 7-year-old brother. Both her parents are Israelis; both hold academic degrees. Leah's mother contacted me during the second week of the Gulf War (1991), but said that she had been referred to me nine months earlier. During the war, Leah's fears intensified to the point where her mother felt that she had to ask for professional help. Leah's mother is the elder of two sisters whose parents came to Israel from Europe in 1932. The father is the younger of two siblings. Both his parents were Auschwitz survivors. Leah's father was against seeking professional help because he did not think that Leah's fears signified a real problem. Only the mother came to the first parental clinical interview.

When I first met Leah she looked very pale and frightened. Verbal interaction was very difficult. She responded to my questions with few words and in a very low voice. She sat in a frozen position and

153

did not approach the box of toys, nor did she look around the new and unfamiliar room. After some initial questions, I suggested that we play the "squiggle game" (Winnicott, 1971b).

The exposure of the family and the emergence of the monsters

Within the interaction of the squiggle game, which continued in the following sessions, "strange" and "crazy" things continued to appear, such as many-faced monsters and robots. I sensed that our interactions provided Leah with the opportunity to express her strange and crazy images. She was proud of her drawings and connected her drawing ability to her paternal grandmother with whom she was very close. At this stage, the father agreed to meet me together with his wife. The father told me that he could not stand his mother, but that he had been very close to his father. He mentioned that his father had had a wife and a child who were killed in the Nazi camps, and that he had found out about this only in the last year of his father's life. His mother had only begun to talk about her past in recent years and was interested in writing her memories. Leah's father said that he was not interested in hearing his mother's "stories." He thought that, if she wished, she could tell them to her grandchildren and primarily to Leah, who was her only granddaughter, and to whom he thought she was much attached.

The father was very uncomfortable with my questions about the grandparents and did not understand their relevance to Leah. I sensed that my questions were an intrusion into his personal and secret space. At that moment I asked myself what had made me put pressure on him to reconnect the split-off parts of his self. I wondered what it was that Leah was urgently placing in me, and what was the specific function that she needed me to fulfill in relation to her parents. Leah's parents spoke about some of her obsessive trends and about a deep-sleep phenomenon that Leah exhibited when faced with difficult situations. At this moment, I recalled Leah's drawing of a sleeping girl from the first session, which she drew after I had related to sadness through my squiggle. Her parents also mentioned that they would have to bring their son, who suffered from "absences." I was reminded of some second-generation patients of mine who were children of Shoah victims and who suffered from similar absences (Gampel, 1982). I thought about how the father did not want to acknowledge the emotional turmoil, both in his parents' home as well as in his own home. It seemed to me that he had left his children with an intolerable burden to carry, in the same way that his own parents had placed an intolerable burden upon him by keeping their past secret. At that point, Leah's father began to talk about how his mother had survived the war because she was taken care of by an older cousin who was in charge of the section of Auschwitz designated for twins – the Lager where Dr Mengele carried out his medical experiments. This was mentioned, along with other details about his father and mother, in an obsessional and flat tone that shocked me. The mother also spoke about her family and about her sister, who had had a psychotic breakdown during her army service but who was now married with children and fully functioning. She said that this was a family secret that was never discussed with her children. I thought about how the father grew up with survivor parents who had developed a particular culture where communication and self-expression were severely curtailed (Kestenberg and Gampel, 1983). The veil of secrecy existed in the father's earliest relationship with his parents and the mother's relationship with her family. Perhaps there were many other secrets that we did not yet know about.

The following day, Leah entered the room in tears. Her mother told me that earlier that morning Leah had said that she did not want to come to me anymore, and that an argument had ensued. The mother left, and after a few moments Leah calmed down. I told her about the meeting with her parents and about the long talk I had had with them about their own parents and their childhood. I suggested to Leah that perhaps her anxiety about coming that day was in some way related to my meeting with her parents, and that she was free to ask me anything more that she would like to know. Leah then showed me a book that her grandmother had given her the day before, when her parents had to come to see me. The book was written by an 11-year-old girl who described the life of her grandmother during the Shoah, and which the young authoress had dedicated to her own grandmother.

Leah asked me to continue the squiggle game. The first few squiggles were of the sea and the monsters that lived in it. I then drew a monster disguised as a triangle and a circle (Figure 8.1), thinking about the sack of shapes that she had drawn earlier, feeling that perhaps she had begun to let out some of the different shapes within the sack, which might have had a monstrous quality. She then

drew twin children, attached by their feet and hands (Figure 8.2). I
thought to myself: "What are these twins doing here? What is their
connection to the monstrous shapes? What do they come to represent
among all these threatening monsters?" I drew a gas mask (Figure
8.3) – as mentioned earlier, this treatment started during the Gulf
War in 1991 and all Israeli citizens were equipped with gas masks and
required to keep them accessible at all times. (Was I perhaps trying to
protect myself from monsters, from gases?) She drew a toy elephant
(Figure 8.4). I had the feeling that Leah was talking about some very
distant sea monsters, which now had a strong impact upon her and
which she wanted to get to know about. However, at the very same
time, she did not want to learn more about them and preferred to
return to her toy elephant. With this in mind, I drew a house with a
huge antenna on the roof that picked up even the most distant sound
(Figure 8.5). She then drew a string of pearls (Figure 8.6). I asked her
who had a pearl necklace. She said: "I am too young for a pearl

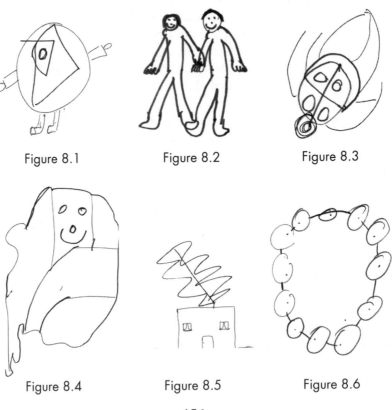

Figure 8.1   Figure 8.2   Figure 8.3

Figure 8.4   Figure 8.5   Figure 8.6

necklace. Mother does not have one either." I drew a picture of an elegant grandmother with a pearl necklace and large eyes who was leaving her house (Figure 8.7). Leah drew the face of an eye monster (Figure 8.8), one that reappeared in each session at some significant moment. I drew a maze for a mouse (Figure 8.9). I thought about her wanting to be so tiny and how her life in the family was like being in a maze. She drew a city with a sign for a supermarket that is open 24 hours a day, with traffic lights and road signs reading: "Beware, children crossing" (Figure 8.10). I thought that she was telling me to proceed with caution, but nevertheless decided to continue with monstrous images, but with the protection of the gas mask. In other words, I suggested that we continue to come into contact with the danger, but with some protection, just like the situation in the reality of the war, when we wore gas masks as a protection against a frightening, unknown, and destructive monster. I drew a ghost with horns wearing a gas mask (Figure 8.11). She drew the neck of a huge giraffe whose body and face could not be seen (Figure 8.12). It was as if she were telling me that the danger was so immense that it could not fit onto the page. I then drew a girl with a bow in her hair, who was looking at the rising sun, the sea, and the birds (Figure 8.13). (Signifying that one is allowed to look, unlike the giraffe). We talked about her curiosity to know more about her parents and her grandparents' past, about the feeling that she knows, and her fear of knowing. Quickly, she drew a snail walking along

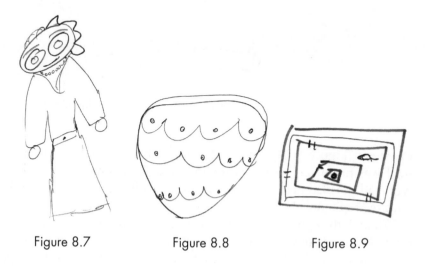

Figure 8.7   Figure 8.8   Figure 8.9

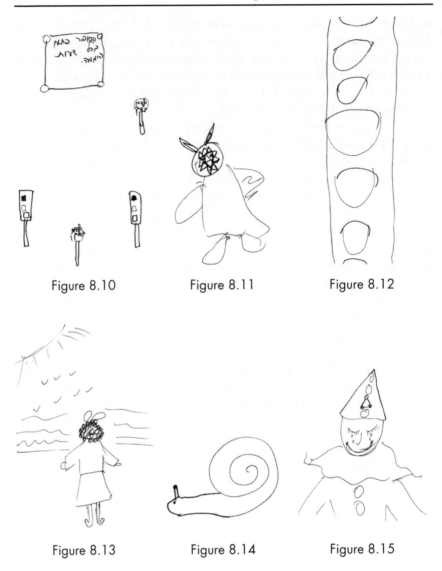

Figure 8.10   Figure 8.11   Figure 8.12

Figure 8.13   Figure 8.14   Figure 8.15

the street (Figure 8.14). Again, she placed herself outside, just as the snail was protected by the armor of its shell. Then I drew a clown who had finished his act and was trying to smile but whose eyes filled with tears (Figure 8.15).

When I thought the session over and got to the picture of the twins, I immediately made the connection between the grandmother's cousin who had helped Leah's grandmother to survive in the Lager

158

for twins, the grandmother who helped her cousin in the Mengele twins' Lager, and the grandmother's pearl necklace, and thought that Leah knew more than a little about her grandmother's secret past. I wondered why I had not made that "simple" connection during the session and was able to do so only afterward. It seemed that I had identified with – and acted out – the wish within this family not to face what they already knew. Up to the end of May, different Shoah themes appeared through drawings and stories. I tried to relate those themes to the Gulf War, to her fears, and to the transference relationship. These sessions were gradually taken up more by verbal interaction than by drawing, until she was no longer relating to me through the squiggle game. In one of our last squiggle games, the following sequence appeared: Leah drew something that resembled a pearl necklace (Figure 8.16) and said, "Don't make me a pearl necklace." I turned it into a lamp, thinking that she wanted and yet was so fearful of having light shone on the things she wanted to know. She drew a man looking at a special television (Figure 8.17), and I thought that she was allowing me to understand that inside her she had something unique and special that she saw. I made her next squiggle into a special pair of glasses (Figure 8.18). She then drew (in her words) "a storm approaching a small village, and all the village people are running for their lives" (Figure 8.19). I thought that perhaps she was telling me that to look too closely at what was inside her could be dangerous and even catastrophic and that it was better to run away from it.

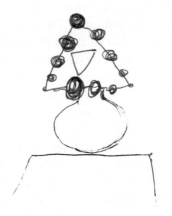

Figure 8.16

Figure 8.17

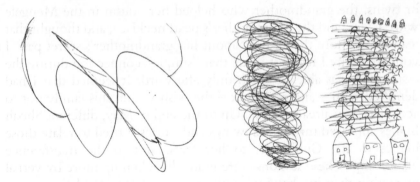

Figure 8.18   Figure 8.19

Slowly, Leah was able to use the psychotherapeutic work, finding moments of pleasure in the experience of self-discovery and spontaneity. It was as if she could expose her capacity to feel and think. By the end of the school year Leah's fears had disappeared completely. Was it a defensive flight into health before the summer break, or was it a reaction to the contract to continue meeting four times a week after the summer?

If we look at the first part of the treatment we can argue that Leah wanted me to contain the unbearable experiences of her grandmother that her father had rejected and was unable to think about because of the intensity of the pain. Leah was probably asking me to accompany her in thinking about these painful experiences.

In our analytic work, it sometimes happens that the psychoanalyst must decline the patient's demands and requests in order to attend to the receptive renderings of the patient's unconscious. Thus, in this case, Leah came to deposit in me an aspect of her self, which was the result of a deposit placed in her by someone else. For my part, I could not take leave of thinking and trying to do something about it, and so I acted. It was as if I entered into a mystery, and I was impelled to resolve it as quickly as possible. Perhaps this sense of urgency is related to the sensation of mortal danger projected onto the analyst. The question then arises: How can one know when immediate reactions (which can be viewed as acting out) are actually therapeutic? Is this an expression of massive projective identification that is being acted out by the analyst through counter-projective identification (Grinberg, 1962)? Or is it the case that, through projective identification, the patient asks the analyst to solve a riddle that he cannot solve alone, and to play out the investigator's role that he cannot fulfill? In this case – and in many others I can recall that were connected to the transmission of some very traumatic elements suffered by parents or grandparents – the transference is not only a matter of mental content transferred to the psychic person of the analyst. It is more a transfer of an epistemophilic demand on the presumed intelligence informing the analytic process (Dorey, 1988; Klein, 1921). It was as if Leah brought to me an insistent willfulness, a strong belief in confirming that which she knew but which was yet unknown (Gampel, 1982). I thought that, for this family, I had been able to fill the role of a transformational object (Bollas, 1987); to transform the radioactive identification that did not permit them to forget things that they had no possibility of remembering by themselves. This "radioactivity" affected the family, and closed them up in such a way that it almost strangled them. Paradoxically, the external "suffocation" imposed by the Gulf War enabled them to treat their internal suffocation (Gampel, 2005).

The reemergence of the fears

Leah did not return in the fall. Eight months later her parents requested urgently that I continue the treatment with her. During the summer vacation Leah had been happy and without fear. She felt free, and her parents saw no reason to bring her back to treatment as we had agreed. Instead, her mother began psychotherapy. But later that year, during Shoah Remembrance Day, a Girl-Scout leader who had just returned from Poland told Leah's group about Auschwitz and her feeling during the visit there. After Leah heard these stories, two fears suddenly manifested themselves. Her suffering was expressed through the fear of taking a shower, lest gas came out of it, and the fear of committing suicide if she were left alone. Leah could not sleep and cried a lot. Was she trying to kill something inside herself that was invisible, inaudible, a pain so impalpable that its intensity could not be tolerated but must be obliterated?

When she returned to treatment she was silent and did not take any initiative in the sessions. I thought about how much rage and sadness she was trying to hold back and repress. This rage had been turned inward and was being translated into mutism and suicidal ideation. We returned to our earlier mode of communication using the squiggle game. Leah was able to respond to this type of interaction. There were ghosts and strangers that had to be met without words. The squiggle game permitted the externalization of the internal persecutory state of conflicts, fears, and rage. Leah led me to understand that she was invaded and overwhelmed by strange and terrible figures and objects.

I was concerned by the question of how to formulate the interpretation. I tried to find one accessible part of her through different ways of interpreting, clarifying, or asking. To every verbal attempt of mine at making a transference interpretation she responded "maybe." My feeling was that she did not really listen to me, and her response was apathetic and autistic. This felt like a much stronger rejection than if she had actively contradicted me or angrily rejected my words. When I finally constructed an interpretation, I felt a sense of personal futility, as if I were talking in a language that she did not understand. There were moments when I wondered if I would ever manage to reach Leah and her sadness again.

Patient and analyst trapped

I decided to give up using verbal interpretations and to try to express my thoughts through the squiggles. It was only much later that I was able to translate these interpretations into words that she could hear and respond to. However, at this point, even with the squiggle game she avoided my overtures. The psychoanalytic framework seemed so hopeless. I really felt Leah's despair and her feeling that there was no way out. Through the squiggle game, a paradoxical situation was manifesting itself. We reached an intermediate space of drawings, where each drawing was a clue that facilitated the slow emergence of material that permitted me to take her beyond the place where she was. On the one hand Leah showed a freedom of expression through the drawings and the stories she told about them, and it seemed as if there were no rigid defense mechanism. She was able to play and to use her imagination. But on the other it was difficult to create a link between these split-off aspects. The images of terrible sadistic monsters and ghosts were in the drawings and in the stories about the drawings, but it was as if they were not really there with us. They had no meaning for her apart from the desire to get rid of some very painful stimulus. It may have been that she was trying to rid herself of parts of the selves of others that had been imposed upon her. Perhaps for her I represented the grandmother in the transference. She was trying to return this raw "material" to me so that I would contain it and not force it upon her again.

As time passed, rather than improving, her condition deteriorated. She became more claustrophobic. Her daily life became terribly restricted as a result of her fears, and she was in an extremely depressed state. Yet she was the best pupil in her class, the president of the students' union, and very athletic. At the same time she suffered from terrible phobias that restricted her activities outside school. She required a constant companion or escort whether at school, at home, or when engaged in other activities.

For ten months we worked exclusively through the squiggle game, meeting four times a week. In this period I related to what was happening to her in the space of the session with me and compared it to her life in the outside world. After this intervention there was a change in the transference climate in the sessions. During the following two weeks Leah recounted details of her family life. She spoke of her friends and members of her family in a factual, robotic manner. She gave a chronological description of when her fears began, at the age of 6, and the development of the fears up to this point. She spoke very quickly and in a detached manner. However, whenever there was a possibility of working together, she closed up and was silent. Her silence contained the essential. I realized that with my interpretative confrontation, which had attempted to connect two split parts of the self, I had left the game, and had taken on the didactic role of the "therapist who is interpreting." I remembered Winnicott's assertion that interpretation outside the ripeness of the material is in fact indoctrination and produces compliance. Such an interpretation, if given outside the area of overlap of the patient and the analyst playing together, arouses resistance. It seems that I was unable to just "be" and to wait in the created space of play. I felt obliged to "do" and to give interpretations.

I felt during these sessions as if Leah's words were coming from somewhere else, and not from the body that sat pale and serious before me. She told me that when she was 6 or 7 her mother was able to calm her fears, and that she had an image of a potato called "Alfie." Thinking about him used to calm her, and at present she was trying to use Alfie – or another image – to help her with her fears, but it was not working. In the next session she continued to talk about the Alfie workbooks she had had when learning to read and write. I told her that we had not found the right workbook with which she would learn to cope with her fears. She told me about how the family had been mobilized to watch over her, and began to talk about her grandmothers. She mentioned an aunt of her father's who came from Slovakia, but said she didn't know much about her father's family. I told her that at the beginning of therapy we actually did open up her father's family workbook and looked inside it. She was silent for a few minutes and began to describe what happened to her when she met me during the Gulf War. She had vivid recollections of the period and of her fears at the time, and she recounted them to me. "I thought Saddam wouldn't send chemical bombs. After the war I was scared when I heard the noise of a motorcycle but I got used to it later." Mentioning her father's family history was conflictive for her, since it aroused anxiety. Her defense mechanism was to recount something familiar, like our common history. And at the same time she felt that I had thrown her into a state of war, and was afraid of being attacked without having the adequate defenses. In the next session she was silent and then commented, "I never think of anything," and spoke of feelings of boredom in different situations. The atmosphere of the session was threatening – meaning she was afraid of what would come out. She was extremely tense, could not think, and used the boredom so that everything would be the same as always. When I tried to comment on this, she said "It irritates me, this silence. Do something. I can't stand these silences." We began to talk through the squiggle game again. From my first squiggle, she drew "a biscuit that grew very, very big in the wonderful oven that Prof. Itzik Levi invented, that makes things bigger" (Figure 8.20). "That's what happened to the biscuit, it went into the oven and grew and now it is five times bigger than the oven." From her squiggle, I then drew "a fisherman in his boat who is trying to fish" (Figure 8.21). She drew two attached snails that were feeding in the field (Figure 8.22). She told me that they divided the food equally and there wasn't much. They both dreamt of a large wide field.

I thought that we were facing a number of layers, and at the same time that it may have been related to the process of transference wherein she felt that I was the professor who was carrying out research on her (my passing from the squiggle to talking) and the fear that I could make something big out of something little in my oven-head-belly. It is interesting that my response to this was to feel that I

164

Figure 8.20

Figure 8.21   Figure 8.22

was out in the open sea trying to "fish" for something out of her unconscious, but in a more natural, easy climate. In her answer there can also be heard the fact that we were both trying to cope with how little there was, and that we were dreaming about emerging from a closed space. However, this content can also be understood as connected to the unconscious transmission and to the way Leah was shut up in the unspoken traumatic family past. It may also have been related to the fact that her grandmother witnessed the experiments of Mengele and the great oven of Auschwitz, and to the grandmother's and her cousin's dreams (told to me by the father) when they were in the camp.

This phenomenon, wherein my understanding of the material pertaining to the total transference situation overlapped with an awareness of the images from her grandparents' life in the camps, continued for a number of months. During these periods all my attempts at interpretations that might bring her closer to herself and to the experience of the here-and-now evoked a terrible sadness in her. I was in the here-and-now, and was waiting. It took her a long time before she could face her horrid monsters, which were such a dominant part of her. Little by little I was able to link images and fantasy to the body and to behavior in the transference situation, using words that she could hear. Her world of fantasy was taking on the feeling of reality and did not have to be a secret or something that was hers alone.

A turning point

I shall present a session that took place eight months later, during which the space of the sessions and the squiggle game evolved into the "squiggle envelope." The themes that came up in this session constituted the outline of several themes that we worked through over the months that followed.

From my squiggle, Leah drew and wrote the following story: "There is a new type of animal. It is called 'Nechbarbo' and the meaning is snake (*nachash*) and swan (*barbur*) together. This 'Snawan' is doing its exercises." When faced with her "Nechbarbo" monster, I thought once again of Mengele's monstrous experiments on sets of twins.

I thought that perhaps Leah was showing me that, with her special way of looking at the world, she could combine two things and create something new that is logically and biologically impossible. We might call this creation a monster that is hinting at psychotic thinking. However, it seemed that perhaps Leah had the capacity to see the characteristics of both the swan and the snake at the same time. For her, this monster existed and did gymnastics. Was this new type of animal the product of our work together? Was this a new type of monster inherited from Auschwitz? Perhaps she was connecting the split-off aspects of her family culture: the snake as the representation of the search for the terrible traumatic truth about the past, and the swan as representing the "false self" of the family? By putting them together, a monster was born. From her squiggle I drew a bird sitting on her egg. Through my response I expressed the wish for the birth of something else, and I was prepared to sit and wait for it. Leah continued her story: "The wind blew and one of the bird's eggs fell out of the tree. The bird went to look for the lost egg." Here, Leah was referring to external influences like the wind that cannot be controlled and that do not permit sitting quietly to wait for the eggs to hatch. Therapist: "The bird tries all kind of paths around the tree. From afar she notices a few round shapes. She goes in that direction. Perhaps one of them is the egg." I wanted to give the search a chance. Leah: "The small bird hatched from the egg. She knew birds flying in the air. She tried to be like them. In the end she succeeded and flew with them." Leah didn't give the mother bird and me the chance to be with her as she was being born, or to teach her how to take the first steps and so create a mental space to register the representations of emotions. It was as if she were telling us: "I can manage on my own … I don't need you." The little bird managed to hatch on its own and learned to fly on its own. Maybe this was the narcissistic fantasy of parthenogenesis. The small bird, Leah, did not need her mother or myself in order to venture out into the world. Therapist: "The small bird is flying through the clouds looking at the world. She sees a house being built and asks herself, Who made it, how did they make it, does she have a mother?" I tried to lead her to an inquiry into origins. Leah: "The bird continues on her way. She meets a strange creature. She thinks perhaps that it is her mother. She asks the creature if this is so. In the end she is sorry when she discovers that it isn't her mother. She continues on her way." Leah seemed very ambivalent about the search for her origins.

Therapist: "The bird continues her search and reaches the sea. She is surprised by the waves, by the beauty, by the sounds of the sea that are different from the sounds that birds make." I tried to lead her to the issues of observation and differentiation.

Leah: "There was once a boy who was always happy. It didn't matter what they did to him, he was still happy. One day he got stuck on a hill but he was still happy." As always, Leah's immediate reaction was to run away from observation and from the search. Once again she was using the multiform defense mechanism and reaction formation that I knew so well. She was telling me that she wanted to be happy and to "not know." She did not wish to discover new things, or new thoughts. I wondered who was speaking at that moment – was it Leah, was it her father, and why was it happening now? What was she talking to me about? Was she refusing to be a witness to the frightening things she might discover if we continued to search for her origins?

167

Therapist: "A girl who sits and thinks thoughts. They are so frightening that her hair stands up on end." Leah: "The girl's mother comes home and doesn't understand why her daughter's hair is sticking up. She gets a shock but then she understands." For Leah it was as if she were unwilling to rescind her own catastrophic and monstrous view of the world. I wondered whether it was solely an expression of a negative therapeutic reaction, or were there reminiscences, or premonitions, or both.

Bion's statement came to mind:

> they come from a domain in which measurement of temporal and spatial time is proper to a constant conjunction of helplessness, omnipotence, idealization, [an] embryonic-sense of reality … transformed for use in a non-sensuous domain of thought without a thinker, from thoughts in which a thinker is itself of the essence of thought.
>
> (Bion, 1975, p. 51)

Were they the counterpart of disturbance, perturbations, turbulences that are violent, invisible, and insensible? This session was a turning point in that it enabled us to disclose the themes that had been expressed in drawings and could now be discussed in words.

The "squiggle envelope" encompassed a number of layers that began to be uncovered as Leah attempted to avoid and to cut off the maternal therapeutic transference. This led us to very subtle interactions that touched on some of her more infantile/primary psychic experiences. It is known that, against the state of helplessness of the infant, the formation of a stable link of exclusivity and of need is necessary. In this session, Leah tried to negate the existence of such a link. The link with the primary object provides meanings. This was evident in the therapeutic process. We also know that the polarity of pleasure–pain provides a first psychic organization: a mental space that is registered as the representations of emotions. Leah was negating the existence of such a mental space.

At the same time, it was the beginning of Leah's hatching from the trans-subjective space to the intra- and intersubjective space. Little by little I was able to convey to her and she was able to understand and tolerate the presence of a split inside herself and how we must negotiate with this aggressive, monstrous, diabolical aspect that was a part of her, perhaps having been transmitted. We continued our work over a number of months, and little by little Leah regained her capacity to express herself through words. She had recovered her freedom to think and to verbalize her thoughts.

What is the correct procedure?

Bion asked:

> What is the correct procedure? To analyse it and make what is implicit and unconscious, explicit and conscious? Or to forget it? But the theory is that you can't forget what you can't remember, and that you have to remember things, otherwise they fester and grow out of control in the unconscious. But as analysts we are not concerned with *theories*; we are concerned with "What shall I say to this man?"
>
> (Bion, 1987, pp. 170–171)

The case of Leah raises many questions about correct analytic procedure. Twenty-five years ago I would have worked in the classical fashion and taken a long clinical history from the parents and begun to work four times a week with the child. There would probably have been many silent and passive sessions, which I would have interpreted. Then, I would not have had the courage to suggest to the silent and uncooperative child something of an active nature like the squiggle game (Winnicott, 1971b). For many years I used the squiggle game only in the first consultation in accordance with Winnicott's approach. However, in this treatment, Leah used the squiggles as a medium for communication over a couple of years. This taught me that for Leah the squiggles permitted contact with the "unthought known" (Bollas, 1987; Puget, 1988), and it was these interventions that gave names to the yet unnamed. The unthinkable was placed within a drawing, or within the words of a story, a scene of the psyche. It became evident that the squiggle game enabled Leah to divest herself of unpleasant painful experiences that tormented her but that she tried to reject. The squiggle game was one way of preventing the repressed from being forced down into the back roads of perverse experience. Leah alternated between insightful "self-holding" moments and moments of "I don't know" and "I can't bear it." Little by little her desires could be assigned a meaning. To accept the bizarreness that was inside her meant that I had, first of all, to accept these bizarre objects. It was a mise-en-scène, a *mise-en-dessin*, a sort of permitted enactment of the repressed in my presence. For me, it was a coming into contact with the deepest part of my own helplessness, my not knowing, not being able to explain. I knew that the drawing projects the spatial qualities of the unconscious fantasy. The verbal material gives us information about the temporal qualities of the relationship. Leah's squiggle game invoked a different principle – one of unknowing and unbinding. The squiggles were "thing representations": undigested facts or "beta elements" (Bion, 1962). I tried to be an imaginative partner, and little by little transformed the squiggle "facts" into psychic elements. It is an interplay between the capacity to say and the image. In this realm we need the drawing and the playing of the squiggle game. There is a presentation and naming in the play that allows us to move the impediments and the images that appear from within. All the scenarios that take place in the secretive internal world – images, drives, the ancestors, and death – emerge. These frightening scenarios may cause something in the mind to become motionless and automatic, and may lead to compulsive repetition instead of a fluent motion that enables projective transformation. Is compulsive repetition only a disturbance? As Bion said, "But repetition compulsion may in fact be a spark of human curiosity which has hitherto failed to be extinguished by any authoritative statements from whatever source" (1976, p. 230).

I think it is very important to contextualize each clinical case illustration, its time and space. The work with this particular case began during the Gulf War (1991) in Israel. This family carries within itself the heavy experience of the Shoah. During the period when I worked with this child, I myself as the analyst was experiencing the Gulf War, so we were living in "overlapping worlds" (Puget and Wender, 1982).

Now we will contextualize Racker's paper, which first appeared in 1951 and opens this book more than 60 years later.

The year 1951 was only six years after the terrible catastrophe of World War II where unimaginable events such as Auschwitz and Hiroshima totally changed our perception of the world.

On rereading the article from that year written by Racker, who had fled Europe during the war, I realized that he lived in Buenos Aires at a time of persecution and social violence, when Peron and Peronism were at their height. Is it possible that this situation did not affect him and his patients?

Following my rereading of Racker's article, I was surprised to discover that this article is "classical" psychoanalysis insofar as it relates only to what happens within the four walls of the consulting room between two people – the analyst and the patient, their conscious and unconscious movement and vicissitudes, with no relation to the events of the external world that could have influenced the transference-countertransference processes. A "classic" allows us to think and ask new questions; it allows for new thoughts to appear.

When I read Racker's book for the first time many years ago, as a beginning analyst, I learned a great deal from him. On rereading him, however, I feel there is something missing. The external social-political violence does not enter the inner world of the subject, or at least it does not appear in the vicissitudes of transference and countertransference.

Racker, who died in 1961, left us a legacy that brought something that was new at that time. Both he and Heimann were very courageous and free-thinking analysts. If Racker had lived longer, I believe he would have changed. He would certainly have included the social-cultural context as a very important element into the psychoanalytic process.

Massive collective trauma structures our representation of the social world. Therapy must include acknowledgment of its historical and political dimensions, whose importance is unique and specific to collective psychic trauma and not present in the same way in individual abuse and accidents (e.g., Caruth, 1995; Freud, 1920). Trauma perpetrated by a nation and sanctioned by a government cannot be worked through via introspection alone, but requires in addition the construction of a historical narrative as well as a collective process of truth-telling if the relationship between self and society is to be repaired. The catastrophic atrocities of the twentieth century have added to our current clinical understanding both the uncertainty and the unpredictability principles (Puget, 2010).

We have described the dynamics of this situation as follows. The traces of the pre-war background of safety created by the family still exist, but at the same time some of its aspects have been destroyed. When everything becomes deadened and homeless, that is when the *Heimlich* becomes a "background of *Unheimlich*" (Freud, 1919; Gampel, 1996). In intergenerational time the life-story of generations scores itself into the memory. In intergenerational time an individual

171

stands face to face not only with his own time but with the time of those who went before him. And in forming this attachment to his predecessors, he identifies with them.

In previous papers (Gampel, 2005; Gampel and Mazor, 2004), I have talked of the difficulty that children touched by sociopolitical violence have in entering into love relationships and enjoying the pleasures of life. On the one hand, it is vital for them to keep up the continuity of generations. And for some of them it is important that the names of the dead should be carried by their children, as a sign of that continuity and as a memorial to the dead who have no marked grave. They are, as it were, declaring a defiance of the extermination Nazi ideology tried to achieve. On the other, something in their being, their psyche, and their body is wounded, shattered, frozen, and their children can sense this without being able to define it. Some of these children require analytic treatment for symptoms through which they are asking questions about their parents' and grandparents' past, without even knowing what their questions are reaching for. It is these questions asked by the second generation and even by the third generation, by the children or grandchildren of those parents who were themselves children during the Shoah, that led me to reflect on how trauma is transmitted, and on the vicissitudes of that transmission. A traumatic event whose effects are transmitted unconsciously has an extremely long life-span and repeats itself endlessly. And it is often hard for children and grandchildren to access the "symbolization" of this trauma through the spoken word and thus to free themselves, at least partially, from its effects.

In many survivors, the capacity to symbolize is damaged because they were unable to reject this past, which then remained untransformed and split off. The transmission to the next generation of something fragmented and non-transformed creates in these children their eccentricities and strange searches. Between the contingencies and constraints of life, an object, a memory that was not told, bursts and is deposited as a trace in mental space for children and grandchildren. These radioactive residues hold something evil. They do burst and create disorders in the evolution of the child. The translation will be psychic and somatic, and can lead to a state of mental confusion. Communication with the inside and the outside is disturbed; their world is torn apart, and self-awareness and the formation of the symbol are prevented. The child feels that it is carrying a foreign body without knowing where it comes from, who

172

it belongs to, and especially what to do with it. This way the son or daughter repeats the traumatic event of social violence in a nonlinear outcome. This is not the return of the repressed, but precisely the return of the non-repressed, of the split-off parts, transmitted earlier through the non-inscription in the unconscious of the parents. This can manifest itself in problems of separation, phobias, destructive behavior, absences, insomnia, and other symptoms that remind parents of their history and their suffering.

As a final point

While on the one hand we are analysts who work with the internal world, at the same time our lives are structured by the external context in which we live. Putting aside or "forgetting" the context is like cutting away an important part of our being in the world.

All this brings up the question of whether it is at all possible to continue doing analysis under these conditions. There are those who think not. I believe that it is possible, even though it demands of us a temporary flexibility with regard not only to the rule of abstinence but to the psychoanalytical framework itself. Didier Anzieu has pointed out that "there is a lack of rigor that alters the transference into a perverse relationship ... but there is also a mortal stringency that kills the psychoanalytical process" (1976, p. 136, my translation).

By containing and transforming the malevolent elements through a psychotherapeutic dialogue (through the digestive, reflective function of the mind of the analyst), we try to put an end to this destructive force of history imposed on the human psyche. To embody it, to represent, to speak and write, will permit the restoration of a space where the "I" may become.

I would like to thank Ms Leiske Bloom for her editing of my chapter.

Notes

1   A holocaust is a religious animal sacrifice in which the animal is completely consumed by fire. The word derives from the ancient Greek holocaustos (Ὀκαυστος from Ὀλος "whole" and καυστός "burnt." In the twentieth century it became strongly associated with

the Final Solution of the Nazis' Third Reich. The Hebrew word Shoah, meaning "catastrophe," denotes the catastrophic destruction of European Jewry during World War II. The word Shoah has no religious connotations whatsoever.

Bibliography

Anzieu, D. (1976) Devenir psychanalyste aujourd'hui. In Favez, G., *Être psychanalyste* (pp. 117–166). Paris: Dunod.

Bion, W. R. (1962) *Learning from Experience*. London: Heinemann.

Bion, W. R. (1970) *Attention and Interpretation*. London: Heinemann.

Bion, W. R. (1975) Book I: *The Dream* (pp. 1–218). In *A Memoir of the Future*. London: Karnac, 1991. First publication: Rio de Janeiro, Brazil: Imago Editore, 1975.

Bion, W. R. (1976) Emotional turbulence. In F. Bion (ed.), *Clinical Seminars and Four Papers* (pp. 223–233). Abingdon, Oxfordshire: Fleetwood Press, 1987.

Bion, W. R. (1987) *Clinical Seminars and Four Papers*, F. Bion (ed.). Abingdon, Oxfordshire: Fleetwood Press.

Bollas, C. (1987) *The Shadow of the Object: Psychoanalysis of the Unthought Known*. London: Free Association Books.

Caruth, C. (ed.) (1995) *Trauma: Explorations in Memory*. Baltimore, MD: Johns Hopkins University Press.

Danieli, Y. (1982) Countertransference in the treatment and study of Nazi Holocaust survivors and their children. *Victimology*, 5(2–4): 355–367.

Danieli, Y. (1984) Psychotherapists' participation in the conspiracy of silence about the Holocaust. *Psychoanalytic Psychology*, 1(1): 23–42.

de M'uzan, M. (1976) Contre-transfert et système paradoxal. In *De l'art à la mort* (pp. 164–181). Paris: Gallimard, 1977.

Dorey, R. (1988) Le désir de savoir: nature et destins de la curiosité en psychanalyse. Paris: Denoël.

Faimberg, H. (1988) The telescoping of generations. *Contemporary Psychoanalysis*, 24: 99–118.

Faimberg, H. (2005) *The Telescoping of Generations: Listening to the Narcissistic Links between Generations*. London: Routledge.

Freud, S. (1912) The dynamics of transference. *The Standard Edition of the Complete Psychological Works of Sigmund Freud* (J. Strachey, trans.), vol. 12: 97–108. London: Hogarth.

Freud, S. (1919) The uncanny. *SE* 17: 219–256. London: Hogarth.

Freud, S. (1920) *Beyond the Pleasure Principle*. *SE* 18: 3–64.

Gampel, Y. (1982) A daughter of silence. In M. S. Bergmann and M. E. Jucovy (eds.), *Generations of the Holocaust* (pp. 120–136). New York: Basic Books.

Gampel, Y. (1986) L'effrayant et le menaçant: de la transmission à la répétition. *Psychanalyse à l'université*, 11(4): 87–101.

Gampel, Y. (1992a) Psychoanalysis, ethics, and actuality. *Psychoanalytic Inquiry*, 12: 526–550.

Gampel, Y. (1992b) Thoughts about the transmission of conscious and unconscious knowledge to the generation born after the Shoah. *Journal of Social Work and Policy in Israel*, 5/6: 43–50.

Gampel, Y. (1996) Between the safety background and the uncanny background: Theoretical and technical aspects of working within the context of social violence. In P. Fonagy, A. M. Cooper and R. Wallerstein (eds.), *Psychoanalytic Theories in Practice: A Festschrift to Joseph Sandler* (pp. 59–74). New York: Routledge.

Gampel, Y. (1998) Reflections on countertransference in psychoanalytic work with child survivors of the Shoah. *Journal of the American Academy of Psychoanalysis*, 26: 343–368.

Gampel, Y. (2005) *Ces parents qui vivent à travers moi. Les enfants de guerres.* Paris: Fayard.

Gampel Y. and Mazor, A. (2004) Intimacy and family links of adults who were children during the Shoah: Multi-faceted mutations of the traumatic encapsulations. *Free Association*, 11(4): 546–568.

Grinberg, L. (1962) On a specific aspect of countertransference due to the patient's projective identification. *International Journal of Psychoanalysis*, 43: 436–440.

Heimann, P. (1950) On countertransference. *International Journal of Psychoanalysis*, 31: 81–84.

Kestenberg, J. S. (1982a) Survivors – Parents and their children. In M. S. Bergmann and M. E. Jucovy (eds.), *Generations of the Holocaust* (pp. 83–102). New York: Basic Books.

Kestenberg, J. S. (1982b) Rachel M's metapsychological assessment. In M. S. Bergmann and M. E. Jucovy (eds.), *Generations of the Holocaust* (pp. 145–155). New York: Basic Books.

Kestenberg, J. S. and Gampel, Y. (1983) Growing up in the Holocaust culture. *Israel Annals of Psychiatry and Related Disciplines*, 20: 129–146.

Klein, M. (1921) The development of a child. In *Love, Guilt, and Reparation, and Other Works, 1921–1945, The Writings of Melanie Klein*, vol. 1: 1–53. London: Hogarth, 1975.

Little, M. I. (1951) Countertransference and the patient's response to it. *International Journal of Psychoanalysis*, 32: 32–40.

Little, M. I. (1986) *Transference Neurosis and Transference Psychosis: Toward Basic Unity.* London: Free Association Books and Maresfield Library.

McDougall, J. (1990) Countertransference and primitive communication. In *Plea for a Measure of Abnormality* (pp. 247–298). London: Free Association Books.

175

Money-Kyrle, R. (1956) Normal counter-transference and some of its deviations. In D. Meltzer (ed.), *The Collected Papers of Roger Money-Kyrle* (pp. 330–342). Strath Tay, Perthshire: Clunie Press, 1978. Reprinted in E. B. Spillius (ed.), *Melanie Klein Today: Developments in Theory and Practice*, vol. 2, pp. 19–28. London: Routledge, 1988.

Puget, J. (1988) Social violence and psychoanalysis in Argentina: The unthinkable and the unsought. *Free Associations*, 13: 84–140.

Puget, J. (2010) The subjectivity of certainty and the subjectivity of uncertainty. *Psychoanalytic Dialogues*, 20: 4–20.

Puget, J. and Wender, L. (1982) Analista y paciente en mundos superpuestos. *Psicoanalisis*, 4(3): 502–532.

Racker, H. (1951) Observaciones sobre la contratransferencia como instrumento técnico. Comunicación preliminar. Paper presented to the Argentine Psychoanalytic Association, Buenos Aires, Argentina, September 1951. In English: Observations on countertransference as a technical instrument: Preliminary communication (this volume).

Racker, H. (1957) The meanings and uses of countertransference. In *Transference and Counter-transference* (pp. 127–173). London: Marshfield Reprints, 1985.

Sandler, P. (1976) Countertransference and role-responsiveness. *International Review of Psychoanalysis*, 3: 43–47.

Searles, H. (1979) *Countertransference and Related Subjects*. New York: International Universities Press.

Spero, M. H. (1992a) Can psychoanalytic insights reveal the knowability and the aesthetics of the Holocaust? *Journal of Social Work and Policy in Israel*, 5–6: 123–170.

Spero, M. H. (ed.) (1992b) Holocaust trauma: Transgenerational transmission to the second generation. Special issue: *Journal of Social Work and Policy in Israel*, 5–6: 7–9.

Winnicott, D. W. (1947) Hate in the transference. In *Through Paediatrics to Psycho-Analysis* (pp. 194–203). New York: Basic Books, 1975.

Winnicott, D. W. (1960) Counter-transference. *British Journal of Medical Psychology*, 33: 17–21. Republished in *The Maturational Processes and the Facilitating Environment* (pp. 153–157). London: Hogarth, 1965.

Winnicott, D. W. (1968) The use of an object. In *Playing and Reality* (pp. 101–111). London. Tavistock, 1971.

Winnicott, D. W. (1971a) *Playing and Reality*. London: Tavistock Publications; New York: Basic Books.

Winnicott, D. W. (1971b) *Therapeutic Consultations in Child Psychiatry*. London: Hogarth; New York: Basic Books.

9

TRANSFERENCE
AND COUNTERTRANSFERENCE
IN CHILD ANALYSIS

Mirta Berman-Oelsner

The place of the child analyst in the session

To begin with I will present three vignettes from three young patients in order to approach the theme I want to discuss here, which is the place of the child analyst in the session, along with the countertransferential feelings that are stirred up in the analyst in consonance with what is transferred onto her, in a process that the patient designs. These three vignettes could well have occurred in the same playroom during the same afternoon. The analyst is the same in the three cases, yet because the place she occupies is that of the transference, in each one of the different sessions she appears to play different roles, possess different qualities, and to experience different countertransferential affects.

Mary

Mary is 8 years old; she attends her sessions punctually and without apparent opposition. However she expresses no curiosity about our work; nor does she seem interested in knowing anything about herself. She does not greet me when she arrives or when she leaves; she takes up her play at the exact point where she left it the previous session. She does a repetitive, very controlling, form of play that she holds on to for long periods of time, of a kind that largely exceeds the typical play of latency. I have to think only about what she allows me to think: for example, about some categories in a game called Tutti-Frutti, and no more. The play consists in both of us thinking and then writing names of people, flowers, vegetables, things, and cities whose names must all begin with the same letter. I don't dare to pull away from the ABC sequence of the game; when I do my words are deprived of meaning.

Frequently I experience feelings of impotence and hopelessness. I nevertheless continue to try to find new perspectives on her activity in order to not be an analyst who repeats interpretations. What Mary does is far from being a creative form of play; instead it offers her a way to restrict her thought processes and to defend herself from her emotions and anxieties. In the session, she enacts the phantasy of keeping her analysis from evolving, and in doing so arrests both mental growth and differentiation. I am meant to be part of her. She needs to cancel any sense of separateness and to hold on to a symbiotic merging in which portions of her functions are deposited in me. Mary attacks her own thinking and tries to immobilize mine in such a way that I really get locked up in her defensive system. When I can realize and interpret how and why she limits and stereotypes my functioning, the dramatization of this phantasy of control starts to crumble.

Andy

With Andy my role is different. He is 12 years old and has a penetrating curiosity, which is not the same as having a genuine interest. He is inquisitive and wants to know all about my private life. He needs to know in detail about who I am inside and my mental contents. He loves drawing; it is his main activity in analysis. He draws and I look. While he displays his sadomasochistic phantasies in his graphics my place is that of a voyeur. During this hour I am a voyeur indeed. This role is quite different from the place I occupied in the previous hour when I was exasperatingly submitted to Mary's control. In his drawings Andy is able to show almost everything: disgusting drooling mouths with rotten teeth, defecating anuses, bleeding bodies, split members. Notwithstanding the strong impact we can expect puberty and early adolescence to have on the mind of a child, his drawings go beyond the themes one would expect at his developmental stage. Disgust, shame, and repression seem not to exist for him. He uses me in order to test and observe the way his works affect me. Since, as he said, "a drawing needs to cause impact, provoke something in the one who sees it," he looks at me looking at what he produces, his eyes controlling my reactions, searching for the feelings the images arouse in me. He needs to create an impact on me just as he tried to strike his mother, a woman whose remoteness was due to a post-partum psychosis. He projects onto me his impotent and helpless self. Having to see awful scenes, I am to be both the object and witness of his anxiety and despair; he then identifies with the cruel, sadistic, and damaging object.

Carol

Next is Carol. She is 6 years old and is in a relentlessly excited state. In session today I am to be a girl that looks at her with envy and impotence. In her dramatization she is grown up, beautiful, wears makeup, has her fingernails painted with a marvelous transparent nail polish, and boasts a cell phone. She talks and moves restlessly. First she is Jane, who walks arm-in-arm with Tarzan in front of all the inhabitants of the jungle; immediately afterward she transforms herself into the Little Mermaid and her fiancé, who do wonders together; she then is Beauty, who walks up and down with a magnificent, ultra-beautiful bridal gown. Exaltation takes over her mind and transforms her. In blotting out the differences, she is oblivious of the fact of her being small and my being big; she is unable to trust that if she only waits long enough she will grow up too.

For the time being, I am the one who must tolerate the feelings of exclusion, rage, and excitement, and all the despairing suffering Carol experiences with regard to her phantasies about the parental couple. Suddenly the situation turns around. My necklace catches her attention. She approaches me seductively, she touches it gently, she begs me charmingly to give it to her; she only wants me to lend it to her for a while. But the impossibility of obtaining it transforms her again; resentment infuriates her, and an escalating defiant destruction begins. She pulls the chain of my necklace, tries to tear it, and wants to break it. She tries to scratch me and kick me; she throws water at me. She searches for my boundaries, hoping to find her own, which get blurred in this merging phantasy in which she wishes to own all I have.

From adult psychoanalysis to child psychoanalysis

Although Freud focused mainly on adult patients, both infancy and children were from the very beginning present in his psychoanalytical conceptualizations. We see the relevance of the prenatal and early years of life reflected in his concept of the *complementary series*, in which elements of the infant's innate constitution, in interaction with early infantile experiences, are combined to configure the disposition upon which other factors later impinge in the causation of mental illness. Freud's analysis of the infantile memories of the patients known as the Wolf Man (1918) and the Rat Man (1909b) have laid the grounds for understanding important aspects in the later developments of psychoanalysis, from theoretical as well as from a psychopathological perspectives. To mention only a few, the concepts of infantile neurosis, the primal scene, and *Nachtraeglichkeit* (deferred action) all came from his analysis of these clinical cases. Little Hans is considered the first child analytic case in history. Although Freud did not work directly with the boy, he guided and supervised the work the father, a medical doctor himself, was able to do with his child. The father's report was based upon observation of the child's behavior, on some of his play, and on his dialogues and questions. Little Hans was a smart observer of reality and needed, as do all human beings, to find answers to all his questions, following his epistemophylic impulse. This child has given us a clear insight into the way infantile sexual theories are constructed. He has let us know how these conflicts force the infantile mind to pursue diverse roads in order to relieve anxiety and suffering. This case can also be seen to have been an early demonstration of the way psychoanalysis regards the unceasing interplay between internal and external realities. However, while this case was important in supporting Freud's theories, at that time he did not think that psychoanalysis was appropriate for children. Nevertheless, the important place of children in society was without question one of the major contributions Freud offered to twentieth-century culture. As the myth of the immaculate, innocent child broke down, infantile sexuality began to be acknowledged, and a new idea of the infant emerged, one in which the infant experiences love, needs, and desires, but also pain, fears, and suffering that need to be relieved.

The play technique

It took many years for child analysis to be accepted in the psychoanalytic world; this was due to mainly to two factors. One relates to the way the child's playing and acting prevail over the use of verbal communications. Psychoanalytic technique was originally based on the method of free association and spoken words, so much so that children were considered apt subjects for psychotherapy but not for being analyzed. Freud wrote in 1914 that

> An analysis which is conducted upon a neurotic child itself must, as a matter of course, appear to be more trustworthy, but it cannot be very rich in material; too many words and thoughts have to be lent to the child, and even so the deepest strata may turn out to be impenetrable to consciousness.
>
> (Freud and Ferenczi, 1914, p. 545)

The "too many words and thoughts" that had to be provided to the child by the analyst resonated for many years, and preverbal expressions of phantasies were undervalued by psychoanalysts. Melanie Klein's play technique made psychoanalysis possible for children. As she wrote in a manuscript in 1925,

> The child expresses his phantasies, wishes and actual experiences in a symbolic way through play [...]. In doing so, he makes use of the same language that we know from dreams, which after all also originates from the infantile inner life. It is reasonable that when an understanding of this language originating from infantile inner life is of such importance in adult analysis, one of the fundamental requirements of child analysis is to take account of it. It is an archaic mode of expression, one that we know to be phylogenetically acquired, which the child uses and we can understand it fully only if we approach it in the way Freud has taught us to approach the language of dreams. Symbolism is only a part of it; if we wish to understand the language of play correctly in relation to the child's whole behavior during the analytic session,

181

we must take into consideration the mechanisms we know from the dream work – displacement, condensation, reworking to make something representable (of which symbolism is again only a part), secondary revision and all the methods of representation employed in the dream.

(Frank, 2009, pp. 7, 8)

According to Klein's postulates, infantile and adult psychoanalysis are based on the same grounds although the technical approaches are different. With its phantasies, anxieties, and defenses, the transference emerges in the psychoanalytic hour in both instances.

Transference neurosis and negative transference

The second reason the utility of child analysis was at first called into question as analytically effective was the belief that children – unlike adults – do not develop transference neuroses. The status of this concept was part of the controversies between Anna Freud and Melanie Klein in the early 1940s. Both women developed different theories and in consequence very different techniques in their psychoanalytic approach to children. Anna Freud postulated that it was impossible for children to establish transference relations owing to their immaturity and their actual dependency upon the real parental figures.

Affectionate attachment, the positive transference as it is called in analytic terminology, is the prerequisite for all later work ... The analysis of children requires much more from this attachment than in the case of adults. There is an educational as well as an analytical purpose ... The really fruitful work always takes place with a positive attachment.

(A. Freud, 1926, p. 37)

Again, in 1927, she wrote that she considered the child's negative impulses toward the analyst as being "essentially disturbing and should be dealt with analytically as soon as possible. The really fruitful work always takes place in positive attachment" (A. Freud, 1927, p. 41). Klein's position was different and her thoughts on what it is that is being transferred were innovative. Klein's conceptualization of internal objects populating the child's inner world opened a new dimension in regard to the function of transference. She postulated that the anxiety triggered by conflicts with and among these internal objects is sent, via projective identification, into external objects. As a result, the analyst is then perceived as being invested with the qualities of the internal object or with aspects of the self. Grinberg (1997) puts it this way: "The transference thus consisted in equating the analyst (the external object) with the internal object or with aspects of the self, by the mechanism of projective identification. The analyst might represent part of the patient and any part of his internalised objects" (pp. 2–3). For Klein (1949), transference phenomena occurred as early as the beginning of a child's analysis and should be addressed as soon as possible. Awareness and immediate interpretation of the child's main anxieties and sense of guilt, usually related to negative transference, was what she thought would allow the analytic situation to be established, so that the positive transference would be reinforced and the transference neurosis could develop. Though Anna Freud later changed her view and thought that negative transference did take place in child analysis, reinforcement of the attachment and the positive transference have been essential features in annafreudian technique. Whether one regards the activity of a child in a psychoanalytic hour as evoking either positive or negative transference depends on the theoretical lens one uses to look at it, which in turn has consequences for the technique the analyst employs, as well as it being influenced by it.

> [W]hether the child develops a transference neurosis, and if he does, how it is utilized for the work of analysis, will depend not only on his level of development and his individual psychopathology, but also on the theoretical position of the analyst. The analyst's theory and his expectations, regardless of his neutrality, always influence his perceptions and his technique.
>
> (Chused, 1988, p. 52)

Concepts like projection, introjection, projective identification, internal world, and psychic reality allow us to think of the transference as a phenomenon taking place early on in the mind of children. Meltzer (1973) wrote that

> The really important modification of our view of children was the growth of the rich concept of "psychic reality", which is by

no means a mere euphemism to imply that children set great store by phantasy. It is a rigorous scientific concept which recognises that the growth of a child's mind takes place by a continually oscillating process, in which his activities with figures in the outside world modify the qualities of internal figures in conscious and unconscious phantasy.

(Meltzer, 1973, p. 31)

As an expression of early infantile patterns, transference occurs early in life and is externalized onto objects of the outside world, just as it happens with adults. The early ego, the existence of primitive infantile object relations, and an internal world populated by internal objects make the child's transference flow in the playroom of a child analyst, even in very young patients. The infant internalizes his parents who become his internal objects early in life. These internal objects are built up in the mind of the child in an active way as the result of processes of projection and introjection, and although they are based on the real external mother and father they are not at all a facsimile of them. The impulses and phantasies that a child experiences during the introjective process influence the way the object is experienced internally. Parents introjected with sadism or oedipal hate will be experienced internally as harsh and sadistic rather than loving and kind. Oftentimes we see in the playroom that the child's transference externalizes introjected parents that are far more strict, harsh, or cruel than the real ones. In the clinical vignette that follows I would like to show how I understood the transference in the play of a young patient who at that time was not yet able to speak.

Bea

Bea was 17 months old when the parents came to see me. The family had had a car accident when she was 4 months old that was certainly shocking to her but caused her no physical damage. Mother reported that since then Bea's development had stopped. After the accident, when she was between 5 months and 7 months old, Bea was hospitalized three times due to respiratory problems. At the time of the consultation she did not crawl and could not remain seated for more than a couple of minutes although nothing organic could be found to explain her difficulties. Mother and father were very busy professionals. The mother was emotionally remote, though she was concerned about Bea's development. Bea's mother also traveled frequently for professional reasons, so separations happened often in the child's life. Bea was regularly brought to the sessions by her nanny, and meetings with parents were difficult to arrange because of the parents' busy lives.

By the time of the fragment I wish to report Bea was 20 months old and I had not seen her for two weeks. These are my notes from that session:

> When I meet her in the waiting room she does not greet me happily as she usually does. She is sleepy, cries, and wants to be on her nanny's lap. When seated on the carpet in the playroom she soon lies on her back and rolls away from me. She then holds her head with her hands and cries as if she were in pain. I say to her that I am bad today because I left her alone for many days. She looks at me and makes eye contact for the first time. I offer to help her sit which she accepts. She looks around and starts throwing away the toys that are close to her. I say that I am bad because I pushed her away. She then grabs a little bear. For the first time since I have seen her she starts throwing it away and bringing it back several times. I say to her that she now enjoys pushing me away and bringing me back. Bea's next play is with the dollhouse. She opens and closes its door and windows and I play with her, saying hello and good bye. I am seated on the carpet close to her. She pushes me, playing that she throws me away. Each time I go down on my back onto the carpet she laughs and repeats the play with pleasure, again and again for a while.

This young patient did not say a word, but in my view her play revealed what she transferred to our relationship from her internal world of object relations. Her internal mother was not strong enough to support her and hold her together. She expressed her despair and pain for having been left alone. The abandonment was projected into the toys that were expelled while at the same time she identified with an expulsive mother. A shift happened when in her play the object was not only thrown away but also recovered. Bea was then able to do actively what she felt had been done to her. The playing with the bear looked like the fort-da game that Freud observed his grandson play while he was dealing with the pain of losing his mother and the joy of recovering and controlling her. Opening and closing the dollhouse door and windows revealed phantasies related to the presence and the absence of the object. At the same time it was a way to express her curiosity about my mind as well as about the interior of mommy's body.

Projective identification, projective counter-identification, countertransference and enactment

Heimann's (1950) and Racker's (1953) contributions helped to make countertransference be understood as a source from which to gain further comprehension and knowledge about the patient's unconscious. The countertransferential feelings are conveyed to the analyst via projective identification. This powerful mechanism, described by Melanie Klein in 1946, is evacuative, pathological, and sparked off by envy; it is the result of the splitting of the self, which is followed by the projection of fragments of what are felt to be dangerous substances. These are then expelled with hate into an object in a process where the differences between internal and external objects become blurred due to the subject's identification with the recipient, which happens as a result of the projection. Klein categorizes this mechanism as the prototype of an aggressive object relation. It is a one-person, intrapsychic model in which an unconscious phantasy is active within the psyche of the subject (Grotstein, 2002). Later on, Bion (1962), in addition to acknowledging the pathological and impoverishing aspects of this process, emphasized its more positive communicative aspects. Evacuation and projection are normal aspects of the process of mental digestion. There are evacuations that are necessary and unavoidable, like freeing oneself of mental waste material. From this standpoint projective identification is a normal developmental mechanism, originally occurring within the container–contained relation between the mind of the mother and that of the baby. Unlike Klein's original concept, this is a two-person model (Grotstein, 2002). The mother with a capacity for reverie can receive in her mind the contents the baby cannot tolerate, take charge of and modify them, and give them meaning.

Reverie refers to the normal mental state of the mother receptive of the projective identifications of her baby, which enables her to introjectively identify with it. It is not a state that will allow her to Know but to Intuit. Reverie allows the mother to "dream" the baby and its emotional experiences, giving it containment through finding symbolic meaning in its projective identifications. It is not *the* symbolic meaning but instead *one* possible meaning.

(Oelsner, 1996, n. p.)

When thus transformed and drained of their persecuting meaning, projective identifications may be reintrojected by the baby, who then also introjects the model of a container–contained function.

The concept of enactment has been particularly interesting for the way it has shed light on some aspects of transference and countertransference in child analysis. Grinberg, for example, described what he called projective counter-identification. He found, in precisely the excessive quality of projective identification, the key reason for the unconscious response of the analyst, who is "passively 'led' to play the sort of role the patient hands over to him" (Grinberg, 1962, pp. 436–437). In such an enactment, the analyst – instead of receiving and understanding the patient's communication – reacts to it by rejecting the material and in turn responding with a projective identification into the patient, creating a harmful vicious circle.

Sandler wrote about the significance of role responsiveness in the analyst's countertransference, and, although he does not mention it, projective identification seems to be the mechanism that underlies enactment. He used the terms "actualization" and "actualize," as defined in the *Oxford English Dictionary*, with actualization referring to " 'a making actual; a realization in action or a fact' and actualize as 'to make actual, to convert into an actual fact, to realize in action' " (1976, p. 44). Sandler describes a particular type of acting that consists in the analysand's actualizing in the transference *"in a disguised way"* a phantasy that involves the analyst, whom he nudges into playing a particular role. The patient's unconscious wishes are expressed in unconscious fantasies in which self and object play roles. Through the transference, the patient, in an attempt to actualize the infantile unconscious relationship, tries to play it out with the analyst in the here-and-now of the session. In this playing, both of them actualize that infantile relationship, which they are not aware is being enacted in the session. It is neither a conscious phantasy nor anything represented in the symbolic discourse of the patient. It is a form of "acting" that, according to Sandler, enables the "actualization" of preverbal mental states in the transference. Borensztejn (2009) distinguishes two different moments in the enactment. In the first

187

one the analyst suddenly, while talking to the patient, is aware of the involuntarily role that he is being pushed into. The second moment corresponds to the interpretation of the enactment, since it is only when the analyst is aware of what has been enacted and is able to understand it and to interpret it that it can become integrated into the texture of the analytic treatment.

Betty Joseph (1985) emphasizes that

> Much of our understanding of the transference comes through our understanding of how our patients act on us to feel things for many varied reasons; how they try to draw us into their defensive systems; how they unconsciously act out with us in the transference trying to get us to act out with them; how they convey aspects of their inner world built up from infancy—elaborated in childhood and adulthood, experiences often beyond the use of words, which we can often only capture through the feelings aroused in us, through our countertransference ...
>
> (Joseph, 1985, p. 157)

The enactment of a phantasy is precisely the way the patient displays in the transference his internal object relations. It has both a defensive and a communicative purpose. In these actualizations we can see, on stage, acted and dramatized, what is being transferred and cannot be conveyed otherwise. On the one hand it is the way the patient presses on the analyst to have him play a role according to an unconscious phantasy; at the same time it has a communicative function: it makes the analyst be aware of something that can only be conveyed in this way. The recognition of the enacted dramatization of an unconscious phantasy into which the patient tries to nudge us, provokes feelings in us and enables us to have better access to understanding what is being transferred. In child analysis enactments are almost the rule, since quick action and fast rhythm are inevitable ingredients of playing and of the child's interaction with the analyst. However, we can make a distinction between symbolic play and enactment. In the vignettes I presented earlier, Mary is far from displaying a symbolic play; hers is a repetitive, almost compulsive activity. Some sequences of Carol's actions feel as if they are closer to a motor discharge that is more of a discharge of despair and an attack than play; she misses the possibility of expressing, by means of the "as if" state of mind that is involved in play, those feelings of pain and despair that invade her. It is thus of utmost importance for the analyst to maintain his place in thinking, understanding, and interpreting both the play and the enactment that are unfolding in the playroom. For the child analyst, it is particularly important to deeply accept the value of enacted material as well as genuine play in order to access these young patients' unconscious.

What is exclusive to child analysis

In my experience, analytic work with children sensitizes the analyst's mind; through it one can more easily grasp early conflicts in adult patients as well. The evolution of the human psyche is characterized by its continuity, and mechanisms that are present in childhood are also regularly to be found in adults, although the means through which each group expresses them are different. Children resort to play to externalize their transferences owing to the fact that the infantile ego has not yet mastered verbal communication. This will be acquired later. The action that for a child is present in his playing is presented in the adult in an idiosyncratic use of words. As Anderson (1997) states, "we see adult material as consisting of a constant process of action through words, that it is not so much that children are like adults in the analysis, but rather that adults in analysis continue to be children" (p. 415).

Though usually child analysts work with adult patients as well, one can observe that, over time, most of them tend to abandon or to reduce their analytic work with children. Some experienced child analysts choose to be consultants or supervisors rather than continue to be involved directly in the work with children. One of the reasons for this lies in how demanding the task in the playroom is, both physically and emotionally. In his work with children the impact on the analyst's transference and countertransference adds complexity to his task. Three very challenging elements for the child analyst that may together explain why he may burn out over time include:

1   The play technique, which demands of the analyst a regression to a form of language long ago overcome;
2   The persistent challenge to the rule of abstinence, in that a child analyst is often compelled to "do" things for a young child, or compelled to play with him, and thus needing to constantly measure where the boundary lies between technically correct action and acting out;

3   Last but not least, there are the real parents, whose cooperation and support is essential, but whose own conflicts may disturb the process of the child, and that cannot be resolved interpretatively. I will say more on this point below.

All these factors impinge heavily on the analyst's countertransference to the child in analysis, to the extent that he may wish to leave this hard task to his younger colleagues.

A playroom and the analyst's countertransference

As we know, the play technique requires a particular framework. It is convenient to create a setting that is adapted for the child so that the child may experience both an adequate physical and psychological ambience in which he may feel able to bring to analysis the totality of his self. The analyst can thus observe, think, feel, and sort out what originates in the child and what in himself (Joseph, 2000). By adequate physical ambience I mean a space where the child can unfold his play and give way to his phantasy and where the analyst has the peace of mind to observe and think without having to worry about the furniture or the objects in the room. This enables him to concentrate on that part of his feelings that originate in his countertransference. In other words, since we surely agree that what is central is the state of mental availability of the analyst, the more comfortable he is in the ambiance in which he works the more he is allowed to devote his mind to the child. Exceptionally, we may from necessity have to work in less ideal places and still make some headway in our task. Here we need only recall the inappropriate characteristics of the playroom where Melanie Klein analyzed little Richard (Klein, 1961), which nevertheless did not prevent her from writing what is still regarded today as the most complete and magisterial narrative of a child analysis.

The parents, their transferences,
and the analyst's countertransference

As noted above, the real parents play an indispensable role in child analysis, which can only happen with their support. The decision to bring a child to analysis and to support the treatment implies an intense emotional investment that mobilizes unconscious and conscious conflicts in the parents. The analyst has to attend to the parents' transferences but cannot interpret them. To create and maintain a therapeutic alliance with them can only happen successfully if the parental unconscious negative feelings toward their child, or toward the analytic couple, are not too powerful. Strong feelings of guilt about their child's illness, rivalry or competition with the analyst, or envy directed at the analyst because he can do for the child what they could not, might work against the continuity of a therapeutic process. It is well known that the continuity of the treatment will hold as long as the parents allow it. A child analyst is familiar with the frustration and impotence that abrupt terminations cause him, and sometimes he is the one who must carry the sadness of an unfinished process and a sudden separation. The child analyst has to work on his own countertransferential feelings related to the parents, feelings that sometimes are as intense as the emotions triggered by the child patient. The analyst may be counter-identified with the parents against the child, or may be counter-identified with the child against the parents while having the phantasy of being a better parent than the parents. Of course the measure to which he has overcome his oedipal conflicts with his own parents is crucial. The child analyst could also regard the child's parents as his own parental couple – as rivals who he would tend to have critical and competitive feelings about. This may interfere with the analyst's neutrality in assessing the material of his child patient. Conversely, the analyst may feel persecuted, examined, and diminished by the child's parents if his neurotic countertransference (unresolved oedipal conflict) gets triggered by the triangular situation.

Boundaries and the rule of abstinence

Another exclusive challenge for the child analyst is the fact that he faces technical situations that are not usual in work with neurotic adults. Some children express their transferential phantasies in such an intense mode that they cause strong reactions in the analyst. Violent physical attacks, persistent search for physical contact, erotized acting in, boundary issues, destruction of the play material, mess and chaos in the playroom are only some of the issues we struggle with daily. When we have a young child in the playroom dependency is not simply a phantasy or a feeling. It may reflect the child's concrete need for assistance with functions he cannot perform by himself. To follow the directions of a demanding, controlling, or manically excited child may be exhausting for an analyst, who must find a mental space for observing and thinking about the transference and his countertransference. During these not infrequent phases we have to work, as Bion once said, under fire. The countertransferential responses are intense, and stir up a broad range of emotions that range from love to hatred and include tenderness, pity, guilt, and rejection. A clinical vignette from a session with Carol will show some of the complexity I am describing.

Carol

At one session Carol strives to get hold of my necklace. She tries to find my boundary in order to find hers. She is excited, she gets confused, and she searches for body contact and tries to touch me, challenging all my limits. She is provoking and wants to annoy me because she is in despair. She keeps trying: does her writing on the walls bother me? No, since it does not seem so, so she stops. And her wetting the floor of the playroom? Not that either, since I can go on observing, thinking, and telling her what I think. She tries to scratch and kick me but I am able to protect myself. Then, soaked in green glue, she jumps on me and messes my clothes up. Now I do indeed feel irritated and have fantasies of using my physical force not only to hold and stop her but to teach her a lesson. What is the matter with Carol? And what has happened to me that we came to this? It is no longer easy for me to think; I am aware of her trying to provoke me to become violent and get confused. Might she be trying to make me fly out of control? Her wanting to take possession of what she so much desires is very intense. The challenge is either to possess the object or to destroy it. She is provoking me both to punish her and to submit to her in order to satisfy the masochistic aspects of her character. We see we are abandoning the area of knowing about and understanding Carol, and falling into the pit of cruel and destructive phantasies. If I respond violently, I will no longer be different from her. She spits at me, and when I say something about it she corrects me and says "I am not spitting. I'm vomiting." I then propose to call what she does "an enraged and desperate vomit." She then repeats, amused, "rage vomit, rage vomit." And the atmosphere changes entirely. I know from previous experience that I must avoid physical contact and struggling since I have observed that this gets her aroused. The risk then is enacting with her and, in doing so, satisfying her sadomasochistic phantasies.

Yet all these rather grim images of child analysis for the analyst are not the full picture. It is fair to say that it is also an amazing emotional experience. It is a deeply moving experience when a child I meet for the first time in the playroom starts playing or drawing in my presence and allows me to know about his feelings, his fears, and his struggles. To work analytically with a child requires that the analyst be receptive, containing, and understanding of the child's anxieties. For the child, it means an opportunity to work through with his analyst his own conflicts, to modify his anxieties, to know and understand more about himself and how his mind works. Child analysis is an effective way to spare a person suffering and pain later in life. In his discussion about Little Hans's analysis Freud wrote:

> It may be that Hans now enjoys an advantage over other children, in that he no longer carries within him that seed in the shape of repressed complexes which must always be of some significance for a child's later life, and which undoubtedly brings with it a certain degree of deformity of character if not a predisposition to a subsequent neurosis.
>
> (1909a, pp. 143–144)

These noble aims enhance the child analyst's positive counter-transference and offer an encouraging perspective that can keep him going.

Bibliography

Anderson, R. (1997) The child in the adult: The contribution of child analysis to the psychoanalysis of adults. In R. Schafer (ed.), *The Contemporary Kleinians of London* (pp. 414–425). Madison, CT: International Universities Press.

Bion, W. R. (1962) *Learning from Experience*. London: Heinemann. Reprinted in 1984 by Karnac, London.)

Borensztejn, C. (2009) El enactment como concepto clínico: Convergente de teorías divergentes. *Revista de Psicoanálisis*, 64: 177–192.

Chused, J. F. (1988) The transference neurosis in child analysis. *Psychoanalytic Study of the Child*, 43: 51–81.

Frank, C. (2009) *Melanie Klein in Berlin: Her First Psychoanalyses of Children*, E. Spillius (ed.) and S. Leighton and S. Young (trans.). London: Routledge. New Library of Psychoanalysis. First published as *Melanie Kleins erste Kinderanalysen*. Stuttgart: Frommann-Holzboog Verlag, 1999.

Freud, A. (1926) *The Psychoanalytic Treatment of Children*. New York: Schocken Books.

Freud, A. (1927) The role of the transference in the analysis of children. In *Introduction to Psychoanalysis: Lectures for Child Analysts and Teachers* (pp. 36–49). London: Hogarth.

Freud, S. (1909a) Analysis of a phobia in a five-years-old boy. In *The Standard Edition of the Complete Psychological Works of Sigmund Freud*, J. Strachey (ed., trans.), vol. 10: 5–149. London: Hogarth.

Freud, S. (1909b) Notes upon a case of obsessional neurosis. *SE* 10: 155–318.

Freud, S. (1918) From the history of an infantile neurosis. *SE* 17: 1–122.

Freud, S. and Ferenczi, S. (1914) Letter from Sigmund Freud to Sándor Ferenczi, 11 March. In E. Brabant, E. Falzeder, P. Giampieri-Deutsch (eds.), *The Correspondence of Sigmund Freud and Sándor Ferenczi*, P. T. Hoffer (trans.). Vol. 1, 1908–1914. Cambridge, MA: Harvard University Press, 1993.

Grinberg, L. (1962) On a specific aspect of countertransference due to the patient's projections. *International Journal of Psychoanalysis*, 43: 436–440.

Grinberg, L. (1997) Is the transference feared by the psychoanalyst? *International Journal of Psychoanalysis*, 78: 1–14.

Grotstein, J. S. (2002) Projective identification and its relation to infant development. In S. Alhanati and J. V. Buren (eds.), *Primitive Mental States*, vol. 2, 67–98. London: Karnac.

Heimann, P. (1950) On counter-transference. *International Journal of Psychoanalysis*, 31: 81–84.

Joseph, B. (1985) Transference: The total situation. In M. Feldman and E. B. Spillius (eds.), *Psychic Equilibrium and Psychic Change* (pp. 157–168). London: Routledge, 1989. New Library of Psychoanalysis, 9. (Paper written in 1983.)

Joseph, B. (2000) Thinking about the playroom. Unpublished.

Klein, M. (1946) Notes on some schizoid mechanisms. In *Envy and Gratitude and Other Works, 1946-1963* (pp. 1–24). New York: The Free Press.

Klein, M. (1949) *The Psycho-analysis of Children*, A. Strachey (trans.). London: Hogarth. First published as *Die Psychoanalyse des Kindes*. Vienna: Internationaler Psychoanalytischer Verlag, 1932. Reprint: *The Psychoanalysis of Children*, New York: Vintage, 1997.

Klein, M. (1961) *Narrative of a Child Analysis: The Conduct of the Psycho-Analysis of Children as Seen in the Treatment of a Ten Year Old Boy*. International

Psycho-Analytical Library, 55: 1–536. London: Hogarth Press and the Institute of Psycho-Analysis.

Meltzer, D. (1973) From pain-and-fear to love-and-pain. In *Sexual States of Mind* (pp. 28–34). Strath Tay, Perthshire: Clunie Press.

Oelsner, R. (1996) Transferencia-Countertranferencia: Un sueño de dos (Transference-Countertransference: A dream of two). Paper presented at the XXI Latin American Conference of Psychoanalysis.

Racker, H. (1953) A contribution to the problem of counter-transference. *International Journal of Psychoanalysis*, 34: 313–324.

Sandler, J. (1976) Countertransference and role responsiveness. *International Journal of Psychoanalysis*, 3: 44–47.

THE PSYCHOANALYTIC COVENANT

"Human sacrifice" as the hidden order of transference ↔ countertransference

James S. Grotstein

Introduction

The concept of transference has long dominated psychoanalytic theory and practice (Freud, 1912), but it was only within more recent times that its corollary, countertransference, emerged from its former status as an inevitable but regrettable occurrence in psychoanalytic treatment to become a most highly important psychoanalytic function and source of highly valued clinical data – so much so, in fact, that it is increasingly written about and spoken of as if it were inseparably connected with transference, as a single entity: transference-countertransference, as an example of a "binary-oppositional structure" (Lévi-Strauss, 1958).[1] I shall make that assumption in this chapter even when I seem to separate one from the other for purposes of individual discussion.

The concept of a hidden order

I am using the concept of "hidden order" to reveal what I believe to be the fuller nature and deeper roots of transference and countertransference and of their interaction. In order to achieve this goal I shall begin by deconstructing each of the terms in regard to their traditional and conventional usages and seek their origins in infant development theory as well as their counterparts in religious and anthropological settings, thereby broadening and extending their respective as well as combined functions.

"Human sacrifice" as the hidden order of transference and countertransference

Note: in what follows I am considering the practice and ritual of "human sacrifice" to be principally a metaphor, that is, as if its occurrence lay on a gradient originating first as a prehistoric and ancient practice and then displaced to animals, but that yet continues to this very day in highly derivative forms between ourselves and our loved ones, as well as others. As every infant soon learns, the act of being alive involves his entering the private spaces of others – and vice versa – and tallying the cost of the impact of these intimately personal entries over a lifetime. We universally misuse (sacrifice) the ones we love and trust the most because we can trust their love to bear it. I shall use quotation marks when I use the term "human sacrifice."

I hope ultimately to demonstrate that the theme of "human sacrifice," mainly in its derivative symbolic or generic sense, but once actually in its literal sense, constitutes the hidden order of the transference ↔ countertransference situation (as well as of infant development and, for that matter, daily human interaction). I also believe that psychoanalysis constitutes a "passion play"[2] that is comprised of positive and negative transferences, but one in which the positive transference is required to support the special therapeutic covenant between the patient's negative transference and the analyst's countertransference (Grotstein, 2009b, 2009c, 2009d). I associate this covenant with the religious anthropological rite of "*exorcism.*"

Infantile neurosis → transference neurosis

I begin with Freud (1912), who originally speaks of transference as the analysand's displacement of past object cathexes to the analyst. He states that psychoanalysis is unable to treat a psychoneurosis; it can only treat a transference neurosis, which requires that the patient's infantile neurosis, the template of his psychoneurosis, be *transferred* to a transference neurosis, where it *can* be treated as an "analytic drama" or "play" (Freud, 1920).

197

Transference neurosis ↔ countertransference neurosis (negative transference ↔ countertransference)

When I was in analysis with Bion, he mentioned to me on occasion that, as the analysis progresses, I shall be analyzing him while he was analyzing me. He went on to say that everything he said, the way he said it, and what he didn't say would reveal something about his personal choices to me, the patient. He said three other related things that really moved me:

(1) "Psychoanalysis must help the patient end his blind *endurance* of his pain and enable him to *suffer* the pain with the analyst's help – so that he can recognize and own his suffering." (2) On another occasion he stated that "*The patient will not fully believe the analyst's interpretation if he feels that the analyst doesn't also experience it.*" (3) Yet another idea he mentioned and had also written about was that *the analyst should experience anxiety in every session.*

His first statement introduced to me the idea that, in the course of my choosing him as my analyst, not only was I allowing him to enter *my* private, personal space; I would be let into *his* private, personal space and be able to judge and misuse *him*. That, in addition to his three following statements, set the stage for me to examine possible connections between "human sacrifice," transference, countertransference, enactments, intersubjectivity, analytic fields, shamanistic "analysis," "exorcism," and more.

There were at least six layers to this unveiling:

1 The idea of passion as suffering led to the idea that the analyst as well as the patient are mandated to suffer, and ultimately each is to "become" a symbolic, emotional, and ritualized "human sacrifice" to and for the other.
2 The theme of "human sacrifice" might qualify as a "hidden order" that supraordinates the psychoanalytic conception of infant development – along with the infant's need to fully use his objects as victims of his developmental agenda in order to experience and express the full range of his vitality, and to "rehearse" (Bion, personal communication) his evolution-ordained (Darwin, 1859) strategies for prey–predator success (Bowlby, 1969), which I shall explicate later. Along with this agenda he must experience the guilt for what he, in retrospect, learns that he has done to his objects and, conversely as well as

paradoxically, about how he failed to use them effectively, as we shall see happened with Oedipus.

3   I then instantly thought of related themes, such as "exorcism,"[3] "innocence," "covenants," and the infant's sense of responsibility for his covenant with Truth in the depressive position. The patient is responsible for experiencing his own pain and, again paradoxically, needs the help of his putatively "wounded" mother (and father) to help him process his pain.

4   The current concept of Bion's (1962) "container ↔ contained" should be extended in light of its putative connection with "exorcism" and "human sacrifice," to include the analyst's (as well as the mother's) sublimated masochistic stance in regard to being ready and willing to "suffer" in their obligatory role.

5   Furthermore, one must consider the case of the infant who in his unconscious phantasy believes that he is a "failure as an infant" and therefore will be – and should be – "sacrificed" by his family.

6   Finally, I examine some hidden orders involving the Oedipus complex.

When Meltzer (1978) stated that the truest meaning of transference was the "transfer" of mental pain from one person to another, he, utilizing Bion's concept of container ↔ contained, clarified an important aspect of Klein's (1946, 1955) concept of projective identification. His clarification of Klein's concept was to specify that when the infant evacuates his emotional pain via projective identification, the mother – as well as the analyst – is mandated to contain, or absorb or take over, the patient's pain.

When we combine Bion's and Meltzer's hypotheses, we uncover a hitherto hidden function of *counter*-transference, that of curing the patient of emotional pain by enabling the "transfer" ("exorcism") of mental pain ("demons") from him to the analyst for the latter to absorb, personally experience ("metabolize"), "become" (– the transmogrified "demon"), dream, and ultimately interpret to the patient in tolerable and useful form. In this process the analyst begins to feel (believe) that he has become not only the patient's transferred intolerable demons ("concordant countertransference" [Racker, 1968]). He also becomes the patient's appointed "scapegoat" ("complementary countertransference" [Girard, 1986; Racker, 1968]).

Once we arrive at the juncture of this putative revelation, we can conclude that the protocol of the psychoanalytic healing process is ultimately grounded in, once the practice, now the derivative or generic idea, of "human sacrifice," which constitutes the hidden order of transference ↔ countertransference.

Projective identification, suffering, and the paranoid–schizoid position

In the paranoid–schizoid position the infant (or infantile portion of the adult personality) seeks to protest its suffering by projecting it into the caretaker (mother, analyst), in order to abrogate its responsibility to suffer the pain of being vulnerable and needy, and thus to projectively reassign its pain and the responsibility for it to the caretaker for the other to suffer – causing retaliatory persecutory anxiety.[4] It is only in the depressive position that the infant accepts his or her own responsibility for his or her pain, not the cause but the responsibility for, how he or she experienced or processed ("dreamed") it. This epigenesis will turn out to be of great importance later in this presentation. A female analysand entered the consulting room recently and grumpily uttered: "I'm back for more torture! I wonder what's on your agenda today."

The tale of the orphaned bear–cub

In the midst of being inundated with these "wild thoughts" I happened to recall a movie I saw about a young bear who became orphaned by the death of his mother. He became "adopted" by a roving adult male bear. A hunter shot this father bear, wounding him severely. The anguished orphan-bear thereupon licked his newfound father's wounds. It was only in my *recollection* of this scene that I suddenly realized a deeper emotional meaning of Bion's concept of the "container." I had uncovered its hidden order, a sacred covenant, a bond of love and sacrifice following violence.

Following this, I "recalled" three memories from the past. The first was that of Bion, telling me the following. First, he said, "Freud never seemed to grasp the existence of the religious instinct, which is as important, if not more important than the libidinal instinct." Sometime later, he stated, "Infancy and childhood constitute rehearsals for adulthood, the thing-in-itself." Finally, I recalled the occasion, which I alluded to earlier, when he said, "When you offer a patient an interpretation, they won't really believe you if they sense that you don't feel what they feel."

The first statement was a mind-opener about an entirely new metapsychological dimension, one that opened up a new camera-angle on transference and countertransference as a parallel with the Crucifixion and the Eucharist. The second was a radically new angle on infant development, one that had clear Darwinian overtones. The third was the resounding entry of a totally new view of countertransference (reverie) and especially of the absolute necessity, for the cure, of the emergent role of negative transference and its obligatory connection with "human sacrifice" and "exorcism" in the containing countertransference.

Next, a memory of a long ago conversation with John Bowlby came to mind, in which he stated, "Man, like all animal species, is born with a prey–predator instinct, which is honed by attachment to caregivers." I then hypothesized, upon this recall, that the prey–predator instinct was (a) connected with Bion's idea of "rehearsal," and (b) subordinated the entirety of the developmental protocol of autoerotism and infantile sexuality with part-object relations. An outgrowth from Bowlby's idea was that the prey–predator instinct mediated such functions as sex as well as hunting and mastery of the object, and, when subordinated to the influence of adaptation (Hartmann, 1939), facilitates the development of an altruistic, sublimated "masochistic stance" for nurture and healing of agonized objects.

Then, with Meltzer's statement, to which I have already referred, and juxtaposed with Bion's third statement, I was led to the concept that transference ↔ countertransference may be better understood as the religious-shamanistic practice of "exorcism," which I shall argue also constitutes the quintessence of Bion's "container ↔ contained" and the covenant that binds and defines it – and inescapably invokes the themes of "human sacrifice" and the substitutive use of the scapegoat. The sacrifice of an innocent human being is meant not only to pacify a cruel and demanding deity (Frazer, 1922a, 1922b). It more commonly seeks to absorb a loved one's intolerable suffering. Someone, out of mercy and love, must agree to become sacrificed so as to absorb the sufferer's intolerable demons.

"Transference" ultimately constitutes the "transfer" (projective identification) of demons from one who cannot bear to suffer them to one who can and who is willing to do so (countertransference)! This reading of Meltzer and Bion calls for an expanded role for containment. The container must be innocent so as to absorb (exorcise) the patient's demons and become saturated with them and sacrificed!

An anthropological contribution

I found that the following contribution, based on the work of the anthropologist Claude Lévi-Strauss, cited in Barratt (1993), offers us an interesting and partially supportive parallel from the perspective of shamanistic practices among the Cuna Indians:

> In the case of a protracted labour endangering both a pregnant woman and her unborn child, the midwife called for the services of a shaman. The latter ... never touched the patient, but he performed a lengthy chant, invoking his tutelary spirits to do battle with Muu – the spirit of the woman's womb, responsible for procreation and fetal growth ... The shaman narrates the journey of his helpful spirits, up the patient's vagina and into her uterus, vanquishing all mythical monsters on the way. In this way the narrative details what is happening to the patient, merging a mythical account with [a] description of the woman's internal sensations and the external events in which she participates. The helpful spirits eventually prevail over those who are resisting delivery, the baby is born, and the incantation ends ...
>
> (Grotstein, 2009c, p. 65)

In this anthropological account one can observe the rite of exorcism but not the countertransference of the shaman. A brief anthropological account mentioned by Brown (2011) may reveal this:

> Before diagnosing a patient's illness, the folk doctor often chews coca leaves ... or alcohol to prevent diagnostic mistakes. The folk doctor rubs the patient's body from head to toe with a live *cuy* ... Then he slits the animal's abdomen, examines the rodent's organs and either diagnoses the illness or pronounces the patient's cure.
>
> (Morales, 1995, pp. 47, 75)

A religious contribution

The anthropologist René Girard, who has studied "human sacrifice" and its substitutive derivative, the use of the scapegoat, states the following:

Does the idea of the unconscious belong to the Gospels? ... The sentence that defines the unconscious persecutor lies at the very heart of the Passion story in the Gospel of Luke: "Father, forgive them; they do not know what they are doing." (Luke 23:34) ... If we are to restore to this sentence its true savor we must recognize its almost technical role in the revelation of the scapegoat mechanism. It says something precise about the men gathered together by their scapegoat. *They do not know what they are doing.* That is why they must be pardoned ... In this passage we are given the first definition of the unconscious in human history, that from which all the others originate and develop in weaker form . . .

(Girard, 1986, pp. 110–111)

Conclusion: *The crucifixion of Christ and the rite of the Eucharist, which continues it, constitute the rite of human sacrifice in the service of putative therapeusis, and thus describe the exorcism (transference) of demons (infantile neurosis) from the sufferer(s) (patient) to one who is willing to bear them and to become them (countertransference).*

The concept of a "covenant"

The analytic relationship, in parallel with the relationships of infant development, is bound by a covenant between two or more individuals who promise to respect and protect each other from abuse or negligence by either participant and by any third parties on the outside (or inside) – so that the optimum development, for the infant, and the "sacred passion play of therapeusis" for the analysand, which I am asserting psychoanalysis ultimately represents, may proceed.

I also believe that the infant's state of continuing "innocence" depends on his or her loyalty to the depressive position, which predisposes him or her to loyalty to their personal and private covenant with "Truth" about "Reality" ("transformations in O," as well as with truth about reality (see more on transformations from O to K in Bion [1965, 1970]).

A covenant must exist between the patient and the analyst to honor, protect, and facilitate the welfare of the "analytic third" (Ogden, 2004), the "once and forever unconscious infant of analysis." A special covenant exists, furthermore, between the patient's transference and the analyst's corresponding countertransference (exorcism).

Two hidden orders of the Oedipus complex

We know a great deal about the myth of Oedipus from Sophocles' tragic plays. We know, for instance, that he committed incest with his mother, Jocasta, and parricide upon his father, Laius. We also know that he was born predestined to do so because of a curse cast upon the Labdacid house (all the way back to Cadmus). Earlier, his parents had also consulted an oracle, learned the same prophecy, and decided (principally Laius) to sacrifice him in the archaic Greek manner, exposure on Mount Cithaeron (the "Laius complex"). Thus, we can say, and I shall deal at greater length with this notion as I proceed, that Oedipus was born paradoxically both innocent and unwittingly guilty of a "memoir of the future," as Bion would mystically term it, but also from a curse from the past, of which he was totally innocent.

The Greek scholar E. R. Dodds (1951) offers us another reading of Oedipus' guilt, however. Oedipus, as we know, had been rescued by a shepherd from his would-be fatal exposure on Mount Cithaeron, brought to Corinth by him, and was adopted there by the royal family. At age 18 Oedipus consulted an oracle and received the same prophecy that his natural parents had encountered. Out of love for both his (Corinthian) parents, he exiled himself from Corinth, only fatefully to find himself at the crossroads at Thebes, where he unwittingly carried out the oracle's prophecy after all.

Dodds essentially states the following: The deepest, most authentic level of guilt in the tragedy of Oedipus transcends that of incest and parricide. His most meaningful guilt was due to his attempt to avoid his fate by leaving Corinth for Thebes. The ultimate guilt of Oedipus is ontological (existential) and therefore an utterly unavoidable guilt. I immediately saw the relevance of this idea to infant development, as I shall later explicate.

The other hidden order in the oedipal myth is the occurrence of human sacrifice, first of the erstwhile innocent Oedipus and then of his father and mother. Thus, the Oedipus complex constitutes an ontological fate dilemma, and the Justice-required sacrifice of an innocent child as well as the sacrifice of his mother and father as well as his daughter, Antigone, and his two sons, Eteocles and Polyneices. Dodds informs us that when a crime or "pollution" occurred in the Greece of antiquity, Justice and Fate ordained that an innocent descendant of the perpetrator of the crime shall be sacrificed.

One can readily see how this latter phenomenon finds its way into the intergenerational neurosis. But what is relevant for this presentation is the infliction of sacrifice of the innocents imposed by the truly guilty ones; that is, an innocent descendant is chosen by Fate and Justice to suffer in order to rectify and redeem an ancient taint.

One can now begin to see that *the "innocent descendant" may be the analyst as expressed and experienced by his countertransference.*

Hidden orders in infant development: P-S → D (Klein); P-S ↔ D (Bion); D → P-S ↔ D (Meltzer)

Klein (1955) states that the infant is born into the paranoid–schizoid position, which is actually attained at 3 weeks post-partum, and attains the depressive position at 4 months, providing an epigenetic (consecutive) protocol for both the paranoid–schizoid and the depressive position. In other words P-S → D. Bion (1992, pp. 199–200) modified this protocol as follows: the infant is born simultaneously into the Positions (P-S ↔ D), as shown by the reversible arrow; each position dialectically mediates the operations and functions of the other, creating a binary-oppositional (collaborative) organization.

Meltzer (1978), following and extending Bion, believes that the infant is born immediately into the depressive position and reverts to the paranoid-schizoid position in default (D → P-S → D). The "hidden order" or implicit assumption of importance here has to do with the ontological and clinical consequences for the infant and patient, as I plan to show presently.

Case example from the infant development perspective

Early in my analysis with Bion I had had two successive dreams one night. In the first I had entered a supermarket in order to purchase some meat (white but indefinite – fish? chicken?), which I thereupon took home and ate. I was alone. While I was eating the white meat, I suddenly, and I mean suddenly, realized I had been eating a human breast! I fell into stark terror and unfathomable remorse. I realized that it was too late to rectify the horrifying act. I could never restore it! It was too late! I had to live with this agonizing guilt for the rest of my life.

In the second dream that night I found myself sitting in a chair by a hospital bed with a middle-aged woman who was lying there with surgical dressing wrapped around her chest. My eyes were cast downward, and hers looked wanly elsewhere. The scene closely resembled one I had observed long ago on a TAT card.[5]

Apparently, I must have had some unconscious (preconscious?) awareness or premonition of the depressive position all along, and it suddenly sprung into my conscious awareness *after the fact! – as if the scenes had been mysteriously pre-scripted! I* had *to do what I did so that I could become guilty – retrospectively – for a destructive attack on a loved one.*

One association had to do with my premature birth and the perilous state of my mother's pregnancy that necessitated it.

My earliest memory is of a visual scene in my mind, one of fantastic cosmic beauty and serenity, which is abruptly interrupted by a horrible scene of a barbed-wire fence dripping in blood (the premature delivery). Then I recalled an ancient nightmare that was intimately associated with the earlier visual image. In this nightmare I was in a high but small, closed room filled with countless medieval warriors on horses violently striking each other with swords and spears. I am aware that I am not including Dr Bion's counter-transference experiences – for obvious reasons, but let me at least hint at my phantasy about his painful response shortly.

At the time of this analysis we at LAPSI[6] were undergoing a virtual civil war because of what was regarded as the Kleinian pollution (invasion). After a site review the American Psychoanalytic Association put us on suspension because of it. I had been prominently involved in bringing Wilfred Bion, Albert Mason, and Suzanna Isaacs-Elmhirst over here from London and witnessed their being marginalized and publicly abused. My psychoanalytic rebirth had joined forces in my mind with my biological birth to bring harm to my analytic parents. But my guilt was even further compounded. Not only had I put my imported English colleagues in jeopardy, I had also put LAPSI, my native institute, my "analytic birth mother," in jeopardy with the American Psychoanalytic Association by my having succumbed to becoming a "Kleinian heretic."

As one can see, I am focusing on my experience of profound, ineradicable guilt about an *unconsciously* phantasied act in which I *consciously* but *unwittingly* harmed my mother's body (and the above-mentioned derivatives) by my birth, and devoured the maternal breast. Like Oedipus, *I was caught in an ontological dilemma, a paradoxical one, in which guilt awaited me if I swallowed the maternal breast (not just its milk) but also if I did not.*[7] My primal innocence had been confronted by my fateful entelechy (the prearranged pattern of my genetically determined development and evolvement).

I obviously do not have any data on Bion's countertransference or reverie but will cite a mournful but I believe related and applicable passage from his *Cogitations*:

> The relationship between me and my colleagues here in Los Angeles could accurately be described as almost entirely unsuccessful. They are puzzled by, and cannot understand me … There is, if I am not mistaken, more fear than understanding or sympathy for my thoughts, personality or ideas.
>
> (1992, p. 334)

Note: I am arbitrarily using this passage in two separate ways, in each case as my personal phantasy: (1) I was an agent in bringing Bion to Los Angeles and therefore became an agent in his experience of rejection by my "analytic relatives"; and (2) he may have thought of me as one who had not appreciated him as my analyst.

Conflation and integration

I now see infant development as:

1 Part of a genetically planned pattern of protocols of aided rehearsals (Bowlby and Bion) (hidden orders or organizing assumptions, entelechy) ("Darwinian boot camp" or "wilderness training" in preparation for survival) for strategizing one's way in the adult world, as for example hunters, warriors, lovers. The "rehearsing" infant is mandated to "practice" his life-affirming needs and skills on his caregivers, who must suffer the full range of expression of the infant's enthusiasm (as also in analysis). The infant is mandated to use – and even misuse – the breast in order to learn his limits, and thus to experience his guilt for believing he damaged and ravaged the needed breast, only gradually but fatefully to realize, but always in the irony of retrospect, that the breast was his mother! Such is the preparation for horror, guilt, repentance, reparation,[8] and gratitude – each of which must arbitrarily be on his developmental agenda or checklist.

2   The developmental stages of orality, anality, urethrality, and genitality can be subsumed under the overarching canopy of prey–predator rehearsal development (Bowlby, 1969), which also governs sexual competence. Sadomasochism can now be seen as two-pronged: (a) as a specific aspect of a prey–predator relationship in which the infant is able to enjoy inflicting pain in objects and the reverse; and (b) as a necessary stage of development in infant–mother relationships as well as in analysand–analyst relationships, involving the covenant of altruism, compassion, responsibility – in agreeing to suffer a loved one's (or patient's) pain.

The infant who in using the breast begins in retrospect to feel that he, as predator, has misused it as prey – and acknowledges it – has retained his own covenant (his contact with the responsibility for the acceptance of Truth about reality) with the incipient depressive position. In his "pilgrim's progress," he has journeyed forth from Primary Innocence, has faithfully met the challenge of confrontation with his persecutors in the "Forest of Error," and has achieved Higher Innocence (William Blake, 1789–1794). His unfailing contact with emotional Truth is his saving grace.

Conclusion

Infant development inexorably mandates that the infant should not only *use* the breast but cannot avoid believing in unconscious phantasy that he has (or must have) *misused* it, thanks to his prey–predator "rehearsals-requirements." Mother becomes both the "human sacrifice" (but initially, according to plan, unrecognized as such) for her infant, in unconscious phantasy, during the infant's "rehearsals" in the paranoid-schizoid position, and she also becomes his "counter-predator," a retaliating persecutor to his being her prey, thanks to projective identification and its role in creating persecutory anxiety, the anxiety of her retaliation.

It is only when the infant achieves the experience of the depressive position and becomes aware retrospectively that he had attacked not just the breast, but its owner, his mother, that he only then realizes with horror and contrition that his mother had been his loving, altruistic prey all along and had been his "rehearsal sacrifice." With the phantasied murderous sacrifice of his mother, and later, of his father, and his soulful, after-the-fact recognition and acknowledgment of this virtual "murder," the sacrificed parents become sacred and forthwith internalized as "awe-some" superego figures imbued with august authority and reverence (Bion, 1992, pp. 284–292; Freud, 1913).

With the sacrifice of the innocent infant: (1) Abel and Jesus Christ, Scripture's version; (2) the ego ideal, Freud's (1914) version; and (3) *Billy Budd* and *Moby Dick* in Melville's (1924, 1851) versions, (s)he also becomes sacralized and becomes the third member of this asexual, nonsensual inner divine trinity – as Freud (1913) suggested with regard to the father in *Totem and Taboo*.

Why the emphasis on transference?

Freud (1920) states that psychoanalysis is ineffective in treating a *psycho*neurosis. It is effective only in treating a *transference* neurosis. Thus, in the analytic process the infantile neurosis, which constitutes the template for the current psychoneurosis, must first be transferred (transformed) into a transference neurosis. Freud is saying, in effect, "I cannot treat what you are now suffering from. You must enter psychoanalysis and allow a fiction to occur, a fiction or phantasy in which you may 'rent my image' so as to let me be thought of as any and all the principal persons in your life, especially your mother and father and even yourself. You will develop many feelings toward me, from positive to negative. I invite you to say anything about yourself or me. In what happens here between us we shall be able to observe and experience the truth of your life in what is repeated and co-constructed by us." A "passion play" must be created so that the truth of the "political situation" between the self and one's internal demons (objects and part-objects) becomes patent ("The play's the thing / wherein I'll catch the conscience of the king!").

Why the emphasis on negative transference?

Psychoanalysis resembles the medical treatment of physical abscesses: the physician places a poultice on top of the abscess with the expectation that the poultice will *selectively* draw the purulence of the abscess from within and absorb it (negative transference "as the exorcism" of demons).

Why the emphasis on countertransference?

If negative transference corresponds to the purulence of the abscess, then countertransference corresponds to the poultice, which attracts and absorbs (contains and processes, or employs alpha-function to) the purulence.

Robert Fliess (1942), in his "The metapsychology of the analyst," states:

> [Psychoanalysis] ... requires that the analyst step into his patient's shoes and obtain in this way an inside knowledge that is almost first hand ... a person who uses empathy on an object introjects this object transiently, and projects the introject again onto the object.
> (cited in Brown, 2011, p. 25)

When the analyst is in a state of total identification with the patient, he then finds himself as collusively fused with the patient in a state of folie à deux.

The intersubjective "ventriloquist"

I should like to put forth the idea, one which I have developed elsewhere (Grotstein, 2009a), that the analytic relationship between Systems *Ucs.* and *Cs.* can be thought of as similar to the verbal game of charades operating as a ventriloquistic exercise. The *Ucs.* of the patient knows what it wishes to express but is unable to so directly. Unconscious communications must first be (1) transduced from infinity to finite status, and (2) censored and/or encoded for transmission from *Ucs.* to *Cs.* The *Cs.* and *Ucs.* of the analyst must be so geared that the patient may intuitively act unconsciously as a veritable "ventriloquist" and be able to communicate with his/its extension, the "dummy," which he has unconsciously projected into the analyst's receptive unconscious. When all goes well, the analyst unconsciously experiences a unique combined, co-constructive capacity in which he speaks mysteriously as if "he is being spoken," not only by himself but also by a mysterious other. In states of resistance, however, the mysterious other voice may be that of the patient's "internal saboteur" (Fairbairn, 1944), who seeks to mislead or miscue the analyst.

Summary

The hidden order of countertransference is the analyst's mercifully "masochistic" and dedicated willingness to contain, or as we now say "absorb," "suffer," and "become," or "wear" (Grotstein, 2009b, 2009c, 2009d) execrable and detestable assigned roles (assigned by the "subjugating third subject" [Ogden, 1994, 2004]), or by the "dramaturge" (Grotstein, 2009b, 2009c, 2009d) in the act of lending himself to "exorcism." The analyst must be willing to "become" the patient's unconscious demons (the "Pietà of transference – countertransference").

The analyst is the innocent scapegoat, and the projecting patient (protesting unfairness) seeks to redress his loss of innocence by purloining it for himself from the analyst. (In unconscious phantasy, if not in actual reality, it once-upon-a-time *was* his until it was damaged and then stolen.)

In the depressive position, however, the patient, having successfully negotiated the required obstacles that P ↔ S ordains, now reverses his position and seeks to heal the wounds that he only now regrets that he caused his analyst to suffer. The covenant is the special bond that unconsciously exists between the infant and his parents and between the analysand and analyst that constitutes a sacred cooperation that facilitates healing, growth, and becoming evolved.

The infant, compelled by evolution's instincts, must become a successful predator to mother's prey – and vice versa – and the same with father. The mother and father, on the other hand, must accept the terms of the covenant to absorb this evolutionarily planned suffering for the sake of the race, and vow to spare and protect the infant and child-to-be as their sacred trust. This same covenant applies to the analysand and analyst.

In scripture (Genesis), God placed a mark on Cain's forehead both to signify that he had murdered his brother, Abel, but also to give him His protection against those who would attack him. I interpret that the hidden order of Cain's murder of Abel was out of his envy of him, and that it was really meant to attack God. I also interpret it as Cain's slaying of his own alter ego, in which Abel represented his purest, most innocent aspect (Christ, Billy Budd). But mostly, I consider the "Mark of Cain" to be the ever-living sign of his acknowledgment of his unavoidable sin as well as the ratification of his redemption by his acceptance of his guilt and responsibility.

Epilogue

Transference ↔ countertransference is the quintessence of "suffering love," which constitutes the hidden order of sadism and masochism's original altruistic and loftier as well as baser mandate. "Suffering love" (Nancy Goodman, personal communication, 2011) is also the hidden order of envy. The suffering analytic infant must projectively *transfer* his or her violent and painful demons into the analyst-parent, in whose love he feels secure, and the analyst-parent must, out of merciful self-sacrifice, be able to absorb ("lick") them and ultimately *become* them. Suffering another's pain is love's therapeusis. This consummate act of tolerance ("mimetic desire") is the surest antidote to violence, hate, and envy. This is the covenant sworn between analysand and analyst. Each of them is a trustee for the welfare of the true "analytic third," the once-and-forever-and-ever-evolving-unconscious-infant-of-psychoanalysis.

Such is the deeper mission and hidden order of countertransference in its relation to transference and its especial rendezvous with the negative transference.

Notes

The material in this chapter was originally presented at the Franz Alexander Memorial Lecture to the New Center for Psychoanalysis, Los Angeles, March 17, 2011.

1   I conceive of the two entities as paradoxically both indivisible *and* separate as well as collaborative *and* mutually opposing at the same time (as a "binary-oppositional" *and* interconnected as well as mutually defining structure, as follows: "transference ↔ countertransference").
2   Like Bion (1963, p. 11), I use "passion" in its biblical sense of "suffering," as in the "passion of Christ."
3   "Exorcism" has been introduced earlier.
4   Persecutory anxiety is comprised of the projecting subject's abandoned, lost selves, seeking repatriation.
5   Thematic Apperception Test.
6   The Los Angeles Psychoanalytic Society and Institute.
7   But what might I have felt if I had demurred from importing Bion, Mason, and Isaacs-Elmhirst?
8   Reparations for damage to an object are really impossible; moreover, the continuation of the guilt allows for the formation of a healthy superego.

Bibliography

Barratt, B. (1993) *Psychoanalysis and the Postmodern Impulse: Knowing and Being Since Freud's Psychology*. Baltimore, MD: Johns Hopkins University Press.

Bion, W. R. (1962) *Learning from Experience*. London: Heinemann.

Bion, W. R. (1963) *Elements of Psycho-Analysis*. New York: Basic Books.

Bion, W. R. (1965) *Transformations*. London: Heinemann.

Bion, W. R. (1970) *Attention and Interpretation*. London: Tavistock Publications.

Bion, W. R. (1992) *Cogitations*, F. Bion (ed.). London: Karnac.

Blake, W. (1789–1794) *Songs of Innocence and Experience*. Oxford, UK: Oxford University Press, 1967.

Bowlby, J. (1969) *Attachment and Loss. Vol. I: Attachment*. New York: Basic Books.

Brown, L. (2011) *Intersubjective Processes and the Unconscious: An Integration of Freudian, Kleinian and Bionian Perspectives*. London: Routledge.

Darwin, C. R. (1859) *On the Origin of Species by Means of Natural Selection*. London: John Murray.

Dodds, E. R. (1951) *The Greeks and the Irrational*. Berkeley, CA: University of California Press.

Fairbairn, W. R. D. (1944) Endopsychic structure considered in terms of object-relationships. In *Psychoanalytic Studies of the Personality* (pp. 82–136). London: Tavistock, 1952.

Fliess, R. (1942) The metapsychology of the analyst. *Psychoanalytic Quarterly*, 11: 211-227.

Frazer, J. (1922a) The transfer of evil. In *The Golden Bough: A Study in Magic and Religion* (pp. 624–632). New York: MacMillan.

Frazer, J. (1922b) Human scapegoats in classical antiquity. In *The Golden Bough: A Study in Magic and Religion* (pp. 669–679). New York: MacMillan.

Freud, S. (1912) The dynamics of transference. In *The Standard Edition of the Complete Psychological Works of Sigmund Freud*, J. Strachey (ed., trans.), vol. 12: 97–108. London: Hogarth Press, 1958.

Freud, S. (1913 [1912–1913]) *Totem and Taboo. Standard Edition*, 13: 1–64. London: Hogarth Press, 1957.

Freud, S. (1914) On narcissism: An introduction. *Standard Edition*, 14: 67–104. London: Hogarth Press, 1957.

Freud S. (1920) Beyond the pleasure principle. *Standard Edition*, 18: 3–66. London: Hogarth Press, 1955.

Girard, R. (1986) *The Scapegoat*, Y. Freccero (trans.). Baltimore, MD.: Johns Hopkins University Press.

Grotstein, J. (2000a) *Who Is the Dreamer Who Dreams the Dream? A Study of Psychic Presences*. Hillsdale, NJ: Analytic Press.

Grotstein, J. (2009b) *"... But at the Same Time and on Another Level ..."*: *Psychoanalytic Theory and Technique in the Kleinian/Bionian Mode. Vol. 1.* London: Karnac.

Grotstein, J. (2009c) *" ... But at the Same Time and on Another Level ... "*: *Clinical Applications in the Kleinian/Bionian Mode. Vol. 2.* London: Karnac.

Grotstein, J. (2009d) "The play's the thing wherein I'll catch the conscience of the king!" Psychoanalysis as a passion play. In A. Ferro and R. Basile, R. (eds.), *The Analytic Field: A Clinical Concept* (pp. 189–232). London: Karnac.

Hartmann, H. (1939) *Ego Psychology and the Problem of Adaptation.* New York: International Universities Press, 1958.

Klein, M. (1946) Notes on some schizoid mechanisms. In M. Klein, P. Heimann, S. Isaacs, and J. Riviere (eds.), *Developments in Psycho-Analysis* (pp. 99–110). London: Hogarth Press, 1952.

Klein, M. (1955) On identification. In M. Klein, P. Heimann, S. Isaacs, and R. Money-Kyrle (eds.), *New Directions in Psycho-Analysis* (pp. 309–445). London: Hogarth Press.

Lévi-Strauss, C. (1958) *Structural Anthropology*, C. Jacobson and B. Grundfest Schoepf (trans.), vol. 1. London: Penguin, 1972.

McDougall, J. (1985) *Theaters of the Mind: Illusions and Truth on the Psychoanalytic Stage.* New York: Basic Books.

Meltzer, D. (1978) *The Kleinian Development.* Strath Tay, Perthshire: Clunie Press.

Melville, H. (1851) *Moby Dick, or the Whale.* New York: Harper and Brothers.

Melville, H. (1924) *Billy Budd and other Tales.* In the *Standard Edition of Melville's Complete Works*, vol. 8. London: Constable and Company. Reprinted New York: Signet, 1961.

Morales, E. (1995) *The Guinea Pig: Healing, Food, and Ritual in the Andes.* Tucson, AZ: University of Arizona Press.

Ogden, T. (1994) *Subjects of Analysis.* Northvale, NJ: Jason Aronson.

Ogden, T. (2004) The analytic third: Working with intersubjective clinical facts. *International Journal of Psychoanalysis*, 75: 3–20.

Racker, H. (1968) *Transference and Counter-transference.* London: Hogarth Press.

11

TRANSFERENCE –
OR CAESURA?

Arnaldo Chuster

Rephrasing Freud's statement for my own convenience: There is much more continuity between autonomically appropriate quanta and the waves of conscious thought and feeling than the impressive caesura of transference and counter-transference would have us to believe. So ...? Investigate the caesura; not the analyst; not the analysand; not the unconscious; not the conscious; not sanity, not insanity. But the caesura, the link, the synapse, the (counter-trans)ference, the transitive-intransitive mood.

W. R. Bion, 1977b, p. 56

Introduction

This chapter aims to investigate the connections between two terms, "transference" and "caesura," in the light of W. R. Bion's work "Caesura" (1977b). I have chosen to develop this theme because I understand that it is in that paper that the two terms become interchangeable. Therefore, I propose to explore this vertex that allows for the possibility of exchanging the first and better-known term, whenever it is needed, for the second term, one that is much less saturated with meanings and so essentially more thought provoking. I will also complement these theoretical developments with some clinical material.

What is transference in Bion's works?

On many occasions, Bion exposed his concerns about words, using the metaphor of coins. As time goes by, coins lose their value marks as a result of long use. Similarly, instead of conveying an accurate communication words may cause many mistakes and misunderstandings. Sometimes they acquire a totally opposite meaning (Bion, 1976b).

In psychoanalysis, as in any other human activity, it couldn't be different. Although dealing with this problem constitutes a fundamental part of the analytical process, some theoretical terms also have suffered this unavoidable destiny in a short time. One could say that for Bion transference might be one of them. It is not difficult to recognize that the word transference, in addition to being a major part of analytic theory and the main therapeutic instrument of psychoanalysis, is a word that has also became part of ordinary speech, almost an institutional jargon. It suffers a clear saturation of its original meanings, and therefore, as one sees in many moments of his work, while taking care of the epistemological issues behind this problem, Bion introduced a progressive change in his psychoanalytical model that reached its summit in his theory of transformations (1965a, 1965b). In *Transformations*, he proposed: "I suggest a method of critical approach to psycho-analytic practice and not new psycho-analytical theories" (1965a, p. 6).

In Bion's work we will notice that transformations essentially come from something unknowable, ineffable, and unreachable, which he denominated "O" (1965a). It is the effect of this unknowable, ineffable movement – the evolution of "O" – that is at the bottom of any movement in the psychoanalytic link, which is then described in the languages of different psychoanalytic theories.

But in fact if transference is an evolution of "O" it cannot really be reported; it cannot really be written down as a text or easily translated as a speech, a circumstance that generates the well-known constant insufficiency in all the reports of analysis, whatever their outline. Indeed, a proper means of conveying in writing what analysis consists of has not yet been created. Nevertheless it can be emotionally felt and lived (one may call it an acquired *wisdom of the link*)[1] for those who have had the experience of being analyzed. It is an open system ruled by uncertainty and incompleteness.

Some aspects of the development of the concepts in Bion's work

When writing his first work on psychoanalysis, Bion used one of Freud's significant ideas, which is the presence of *surprise* that characterizes transference. Although "The Imaginary Twin" (Bion, 1950) does not mention Freud's well-known work "The Uncanny" (1919), the ideas are somewhat similar. The imaginary twin might be considered a "double" in the fullest Freudian sense: it emerges with feelings of surprise, as does the uncanny, causing wonder or fear or terror. In Bion's clinical examples one can notice these features in the interaction between the patient, the analyst, and the third element: the reality of a daunting rival unborn baby.

Later Bion will expand and describe those "uncanny" elements, spread more widely, as *emotional turbulence* (1976a, 1977a, 1977b, 1977c, 1979). They might be dealt by the *link* if both participants can make "the best of a bad job": One *"does not immediately know what the emotional storm is, but the problem is how to make the best of it, how to turn the adverse circumstance – as I choose to call it at the moment – to good account"* (Bion, 1979, p. 245, emphasis added).

In the 1950s, when investigating what are called "difficult" patients, Bion described a peculiar kind of transference – hasty and fragile, supported by a deep, constant terror of forthcoming annihilation that causes hatred for internal and external realities and for the mental apparatus capable of making contact with those realities.[2] He also described a predominance of destructive impulses to the point where they dominate the loving ones and transform them into sadism. Those features were the origin of his striking work on the twofold configuration of the *psychotic personality* versus the *non-psychotic personality* (1957).

In "On Arrogance" (1958), one can say that this configuration is described through the new vertex of the arrogance of the characters of the oedipal myth. Their struggle is around the knowledge of truth. Sexuality is no longer in the center of the field but at the outside edge. At this point, it is possible to think of transference as a twofold configuration in which one part is seeking and another part is rejecting the presence of an unattainable truth. Therefore, one can think of transference as a movement one may call a "tragic ethics": the mind needs the truth to survive but at the same time the truth is impossible to reach, and thus the only possible path is to *create something in order to fill the emptiness left by its absence.*

217

Because *thoughts* are the most important and common elements that are being created, all the time, Bion's "A Theory of Thinking" (1962a) naturally followed this vertex and led him to an amplification of his theory of the unconscious. This theory has the concept of *preconception* as the inaccessible root of the unconscious in the process (realization) of "giving birth" to *conceptions* (thoughts). "A Theory of Thinking" brought to light an idea of a constant tension: something *unfinished* and *incomplete* is present at the root of all achieved knowledge: truth. Therefore, one might say that in Bion's work psychoanalytic technique became a matter of approaching the place of truth in our lives. But this is not a truth one should identify with, but a terrible truth that one should try to learn to live with, in order to "learn from experience," which is the innermost feature of each creation and of our evolving human condition.

In *Learning from Experience*, Bion explains one of the basic clinical reasons for the change in this model:

> the phenomena present in the analysis cannot be identified with Freud's description of personality, which acts, during the phase when the pleasure principle predominates, to free itself of additional stimuli. Such a personality is, within certain limits, normal; the one which I am describing is quite abnormal. The activity which is manifested under the denomination of the pleasure principle, to free the personality from additional stimuli, is substituted, in the phase where the reality principle predominates, by the evacuation of the undesirable beta elements. A smile or a verbal affirmation is interpreted as a movement of evacuation and not as a communication of feeling.
> (1963b, p. 29, my translation)

On the other hand what is defined as "evacuation," caused by the existence in every individual of an "abnormal" personality, implies a link with space and time that needs to be investigated from a new vertex, which is provided by Bion's object of psychoanalysis: the *psychoanalytic object* (1962b, pp. 66–71) with the four elements he ascribes to it: the *preconception* ψ (ξ); the *realization*; the creation of *conceptions* (thoughts) in the narcissism–social-ism spectrum he terms ($\pm$Y); and the constant influence of biological *complexity* (M) (action) on the creation of conceptions.

The psychoanalytic object in turn leads to the idea of a *psychoanalytic field*, where the analyst works, investigating and observing the

218

preconceptions unfolding and sprouting in conceptions through *emotional experiences* (in the triangle of L, H, K). The whole concept seeks to clarify that what we can describe about transference is a limit that is only able to be determined just to some extent, because its real effects are felt in the sphere of an *indeterminate subject*, either in relation to an inaccessible origin in the past or in relation to a future that has not yet occurred. Thus we always have a complexity embodied in our analytic observations, although this theory was not available to Bion at that time (Chuster, 2010). Yet it was in the range of his wide scientific intuition.

In *Elements of Psychoanalysis* (1963a) and later in "The Grid" (1977a) Bion's attempts to systematize the *analytic field* simultaneously included the Freudian and Kleinian concepts of transference, while adding the idea of a *selected fact* captured by the psychoanalytic function of the personality of the analyst as well as the analysand.[3] His clear position is that what really matters is the *link* between the objects, and not the objects involved as such. This vertex of the link could be seen as making the difference between growing and deterioration.

The *analytic field* can be seen as an epistemological requirement that conceives of transference as a movement having the most heterogeneous components, any of which may contribute to the evolution (positive or negative) of an analysis. Subjectivity is not only created in the process of the development of psychogenesis (as described in the vertical axis of the Grid), which begins with "objects" at prenatal levels that cross the caesura of birth to go on developing from the experiences with the breast (plus the united sexual parental couple, the society, and the creative mind), and moves toward the acquisition of deductive scientific systems and sophisticated abstractions. Subjectivity is also simultaneously created to be *used* (the use being described in the horizontal axis of the Grid, in the sequence that begins with the definitory hypothesis – the element ψ – the interface of true/false or the defense against the unknown, and notation, attention, inquiry, and continues in an infinite variability of actions). The whole of the Grid provides the social, historical, and linguistic dimensions of the theoretical and practical change brought about by the model of the psychoanalytic object.

In *Transformations* (1965a) the concept of "O" and the evolutions of "O" are mainly seen as offering a way out of the repetitive impasses of the structures[4] that are not prepared to handle the complexity of the mind. Bion gives the examples of those patients who can laugh but cannot smile, or can be neither awake nor asleep, or who do not learn from their emotional experience, or who feel pain but do not suffer it, or who do not transmit meaning in their words and gestures, but instead convey inanimate objects and bizarre objects, placing into the analyst the effects of what he initially called the *beta-screen*: the result of alpha function failure we observe in its many degrees and possibilities.

Is transference just one of the possible transformations?

Even the wrong interpretation causes change; misinformation in the form of false—deliberately false—statements changes the situation. … [and then] how quickly can we see what good use could be made of that changed situation even though adverse?

(Bion, 1977b, p. 46)

As I noted earlier, Bion's theory of transformations represents an effort to introduce a methodological modification in the established and widely accepted relationship between structures and transference in traditional psychoanalysis. In fact, one might consider his theory of transformations as a scientific leap in relation to Freudian and Kleinian theories. In earlier works (Chuster, 1999, 2002, 2005a, 2005b, 2010) I sought to show that one of the possible ways of understanding this leap is to consider that Bion works with *spectral, non-structural models*, whose subject is *nonlinear* and *non-hermeneutic*: the truth as a never-attainable object.

Bion's description of these transformations had its origin in a Kleinian spatial metaphor: "the distance to which an object is projected is related to the duration and intensity of the projective identification" (Bion, 1965b, p. 21, my translation). According to the intensity, we have increasingly distinct degrees of perceptive distortion of psychoanalytic objects, in the following sequence: transformations in K, rigid-motion transformations, projective transformations, and transformations in hallucinosis.

Transformations in O are distinct from other transformations because their action does not occur in the field of knowledge, but in the domain of *becoming*. They occur in another system that does not involve the same problems of perceptive distortion present in the other types of transformations. We have here a movement where the meaning acquired through an emotional experience carries forward the existence of the subject's "truth." Bion wrote this process as K → O. The person *becomes* instead of "knowing about" himself. The aspect common to the other transformations is the fact that it occurs in the always-moving space between analyst and patient, characterized by the signs Tαα, Tαβ, Tρα, and Tρβ.[5]

Additionally, I think it is very important to mention the implicit question of *temporality* that complements the spatial parameter taken from the Kleinian theory. I think if one also follows the patient's transformations from the vertex of *twofold* space-time, it allows a better understanding of the model developed by Bion and its differences from previous models. Therefore, one may say that Bion's theory of transformations (1965a, 1965b) is in general a *spectral model* for observing transference as a transitory link between emotional experience ↔ spatiality ↔ temporality. One can also speak here of the matter of communication inside the Self, which contains elements we call "the body" (a space for the past or memories, notations, etc.), "the mind" (emotional experience in the present), and a "mental space" for further thoughts (future time).

In transformations in O, temporality is the *inaccessible element of the present*, although the "becoming" gets close to what one feels should have always been. One can speak of something like "incarnation" of a full meaning (Bion, 1965a, p. 163), the creation of wisdom being one of its facets. As wisdom never ceases to grow one has an open system.

Transformations in K involve processes of knowledge in general: thoughts that a thinker had previously thought. Any knowledge installs a split in temporality: one time before knowledge, and one after knowledge. It is a matter of a *referential temporality*. Here time can be used as a synonym for knowing something.

On the other hand, Transformations in K can be seen as a minimum level of transference. They could be something that Meltzer (1992) called a pre-formed transference. But besides this, in analysis, as in life, we can (and are obliged to) speak of an *objective time*. The session begins at such and such time and ends after 45 to 50 minutes, so many times a week, for x months and y years. The analyst, as well as the patients, takes holidays, speaks about dates of payment, discusses the interruptions, talks about late or early arrival and changes in the time of the consultations, and so on. But these discussions are not restricted to the mere formality of an agreement between the two parties. Patients can understand the most formal of agreements in a sense that is quite different from common sense. And this will not be noticed unless the analyst puts on his internal agenda another dimension of the mind that has nothing to do with common sense and rationality. Here we should note that, in the mind's subjectivity, there are various kinds of time – or a variety of ways of experiencing time.

Rigid-motion transformations correspond to the original definition of transference by Freud: past ideas, feelings, and emotions are transferred to the person of the analyst.[6] The past, as an irremediable absence, becomes a constant presence – as if it could replace the present. The feeling of a *circular temporality* results from the movement that occurs between being in the present and at the same time an absent-being in the past, which favors the linear conception of a deterministic subject.

Projective transformations correspond to Melanie Klein's original definition of unconscious phantasy. Their presence implies the problem of using adequate language, or any words at all, to convey the meaning that comes from a vision of the world dominated by tyrannical and uncontrollable forces. The means of expression that are available can result in some cases in responses that belong to the range of phenomena known as psychosomatic. The temporality is oscillatory, but although each action has an equal and contrary reaction it is not directly perceivable since the language to adequately express the link is lacking. The phenomenon can be metaphorically compared to water flowing within or filtering through a wall: we do not know where it started, but we know that the water should not be running through there. However, in some individuals, the "infiltration" finds its way out as an artistic expression.

Transformations in hallucinosis expose at first how the nature of time in its totality is impossible to apprehend. For some patients, the aesthetic experience of this impossibility, resulting from the incompleteness and infinitude experienced *vis-à-vis* the unconscious, is not tolerated. As a result, their emotional experience is defensively fragmented by rivalry with O, by the cruelty of the superego, and by moral logic. The practical result of these features is *atemporality*, not in the sense of the nonexistence of time, but in the sense of a confusional state, where the past, the present, and the future become indistinguishable one from the other, a state that is accompanied by a feeling of concreteness that must triumph over any opposition. *Transformations in hallucinosis* promote an excess of sensoriality, through the stimulation of memory, desire, and the need for comprehension, and favor the installation of a system of values that promotes acting-out with no regard for any consequences, like the states that can be found in drug addictions, compulsive behavior, and so forth.

Should we use the term caesura instead of the term transference?

The caesura [...] is the important thing; that is the source of thinking.

W. R. Bion, 1976b, p. 53

If transference is a movement that causes emotional turbulence in the analytic link (affecting both participants), one can say that it is not the repetition (defining transference according to Freud and Klein) that matters to Bion, but rather the new and unknown that may emerge – in addition to the fact that there is no identical repetition; something is always modified by the factor M (complexity) of the psychoanalytic object. This position is very clearly established throughout the his chapter "Notes on Memory and Desire" (1967) and in *Attention and Interpretation* (1970a, p. 4; 1970b).

The term *caesura* as used by Bion fundamentally conveys this quality of something constantly new and unknown moving in the work of analysis. Thus, when he quotes Freud – "There is much more continuity between intrauterine life and earliest infancy than the impressive caesura of the act of birth allows us to believe" (1976b, p. 59) – he reintroduces the vigor contained in the meanings of generation and upbringing, links and transit, birth and death, hidden and explicit, blindness and perception of the unexpected. But whenever or wherever it is, it is something that emerges with a twofold movement: (counter-trans) – ference.

Faced with the many meanings brought by the complexity of the Self,[7] the analyst needs to be cautious, which means to develop a negative capability – an expression that Bion borrowed from the poet Keats, referring to the capacity to tolerate mysteries, half-truths, and uncertainties. It is a mental state equivalent to the state of mind without memory, desire, and the need for comprehension, which is free to interact with the transformations of the analytic link. "The analyst needs to be divested or denuded of his memories and his desires so as to leave room for him to be open to the present" (Bion, 1997, p. 44).

223

In other words, when transference is expected, when it is hoped to be found, when there is a theory pushing to interpret it, what appears in its proper place is the *transferred* (the contained), through which it can be believed that transferential interpretations are possible, simply by mechanically following the associative flow, as if sonority or common logic could account for the actual caesura of the link. The transferred constitutes a part of transience, but it does not produce transience.

From the point of view of the effect of interpretations, the link is not so much altered by what is transferred; the link is altered *by the elements that produce the transience* (the container and alpha function). That is to say, altering the container, amplifying the mental space, problematicizing.[8] Thus the movement of transference does not occur without producing a change from one mental state to another – *it is the thing-in-itself that moves for both participants* that constitutes transference.[9] Therefore, analysis must always speak the language of emotional experience (passions, as the main source of meanings, always return to the surface), confirming Freud's idea that transference is that which expresses the "essential" (1914).

The emotional turbulence–caesura spectrum model as a condition for the observation of transference

> We must consider the transitive characteristic of the free-association and the interpretation.
>
> W. R. Bion, 1977b, p. 51

One of the consequences of working with the idea of *caesura* is to establish a critique on the simplistic method of regarding transference as a way to extrapolate knowledge from one state of mind to another, as this tendency may paralyze creative thought and the capacity to observe. The fact that something might be considered simple should not be taken as a simplification.

It is clear that Freud's phrase about the caesura of birth was intended to *make a critique* on Otto Rank's broad use of the idea of birth trauma; there is much more continuity between intrauterine life and earliest infancy than the impressive caesura of the act of birth allows us to believe. Wide uses usually are simplifications that create a rationality that is doomed to be a closed way of thinking.

Thousands of examples to illustrate this point can be given, for instance, the Euclidean geometry and its five postulates. The most famous one is that parallel lines can never meet. No one ever dreamed of contesting this, and yet there came a day when mathematicians showed that it was possible to create other geometries, non-Euclidean geometries, which turned out to be much richer and more creative. As a consequence different concepts of certain "spaces" were produced, paving the way for Einstein's Theory of Relativity. Without the postulation of a caesura, this discovery would never have been possible. In this sense, the concept of caesura questions habitual ways of thinking, enabling us to direct our thoughts toward new possibilities.

Psychoanalysis implies the careful observation of facts in order to capture the emergence of *new and unknown* elements. This observation is not random, but is planned to occur in a specific space, and requires determined principles to support the procedures. As the ethics of observation are unavoidably associated here with the creation of an interpretative language, I have called these principles *ethical-aesthetics* (Chuster, 1999, 2002, 2005b), with the main intention being to emphasize the complex essence and infinite reality of the unconscious.[10]

We may approach the matter by considering the problems involved in perceiving the fundamental nature of emotional turbulence implicit in each session of analysis, and the conditions that allow it to be brought into language capable of producing a *transformation in psychoanalysis*.[11] The theme is obviously not new, but it constitutes Bion's personal approach, a particular way of presenting transference as a phenomenon "in transience" that *always refers to a caesura* between two diverse mental states.

The term *transience* points to the German title of Freud's 1916 article, *Vergänglichkeit*, and stresses the intrinsically transitory nature of psychoanalysis as *a process linked with life*. If we do not appreciate this characteristic, there is no way of making use of the process, no way of "making the best of a bad job" (Bion, 1979). In other words, it is fundamental that, as psychoanalysts, we observe that human beings and the human condition are constitutively historical. This means that we cannot approach the human condition if we do not understand and interpret what is acquired and created in the course of history. At the same time, analytic history is constructed, and generates instruments that the relationship itself might use to expand such history. Here among those instruments one may find what Bion called *private myths* (a way to facilitate – or not – the transference-countertransference movements) and their significance, as regarded from the vertex of the Freudian concept of "Constructions in Analysis" (1937).

In a broad sense, in any analytic process it is a matter of re-signifying the history, valuing and stressing its singularities, and investigating the process of thought and the events that this investigation may produce.

The turbulence–caesura spectrum model and the creative imagination

> I would suggest that we need to consider the future of an analogy, the future of an 'illusion', the future of 'transference' which is the name given by psycho-analysts to a particular and potent form of relationship. If one could arrange the term, spectrum-wise, in ascending power of emotional drive it could be: generation → analogy → transference → delusion → illusion → group illusion → hallucination → asymmetry → degeneration.
>
> Bion, 1977a, p. 26

As has already been said, using a theory of transformations allows for a nonconventional and nonpsychiatric vertex.[12] This permits an *imaginative conjecture* that visualizes the whole population along a *spectrum* that includes at one end a number of infra-analyzable individuals (for whom it would be difficult to establish an analytic process), and, on the opposite end, a much more restricted number of ultra-analyzable individuals, that is to say, individuals who would manage to accomplish their analysis whoever the analyst and whatever the technique were to be. One of these individuals was, no doubt, Freud. On the other hand, it is clear that analytic practice is not absolutely concerned with these extremes, but rather that the result depends decisively on the quality of the experience with the analyst and his background. This is the mainstream upon which analysts and their institutions focus, and which they take responsibility for.

Can we do something to amplify the possibilities of the infra-analyzable fraction of the spectrum, or is this question just a kind of intellectual prejudice that should be excluded from our concerns?

Let us consider for a moment that within every individual there exist all the gradations of the spectrum. What resources exist in psychoanalysis today that can influence the quality of the analysis and of the analyst in dealing with this spectrum? Are there, at the pole of the ultra-analyzable, any elements that we could use with the infra-analyzable?

I think that once again this flexibility can be obtained if one starts from the example of Freud, who, being an example of an ultra-analyzable individual, knew how to take full advantage of what the moment had to offer, that is to say, to go straight to the "key point."

One can see that Freud did not let himself be intimidated by all the explicit tragedy in what his patients were saying. His scientific courage allowed him to turn his attention to the caesura of the explicit tragedy brought by his patients. Despite all the adverse circumstances, one can say that for him the *mystery* of psychic life had always been the object of his investigations and respectful admiration: there has always been much more continuity between ...

But would it not be true to say that all the people who come to us for analysis are in some way "extraordinary"?

I feel that this question only acquires deeper meaning in the universe of the complexity inherent in the human mind. It is from this vertex that people become extraordinary; it is a matter of *turbulence*.

In quantum physics such questions are not unusual. It is said that Heisenberg, on his deathbed, declared that he had two questions to ask God. "Why Relativity and why turbulence?" And he goes on, "I sincerely believe that he must have an answer to the first question ..." (Penrose, 1995, p. 87, my translation).

Although Heisenberg was obviously referring to turbulence in physics, the points in common with the observation of emotional turbulence are clearly quite extensive. After all, both in physics and in psychoanalysis we are observing and dealing with transient systems, that is to say *unstable systems*, which consequently can only exist in three or more dimensions.[13]

Turbulence–caesura is like a *limit* in that it is instability in action, also signifying that a void has appeared. It is the expression of random movement, a witness to the tendency toward chaos. How can one analyze someone who is at the heart of this experience? Very probably we will never have the answer because it is in the field of the unknowable. We can, however, consider that psychoanalysis may help people enormously to free up their words and their ability to take decisions, and in so doing also may liberate their imagination.

It is up to the psychoanalyst to make use of *speculative imagination* in the same way that any scientist would do with the object of his research, and therefore, he or she may cross the caesuras in order to give birth to meanings, ideas, thoughts, feelings, changes. I quote Bion on this matter: "Unless the analyst allows himself the exercise of his speculative imagination he will not be able to produce the conditions in which the germ of a scientific idea can flourish" (1997, p. 46).

Clinical material

Case 1

In the month of December, with Christmas approaching, the late afternoon in Rio de Janeiro is characterized by extensive traffic jams. In the area known as "the lagoon," near my office in Ipanema, the traffic jams are even bigger because of the curiosity of the drivers who – after going underground through a tunnel – slow down to admire the world's biggest Christmas tree, beautifully illuminated and set up in the middle of the lake.

The patient, 42 years old, whom I will call W, is not unaware of the existence of this obstacle after coming out of the tunnel. If he does not take the trouble to leave his work somewhat earlier than usual he will certainly be late for his session at this time of the year. However, he also knows, as a result of his analysis, that he always leaves things to the last minute, making them a source of anxiety and irritation. And it was a repetition like this that occurred, as he let me know, calling me on his cell phone from inside the tunnel that leads to the lagoon neighborhood. He ended up arriving approximately 20 minutes late. He came into my office with an expression which was a mixture of breathlessness and alarm. He was carrying a metal object in his hands and as soon as he was settled on the couch, he began to talk about it.

The patient sought analysis after his third official marriage failed,[14] also associated with developmental difficulties at work. Previously, and in the interval between marriages, all of his intimate relationships had failed. He broke up with all his relatives. But what was shown for me to observe was a person who had explanations for all of his failures and all of his explanations placed the responsibility on other people, never on himself, although he showed himself to be intellectually willing to accept the theory that he had some strong participation in the breakups.[15]

W is an industrialist. He has a small factory that produces precision instruments used in naval technology, and that is why he explained to me that the metal part he was holding in his hands, which he had been developing for a new satellite navigation system, had a flaw that none of the engineers could understand. But, when he was stuck in the traffic, concerned about his lateness, "being forced to look at the horrible Christmas tree," he tried to "switch off" – and it was then that he understood what was wrong with the part, and he proudly began to explain to me the technological alterations that he would have to make. But I interrupted him to ask if we would also have to fail – talking about things that would hold us up in our understanding of what was happening at that precise moment – or if we could think that he managed to discover the flaw because he looked at the tree and not because he avoided it. I felt that he was surprised by my interpretation and remained silent for some moments. He then told me that he had had a bad night because of the part. He had been in an intermediate state between sleeping and wakefulness. He told me that he often finds himself in this peculiar state when he is worried. I said that "peculiar" could be the delay in finding something or someone, including me in that very moment, to solve his problems, which left him with feelings that were difficult to describe. He said that they were thermal sensations, like "cold water running down my spine," or "a progressive dark chill under the skin."

W's mother had a brain aneurysm in the sixth month of her pregnancy with him. She was in a coma for two months but recovered consciousness, apparently without any sequel. The birth was premature; it happened as soon as she recovered from the coma, and she was unable to breastfeed her child, claiming to be too weak and too confused. Everything indicates that she blamed the pregnancy for what happened to her. W complains many times that she was always an emotionally distant mother. I add, in this opportunity to write the words, a "cold" and "chilly" mother, in contrast to how she was with his two younger brothers. What can W do when faced alone with what one might call *the ceaseless motion of the incomprehensible bustle of life?*[16] Many times, the movement that he makes draws him close to objects "in a coma" (I sometimes catch myself feeling sleepy), which produces in him both the failures and the feeling of loneliness, feelings that he does everything to avoid. But how could he manage to face the immense terror?

In the course of the analysis, I have told him in many different ways that he appears to be seeking a situation where he can be married, but neither with himself nor with me or any other person, and that we are in a situation where I become a kind of a distant analyst to him, with whom he can't speak about himself. Yet at the same time this same analyst shows him that there is always something new, like life flowing, which could help him decide to face situations instead of running away from them. Is the analyst acting like Socrates' midwife? Bringing to light the psychoanalytic function of the personality by showing descriptively the emotional turbulence/caesura?

Case 2

M, 33 years old, a lawyer and journalist, frequently brings to her sessions mental states that seem to be the outcome of painful feelings that are not perceivable. The shift from one state to another is dramatic. M says that she constantly finds herself torn between two terrible alternatives that she compares to those in the film *Sophie's Choice*; however this type of emotional experience does not appear in her speech during the sessions. These states, which seem to me to be related to violent and very primitive situations, make possible some imaginative conjectures about the baby that she was. The reminiscences of the baby seem to be present in mental states described as "laziness, ill-will, bad temper." She complained that yesterday's session seems too far away from today and she made a long silence. Interaction with such states may produce sleepiness in the analyst if he loses sight of the suggested caesura. For this reason I can imaginatively conjecture that if she were to go to the opposite, to the "feeling of terror of some Sophie's choice," we would find a situation in which she felt this terror but did not suffer from it – and that what were probably *transformations in hallucinosis* were taking up her objective time.

The hypothesis of a communication (through projective identification) with the imago of a mother physically present but emotionally absent also makes it possible to conjecture that the analyst is being placed in a situation where he can feel what it is like to have a mother like this. But, at the same time, it also makes it possible to feel what it is like to have an adult patient who stays completely motionless on the couch, speaking in an almost inaudible monotone, session after session, about the same things, or remaining in silence for long periods of time. How is it possible to perceive the new, unknown element that emerges in this repetitive movement?

Her reactions to the slightest changes in the analyst or in the setting appear to me to indicate that she seems to be threatened by a transformation in O (what could it mean – "break-down, break-up, break-through?")? So I try to observe her reactions to such changes.

In fact, she frequently behaves as if she were unaware of time. Consequently she does not realize that one can only get from analysis what one puts into it. Sometimes this is true in a broader sense: if she does not change, the most likely outcome is that life will change her, and always for the worse.

In a session in which I was observing her extended silence, there came spontaneously to my mind the image of the *Pietà* – and then I realized that she had spoken to me weeks before about the statue, a replica of which I have in my office. I questioned her about the possibility of her not being able to say everything that came into her mind, because she had a *"Maria's choice"* to make (I said the name Maria deliberately – coincidentally the name of her mother – instead of M, the patient's name). She was surprised and for the first time shed a tear and told me that it was always a risky experience to be sincere with her mother.

In the following sessions, it was possible to think that sincerity, feelings of guilt, punishment, and betrayal of confidence were associated. A dream on this occasion showed *a child wanting to speak but giving up and bumping into a chair*. I said that she was punishing herself for not being able to be sincere to herself, but simultaneously blaming someone for this. This someone, depending on the moment, could be herself, the analyst (in the chair) or any other person. She seemed to understand and agree. But what does it mean to agree with the interpretation? The transformation in K is merely *referential in time*: at that moment something was knowledgeable.

In the next session, after the weekend, she told me that she almost fainted at home while crossing from the bedroom to the kitchen. Alarmed, she went to see a doctor. After the long habitual silence, she said, with her also habitual emotionless discourse: "but that seems to be something that happened years ago," and explained that the doctor had diagnosed high blood pressure, and then she went back to her silence. I described the situation (in my conjectures: a caesura), stressing the absence of any feeling in the face of a situation that on the previous day had visibly alarmed her. She then shouted angrily and in a very sharp tone (generally her tone is low and almost inaudible) that if I was not alarmed by the problem of her high blood pressure it was because I "didn't give a shit" about her state of health. For a moment I observed the surprise of the explosion: How is it that she could speak so loud and not use her ability to express her feelings? Where is the caesura?

I said that she was insinuating that if my feeling were heartfelt then I would confess that I was doing exactly what she said I was doing. If this could be the cause of her blood pressure we were speaking about the pressure that an old repressed hostility, unable to find an outlet, could be causing her.

In the subsequent session she brought a dream in which she was holding a very small child in her arms. Someone said to her very angrily: deliver that baby because this baby is not yours ... Is this dream a picture of that moment of her analysis? I said she oscillates between the fear that the analysis will be successful (being able to hold and be responsible for the baby) and the fear that it will fail (denying responsibility for the baby).

Could we speak further about the perception of an oscillating temporality, in the pressure that goes rapidly up and down, characteristic of projective transformations, and also in a way a transformation in O, in which the primitive language finds expression in the emotional experience: the caesura in the session?

Notes

1 "Wisdom seems to have this capacity for survival by changing its route and then reappearing in unexpected places" (Bion, 1979, p. 256).
2 Realities and new thoughts became the daunting unborn baby.
3 The concept of Poincaré's *selected fact* is deeply connected to Bion's indeterministic model; it stresses the transience of the analytic phenomenon, and may be compared with the modern theories of instability and chaos. This model gives a fundamental meaning to the principle of the arrow of time, without which we are incapable of understanding the main characteristics of nature that are present in the human mind: its unity and its diversity. The arrow of time, common to all parts of the universe, evidences this unity. As for diversity, it is

witnessed by the presence of objects produced by the irreversible processes of non-equilibrium (where life exists, entropy exists and, therefore, so do irreversible processes).

4 "We need to re-view commonplace formulations – psychotic, neurotic, psychosomatic, soma-psychotic and so forth – to consider what we think, from our own experience, those things are when we meet them" (Philips, 1970, p. 22, my translation).

5 Taα represents the transformations of the analyst that produce an interpretation, and Taβ the interpretation. Tpα represents the transformation cycle of the patient, which can be a dream process; Tpβ is a dream or speech of the patient in the session.

6 "This reproduction appearing with unwelcome fidelity always contains a fragment of infantile sex life, therefore of the Oedipus complex and its off-shoots, and it is played regularly in the sphere of transference, i.e. the relationship with the physician." Sigmund Freud, *Beyond the Pleasure Principle* (1920) *SE* 18, p. 18; quoted by Bion (1965, pp. 18–19).

7 These include meanings previously developed by the ideas of the container–contained relationship, of the selected fact, of a preconception seeking a realization to be transformed into a conception, and of the relationship between thing and no-thing and between I and not-me.

8 This also means amplifying the capacity of alpha-function, and modifying the repetitions that originate in the pattern that began with maternal reverie. For the analyst, it always means, as Blanchot wrote, that *La reponse est le malheur de la question* (the answer is the misfortune of the question).

9 Therefore, in order to capture its surprise value, one must try to be free from desire, memory, the need for comprehension, and sensorial interferences (Bion, 1965a, 1967). Analysis is only operative if the analyst manages to divest himself of those elements.

10 I recall here the words of John Milton in *Paradise Lost*, Book III, which Bion quoted so many times: "*The rising world from waters dark and deep ... won from the void and formless infinite*" to express the inaccessible unconscious.

11 Transformations that produce a K → O movement: a transformation that allows the patient to have autonomy in the direction of becoming what he should always have been.

12 I refer to the dialogue between P.A. and Robin in Bion's *A Memoir of the Future, Book 2: The Past Presented* (1977c, pp. 125–126), which we can summarize as follows: the psychiatric concepts conceive of a split person. The splitting is useful for the purposes of articulate speech, but it obscures the thing that transcends the frontiers of grammar.

13 This means that dual or two-dimensional systems are idealized systems; they do not correspond to the realities of nature.

14 "Like birth, the caesura of marriage is dramatic; it may obscure the fact that the events at the time of marriage and after are influenced by events which take place long before the marriage. As Freud put it with regard to birth, events in the patient's mind are greatly influenced by events which were in fact intra-uterine. Using this for theoretical purposes, events which are in the womb of time eventually show themselves in the conscious life of the person concerned who then has to act in the situation which has now become actual" (Bion, 1977b, p. 49).

15 "Some patients repeatedly state that they have some particular experience and then give the reason why – making it part and parcel of their formulation ... But the only world in which causes can be said to be a prominent feature is the world of *things* – not the world of people, or characters, or personalities. The patient who is always telling us that he feels such and such 'because ...', is avoiding a particular relationship which exists between one character and another" (Bion, 1977b, p. 51).

16 A phrase from Gustav Mahler in the lyrics of *The Song of the Earth*.

Bibliography

Bion, W. R. (1950) The imaginary twin. In *Second Thoughts* (pp. 3–22). London: William Heinemann, 1967.

Bion, W. R. (1957) The differentiation of the psychotic from the non-psychotic personalities. In *Second Thoughts* (pp. 43–64). London: William Heinemann, 1967.

Bion, W. R. (1958) On arrogance. In *Second Thoughts* (pp. 86–92). London: Heinemann, 1967.

Bion, W. R. (1962a) A theory of thinking. In *Second Thoughts* (pp. 110–119). London: Heinemann, 1967.

Bion, W. R. (1962b) *Learning from Experience*. London: Heinemann.

Bion, W. R. (1963a) *Elements of Psychoanalysis*. London: Heinemann.

Bion, W. R. (1963b) *Aprender da Experiencia e Elementos da Psicanálise*. Rio de Janeiro, Zahar.

Bion, W. R. (1965a) *Transformations: Change from Learning to Growth*. New York: Basic Books. Also in W. R. Bion, *Transformations*, London: Heinemann, 1965.

Bion, W. R. (1965b) *Transformações: Mudança do aprendizado ao crescimento* (M. Paterson, trans.) (Transformations: Change from Learning to Growth). Rio de Janeiro: Imago, 1991.

Bion, W. R. (1967) Notes on memory and desire. *Psychoanalytic Forum*, 11(3): 271–280. Reprinted in E. B. Spillius (ed.), *Melanie Klein Today*, vol. 2. *Mainly Practice* (pp. 17–21). London: Routledge, 1988.

Bion, W. R. (1970a) *Attention and Interpretation*. London: Tavistock.

Bion, W. R. (1970b) *Attenção e Interpretação*. Rio de Janeiro: Imago.

Bion, W. R. (1976a) Emotional turbulence. In *Clinical Seminars and Four Papers*, F. Bion (ed.), (pp. 223–233). Abingdon, UK: Fleetwood, 1987.

Bion, W. R. (1976b) On a quotation from Freud. In *Clinical Seminars and Four Papers*, F. Bion (ed.), (pp. 234–238). Abingdon, UK: Fleetwood, 1987.

Bion, W. R. (1977a) The Grid. In *The Grid and Caesura*. Rio de Janeiro: Imago. Reprinted in W. R. Bion, *Two Papers: The Grid and Caesura* (pp. 1–33). London: Karnac, 1989.

Bion, W. R. (1977b) Caesura. In *Two Papers: The Grid and Caesura*. Rio de Janeiro: Imago. Reprinted in W. R. Bion, *Two Papers: The Grid and Caesura* (pp. 35–56). London: Karnac, 1989.

Bion, W. R. (1977c) *A Memoir of the Future, Book 2: The Past Presented*. Rio de Janeiro: Imago.

Bion, W. R. (1979) Making the best of a bad job. In *Clinical Seminars and Four Papers* (pp. 247–257). Abingdon, UK: Fleetwood, 1987.

Bion, W. R. (1997) *Taming Wild Thoughts*, F. Bion (ed.). London: Karnac.

Chuster, A. (1999) *W. R. Bion: Novas Leituras – a psicanálise: dos modelos científicos aos princípios ético-estéticos*. Rio de Janeiro: Companhia de Freud.

Chuster, A. (2002) *W. R. Bion: Novas leituras – a psicanálise: dos princípios ético-estéticos à clínica*. Rio de Janeiro: Companhia de Freud.

Chuster, A. (2005a) A Brief Survey on the Difference Between Fantasy and Imagination in the Light of Bion's Ideas. Paper presented to the Massachusetts Institute of Psychoanalysis (MIP), February 2005.

Chuster, A. (2005b) Interpretações analíticas e princípios ético-estéticos de observação. Paper presented to the 44th IPAC, Rio de Janeiro, July 2005.

Chuster, A. (2010) The origins of the unconscious: Framework of the future mind. In J. V. Buren and S. Alhanati, *Primitive Mental States: A Psychoanalytic Exploration of the Origins of Meaning*. London: Routledge.

Freud, S. (1914) The history of the psychoanalytic movement. *The Standard Edition of the Complete Psychological Works of Sigmund Freud*, J. Strachey (ed., trans.). London: Hogarth Press, vol. 14: 1–66.

Freud, S. (1916) On transience. *SE* 14: 303–307.

Freud, S. (1919) The uncanny. *SE* 17: 217–256.

Freud, S. (1937) Constructions in analysis. *SE* 23: 255–270.

Meltzer, D. (1992) *The Claustrum*. Strath Tay, Perthshire: Clunie Press.

Penrose, R. *A Nova Mente do Imperador* (The New Mind of the King). Rio de Janeiro: Campus, 1995.

Philips, F. (1970) Prologue. In W. R. Bion, *Attenção e Interpretação* (p. 86). Rio de Janeiro: Imago, 1970.

12

TRANSFERENCE
MINUTE TO MINUTE
Analysis of an analysis

Robert Oelsner

Freud created a method of listening to patients' free associations with a free-floating, unbiased attention. But he soon realized that while he was doing this some of his patients' powerful emotional links to the analyst contaminated the sterile field of the surgery of the mind he hoped to perform. He called these effects transferences, and then noticed that what had at first looked like a disturbance was actually a rich source of information about the gems of the unconscious that he was seeking. Although he acknowledged that feelings were also stirred up in the analyst when exposed to the transferences of the patients – which he therefore christened "counter-transferences." However he did not think of them in the same way he thought of transferences but only as shortcomings of the analyst, and recommended the analysis of the analysts to overcome or prevent them. This was the origin of the institution of the training analysis. Both Hinshelwood and Faimberg (this volume) have done fine studies of Freud's countertransferences, which he did not then have the tools to use for the benefit of the treatment. Melanie Klein's method did not differ from Freud's in this respect.

As Hinshelwood (this volume) notes, it was around the decade of the 1950s that a shift in the field of observation occurred – although I would rather call it an expansion. This change to the analytic field came to include the analyst's emotional resonance to the patient's communications as an additional tool for the analytic work, which was no longer equated to surgery on a surgical field. Instead, there has been an acceptance that the analyst's mind, both conscious and unconscious, is regularly being engaged in the patient's externalization of the internal conflictive object relations now circulating between patient and analyst. The work of Willy and Madeleine Baranger (1961; Baranger et al., 2009) in Argentina on the psychoanalytic field is a valuable expression of this expansion.

Certainly Klein's model of the mind as an internal world of objects (and not solely the superego, as Freud theorized) in relation to the ego, along with her discovery of projective identification,[1] called for such a shift in the theory of technique. In a sense Klein's internal world is a field created by the relations of the self to its objects and by the objects with each other. The transference-countertransference need not be anything other than a reflection of this.[2]

It is likely that Heinrich Racker in Buenos Aires and Paula Heimann in London are the two analysts best known for their groundbreaking work on the meaning of analysts' emotional responses in relation to those of their patients, and who thus invite us to bring our countertransferences out of the closet. Analysts were no longer to feel ashamed or faulty, and should acknowledge their countertransference as a natural counterpart to the patients' transferences and a normal part of analytic work. Racker in particular devoted his short time as analyst, before being interrupted by his premature death, to an exploration of the valuable aspects of countertransference, its unconscious sources, its meanings, and its technical uses. We can only agree with Hanna Segal (2000–2003), who often remarked that "countertransference is the best of servants but the worst of masters."

A brief vignette may serve to illustrate what I am trying to say.

On a Monday, a male patient reports to his analyst some quite eloquent material about his emotional experience during the weekend break. There are multiple allusions to the transference situation in which he either felt that a father was busy with a child in his arms and someone had to wait. Or a child having to wait for too long for his food. Also his suspicion about the girlfriend not really wanting him other than for his money and then sending him away, and so on. The analyst understood well the transference dimension of all of these pictures but felt tied up when trying to tell the patient what he thought was going on. This was remarkable since this is an experienced analyst who is not typically shy. (But a subtle comment of the patient – that when he wanted to bring things up with his partner they inevitably ended in a fight – could have predisposed the analyst to fear that if he interpreted what he thought was happening, they too would end up in an argument. The analyst indeed commented, when he presented the case, that he thought the patient would dismiss any transference interpretation.) As the report of the session continued the patient talked about his father letting him have a room in his home but not reaching out for a connection with him and asked himself what the father's actual feelings toward him might be since he did not tell him. This gave us the clue to the understanding of the analyst's position: in the patient's view he had "become" the father who would not connect emotionally to the son, manifested in his lack of speaking about what was going on between them – the transference. But on a second stratum the analyst's inhibition in interpreting the transference also indicated a role reversal (see Borgogno and Taglianti, this volume). Here the analyst identified with the son of a cold, dismissive father/patient and therefore was shy of addressing the "here and now between us." He had picked up the role of the patient feeling inadequate and fearing rejection. (The patient would often come late to his sessions or miss them, alleging he had important business to attend to, thus defending himself from a father/analyst who would not engage with him.)[3]

In the example above we can note that just as the analyst had a countertransference response to the patient's unconscious phantasy, so the patient in turn picked up the analyst's countertransference.

An almost humorous situation I recall that may illustrate communication of this kind involved an analyst who would typically look carefully into both his transference and countertransference before making his interpretations. On one occasion when he based his interpretation solely on his observations of the patient's discourse, the patient – a young architect – brought up his concern about a designer on his staff who had come in with a patch on his right eye and had to manage to make his drawings with just the left one! Yet on second thought, it appeared that in his response that day the analyst had also enacted the patient's difficulty in taking into account more than one point of view.

This brings us to the now-renowned concept of enactment, which is the effect of the patient's transferences not only on the analyst's feelings but also on his actions, a response to a large extent based on projective identification. The forerunners of the concept of enactment can be found as early as 1956 and 1958 in Grinberg's concept of projective counter-identification, followed by Bion, who wrote that "The analyst feels he is being manipulated so as to be playing a part, no matter how difficult to recognize, in somebody else's phantasy ..." (1961, p. 149) and further elaborated in his (1962a, 1962b) expansion of Klein's (1946) concept of projective identification. He there posited that even a baby has some innate ability to manipulate the object, just as patients have – with regard to mother or analyst respectively – so as to have an actual effect on them, a process he called "realistic projective identification."

Some stimulating work with British contemporary analysts in London over the past 15 years has led me to incorporate their technical developments in own my work. Joseph Sandler (1976), Betty Joseph (1999), R. D. Hinshelwood (2000), and many others who followed studied the subtle ways in which analysts play roles that their patients in unconscious ways invite them to play. The expansion of the field in which analysts are now "participant" observers requires some modification in technique, which involves the careful monitoring of the two analyses, rather than only one, that are going on in the room – the patient's and the analyst's. It also speaks to the helpfulness of running one's clinical work by a third party, whether this may be a supervisor, a consultant, or an experienced group of colleagues, so as to gain more insight into the unnoticed countertransference blind spots that we are all prone to.[4]

Just consider Freud, for instance, who – had he been supervised by Betty Joseph – would have realized, as Hinshelwood (this volume) notes, that he was enacting with the Wolf Man his patient's idiosyncratic primal scene.

Perhaps Heimann's analysis with Klein would have ended on a different note too had Klein had the tools we now have, which enable us to make better use of our countertransference enactments.[5] According to Elizabeth Bott Spillius (1992), Klein was distrustful about the use of countertransference, feeling that it could lead analysts to put their own unanalyzed conflicts on their patients' shoulders.[6] Could Klein, owing to the state of technique at the time, have perhaps been putting on Heimann's shoulders her own unanalyzed countertransference, as we refer to it now?

Most of the writings of the contemporary Kleinian group regard the observation of the patient–analyst link (and not just the patient's associative material) as the source of data about the relations of the patient's self with its internal objects and the status of his or her contact with reality. For an example, consider Steiner, who wrote:

> When I could examine my own responses it was possible to see how the role I was led to play was, at one level, a way of evading the internal situation which the patients individually communicated through the evocation of states of fragmentation or dissonance. I was instrumental in sustaining a *psychic retreat* which helped them avoid contact with reality and which interfered with their development.
>
> (2000, p. 253)

Following these developments, "clinical material" for contemporary Kleinian analysts is now the totality of the situation that is being structured *between* analyst and patient minute to minute (Joseph, 1989; O'Shaughnessy, 1994; Riesenberg-Malcolm, 1995). Moreover, because Kleinian analysts give special importance to the early levels of psychic development, which are by definition preverbal and preconceptual (Young, 1998), changes both in the mode of observation and in the recollection of the corresponding clinical material are necessary. For the understanding of these early levels of communications we need to look at *the effect in the analyst's mind* of that which a patient has said or done, rather than in the patient's associative discourse. I have always in mind Steiner's statement of 2001: "The patient tells a dream, and if you observe attentively five minutes later he is already acting it out with the analyst in the session." An action is worth a thousand words.

Needless to say, it is essential that for the patient to be able to use the analyst as a supporting actor for his internal dramas he needs to rely on the analyst's capacity to play the roles, experience the pains he has been assigned, feel and contain the anxiety thus created, and be able to go on thinking. The ability to go on thinking shows to what extent the personality and internal objects of the analyst count in actively sustaining the transference.

I shall now illustrate several of the concepts I have outlined with some interesting child material from a talented therapist in Madrid who discussed the case with me.[7] In so doing I hope to reveal how I use the above mentioned conceptual tools in the realm of supervision.

Case material

Note: For the sake of clarity, the therapist's report will appear in italics, while my own interventions will be in roman type.[8] I have respected the report as she presented it to me since what she said and how she said it are both relevant, and also reveal her resonance on the receiving end. What she included and what she did not are of equal importance in the supervision hour. I have recently heard that Faimberg's technique of supervision is quite similar to mine with regard to this matter. She calls it "listening to listening" (1993; personal communication, 2011).

Therapist: *Jose is a 7-year-old boy who is brought to analysis by his parents, as he does not play with boys, only with girls. During breaks at school he remains alone with some storybooks or dolls that he brings from his home. He panics when he hears firecrackers. He is clumsy, does never run nor play football. He only likes girls' play, watching videos and reading tales. Both he and his brother 4 years his junior were born through artificial insemination. At the time of this report I had not been able to inquire about the motives nor the details about the conditions of the insemination. [In Spain it would have been rude and offensive to ask about this.] Both parents, 40 years old, are anxious people. I have seen the child twice a week for the past two months and every fortnight I do a family session. It called my attention to see that the father couldn't stop crying in the first one. I am under the impression that the sexual identities of the parents are reversed. Mother, for instance, made a drawing of Superman for the younger sibling in one of the family sessions, viewed from the front in a menacing attitude in red and black, quite muscular. That struck me being a production coming from a female, specially one a mother makes for her child. In the waiting room there is also a blackboard where she has drawn sometimes and the drawing that was left on it once was that of a warrior, very strong and muscular too. When the father brings Jose, the drawings that remain on the blackboard are tiny flowers. Moreover, the father is quite affected though he has lately grown a beard, which gives him a more masculine aspect. He reported to have suffered the same troubles as his son when he was a child, in his case because he used to be obese and to stammer. He never liked to run nor do any physical activity. Mother has stated her concerns about Jose's sexual identity while father's concern is more about his being rejected by other children. At home Jose likes to put a ribbon on his head and make movements with his hands and head as if*

*he wore long hair and were a girl, but when his mother asks him he
pretends he is a Ninja Warrior.*

*The first time I met Jose I saw an ugly child. His teeth separated and
protruding as well as hairy and merged black eyebrows caused me that
impression. I no longer see him that way. I enjoy working with him. I
believe we have a good relation. What I find more difficult to stand is when
he suddenly loses interest in the session and says he is bored.*

A preliminary approach to the patient's pathology

R.O.: The therapist's report picks up what looks like a complicated
situation for Jose. While she lets us know about the identity problems,
her seeing him as an ugly child (a view that later changed) recreates
right away between the two one of the other complaints, that is, his
being rejected by other children. Then it looks like he has to confirm
that he is the biological offspring of his father with whom he identifies
with his feminine aspects, and also by being like his father as a child,
clumsy and isolated. This may come from an unspoken doubt in the
family about the paternity, furthered by the artificial insemination
and potentiated by the father's weak maleness.

On the other hand he also needs to oedipally satisfy his mother,
becoming the Superman she has drawn for his younger brother: the
Ninja Warrior. But if he satisfies his father he frustrates his mother
and vice versa. He has to face a conflict of loyalties derived from the
double oedipal complex, both direct and inverted, a situation that
seems to sustain his manifest bisexual conflict.

The father, on his side, identifies to such a degree with the child
that he cries as if the child were himself. And to some extent he is.

As for the therapist's early position, we want to notice that she will
inevitably align with the mother insofar as she is concerned about the
gender conflict. In this, she will become – whether she likes it or not
– the mother whose ideal (and likely the aim of the therapy) is to have
Jose satisfy her ideal for a masculine boy, while at the same time her
devoting attention to his isolation will also align her with Jose's father.

Viewed from this angle, the material would orient us toward a
split self. On one side a neurotic infantile self stuck in the classical
Oedipus complex in both its aspects just as Freud described it. The
dominance of the child's erotic feelings toward both his parents and
the desire to satisfy them both leads Jose to become the girl for the

father and the Ninja Warrior/Superman for his mother. Hate seems to have little place here.

But on the other side there is also a perverse aspect of his. We heard that Jose likes to put a ribbon on his head and pretend he is a woman, but lies about this when mother discovers him. This may be due to his bad conscience, a response evoked by his phantasy of having usurped mother's femininity. On the neurotic side of the split, his femininity looks like an amorous reassurance of his father's doubtful masculinity and paternity; on the perverse side it may mean that he can also betray his father, pretending he is a girl just to have him face a male warrior – and so his own homosexuality – that of the father. The hate that does not emerge in his neurotic self finds satisfaction in the perverse. If there were some truth in this, the therapist's viewing him as ugly could also be due to her intuitive contact with this latter aspect.

In both instances a projective identification seems to be operating, with the mother and the father each taking up the role of the other.[9] The difference is that in the perverse version it is robbery and betrayal that prevail, while in the neurotic version the motive is infantile love toward both parents (incestuous desires).[10] Jose's therapist will let us know what comes alive in the analytic transference-countertransference field.

Now, all of the above is just a first orientation, a kind of mapping of the landscape. Nothing of this is to be interpreted to the patient, who will need time and space in order to display his internal object relations in the here-and-now of the transference situation. Let us see how he does it. Both sessions presented were around a year into therapy, and his usual days were Monday and Thursday.

Thursday session

Therapist: *I fetch him in the waiting room where he is with his father and he comes with me as usual without greeting me or looking at me. He sits down and draws a fairy which he immediately erases. He asks me if I know how to do a bow for the hair and begs me to draw one. I draw it and he completes the rest of the figure. He then asks me to draw a boy with a ponytail and wants to know whether it is possible "at [age] 15 to wear a pony tail?" I draw the ponytail and he does the rest. As he has finished he asks me to erase it and to draw it again but closer to the girl.*

He then asks me to add a little bird. I will do it and only ask him where he wants the birdie to be, where it should be looking at. He paints it in blue. [I never draw in therapy with children, but I am doing it here with this child and ask myself if I am not doing wrong. I realize that he seems much more interested in the sessions since I accepted to draw.]

R.O.: We now have the opportunity to observe patient and therapist in action. The supervisory hour is a privileged instance where detailed observation of transference and countertransference can happen; it allows for a microscopic view of the movements in the field created in the session. Checking on the patient's responses to the interpretive formulations and the play behavior of the therapist is part of this task.

In this beginning of the session the therapist notes that she made a breach in what is her regular technique. Not that drawing when the patient asks for it is universally wrong, but for this therapist it meant an exception, which has to call for our attention. The fairy that Jose draws and erases seems to be a magic element that appears and disappears. That is to say he begins the session in a "fairy key," as if he had said: *something magic should occur, a spell.* Let us recall the secret and silent communication he has with his mother through drawings on the blackboard, which is also something like a shared secret code. In this sense the drawing of the fairy is a fleeting communication indicating what he wants from her: "*If you know how to draw a bow you will be a fairy that can give me the femininity, a vagina perhaps. But if you can also make a 15-year-old boy with a ponytail (can 15 year boys have one like that?) you will also be giving me the gift of an adolescent penis.*"

We may witness more eloquently than in any adult analysis what action the patient prods the analyst into. Let us remember once again that the concept of "actualization" or "enactment" (acting a phantasy out) tells us that not only does the patient act, but also that he manages to drive the analyst into playing a role that supports his own defensive system to keep mental pain at bay. Hence the self observation of the therapist, and not simply her observation of the patient, is relevant in testing the meaning of what he – the patient – is doing at every moment in the analytic hour.

He has succeeded in leading the therapist away from her usual technique into drawing elements that for him are sexually charged, and then having her experience remorse. She seemed to have enacted his oedipal phantasy of both being mummy's secret partner as well as having her be robbed of her femininity. He then has the therapist draw the little bird that looks at the couple, but when he takes the drawing from her, she is turned into the onlooker-bird looking at him and the drawing. She is now the child/birdie while he is the creative mother/daddy couple. The drawing became alive in the room.

Let us see how he goes on.

Therapist: *He places the toybox in front of the sheets of paper on which he is drawing some more, so I won't be able to see it. He asks me too to cover my eyes. [He will draw a heart between the two figures, as I get to know much later.] He says he won't show it to me until the Monday session.*

I tell him that he wants me to stay out without seeing anything as happens to him when mummy and daddy leave him outside their room while they kiss and touch each other. [He has often said he imagined that that is what they did.]

R.O.: The therapist, in touch with her countertransference, interprets to Jose the meaning of what he has been doing to her: by covering what he is doing he turned her into the excluded birdie that is unable to get itself into the parental couple.

She accurately shows how Jose has put her in a role and a feeling he cannot bear, while she was able to contain it and interpret to him, taking into account her response to his projective identification. She could have described too in that moment the change of identity in him that ensued, having stolen the identity of the parents in projectively identifying with them "Identijectifying" with them, I add humorously, to highlight the identificatory aspect of projective identification.

Therapist: *He says that sometimes he sees how they kiss and that disgusts him. He makes a rejecting gesture and laughs nervously.*

I tell him that he, in such an instance becomes the bird that does not bear to remain excluded and gets in to see all what mummy and daddy and I and my husband do.

R.O.: It is notable that as soon as the therapist recovers her identity and interprets what Jose projected into her, she obtains a genuine response. And Jose on his side stops enacting the role of his parents.

His disgust at his parents kissing and touching each other (his conception of lovemaking) is a genuine reaction of the infantile self after he recovered his identity too. She then tells him that because he cannot bear exclusion he has to intrude voyeuristically into the parental couple. This formulation is accurate, and one could lay out clearly that as he cannot bear being excluded he must get into them to become them (which as we heard before is what he does behind their back at home). He wants to "be" both parents and also both the therapist and her husband who represent them, and wants each one of them to be left out.[11] His voyeurism is a vehicle used to get inside the parental couple and become them, a rather unexplored side of voyeurism in the service of projective identification. His first drawing also lets us observe the intrusiveness of the eyes of the couple looking at each other, thus representing his projection onto them of his own voyeuristic intrusion.

The motive of this mise-en-scène is clearly what the therapist has interpreted – he cannot bear the primal scene and his inability to participate. (His seducing the therapist away from her usual technique, as we heard in the beginning of this hour, had the meaning of upsetting the oedipal boundary, which is where the therapist's feeling of doing something wrong came from.) But when he asks her to cover her eyes and says he won't show her, he not only wants her to become the bird and to feel curious and frustrated, but he also brings his trickiness into the transference. What she shouldn't see is how he usurps his parents' identity, to their detriment. This helps him to feel omnipotent and defends him against his feeling like a little child/birdie (the little boy he in fact is).

> Therapist: *He gets very nervous, laughs and makes a frolic gesture. He asks me when I will bring him the toys from last year (actually, last year we had not yet met). As I ask him he answers: "those to see what is missing." I realize that he is referring to the Test of Wechsler, which we used for his assessment a year ago.*
>
> *I tell him he wants things not of age 7 but from when he was younger, 6, 5, 4, or even less.*
>
> *He laughs. "Yes. I want to be a baby and play with toys for babies and have many videos."*

R.O.: Now the therapist has picked up Jose's wish to regress, which Jose confirms and completes, stating that it would allow him to "have many videos" – meaning having access to the parental couple in their love scene and therefore regain his imagined lost privileges.

> Therapist: *Jose continues: "I'm bored. What can I do? … Ayyy! I'm bored. Ayyy …"*
> *I tell him that I believe he is not bored but annoyed with me because I am not bringing him what he has asked for and therefore he loses interest in being with me.*

R.O.: This seems to be a very good interpretation rooted in the countertransference. The analyst feels the child is annoyed rather than bored and tells him that that is his reaction to her not having contributed to his omnipotence this time, which she did in the first part of the session by supporting his belief that he could become the parents in the primal scene assisted magically by the fairy-therapist. We must also remember the therapist's sensitivity to the child's boredom, which had her give in to the child's wanting her to draw for him. So, this manifestation of boredom is blackmailing her to again give in to his pressure.

> Therapist: *He now says: "I'm going out to see if Dad is there. Do you say he is or he isn't?"*

R.O.: He still wishes to believe the therapist is a fairy. Now she should be able to guess. But more important than that is that he is withdrawing from her because she was not pleasing but interpreting to him. He wants to see his dad and drop her. It is likely that this response lets us see the beginning of his inverted oedipal cycle, out of frustration with his maternal object. The detailed observation of the transference-countertransference fluctuations allows us to follow the ever-transforming emotional movements of the patient's unconscious mind.

> Therapist: *I tell him that in a few minutes we will have finished and maybe he is able to wait.*
> *"I will make a snail with playdoh." He tries to, but does not achieve it. He gets angry and puts the playdoh away.*
> *I tell him he does like the snail. When he gets angry with me he withdraws and doesn't want to know anything from me.*
> *All his paints fall to the floor. He asks me to gather them.*
> *I tell him he now only wants me in order to do things for him. He picks them up and we finish the session.*

Discussion

In this session Jose tries to seduce the therapist by behaving well and leading her to join him, abandoning her technique. But then she has to let him see "what is missing," what he is missing and what he could not see – ultimately what she does with her husband when he is not there. He eagerly took the therapist's suggestion that he wanted to become a baby as giving him a good reason to have access to the toys and most of all the videos, which to him meant to be able to get back to rejoin his parents in their room, which is what he is always feeling he misses. There is no exclusion for babies, he believes. Maybe he will even want to get back into mummy's belly in order to witness and participate in the parents' intercourse from the inside, like the Wolf Man. If all this fails, he might in the future become addicted to pornography, where you imagine you see it all and miss nothing.

Now, as the therapist does not bring him the Wechsler box (he seems to have taken the previous testing as if she were being exhibitionistic), he will blackmail her with his boredom and will leave her for his father, and if she does not agree he will throw his playdoh and paints to the floor and she will have to be his servant to do the cleaning after he leaves. And she will have earned it!

Monday session

Therapist: *He starts off just like last Thursday, asking me to draw a bow for the hair and he draws the girl and the boy with the ponytail.*

I tell him that these are mummy and daddy when they touch each other (reference to the past session) and that he would like to do the same with me in order to know whether he is a girl or a boy.

He asks me to erase the boy and to make a deer. I draw it and ask myself if he is not making a reference to horns, put horns on ... but I dismiss it as an irrelevant idea of mine. [The Spanish word for horns is "cuernos" and for having horns "cornudo." The latter is slang for "cuckold."]

R.O.: We can see that the weekend break is over and Jose gets back to the theme of the couple. The therapist has joined him again so the two would reconstitute the couple to repair the disruption of the break. She interprets this plus his attempt thus to define his identity in this Jose and mother–therapist couple.

Listening to his response will put us on the right track. He does not seem to confirm the interpretation. He seems to say: "No, I do not want to know whether I am 'one or the other.' I want to be able to transform myself from one figure into another, and in order to do that I need you to assist me as my fairy." The therapist's silent association to the deer/cuckold is likely coming from her countertransferential guilt feeling of having betrayed him by leaving him for her husband. It is this guilt feeling of the therapist that makes her want to compensate him by joining him in his drawings.

> Therapist: *Following this Jose asks me to erase the deer and draw a fairy, which he gives me no time to do.*
> *I tell him that this reminds me that last Thursday he left something hidden here which he said he would show me today.*

R.O.: At this point the therapist remembers he had hidden something on Thursday that she felt excluded from since then, and now she is enacting the role of the curious child, reminding him of his promise.

> Therapist: *He laughs nervously and makes gestures as of shyness. He asks me to cover my eyes. He places the toybox in front of him so I would not see. He takes from his folder the drawing from last session and I see he covers the heart he had drawn then with a black blot. He shows it to me. "Don't you think this bird has the shape of something sinister?" – [I am perplexed at the expression he uses. I ask myself if he is speaking of perverse aspects.] So I ask him what he meant by "sinister." And he replies: "that does bad things."*
> *I tell him that when his parents are together in their bedroom touching each other and leaving him apart he feels his inside becomes filled with sinister feelings and wishes to make bad things to them. [Covering the red heart with a black blot.]*

R.O.: Covering the heart with black is what makes him feel like the birdie, now turned sinister. This is the ugly side of Jose that the therapist saw when she first met him. She makes this precise interpretation about the bad things he imagines when his parents are together in their bedroom. The bad things stand for his masturbatory phantasies, like transforming the mother/therapist into his servant, as was the case at the end of Thursday's session.

Therapist: *He now makes messy lines and blots with his pencil, much like a muscular discharge. He attacks the girl figure with the tip of the pencil and leaves her full of marks.*

I ask him what he is doing.

He says: "That which turns and sweeps all things away … and it is a triangle but an inverted one … but where does it take it to? … What room is it taking it too? … He asks me to hold him tight. He is now in a manic vortex.

R.O.: For a moment he seems to be in the role of somebody powerful who can turn things upside down, the inverted triangle. He is the couple while his internal mummy is under attack. We saw earlier how he had drawn the male figure with the ponytail and then erased it. Now father has disappeared, mother/therapist has been left alone, and he is prey to a sinister masturbatory phantasy where he destroys his internal parents and all becomes chaotic.

Therapist: *I tell him he seems to mean a tornado. And maybe when he feels he has turned sinister he fears he could disappear and wants me to hold him tight.*

The rest of the session he is busy tearing little pieces of playdoh which he recovers, sticking them to a larger playdoh ball that he rolls over them. In the end there results an amalgam of colors all mixed up into a larger ball.

R.O.: He seems to be dramatizing how his attack on his internal parents – mainly deleting his father and stabbing his mother – launches him into chaos. His feeling carried away by his mania, which he lost control over, has him anxiously resort to his therapist, asking her to hold him physically down to earth, lest he go crazy. She manages to comfort him with her understanding words that surround him like a seat belt. And then he picks up the little pieces he had torn into a large colorful ball. It looks like the debris of the tornado.

At the end he might have agglomerated the debris of his parental objects – particularly his internal mother – into a bizarre object (Bion), amalgamating the bits of playdoh into the large colorful ball in which the originals got lost. It will be the task of the therapist to reconstruct for him where this all originated so as to provide him with a consistent internal parental couple to ground his identity in a safer way.

Conclusions

I have tried to illustrate with the material that Ms López has discussed with me the usefulness of the "work after hours" that incorporates the tools of transference-countertransference and enactments to make new findings and inferences about a patient's conflicts and pathology. Looking back at the material together enabled us to observe the totality of the field created between patient and therapist in which the patient's unconscious phantasies came to life.[12]

The observation of Jose's transforming identity and the transformation of his objects showed the kaleidoscopic change of the transference-countertransference configurations. The girl, the boy, and the blue birdie in the first hour represented the mummy–daddy–child situation and the struggle to overcome exclusion. In that hour the therapist was at times the set designer who helped with her drawing in the production of the drama. At times she was the fairy that would by magical means make Jose's life easier, giving him the gift of becoming the parental couple. But then in the next hour the manic (magic) defense collapsed and the blue birdie turned into a sinister figure that reacted to the pain of exclusion, attacking the love relation of his internal parents and fragmenting and deleting them. (The conflicts of his actual parents must have contributed to Jose's omnipotent phantasy of damaging them.) At this point all sense of security went away and the child was left for a while in a psychotic world, the vortex. He resorted to his therapist – now a split reliable good object saved from his manic fury – to fasten a seat belt around him with her arms until the hurricane would be over. This seemed to have a different quality than the times in both sessions when the therapist dropped her usual boundary and agreed to draw, thus reinforcing Jose's omnipotence while she felt guilty. An important moment occurred when her countertransference indicated to her that she was being led to feel curious and excluded in place of Jose, when he hid his drawing from her over the weekend, which she could interpret to him. This seemed to have furthered a withdrawal of his projection into her of the curious excluded child – that is, his having projectively identified her with this aspect of himself – leading him to re-own his projection. So then, when his fury against the excluding couple recurred at an unbearable level and he launched his attacks on the internal couple, his therapist – no longer the excluded blue birdie – was there to contain and save him.

251

Addendum

Throughout this chapter it can be noted that countertransference, as I use that term, encompasses a gradient, some steps of which could be defined as:

1 A conscious feeling or association in the analyst to the patient's material.
2 An unconscious feeling or idea that the analyst can retrieve by doing some piece of self-analysis in or after the hour as he intuits its existence.
3 An unconscious feeling or idea that conflicts with his ego-ideal-superego and causes blind spots that hinder the analysis of the patient, or the analyst's counter-resistance.
4 If the latter becomes a state in the analyst rather than a temporary problem we call it a countertransference position from which the analyst's ego is now perceiving and thinking.
5 The unresolved countertransference is discharged in action in response to the patient's unconscious induction. Its result is a mutual enactment.

The detailed attention after hours to the minute movements and transformations of the transference, when enhanced by the corresponding observation of the countertransference, enables us to do this kind of exploration.

Notes

1 The term projective identification had been used earlier by Edoardo Weiss (1925), and Marjorie Brierley (1945); however, it is Klein who we acknowledge for the discovery of the corresponding omnipotent phantasy of intrusion into an object.
2 Grotstein, in a personal communication (2012), rethought the transference-countertransference as an expression of Bion's contained–container function.
3 I thank Dr Michael Pavlovic from Stuttgart, who discussed the case with me, for his permission to use this vignette.
4 The practice of analytic supervision was started in 1920 at the Berlin Psycho-analytic Policlinic for the interns who were young psychoanalytic candidates. Eitingon and Horney were two of the leaders of the project. It

was then called *Kontrollanalyse* (control analysis), and one of its aims was to enlighten candidates about their countertransferences (see Eitingon, 1923). As we nowadays know that no analyst is exempt from countertransference and enactments, incorporating some form of supervision as part of our own lifelong clinical work has become increasingly common.

5 Grosskurth (1986) tells us about the disagreements between Klein and Heimann around the concept and use of countertransference, and of the way Klein later dismissed her analysand, possibly for being too destructive.

6 This is undoubtedly a risk we need to be mindful of, but it should not make us dismiss the value of countertransference. Any technical tool can be potentially misused or abused.

7 I thank Coral López from Madrid for having enabled me to give an account of this boy's case and her work with me.

8 Square brackets that appear in the material are the therapist's.

9 This double identification is the basis of the masturbatory phantasy.

10 In making the distinction between neurotic and perverse I am following Meltzer (1973, pp. 92–93), for whom perversion is "characterized by perversity of purpose" coming from the destructive part of the personality, that is, Jose's sinister black bird as opposed to the blue birdie. This is clinically different from what analysts have classically understood as a perversion.

11 One sees here the identificatory and the projective aspect of projective identification respectively.

12 This minute work, which includes analyzing the analyst's countertransference, is best done when a trustful relation between supervisee and supervisor has developed, thus reducing persecutory anxieties and guilt feelings in both to the benefit of the cooperative work that assures a creative relation.

Bibliography

Baranger, W. and Baranger, M. (1961) The analytic situation as a dynamic field. *International Journal of Psychoanalysis*, 89: 795–826, 2008 (La situación analítica como campo dinámico). In *Problemas del campo psicoanalítico* (pp. 129–164). Buenos Aires: Kargieman, 1993).

Baranger, W., Baranger M. and Glocer Fiorini, L. (2009) *The Work of Confluence: Listening and Working and Interpreting in the Psychoanalytic Field*. London: Karnac.

Bion, W. R. (1961) *Experiences in Groups*. London: Tavistock.

Bion, W. R. (1962a) The psycho-analytic study of thinking. *International Journal of Psychoanalysis*, 43: 306–310. Republished as W. R. Bion, A theory of thinking, in *Second Thoughts* (pp. 110–119). London: Karnac, 1984.

Bion, W. R. (1962b) *Learning from Experience*. London: Tavistock.

Brierley, M. (1945) Further notes on the implications of psycho-analysis: Metapsychology and personology. *International Journal of Psychoanalysis* 26: 89–114.

Eitingon, M. (1923). Report of the Berlin Psycho-Analytical Policlinic. *Bulletin of the International Psycho-Analytic Association*, 4: 254–269.

Faimberg, H. (1993) 'Listening to Listening' and *après-coup*. In *The Telescoping of Generations: Listening to the Narcissistic Links between Generations* (pp. 76–88). London: Routledge, 2005.

Grinberg, L. (1956) Sobre algunos problemas de técnica psico-analítica determinados por la identificación y contra-identificación proyectiva. *Revista de Psicoanálisis*, 14: 507–511.

Grinberg, L. (1958) Aspectos mágicos en la transferencia y en la contratrans-ferencia. Sus implicaciones técnicas. Identificación y "contraidentificación" proyectiva. *Revista de Psicoanálisis*, 15: 347–368.

Grosskurth, P. (1986) *Melanie Klein: Her World and Her Work*. London: Maresfield.

Hinshelwood, R. D. (2000) What we can learn from failures: Using the analyst and the countertransference 'fit.' Unpublished paper.

Joseph, B. (1989) *Psychic Equilibrium and Psychic Change*, E. B. Spillius and M. Feldman (eds.). London: Routledge. New Library of Psychoanalysis, 9.

Joseph, B. (1999) From acting-out to enactment. Unpublished paper read at the Joseph Sandler Memorial Day Conference, London, March 1999.

Klein, M. (1946) Notes on some schizoid mechanisms. In *The Writings of Melanie Klein,* vol. 3, *Envy and Gratitude and other Works* (pp. 1–24). London: Hogarth Press.

Meltzer, D. (1973) *Sexual States of Mind*. Perthshire, Scotland, Clunie Press.

O'Shaughnessy, E. (1994) What is a clinical fact? In R. Shafer (ed.), *The Contemporary Kleinians of London* (pp. 30–46). Madison, CT: International Universities Press, 1997. Presented to the *International Journal of Psycho-Analysis* 75th Anniversary Celebration Conference, London, October 14–16, 1994.

Riesenberg-Malcolm, R. (1995) Conceptualization of clinical facts. In R. Shafer (ed.), *The Contemporary Kleinians of London* (pp. 51–70). Madison, CT: International Universities Press, 1997. Presented to the *International Journal of Psycho-Analysis* 75th Anniversary Celebration Conference, São Paulo, March 31–April 2.

Sandler, J. (1976) Countertransference and role-responsiveness. *International Review of Psychoanalysis*, 3: 43–47.

Segal, H. (2000-2003) Comments from the London Clinical Seminars, an international clinical group founded by R. Oelsner that has met in London annually since 2000.

Spillius, E. (1992) Clinical experiences of projective identification. In Anderson, R., *Clinical Lectures on Klein and Bion* (pp. 59–73). London: Routledge.

Steiner, J. (2000) Containment, enactment and communication. *International Journal of Psychoanalysis*, 81: 245–255.

Steiner, J. (2001) Comment within the London Clinical Seminars. London: February 3.

Weiss, E. (1925) Über eine noch nicht beschriebene Phase der Entwicklung zur heterosexuellen Liebe. *Internationale Zeitschrift für Psychoanalyse*, 11: 429–443.

Young, R. M. (1998) Being a Kleinian is not straightforward. Paper presented at the 7th Public Annual Conference in the Severnside Institute of Psychotherapy, Bristol, October 10.

13

NONVERBAL CUES IN TRANSFERENCE-COUNTERTRANSFERENCE INTERACTIONS

Reflections on their role in the analytic process

Theodore J. Jacobs

Although from the earliest days of psychoanalysis Freud (1895) and other pioneers (Reich, 1933) recognized the importance of nonverbal behavior in psychoanalytic treatment, this aspect of communication has not progressed beyond the status of stepchild in our field.

The dominance of speech in psychoanalysis – it is known throughout the world as the talking cure – has tended to obscure the role of the nonverbal in analytic treatment. Although an important mode of communication in every analysis, the nonverbal behavior of both patient and analyst is an aspect of psychoanalysis that often goes unexamined. In our institutes there are no courses on nonverbal communication, and rarely in supervision or in case seminars is the nonverbal dimension of analysis discussed. Nor are efforts regularly made to relate this form of communication to the verbal content of a session.

In part, this neglect of the nonverbal is due to a lack of expertise in this area, even on the part of our most experienced teachers and clinicians. Since over the years there has been so little focus on this aspect of analysis, there has not developed a core of teachers skilled in deciphering the nonverbal interactions of patient and analyst that is comparable to the growing number of colleagues who, trained in mother–infant observation and research, have become quite expert in decoding the reciprocal movements of mother and baby.

In recent years, growing awareness of the importance of unconscious communication in analysis has sparked interest in the dance, the nonverbal interactions that regularly take place in treatment, but attention to this aspect of analysis remains sporadic.

In the last two decades, the individual who, more than any other, raised our awareness of the central role of nonverbal behavior in analysis was the late James McLaughlin. In several papers (1988, 1991, 1992), as well as his plenary address to the American Psychoanalytic Association (1987), McLaughlin described in detail the posture and gestures of patient and analyst and demonstrated how much information he was able to glean from paying close attention to this aspect of their communication.

In these studies he was following the lead of Felix Deutsch, who, some forty years earlier (1952), carried out a project in which he charted the movements of patients on the couch and correlated these with the verbal material of the hours. In this way, Deutsch was able to demonstrate a consistent relationship between certain themes in the patients' material and particular bodily movements that regularly preceded and anticipated the verbalization of such material.

Although both were valuable contributions, Deutsch's interesting study and McLaughlin's later papers have met the same fate; they have been largely ignored and have had very little impact on theory or technique. Thus the study and effective utilization of nonverbal communication in analysis remains a frontier that has yet to be adequately explored.

In this paper, I will offer several clinical vignettes in order to illustrate a particular aspect of nonverbal behavior in analysis, and the key role it can play in affecting the transference-countertransference interaction of patient and analyst.

Clinical case 1: Thursdays

My first example goes back many years to my days as a candidate at the New York Psychoanalytic Institute. At that time I was working with a young woman who seemed to make a point of arriving for her hours dressed as indifferently as possible. Her usual outfit consisted of ill-fitting jeans, torn in several places, a blouse that looked as though it had been slept in for several days, and sneakers miraculously held together with masking tape. This was her outfit four days a week. Thursdays were very different. Quite regularly on that day Ms G arrived at my office as a new person. Attired in a stylish dress or fashionable skirt and neatly pressed blouse, she was all but unrecognizable. Ms G's Thursday sessions were different in other respects, too. Most days her hours were filled with recitations of daily events described with little affect. Striking, too, was her clear avoidance of references to her analyst, as well as emotionally laden material of any kind.

On Thursdays, by contrast, Ms G spoke more freely and in a less guarded way. What she said contained more affect, and in her Thursday sessions she was more likely to report a dream or a fantasy. At times she even allowed herself to speak of a reaction she had to something that I said or did.

For quite a long time I was not aware of this pattern. I simply noted that on some days Ms G arrived for her hour looking very different and was freer and less guarded in her sessions. It did not register on me that my patient's altered appearance and behavior regularly took place on the same day of the week. Nor did I have the least understanding of why these changes were taking place. In an effort to learn more about what was motivating this transformation, I tried to pay especially close attention to the analytic material on the days that the changes took place. For many months, however, I was unable to solve this ongoing mystery. Then, at one point, when I was reviewing my notes for a supervision session, it struck me that it was always on Thursdays that the change in Ms G took place.

When I remarked on this fact and asked my patient about it, she quickly cleared up the mystery. From certain changes in my behavior on Thursday, she had deduced that it was on that day that I saw my supervisor. She had noted, she said, not only that I seemed to be more attentive on Thursdays, that I listened more closely, but my posture also seemed to change. She experienced me as being closer to her in the Thursday session. Not infrequently, she said, I leaned forward in my chair and my voice seemed to be coming from a place nearer to her head.

It was on Thursdays, too, she realized that I tended to take more notes – sometimes writing for most of the session. From these observations, Ms G had concluded that I had supervision on that day of the week and that the changes she had noted were in preparation for my supervisory session.

Ms G's detective work was accurate. In fact, I did see my supervisor on Thursdays and no doubt she was correct in concluding that on that day I tended to listen more closely, to lean forward more than usual, and, in order to present process material as accurately as possible, to take more abundant notes.

My patient had the idea that my supervisor was Dr N, the director of the treatment center, who had interviewed her in connection with her application for analysis. She had been told this by another patient who was in analysis through the center, but, in fact, that patient's information was inaccurate. My supervisor was another faculty member.

It was, however, this belief that motivated my patient to change the way that she presented herself at my office on Thursdays.

When I questioned Ms G about this puzzling connection, she explained that she had been very much taken with Dr N, whom she found to be a warm and responsive individual. He had reminded her of her beloved grandfather who had died when she was 7 years old. This grandfather was a very special person in Ms G's life and she looked forward to her weekly visits to his home. He always made a great fuss over her and made sure to compliment her on the specially chosen outfits that she insisted on wearing to their Sunday dinners. His death had been a shattering blow to the child, and Ms G recognized that throughout her life she had been looking for a replacement grandfather.

In Ms G's mind, the link between her grandfather and Dr N was solidified by an incident that took place during her interview at the treatment center. About 20 minutes into the interview, Dr N was called away to attend to an urgent matter that had arisen in the clinic. In his absence Ms G could not resist the temptation to sneak a peek at the few notes that Dr N had jotted down during their conversation.

What she read both pleased her and stirred a host of memories. Dr N had described her as an attractive 22-year-old woman who was neatly and stylishly dressed. In Ms G's mind this view of her coalesced with memories of the compliments her grandfather regularly gave her on the outfits she wore, and forged a link between the two men.

With this connection in mind, Ms G believed that on Thursday I would report about her to Dr N. Wanting him to maintain the favorable impression of her that he had initially, she made a point of dressing neatly and attractively on Thursdays so that in my supervisory session I would present her in a positive way. It was for this reason, too, that she strove to be a good and cooperative patient on Thursdays, one whose lively and productive session I would report to Dr N.

There was, in addition, another important determinant of Ms G's behavior. This had to do with covert negative feelings that she had about me, feelings that she kept strictly secret.

Although she had said nothing about this, Ms G viewed me, as she did her father, as a disappointment. Her father was a quiet and reserved man who was uncomfortable with feelings and who remained emotionally distant from his children. Ms G respected him but also felt rejected by him, and she compared him unfavorably to her warm and loving grandfather.

In a similar way, Ms G was secretly disappointed that it was I, and not Dr N, who was her analyst. As a student, I worked with her in the manner that I imagined analysts should work; that is, with much quiet listening, few interpretations, and little interactive engagement. This style reminded her of her reserved and undemonstrative father, and evoked negative transference feelings. Out of fear that I would become furious at her if I detected these feelings, Ms G concealed them from me, just as she concealed her long-standing resentment of his aloofness from her father; she kept hidden, too, her preference for Dr N, whom she regarded as more engaging, supportive, and helpful. She did not, however, want to hurt my feelings by openly acknowledging this preference, and, in any case, she was quite convinced that if I discovered the way she felt I would no longer want to see her. This was precisely the idea that she had concerning her love for her grandfather. If her father discovered that she much preferred her grandfather to him, she was convinced that he would permanently turn away from her and she would lose him altogether.

Thus in this case, centrally important transference feelings went underground: covert negative feelings that were having a profound effect on the analytic work. It was these feelings, in large measure, that gave rise to the strong resistances that characterized Ms G's treatment.

Although outwardly cooperative, Ms G harbored a secret dissatisfaction that she had been assigned to me. This she expressed not openly but rather indirectly in her manner of dress and in the superficiality of the analytic material. In these ways she expressed her silent protest, one that that was communicated nonverbally, just as I had communicated my own special interest in Ms G's Thursday sessions – the day that I had supervision – through nonverbal means. And it was only by paying close attention to such communications on both sides of the couch that the mystery concerning Ms G's behavior, and its transference meaning, could be solved.

Clinical case 2: fathers and sons

I would like now to describe two other forms of nonverbal behavior on the part of the analyst and, briefly, illustrate the impact that they can have both on the transference and on the overall analytic process.

The first involves a matter rarely mentioned in our discussions of clinical work: the physical appearance of the analyst. We take care to observe the way that patients present themselves each day, paying close attention to their physical appearance and manner of dress, in addition to other aspects of their nonverbal behavior. The same is not true for the analyst. We rarely describe our physical appearance or assess the impact that it has on our patients. This is a significant omission for, as we know, the way the patient perceives the analyst has a substantial effect on the analytic material. This is particularly true when a change has taken place in the analyst's appearance. Such a change, quickly taken in by most patients, not infrequently triggers memories and fantasies that are linked to perceived changes in significant objects in the patient's life. If, as often happens, these memories have undergone repression, a sudden change in the analyst's appearance may trigger associations that help bring the relevant memory traces into conscious awareness.

In the case that I will describe, it was just such an alteration in my appearance that led to the uncovering of a transference reaction that was at the heart of an impasse that had developed in treatment, one that had, effectively, brought the analysis to a halt.

Mr L, a 26-year-old man, sought help because he was floundering in life and had lost all direction. An intelligent and capable young man who, until the age of 18, was considered a star student and a popular and outgoing youngster, he fell apart when, just past his eighteenth birthday, his father developed a progressive neurological disorder.

Mr L's father was a dynamic, outgoing, and strong-willed individual, an athlete and community leader who was a dominant force in his son's life. Mr L was quite dependent on his father, relying heavily on his judgment to help him make decisions in life. When his father fell ill quite suddenly, deteriorated rapidly over a two-year period, and then died in a nursing home, Mr L was crushed. He became agitated and depressed, had difficulty concentrating, and had to drop out of college. He began to withdraw from friends and to spend increasing amounts of time with his mother, who, in her grief, clung to him as he did to her.

When I met him, Mr L had been out of school for more than three years. He attempted to travel in Europe but became so anxious that he cut short his trip and returned home. In this three-year period of time, Mr L held several menial jobs, all of which he quit after a few months' employment. He had very few friends and dated only sporadically. He had no sustained relationships with a woman other than his mother, and if he showed an interest in a young woman, his mother quite regularly dissuaded him from pursuing her.

In my initial consultation with Mr L, I had the impression of a young man who was quite lost. Clearly he was in a regressed state, but his intelligence was intact and his basic ego functions not severely impaired. It seemed to me that Mr L was out of touch with the conflicts in himself that had been unleashed by his father's illness and death, and that he needed an in-depth treatment to help him get in touch with the warded-off and repressed parts of himself that he was attempting, through avoidance and repression, to keep at bay.

Mr L eagerly accepted the recommendation for analysis and launched into the process with determination to get to the root of his problems. For a year and a half he made substantial progress. In fact, Mr L seemed to be a model patient. He was psychologically minded, associated quite freely, reported dreams and fantasies regularly, and was developing quite intense feelings about his analyst. Mr L was also gaining insight into his conflicts and motivations, particularly in relation to his guilt over his aggressive and competitive feelings toward his father.

Then, a year and a half into the analysis, all progress stopped. Instead of engaging in the analytic process as he had done before, Mr L became wary and hesitant to open up. He spoke haltingly, no longer brought in dreams or fantasies, and rarely spoke of the past. Instead, he focused on one subject alone: his relationship with a young woman whom he had met at a party. He talked obsessively about this new girlfriend, describing in minute detail every date they had, and all the ups and downs of their relationship. This focus served to exclude any other material. No longer did Mr L make any comments about me, or what was transpiring between us. It was as though all of Mr L's thoughts and feelings about me had gone underground.

Why such a change had come over Mr L was a total mystery. I strongly suspected that some troubling perception of me was responsible for it, but what that might be I had no idea.

I listened carefully to Mr L's associations, hoping to get a clue as to what had triggered this sudden shift in his behavior, but in this effort I remained frustrated.

Mr L continued to speak almost exclusively about the new girlfriend, clearly utilizing these descriptions in the service of resistance. It was evident that he had gone into hiding.

It took enactments on the part of both patient and analyst to clarify the situation and for me to learn what lay behind Mr L's change of behavior.

At that time, Mr L had early-morning appointments in my home office. It was winter then, and when I rose and dressed for the day it was not yet light. So as not to waken my wife at this early hour I was in the habit of dressing in the dark. Ordinarily I had no trouble doing this, but one morning when I'd had little sleep and felt quite tired, I mistakenly took from my closet the jacket from one suit and the trousers from another. They were quite similar in color but very differently patterned.

When I greeted Mr L in the waiting room, he looked at me in a quizzical way, but said nothing. In his sessions, however, he made reference to an offbeat teacher of his and to a psychiatrist friend of his mother's who went around town sporting an earring, cape, and walking stick. Then, at the end of the hour, as he was headed to the door, Mr L turned and looked at me in a piercing way.

It was not until sometime later when my wife alerted me to my mistake – she could not help laughing at the way I looked when I entered the kitchen – that I understood Mr L's behavior and the material of the hour. For good reason he had viewed me as quite daft – or worse, as a psychiatrist who was becoming demented.

As I thought about my mistake I realized that it was not an isolated one.

In fact, for over a month I had been making errors of one kind or another, losing my appointment book, forgetting to hand out some bills, misremembering the time of professional meetings, and the like. In short, I was acting in a disorganized way, clearly symptomatic of something that was troubling me.

As it turned out, Mr L had noticed these lapses and they worried him. And when he encountered me in a mismatched suit, looking like someone with a rapidly advancing case of Alzheimer's, he became truly alarmed.

For my part, I was aware that I was making errors, but I rationalized these as due to overwork, fatigue, preoccupation with family issues, and similar concerns. It was only after the mismatched suit incident that I recognized what was actually happening.

My father had had a serious stroke a few months earlier that resulted in a number of cognitive and expressive defects. A man who had always been fastidious about his clothing, he now dressed carelessly, seeming in his confusion to select his outfits in a quite random manner.

My father's illness had a profound effect on me as well, and in an effort to cope with the feelings of loss that I experienced I had identified with his condition. I, too, was acting like a deranged person.

Observing me, Mr L was terrified. He feared that I, like his father, was suffering from an incapacitating illness. So frightened was he, both of what he imagined was happening to me and of the retaliation that he expected for the hostile and competitive feelings that he harbored toward me, that he could not speak about his fears.

It took an enactment on his part for him, finally, to confront the truth and to begin to deal with his profound anxiety.

One day when I entered the waiting room to fetch Mr L for his appointment, I noticed that he looked up from the magazine he was reading and, for a moment, seemed to stare at me. On the couch, Mr L began, as usual, to recount the previous day's events, including several hours spent with his girlfriend. When there was a pause in his narrative, I intervened and drew Mr L's attention to what had happened in the waiting room. I remarked on the intense look that he had given me and asked if he could say anything about what he was experiencing at that moment.

Mr L remained silent for some time. Then, suddenly, he spoke up.

"Is there anything wrong with you?" he asked, "or do you always buy your clothes at a Salvation Army store?"

I laughed, and with the tension broken Mr L opened up. For several months, he said, he had been aware of mistakes that I had been making. These had caused him to be concerned about me, but when I appeared in the bizarre-looking mismatched suit, he found himself feeling terrified, convinced that I was becoming demented.

In the ensuing weeks, Mr L revealed how strong his feelings had become for me, how much he relied on me, and how he had, in a sense, turned himself over to me. He felt that he could not make any decisions without me, and the idea that I would no longer be available to him as his "seeing eye" practically paralyzed him. At the same time Mr L recognized that he hated being so dependent on me and also resented me for being the one who was so admired and needed.

The strength and intensity of Mr L's transference feelings put him in touch with the way that he both idolized and resented his father, and with the extent of his dependence on and resentment toward him. This work, ultimately, had the effect of freeing Mr L from the grip that, in death as in life, his father had on him. And it was enactments on the part of both patient and analyst, enactments carried out entirely in the nonverbal realm, that opened up the powerful transference-countertransference feelings that were at the root of the patient's resistance.

Clinical case 3: love and distance

As my final example, I will describe a situation in which transference-countertransference feelings, played out nonverbally, had a strong impact on the issue of termination of analysis.

This question arose in the treatment of Mr C, a rigid and obsessional man whom I had been seeing in analysis for many years. The work had proceeded very slowly – on one occasion, I had the image of two alligators swimming upstream in a sea of molasses – but small gains were evident from year to year. They were evident, that is, until, in the ninth year of treatment, progress stopped – or seemed to. For weeks on end we covered the same ground without anything new being added. After a time, the patient brought up the idea of ending. This surprised me since he never initiated anything, especially the ending of relationships. The idea of termination seemed reasonable, however, in light of what was happening and I very nearly agreed to setting a termination date. If I had done so, on the face of it, it would have been quite a reasonable decision.

Something made me wait, though. Something did not seem to be quite right. As it turned out, Mr C had picked up my feelings of frustration and the fact that, in the face of the stalemate that had developed, I had begun to withdraw emotionally from him. On several occasions I found my mind wandering in sessions with Mr C, and once or twice I almost drifted off into sleep. Furthermore, I noticed that I no longer observed Mr C on the couch as carefully as I had done before, and, at times found myself sitting with my body slightly rotated away from him. These were enactments both of my frustration with a patient whom I found increasingly difficult to reach, and irrational annoyance at him for making my work so difficult.

Although I said nothing about what I was experiencing in sessions and thought that I had managed to conceal my feelings from my patient, they clearly were transmitted to Mr C. Very sensitive to slights and rejections, he had launched a preemptive strike and had proposed ending. What transpired between us was of the greatest importance. Our interaction contained a good deal of my patient's neurosis – and a good deal of mine. It proved essential to translate our nonverbal enactments into words and to bring into the open the message that each of us was transmitting to the other. Once this was done and we no longer were communicating covertly through actions, meaningful work could be done, not only on this issue but on the source of the stalemate. This was primarily related to Mr C's tenacious defenses against his growing wish for my love, and my enactment of the frustration and anger that I experienced at his keeping me at so great a distance. Once these issues were dealt with openly and explored in treatment, we were able to continue the analytic work in a productive way for two more years. These two years, in fact, turned out to be the most valuable period in Mr C's analysis.

What I found to be of particular interest in this case is that, unknown to me, my behavior was influenced by something that my analyst had said some years before. At that time – it was long after my analysis had ended – he was the discussant at a case conference involving a lengthy, but stalemated, analysis.

"If you have not broken through after nine years of treatment," I recall him saying, "perhaps you should acknowledge that further progress is unlikely."

It was in the ninth year of analysis that I found my doubts about the treatment increasing. For reasons that were not clear to me then, I experienced more frustration and became less hopeful about the outcome at that time. No doubt this attitude communicated itself to my patient and, in leading to emotional withdrawal on my part, was largely responsible for his wish to end the analysis. My recollection of the conference involving my former analyst, which arose suddenly one day as the patient and I were discussing termination, was a clue to important transactions that were taking place between Mr C and myself. I realized that my identification with my analyst carried within it a long-standing wish for his love and approval. And it was just this kind of yearning, increased by my subtle withdrawal from him, that my patient was protecting himself against by the employment of rigid defenses; defenses that were off-putting to me and to which I, in turn, reacted by pulling back.

This experience, perhaps more than any other, served as proof for me of the enduring quality of our transferences to our own analysts and of the need for us, as clinicians, to be aware that even years after our own treatment has ended, being in the presence of our former analyst – even when this is at a distance and no words are exchanged – can revive transference feelings in a way that can exert a significant influence on our work with patients.

I have cited these examples, then, in an effort to illustrate the impact that the nonverbal communications that regularly take place between patient and analyst can have on their transference-countertransference interactions. Ordinarily when we examine this centrally important aspect of the analytic situation, our focus is on the verbal sphere, and what is communicated overtly through language. Equally important in affecting transference and countertransference, however, are the subtle, often unconscious, influences that are expressed through nonverbal enactments. Awareness and interpretation of the impact of behaviors of this kind, which are carried out by both patient and analyst, constitute an essential element in dealing effectively with the transference-countertransference dimension of analytic work.

Bibliography

Deutsch, F. (1952) Analytic posturology. *Psychoanalytic Quarterly*, 21(2): 196–214.

Freud, S. (1895) Frau Emmy von N. *SE* 2: 48–105.

McLaughlin, J. (1987) The play of transference: Some reflections on enactment in the psychoanalytic situation. *Journal of the American Psychoanalytic Association*, 35: 557–582.

McLaughlin, J. (1988) The analyst's insights. *Psychoanalytic Quarterly*, 57: 370–388.

McLaughlin, J. (1991) Clinical and theoretical aspects of enactment. *Journal of the American Psychoanalytic Association*, 39: 595–614.

McLaughlin, J. (1992) Nonverbal behavior in the analytic situation: The search for meaning in nonverbal cues. In S. Kramer and S. Akhtar (eds.), *When the Body Speaks: Psychological Meaning in Kinetic Cues* (pp. 131–162). Northvale, NJ: Jason Aronson.

Reich, W. (1933) *Character Analysis*. New York: Orgone Institute Press, 1945.

14

THE ANALYST'S SELF-REFLECTIVE PARTICIPATION AND THE TRANSFERENCE-COUNTERTRANSFERENCE MATRIX

Steven Cooper

In this chapter I shall try to elaborate what I believe to be a few under-theorized points about the transference-countertransference matrix. I will explore an element of the analyst's self-reflective participation that involves his attitudes about the transference-countertransference – attitudes that influence how he thinks about and uses this realm of clinical information. I introduce a related concept, the "transference-countertransference surround," to refer to a number of factors and attitudes held by the analyst that surround the concept of understanding, using, and interpreting the transference-countertransference. In total, the transference surround may be usefully understood as a part of what Racker (1968) refers to as the analyst's "counter-resistances."

I include several factors in the notion of the transference surround. One important dimension is the analyst's effort to create degrees of significance about examining the transference-countertransference. Patient and analyst collaborate in the examination of what they form together as a unity in the communication of unconscious minds and experience. Part of the analyst's work is to create an atmosphere or culture for examining this unity. The analyst's relationship to the idea of analyzing transference-countertransference is not just a function of his countertransference to the patient but is also determined by other factors such as his countertransference to the psychoanalytic method. Another important dimension is the fact that some analysts prefer to work with the transference-countertransference during all phases of analysis while others are most interested in working in displacement. I also include the ways that the analyst thinks about himself as both an old and a new object. All these factors related to the transference-countertransference surround relate to some extent to the analyst's transference-countertransference to the psychoanalytic method (Cooper, 2010a, 2010b; Parsons, 2006).

I believe that psychoanalysis is entering a phase of theory development in which it is necessary to think of concepts such as the transference-countertransference surround that bridge different theoretical orientations. There has been enough interpenetration of theories that we are now ready to speak of concepts that are important across theoretical approaches as well as how we use these concepts, since many of us are not clearly identified with one theoretical model.

I think about transference and countertransference phenomena in clinical work as a unity. I find it meaningful to think about the two as a unity because it is difficult to understand one person and the kind of transference that he might form without knowing something about how it is being experienced by another person. Since I believe that patients recruit us into particular kinds of familiar internalized object relation patterns and unconscious conflicts and fantasies, it is usually necessary to try to understand how the analyst is experiencing this form of recruitment and how he participates in its development. Often, as we learn about this participation we also learn how the analyst's responses to his patient's internalized objects and relational patterns and engagement, in turn, affect the patient.

The notion of a transference-countertransference unity takes as a given that as a patient feels safe enough to communicate deeper levels of affect and meaning, that he or she will engage the analyst in particular kinds of understanding and responses. One of the most difficult parts of the analytic process involves the efforts of the analyst to get "inside" the patient's internalized world while trying to understand this world and his own responses to the patient.

There are many ways that I agree with Feldman (1997) and many other contemporary Kleinian analysts about how the patient attempts to reduce the discrepancy between an internalized object relation or unconscious fantasy and the actual behavior of the analyst. To the extent that an internalized object relation is a comfortable or congruent one for the analyst, he may not be able to interpret for the patient what is being projected and recruited. I am also quite interested in how the analyst finds himself able to succeed in examining these transferences and how he is limited in doing so. What kinds of countertransference does he experience with the patient about what he observes and interprets? These phenomena are also always well described at the level of the analyst's counter-transference to the analytic method.

I tend to think that the analyst is always involved in some form of enactment in the transference-countertransference. This does not mean that these forms of enactment are always problematic. In fact, I think that a hypervigilance toward various modes of enactment creates its own problems and illusions.

Creating significance about the idea of transference-countertransference

In agreement with Racker (1968) and Balint (1968) I believe that analysts of all theoretical persuasions indoctrinate their patients. I rarely say things to my patients that are explicitly orienting or educational, though I have done so before and don't take a position about the value or meaning of this without a particular clinical context to draw from. But there is no mistaking the idea that we communicate to our patients what we value about examining their inner lives. Patients learn early on whether the analyst is interested in the patient's allusions to the analyst, direct and indirect. They learn whether the analyst makes inferences about the nature of the transference from extra-transference communication and displacement. They learn early on whether the analyst ever makes indirect use of his counter-transference reactions and the like. They learn whether the analyst is likely to make use of the transference-countertransference early on in analytic work or whether he is prone to wait for a longer period of time before referring to the transference.

Apart from the analyst's theoretical model and the degree to which he values the transference-countertransference entity, there is the question of how explicitly he draws the patient's attention to this unity. For example, Merton Gill's extensive elaboration of the transference in the early stages of analysis was different in part because of the degree to which he explicitly drew the patient's attention to the transference. One can make use of the transference-countertransference in our understandings of the patient without making these understandings explicit to the patient.

The issue I wish to place into focus is how the analyst attempts to draw the patient's attention to the significance of the transference-countertransference. For example, when relevant, I try to catch moments of the patient's seemingly banal questions or associations and draw out their significance in terms of multiple and evocative expressions of possible meaning regarding what is being communicated by the patient. I am always struck by the power of the meaningful connections that I can make in connection with a patient's associations that they believe to be trivial or meaningless. When there is something to be interpreted in these moments it can help to expand the patient–analyst framework of meaning. Sometimes the simplest of questions from patient to analyst are saturated with meaning. Even a question such as "Why do I keep doing this?" may have many different meanings. It may represent the patient beginning to move into a different kind of self-reflection about his own behavior or mind. It may constitute the first time that the patient is allowing himself to be more dependent and in a more regressive transference to the analyst. It may signify or mark a level of curiosity and conflict that the patient has been able to move toward from positions of relative comfort with various kinds of compromise formations.

For three years prior to receiving formal analytic training I studied with Merton Gill, who was at the time immersed in his work on the early interpretation of transference. Gill's notions of transference taught me a number of useful lessons in working with the transference but also, as I discovered, interfered with others. Gill was developing a very persistent, perhaps it might even be said relentless, curiosity about the patient's tendencies to allude to the transference. This way of listening, no matter how illuminating, could become a kind of enactment of a narrow form of engagement and participation with a patient. For me, the narrowness lies in trying to grab on to meaning too quickly, in contrast to letting the characters in the play get developed (Ferro and Basile, 2009). Gill's focus on the patient's experience of the analyst as a part of the transference was a much-needed correction to the analyst's focus on transference as more exclusively unconscious. Yet taken to its extreme it can make the analyst less attuned to the behavior of the patient, to words as actions, and to the transference as a "total situation" (Joseph, 1985).

The analyst's attitudes toward the
transference-countertransference

Parsons (2006) suggested that all analysts have various versions of countertransference to the psychoanalytic method, and my focus here is on only one dimension of that method. Perhaps one reason that we haven't vigorously explored the analyst's experience of being a transference object is because we fear that in doing so we might undermine the method itself. If analyzing transference were our job – our medium as well as our work in understanding our own countertransference – then why would we think about or perhaps even legitimize the idea of considering how it feels to be a particular kind of transference object?

While it is next to impossible to differentiate the analyst's attitudes toward the transference-countertransference from his theoretical orientation, I believe that is useful to try. For example, some basic questions arise: Does the analyst welcome transference reactions or does he feel alienated by them? Is he likely to feel like an excluded observer (Steiner, 2008) if the patient tends to not allude to or work with his feelings to his analyst in a direct fashion? Conversely, does the analyst feel alienated by the patient's tendencies to see him exclusively in a particular transference mode as opposed to some sense the analyst has about his own experience of the patient within the transference-countertransference? Does the analyst think about the transference-countertransference in a relatively consistent way or is he trying to step outside his own residence, as it were, to see things from outside the transference-countertransference matrix?

Psychoanalysts are always in a relationship both with their patients and with the psychoanalytic process. While many elements make up the analyst's object relationship to the psychoanalytic process, my focus here is on one that is at the heart of method: his reactions not only to being a particular kind of transference object, but also to the basic fact of being a transference object. The centrality of transference to method makes it particularly difficult to think about. Generally, psychoanalysts tend to think about this kind of transference or countertransference to method as overdetermined by work with a particular patient. Yet we are each quite different in our relationship to receiving and participating in the analysis of transference – in how enthusiastically we embrace, feel gratified, idealize, devalue, or resent the method. We are each different in the degree to which we are likely to feel at home with being an object of transference, alienated by the notion of transference, and the like. There are also the general matters of whether a particular analyst is most at home in working with transference through displacement or taking it up more directly.

The act of giving ourselves over to receiving the patient's transference partly defines us as analysts and shapes what we are trying to accomplish. When we work with our internal reactions and experiences about being transference objects within the particularities of any analytic dyad, we always run the risk of collapsing the patient's analytic space itself, taking away this precious opportunity to understand our old objects, the ghosts that haunt us and accompany us in the present. Unconscious enactment is related to working with feelings about being objects of transference, yet since it is a lynchpin of technique it may sometimes be quite difficult to see.

The notion of the analyst "being" a transference object doesn't imply that the analyst occupies a static, one-dimensional form of object relating or affective experience for the patient as the patient expresses unconscious feelings for the analyst in the form of transference. By "being a transference object" I simply refer to the patient's conscious and unconscious experience and participation in that affective realm that both patient and analyst recognize as a part of transference.

Psychoanalysts have been more likely to focus on the patient's resistance to the transference (e.g., Sandler and Sandler, 1994) versus the analyst's resistance to observing the transference. Bird's (1972) description of these forms of resistance in the analyst is one exception to this generalization, and Joseph (1985) and Feldman (1997) offer others. Each of these authors in different ways provides the analyst with an expanded lens for observing both the transference and his own resistance to observing the transference, while the transference involves "obvious but unseen" expressions by the patient about how he experiences the analyst within his internalized object world.

Our more general reactions to being a transference object often help inform us about the nature of specific transference and countertransference reactions with a particular patient, just as they are affected by the content of particular transferences. For example, the analyst may have a distant relationship to what the patient attributes to him, or an intimate experience of these attributions. This may be related to defensive aspects of how the patient is relating to the analyst, or may correspond to the analyst's particular kinds of experience in response to the patient. The analyst's wish for

274

recognition may become prominent at various stages of analytic work (Steiner, 2008). In the same way there are aspects of the analyst that he may wish to not be recognized by the patient. It is easy for the analyst to attribute or consign disavowed parts of himself to the patient's "transference," or to be overly literal in failing to see, as transference, elements of the patient's perceptions of the analyst that resonate with the analyst's perceptions of himself. For example, experienced analysts have the opportunity over time to determine whether they tend to be more comfortable with elements of erotic or hostile transferences, and of course whether they tend to experience more frequently one form of transference rather than another.

I view it as axiomatic that the analyst is in various modes of conflict with the idea and experience of being a transference object, just as he is in one state of conflict toward everything else in psychic life (Brenner, 1982; Smith, 2000). Moreover, one part of the various targets of conflict – and the ways that conflict is expressed – lies in the analyst's relationship to our method and its status in working with and in the transference.

Perhaps it could be said that we have particular forms of compromise formation related to being transference objects that involve occupying a position between a methodological ideal (e.g., what the analyst aims to receive and interpret) and a clinical reality (the analyst's constraint in interpreting particular clinical phenomena). For example, when the analyst notices that he is in a kind of postured position with his patient related to this type of compromise, it is often a sign that he might try to understand the relevance of this countertransference situation to the notion of transference in the "total situation" of psychoanalysis (Joseph, 1985). In other words, the analyst might question what these compromises repeat or how they might be seen as a form of enactment of previous or new forms of object relating. This view is consistent with Feldman's (1997) view of the analytic situation as one in which the patient projects both a fantasy of an object relationship and a propensity toward action. Within this view, the patient is trying to reduce the discrepancy between this internalized object relationship and his experiences in the analytic situation. If the analyst receives these attributions with too much of a sense of congruence between the internalized object relation or fantasy and the experience of the analytic situation, he is often unable to observe various modes of conflict and defense related to the meaning of these unconscious object relations.

For example, I have several times noted a particular kind of countertransference reaction to patients who were particularly envious of me and angry in the transference. With one patient in particular I was seen as a father who had much to give and selfishly refused, instead deciding to withhold love from him. I began to feel that something was being extracted and stolen from me that I wanted to get back. I felt that what I had to give was continually minimized or not even perceived. This patient stimulated a vengeful fantasy about not wanting to give, and I noted myself withdrawing from him at particular moments when I knew that I had something useful to say to him about what he was overlooking and unable to take in from me. I had felt that I was giving my all and it was not enough. My patient wanted me to change the inherent and institutionalized restraints of being an analyst so that I might spend more time with him, time that would be outside our analytic hours and time that he would not pay for. Interestingly, my vengeful fantasy of withholding from him reflected an actual inhibition on my part about interpreting more actively the ways in which he felt that I wasn't giving enough and that I couldn't give enough. I have referred to this as a form of the analyst "working backwards" – discovering and hearing a new formulation that is implicit or embedded in a comment that we have just made (Cooper, 2010b). Ferro (2005) has written extensively about these phenomena as he illuminates the evolving narrative and elaboration of the patient's unconscious, internalized world.

Feldman (1997) has noted that what is projected into the analyst by the patient is a fantasy of an object relationship that "evokes not only thoughts and feelings but also propensities toward action" (p. 238). Thus a fantasy of an object relationship essentially impinges upon the analyst in one manner or another. Feldman states that the analyst may feel varying degrees of comfort with this projection or he may be prone to enact. In Feldman's terms the enactment may represent the analyst's attempt at restoring or bringing a less-disturbing fantasy to the forefront of the interaction. Feldman seems to be implying that there is an optimal level of receptivity to these projections in which the analyst will not be prone to restoring or revising the patient's elaboration of his fantasy. While I agree with the notion that there is an optimal level of receptivity to the patient's projections, I also believe that the analytic pair is always in some form of enactment. I would tend to think that, whether the analyst is comfortable or not with these projections, he is positioned in a particular place – via unconscious process that may reveal itself at one point or other as a form of enactment. But I find quite useful Feldman's notion of thinking about projection in terms of the projection of a particular kind of object relationship that evokes or recruits (Sandler, 1976) particular kinds of actions. This points the analyst to consider more specifically how he feels about being pointed in particular directions by the patient and how it differs from the patient's earlier propensities for action.

Somewhat similarly to Feldman, Caper (1997) describes the need for the analyst to discover both his relationship to receptivity to the patient's transference ascriptions, and his need to stand outside these ascriptions with "a mind of his own." When the analyst identifies too much with the patient's projections, or what Strachey (1934) called "external phantasy objects," he is unable to survive these projections and cuts off his access to his internalized objects that allow him some interpretive purchase. Caper offered a view of his own attempts to position himself in relation to his own analytic attitude by emphasizing the importance of the analyst establishing "a mind of his own."

I appreciate Caper's focus on the need to not be too subsumed by the patient's unconscious wishes to create in the analyst too great a receptivity to the patient's projected internal world. Caper's concern about the analyst's susceptibility to being "too receptive" might prevent his or her achievement of the position from which interpretations about the patient's inner life may grow. Yet I also try to be attuned to the ways in which the analyst's inner object world is experienced by the patient. We can't always determine that the analyst's "receptivity" to the patient involves simply the analyst's identification with the patient's projections as a problematic or pathological receptivity to the patient. In my view there are elements of reciprocal exchange between the inner object world and ascriptions of external phantasy objects from each participant.

I think it fair to say, since the method of psychoanalysis is so centrally defined by the analysis of transference, that we have been more prone to focus on the analyst's attempts and wishes to bring the transference into focus (Steiner, 2008). Sandler and Sandler's (1994) classic paper on the anti-regressive tendency also spoke to the patient's anxiety and inhibition, which prevent him from using therapeutic regression and building the capacity to work in the transference.

Analysts have written less about the sense of alienation that can accompany listening to the myriad ways that patients experience us in the transference. Sometimes I think of being a transference object as a kind of uprooting, being an alien in a strange land. There can be a sense of inhabiting a self as experienced by another that is sometimes unfamiliar or at other times uncomfortably familiar, in that the patient recognizes parts of us that we might wish were less recognizable. In our acceptance of this role as analysts, and indeed in our invitation to work with transference without really knowing what we're getting into or how it will go, our work of psychoanalytic treatment begins with an act of uncertainty and risk for the analyst even if the risks are not as great as for the patient.

To some extent the analyst pushes aside his personal concerns about this risk in favor of his method, which he believes will be helpful to his patient. The notion of pushing aside personal concerns is, however, always a mix of investment in the patient and the analytic process, as well as potentially having available to the analyst elements of useful information. An obvious caveat to this investigation is the need for the analyst to always consider first that his "objections" to being seen in the transference may involve any one of a number of problematic features – a rejection of the patient's unconscious fantasy life, a need on the part of the analyst to be seen "as he is" rather than as the object in the patient's mind, or a wish on the part of the analyst to dictate psychic reality rather than explore the patient's psychic reality.

At the beginning of analytic work there is a kind of agreement involving the analyst's invitation for the patient to say what comes to mind. Since the analyst cannot know everything about his unconscious reactions to this invitation, inviting patients to say what comes to mind, as we know, is a limited invitation. There are some rules of engagement, however uniquely defined, in sex, visual art, literature, and athletic activity as well. While different than the faith of the patient, the analyst's invitation may involve a potentially counterphobic defense inasmuch as he doesn't yet know whether he really wants the patient to say what comes to mind. Ogden (1996) seems to implicitly address this complexity in outlining that he also wishes to let his patients know that they, like he, may want their privacy as well. Ogden may, in effect, be making an interpretation about the analyst's countertransference to his method, one that involves a particular kind of enactment in this invitation that doesn't pay enough attention to both the lack of certainty about what we want and the need for privacy as well as expressiveness. He is implying a kind of posturing, as it were, on the part of the analyst's invitation.

This partial posturing may even be seen as a kind of institutionalized enactment of our countertransference to the method of psychoanalysis.

I would suggest that the analyst's stance regarding inviting the patient to say what comes to mind is always an adapted stance that the analyst has not yet fully come to experience as his own stance. He is consciously wishing to extend the invitation because of his belief in the method, but he doesn't yet know whether he really wants to hear what the patient has to say. At the very least, he knows that a new patient, a stranger as it were, will be telling him the most intimate details of his or her life. What has prepared the two for this? The postured part of his stance relates to the fact that the analyst commits himself to this method because he believes in it. But he is often filled with complex feelings that are sometimes not attended to and may be important.

Thus, at the beginning of an analysis, our surrender to being transference objects and translators of the language of transference has elements of posture because we don't yet know the patient well, just as we do not know how the patient experiences us. We don't necessarily understand the origins of the ways the patient sees us – whether it is based in early history and/or is currently unfolding in aspects of the interaction with the analyst. We don't yet understand how we have become implicated in the patient's inner object world, nor how we will contain, enact, and analyze this inner world with its attendant feelings. At the outset, the analyst's receptivity to the patient's transferential experience is established more by fiat, and by the analyst's good intentions, and grows out of our dedication to helping our patients. It is a partly postured stance that is part of our clinical, human, and technical responsibility, but probably different than it will be over the course of analysis.

This invitation by the analyst is, of course, far more than postured. His genuine concern for the patient is quite important in understanding the analyst's countertransference to the analytic method. I imagine that for most analysts there is a period of time, a transitional time, during which they need to translate their method of being a person who is listening as we do outside analysis, to the ways in which we listen with our method of psychoanalysis. For example, when I begin working with a patient in analysis I often initially have an intensity of focus that unwittingly limits my experience of my own reactions and person. I would say that I am less "adrift" in my own associations and reverie as I'm trying to simply learn about the patient and get the "facts" surrounding their actual and not only psychic lives. I have had experiences as I begin an analysis in which it is common for me to see things very close to the way that my patient is seeing and describing things; I don't have my usual accompanying ability to step back and consider a variety of ways of thinking about what he is saying. It as if I'm psychologically devoted to seeing things as he does, colonized in an easy and seamless way by the patient's sensibility and concerns, and some other part of my mind is either constricted or on hold. While this empathic capacity is always a valuable, necessary analytic function during all phases of work, I usually find that it is not sufficient.

Over time, my mind is freer to work and function as a separate entity. I have, in Caper's (1997) words, more of a mind of my own as things develop. I can observe how I view the patient more distinctly from how I experience how the patient sees things. My devotion to the analytic task becomes less postured, more genuine, to the extent that I feel a more distinct sensibility within myself that can move back and forth between immersion in the patient's psychic reality and our overlapping and distinct psychic realities. In a sense, during this early process, I've shut down a part of my mind that would think more analytically and in a more complex and supple way because, at some unconscious level, I don't feel comfortable thinking that way with someone whom I don't know very well. We are taught to not talk to strangers, particularly about something as private as the ways in which the patient has managed conflict, or in effect his self-cure (Khan, 1973). Of course, these are generalizations, since among the things that make analytic work so interesting are the analyst's vicissitudes in listening and participation.

One might usefully ask questions about why I would emphasize, in the act of beginning an analysis, elements of the analyst's posture rather than simply refer to it as a kind of unobjectionable participation or dedication to the work task. I want to emphasize that psychoanalysts do well to stay close to the nature of their personal participation and, if you will, impersonal participation.

Regarding the analyst's countertransference to method, I have heard some patients complain that their analyst loves his technique more than the patient. To some extent, of course, this is an epic battle for each patient as he tries to get the analyst to love him, while the analyst's job is to understand him and show him how to understand himself. Partly the analyst's love of his method allows him to work with and know his patient in a way that is unique and distinguishable from other forms of intimate contact. However, there is something to the idea that if the analyst is too in love with his method it can become an obstacle to analytic work. If the analyst is absorbed by his method and theory, too much in love with those objects, as it were, then he will not have enough left over to engage with a patient. There is a difference between the use of theory as usurping versus facilitating our formulations, interpretations, and participation in the analytic process. Being too in love with method is a kind of degradation of the psychoanalytic process that, after all, is a method that allows for us to intimately and uniquely understand each of our patients. Just as the analyst helps the patient to examine his method of self-cure, which interferes with him giving up old, ineffective solutions to problems and resolving conflicts, the analyst must also examine his own relationship to self-cure, since this inevitably goes to the core of his blind spots in understanding his patient. In this way the analyst must surrender to his patient. He must move beyond his fixed ideas and selected facts (e.g., Bion, 1962; Poincaré, 1908). This includes examining the degree to which his relationship to his method may serve as a resistance to analyzing the patient. In a sense, the notion of the analyst as a new object in the therapeutic action of analysis is not only related to the patient's increased freedom in finding new affective pathways associated with object ties (Loewald, 1960). It also includes the fact that the analyst has to become a new object to his self, and his self's relationship to the analytic method (Cooper, 2004, 2010a; Slavin and Kriegman, 1998; Symington, 1983).

If the analyst is too attached to being seen as a transference object closely tied to the patient's conscious perceptions and fantasies, this can also be problematic. Feldman (1997) puts this well when he comments on a "comfortable, collusive arrangement, in which the analyst feels his role is congruent with some internal phantasy" (p. 238). This "comfort" may also become an idealization of being a particular kind of "transference object" that can, in turn, involve a degradation of the analytic method since it may involve the analyst's compromised ability to reflect on transference in terms of the patient's unconscious participation or the total situation of transference.

Sometimes the analyst is too attached to or falls back on encrusted ways of being observed and experienced by the patient that, in turn, become sources of resistance to analytic work. The "method" is memorialized through previously offered interpretations of transference rather than given life in the form of curiosity and exploration. It can be tiring to be stuck in places of transference–countertransference entanglement that are difficult to change. Often, as the patient and analyst get engaged with the patient's most refractory conflicts, they get into habits, if you will, that are related to this transference-countertransference engagement. As one of Samuel Beckett's (1954) characters said: "habit is a great deadener." I think that every dyad, including in analyses that are productive, going concerns, may get habituated to transference and stuck in particular places that involve acclimating to each other for better and sometimes worse. For the analyst to get habituated to the patient's perceptions and experience seems as potentially problematic as the patient getting habituated to the analyst's limitations. Similarly, Joan Didion (2006) wrote of the dissociation related to the stasis of everyday life as a kind of disconnection that can go almost without notice. Sometimes it is important for the analyst to check in with himself about whether forms of distancing and disconnection are a part of ongoing engagement or disengagement with the patient. Method in these instances is associated with deadness.

In this sense, the analysis of transference and countertransference can sometimes be the stuff of dissociation – the stasis of everyday life – a kind of force of habit for both the patient and analyst. In this context, so-called interpretations of transference provide more distant and static observations instead of new information about the patient's unconscious experience. The analyst should thus be prepared for the emergence of aspects of habit. At first, transference is new and in some sense unfamiliar, "*unheimlich*" (Freud, 1919). Yet over time the very nature of transference as unfamiliar may change and become part of our habitual modes of relating to each other.

Various types of collapse can be occasioned by the analyst's dissociated states that prevent him from being a transference object, or by the patient's dissociation within an embedded and repetitive transference experience. It is particularly when strong affective expressions in the areas of longing, desire, hostility, and attachment are directed toward the analyst that he may become dissociated. Sometimes the analyst's distancing from these affects involves a kind of compromise between saying more of his thoughts about the patient versus not doing so for fear of hurting the patient. Analyst and patient alike can retreat from the daunting uncertainty of new and spontaneous interpersonal relatedness by viewing each other, over extended periods of time, in the familiar safety of mutually agreed-upon transference-countertransference understandings. This retreat is well described as a kind of interpersonal compromise formation (Cooper, 2010b) and often takes one form or other of analytic posturing.

Put another way, the interpretation of transference as an action or a form of enactment has been a much ignored and neglected area of focus in analytic work because the interpretation of transference is our most revered form of technical activity. Nevertheless it is no less likely to involve compromise formation, repetition, and enactment than other forms of analytic activity.

New good and bad objects and countertransference to the analytic method

Related to the elaboration of the analyst's attitudes toward the transference-countertransference is his view of himself as a new and old object over the course of analytic work. In many discussions about the new-object concept there is a conflation between how the patient experiences the analyst and how the analyst is intending to function. For example when the analyst is able to interpret the patient's attempts to recruit him to engage in particular versions of internalized object relations (Feldman, 1997), we might say that the analyst is functioning as a good analyst and a new object. The patient, however, may be disappointed and angry that the analyst is not acting in ways that are familiar to the patient and thus the analyst becomes a "bad" object. When the analyst enacts particular elements of the patient's recruitment (Feldman, 1997; O'Shaughnessy, 1992) we might say that he is not a "good" object or effective analyst, but that the patient is experiencing the analyst as a familiar/good object.

From the patient's point of view the analyst may be experientially a bad object at a few levels. He may be experienced as bad to the extent that he doesn't fulfill the patient's expectations for his behavior from the point of view of the internalized fantasy. As analysts observing this situation, we are likely to view the analyst in this situation as a "good" analyst doing his job, and ultimately as a good object. In the context of trying to interpret the patient's attempts to repeat these earlier relationships, the patient's experience of the analyst as a bad object may or may not be connected to the notion that the patient is experiencing a negative transference in the form of a repetition of a reaction to an earlier disappointing object. It is commonly observed by analysts from various theoretical schools that negative transference often proceeds from deep levels of trust between patient and analyst. The analyst may simply be frustrating to the patient to the extent that the ways that he is psychoanalyzing him are not in line with the patient's modes of self-cure (Freud, 1912; Khan, 1973). In fact, Freud (1912) emphasized that transference was among the most important forms of self-cure. Of course, the analyst may also be experienced as a bad object as the result of empathic failures based less on this discrepancy between internalized fantasy and real behavior, and more on the fact that the analyst has simply not understood or is unable to contain something vitally important to the patient.

From the point of view of analytic technique, there are several surfaces that I think about in terms of the analyst's function as a good analyst/object, functions that are not necessarily equated with the patient's experience of the analyst as a good object. First, the analyst who tries, more or less consistently and empathically, to draw the patient's attention to the discrepancy between the patient's internalized fantasy and the analyst's differences from those fantasies functions as a good object (Feldman, 1997; Strachey, 1934). He might also be considered a good-enough bad object (bad referring to the patient's experience of bad, and good with regard to the analyst fulfilling the aim of interpretation). In this sense, the analyst who tries to or is able to stay close to the aims that Strachey (1934) and Feldman (1997) have spelled out is functioning as a new good object, while the analyst who is unable to see the patient's efforts to recruit him in coordination with his internalized fantasies is a new bad object. He is an old object in his congruence with the internalized fantasy but is a new bad object in the sense that he is the patient's analyst who is supposed to be pointing out what he sees. He is new especially in how he will, in very particular ways, bump up against his inability to implement analytic tools and to work with the analytic process in helping the patient to observe the unfolding of transference and unconscious fantasy. For example, Feldman (1997) observes how the analyst's experience of congruence and easy acceptance of the patient may often belie various forms of blind spots and be a fertile ground for enactment. I believe that sometimes these limited failures or blind spots of the analyst's are quite productive and generative in terms of promoting deeper understanding of the patient's unconscious communications.

Second, I agree with Ferro (2005) and Ferro and Basile (2009) that psychic reality in the field is often more virtual in nature, involving "characters who are progressively subjected to a process of casting in order to express the types of functioning active in the field" (Ferro and Basile, 2009, p. 2). This means that the analyst's predilection to fall into particular kinds of recruitment is often helpful and necessary in terms of understanding new and deeper levels of the patient's psychic reality. It is often difficult to know for periods of time the meaning of transference because meaning is communicated not only in the use of words but in the use of words to carry out actions (Joseph, 1985). It is also the case that the minds of the analysand and analyst form a novel structure, a transference-countertransference entity that is at times only understood through the analyst's capacity to retrospectively examine his previous blind spots.

For example, enactments of many kinds occur when the analyst finds the patient's recruitment so congruous as to not be able to have interpretive purchase on what is occurring between them. Some analysts are engaged in this recruitment even as they think that they are analyzing particular parts of the patient.

I have noticed at least two extremes of the analyst's countertransference to the analytic method related to new object experience. One involves the analyst's too-active attempt to become a new object through the circumvention of conflict rather than through the analysis of the patient's internalized world and the ways that it engages the analyst in particular modes of understanding. Sometimes the analyst's countertransference prevents him from perceiving how the patient is unconsciously expressing new thoughts and feelings about him. Sometimes the analyst may also fail to see how his own stance toward the patient's conflicts reflects his patient's changes. In these instances, sometimes the analyst is in the process of but not yet fully able to see how he is becoming in some sense new to the patient, or to himself in relation to the patient.

A great deal of terrain can be found between these two extremes of the countertransference. Part of the analyst's responsibilities lies in creating significance when the patient is able to experience new parts of unconscious conflict, or is displaying new elements of integration of various parts of self and experience. These new moments of significance are often cloaked in familiar, old trappings such as the patient's modes of "self cure" (Freud, 1912; Khan, 1973) that make seeing these moments more difficult than we sometimes realize. Mitchell (1988) suggested that analytic inquiry itself, when involving observation and participation, often promotes the discovery of emergent self and object representations within the patient.

There is little doubt that the dangers linked to the analyst's trying too hard to be a new object are perilous; they certainly fit well in the category O'Shaughnessy (1992) termed "excursions." A related form of countertransference to the analytic method has been well elaborated in post-Bionian explications of the field concept. Ferro and Basile (2009) suggest we are wise to not seek hidden meaning at the expense of viewing the analysand's efforts to express new, evolving meaning, and feel that it is important for the analyst to be able to think for himself. Thus excursions may be manifested through too much focus on either repetition or newness.

If the analyst is to interpret the patient's attempts to reduce the discrepancy between the archaic internalized object and that of the analyst, in my view it is also important to underscore that, in the conduct of many analyses, the patient is experiencing elements of the analyst's conflicts and potentially problematic countertransference both to the patient and to the analytic method. In this way, the analyst is a new bad object. To the extent that the analyst is recruited, enlisted, or is drafted into service in fulfilling these roles, he is contributing to the perpetuation of the patient's problematic adaptations, while, in turn, the analyst's participation in them becomes an obstacle to analytic change and growth.

It is worth including these elements of the analyst as "new" for a few reasons related to both clinical work and theory. The concept of newness is in need of being redefined and modified in our clinical theory because it does represent elements of the analyst's participation in the enactments that occur. It is also important to include a concept of the analyst's newness since, in a certain sense, it relates to the particularities of the analyst's person and his personal participation. In a certain sense it is the analyst's and the patient's encounter with the elements of the analyst's new bad object participation (his struggle in interpreting elements of the patient's internalized world). I believe that it is rarely necessary for the analyst to draw the patient's attention to the analyst's struggle with these elements of participation. The analyst's modes of self-reflection are chiefly organized around his own investigation and observation of his struggles to see the ways that he is being invited into the patient's familiar patterns and modes of engagement with the patient's internalized, unconscious life.

Bibliography

Balint, M. (1968) *The Basic Fault*. London: Tavistock Press.

Beckett, S. (1954) *Waiting for Godot*. New York: Grove Press.

Bion, W. R. (1962) *Learning from Experience*. London: Heinemann.

Bird, B. (1972) Notes on transference: Universal phenomenon and hardest part of analysis. *Journal of the American Psychoanalytic Association*, 20: 267–301.

Brenner, C. (1982) *The Mind in Conflict*. New York: International Universities Press.

Caper, R. (1997) A mind of one's own. *International Journal of Psychoanalysis*, 78: 265–278.

Cooper, S. (2004) State of the hope: The new bad object in the therapeutic action of psychoanalysis. *Psychoanalytic Dialogues*, 14: 527–553.

Cooper, S. (2010a) The analyst's experience of being a transference object: An elusive form of countertransference to the psychoanalytic method. *Psychoanalytic Quarterly*, 74: 349–382.

Cooper, S. (2010b) *A Disturbance in the Field: Essays in Transference-Countertransference Engagement*. London: Routledge.

Didion, J. (2006) *The Year of Magical Thinking*. New York: Random House.

Feldman, M. (1997) Projective identification: The analyst's contribution. *International Journal of Psychoanalysis*, 78: 227–241.

Ferro, A. (2005) *Seeds of Illness, Seeds of Recovery*. New York: Brunner-Routledge.

Ferro, A. and Basile, R (eds.) (2009) *The Analytic Field: A Clinical Concept*. London: Karnac.

Freud, S. (1912) The dynamics of transference. *The Standard Edition of the Complete Psychological Works of Sigmund Freud*, J. Strachey (ed., trans.), vol. 12: 97–108. London: Hogarth Press.

Freud, S. (1919) The uncanny. *SE* 17: 217–256.

Joseph, B. (1985) Transference: The total situation. *International Journal of Psychoanalysis*, 66: 447–454.

Khan, M. (1973) The role of illusion in the analytic space and process. *Annual of Psychoanalysis*, 1: 231–246.

Loewald, H. (1960) The therapeutic action of psychoanalysis. *International Journal of Psychoanalysis*, 41: 16–33.

Mitchell, S. (1988) *Relational Concepts in Psychoanalysis*. Cambridge, MA: Harvard University Press.

Ogden, T. (1996) Reconsidering three aspects of psychoanalytic technique. *International Journal of Psychoanalysis*, 77: 883–899.

O'Shaughnessy, E. (1992) Enclaves and excursions. *International Journal of Psychoanalysis*, 73: 603–611.

Parsons, M. (2006) The analyst's countertransference to the psychoanalytic process. *International Journal of Psychoanalysis*, 87: 1183–1196.

Poincaré, H. (1908) *Science and Method*. New York: Science Press.

Racker, H. (1968) *Transference and Counter-transference*. New York: International Universities Press.

Sandler, J. (1976) Countertransference and role-responsiveness. *International Journal of Psychoanalysis*, 3: 43–47.

Sandler, J. and Sandler, A. (1994) Theoretical and technical comments on regression and anti-regression. *International Journal of Psychoanalysis*, 75: 431–439.

Slavin, M. and Kriegman, D. (1998) Why the analyst needs to change: Toward a theory of conflict, negotiation, and mutual influence in the therapeutic process. *Psychoanalytic Dialogues*, 8: 247–284.

Smith, H. (2000) Countertransference, conflictual listening, and the analytic object relationship. *Journal of the American Psychoanalytic Association*, 48: 95–128.

Steiner, J. (2008) Transference to the analyst as an excluded observer. *International Journal of Psychoanalysis*, 89: 39–53.

Strachey, J. (1934) The nature of the therapeutic action of psycho-analysis. *International Journal of Psychoanalysis*, 15: 127–159

Symington, N. (1983) The analyst's act of freedom as an agent of therapeutic change. *International Review of Psychoanalysis*, 10: 283–292.

15

ROLE-REVERSAL AND THE
DISSOCIATION OF THE SELF

An exploration of a somewhat neglected
transference-countertransference dynamic

Franco Borgogno and Massimo Vigna-Taglianti

Introduction

Within a historical-clinical framework in which the development of psychoanalytic thought on the process of transference-countertransference is underlined in light of the (often conflicting) binomial "acting cure–talking cure," we would like to present our thoughts on role-reversal, and on why this primitive inter- and intrapsychic dynamic, at the forefront in our practice and at the center of what is repeated during the longer-term wave of an analytic treatment, has not yet been explicitly granted sufficient theoretical space in our literature, despite being precociously identified and explored by Ferenczi.

The phenomenon of role-reversal will be presented and clinically and theoretically discussed in its two principal aspects – the unconscious identification with parents and their psychic culture, and the concomitant dissociation[1] of the suffering infant part of the self – with particular attention paid both to the affective-cognitive conditions that favor its occurrence and transformation, and to the principal characteristics with which it prevalently manifests itself during the analysis, while also indicating the various types of mental suffering and psychic conflict at work.[2]

Aside from its specific focus on role-reversal, our work aims to propose some considerations on the inevitability of *enactment* in the analyst's management of the typical sequence "remembering, repeating, and working-through" that the analytic path encounters in these cases, and to underline how it can sometimes become a profound preliminary matrix of the traditional mutative interpreting activity if it is recognized and worked through. In other words, we would like to anticipate that "interpreting" signifies for us not only the elective activity of verbalizing those mental events that emerge in the session, but, above all, the willingness of the analyst to become an "interpreter" – in the literal sense of the word – of the painful events that the patient brings to the analytic scene, in the hope that they will be witnessed and understood through a long process of *working-through*. It is precisely this testimony – which the analyst can offer through his willingness to experience (at first not knowingly) in his own skin and body all the roles that every analysis requires the analyst to take on, an aspect pointed out earlier by Melanie Klein in 1929 – that, with time, allows the patient to feel "real" (in the sense of Winnicott's "realness") and to find his lost emotional experiences, or sometimes to experience them for the first time, consequently promoting the integration of what had been dissociated and the healing of the patient's psychic wounds.

Primitive transference, symbolic transference, and repetition

We think that transference – the elective scene in which the past comes back to life – will manifest itself in analysis under different forms, and not always at a symbolic level (Freud, 1912, 1914). For instance, in patients whose psychic suffering originates in the area of preverbal trauma – in the area of the "basic fault" (Balint, 1968) – transference occurs mostly at a more primitive level of expression (Winnicott, 1967a, 1967b) that involves in an unconscious way, at least initially, not just the patient but also the analyst. In such situations we are in the domain of non-completed symbolization; with the passing of time, the symbolization can slowly be reintroduced into the analysis by the functions that the analyst performs, so that the patient will eventually be able to find it within himself.

The symbolization that has to be constructed obviously implies much more than the simple activity of verbalization on the analyst's part: it is a matter of concretely creating the affective interpsychic conditions so that the emotional alphabet necessary for mastering the lived experience can be transmitted and learnt. In short, it is a matter of creating the conditions for the symbolization process rather than repairing or rerouting it, so that in such cases the analysis is, more than ever, a chance for making a new experience happen, an experience which could have never occurred before (Balint, 1952; Beres, 1957; Greenacre, 1968).

There is no doubt that transference manifestations – new editions or facsimiles of impulses and phantasies that have to be reawakened and rendered conscious during the analytic process and in which the analyst takes on, or is substituted into the role of a figure from the patient's early history – can be, at times, from the very outset, immediately decoded and interpreted. This occurs also thanks to the different levels of symbolic representation, more or less evolved as it may be, that transference manifestations can take on during the sessions. But the point is that nowadays what happens, especially in the case of neurotics and personalities close to so-called normality, is not to be found in many patients who ask for our help. On this matter, even if it is certainly true that contemporary clinical practice stresses that a lengthy amount of time must pass before the transference can emerge in a decipherable guise, without being precociously induced or led toward particular forms by the analyst's interventions, it is also true that there may be contingencies in which the minimal psychological conditions for the development of a transference and a countertransference, distinguished one from the other, have not yet been constituted. When this is the case, what is missing is a piece of experience connected to subjectivation (Balint, 1963; Botella and Botella, 2005). Trauma, in these circumstances, would consist of the very fact that something that should have happened has not occurred (Bokanowski, 2005; Borgogno, 2007; Ferenczi, 1988; Winnicott, 1963).

We would like, therefore, first to consider once again the fact that these more archaic forms of the transference-countertransference intertwining frequently do not depend on the verbal contents, but take shape in the analytic setting or in its framework through actual reciprocal "enactments" (Boesky, 1982). These enactments do involve the analyst as well, who, in an unconscious manner, finds himself experiencing emotional feelings and roles that, only if adequately worked-through in the long wave of the analytic encounter, will acquire, with their reiterated re-proposal, a rich communicative meaning, allowing a higher degree of understanding of the situations in which the analyst finds himself ensnared.

Precisely this understanding will be the main transformative engine in analysis and, in line with this point of view, our commitment in these clinical cases must be of two types. On the one hand, it will involve welcoming the patient's repetition as his attempt to resolve a task that was left suspended, with his expectations of finding an "encouragement to feel and to think the traumatically interrupted mental experiences to their very end" (Ferenczi, 1955, p. 243). On the other hand, the analyst has to offer the patient the type of mental activity capable of bringing back to life and restarting what has been left unmetabolized at the level of perception and affective significance (Lagache, 1952).

Moreover, it is not rare for these enactments to happen through the "dissociation within the analyst" of the infantile and suffering part of the patient – because they occur through an inversion of roles. In the history of psychoanalysis, role-reversal is, as we have noted, an investigative field onto which little light has been shed due to the great psychic effort that we as psychoanalysts have had to make in order to have access to a psychoanalysis truly based on learning from one's own and from the patient's experience. Only after this long and tormented journey have we become able not only to generically recognize ourselves in the roles of fathers and mothers as objects of transference (a position quite often readily accepted, excluding of course the difficulties in identifying with images of fathers and mothers completely different from the repertoire of affects and manners of being and feeling available to each individual analyst), but also to be really willing to distinguish, within this explorative direction, what kind of father or mother we have contributed to bringing about during our analytic interactions.

Furthermore – and this is a more recent achievement – when it is a case of personifying and literally "embodying" on a conscious level within the analytic scenario not only the parents but also the infantile suffering and traumatized aspects of the patient in contact with a truly improper caregiver, and of identifying ourselves both with the reasons and needs of the child and with the suffering and madness of the parents, the price of recognizing ourselves in these new parts has become even more elevated at the level of the working-through of one's own countertransference, as well as of one's own indispensable *affective response* to what the patient asks us to welcome and host

292

within us. In the increased emotional demand that is progressively required of the analyst, two new voices, which we will discuss in greater depth later, enter the scene. Here we have not only the difficulty of being in vivo the suffering child and sometimes also the traumatic parent, but also that of accepting the lengthy time needed to enucleate the transference, to disentangle it from one's own personal elements (the analyst's transference neurosis, and for Racker [1968], countertransference neurosis too), and to be able finally and mostly *après coup* to interpret it in the most effective manner for the evolution of a treatment.

To summarize, everything we have said so far leads us to advance the following three considerations.

1 The first is that the analytic mirror can no longer be directed merely at reflecting back to the patient, in the most accurate way possible, only his emotional contents; on the contrary, it must unfailingly strive to become aware of and be responsible for that additional part that must necessarily refract, so that true psychic and affective recognition is possible. In other words, in this light we can say that what it has to reflect back, in order to make real recognition possible, has to do not so much with our brilliant understanding of the subject, but rather with something that authentically comes from our own selves.

2 The second is that, in order to make the Goethian "*Werde, was Du bist*" ("Become what you are") possible, at least in the clinical situations we have in mind while writing these reflections, the "construction" needed is indeed the construction by the analyst of an affective "effective" reality, which is preliminary to the construction of a memory (*Wirklichkeitsgefühl*). The construction of the reality we are referring to lies – we must specify – in a more complex operation than the "intellectual-cognitive" one underlined by Freud when, emphasizing the effects of narcissistic traumas that exceeded the common neurotic defense mechanisms, he spoke of "constructions in analysis" (S. Freud, 1937). In brief, unlike Freud, we believe that recovering an unsymbolized and inaccessible historical past (inaccessible through the usual recollections on which analysis hinges) requires more libidinal investment and effort on the part of the analyst. This extra investment and effort on the analyst's part is, in addition, often felt as "dirty" because, in these circumstances, in order to be able

293

to later emerge as distinct and capable of thought, we must earlier be closely involved and not afraid of being and of showing ourselves "mishmashed" and *mestizo* (Borgogno, 1999, 2011) in the dynamics of transference-countertransference. We must, as well, not let ourselves be seduced by our wish to "unplug" (Vigna-Taglianti, 1999, 2002) with regard to the suffering and conflicts that derive from the disturbance that contact with the patient creates in us. Here, Kleinians would say that the analyst must always keep alive his interest in knowing, and stay on guard for the inescapable urge to avoid this. (For more on this, see Brenman-Pick, 1985; Britton, 1998; Feldman, 2009; Joseph, 1989; O'Shaughnessy, 1992; Steiner, 1993.)

3   The third consideration is that the analytic working-through of the countertransference response – which the patient continuously demands of us – cannot be achieved right away, as everyone accepts today.

Role-reversal: clinical phenomenology and the history of a concept

Let us look a little closer at the dissociation of the patient's infantile self in the analyst, and at the resulting role-reversal (in this case, the patient is, in fact, unconsciously identified with the caregivers and with their psychic culture), before providing some clinical vignettes that illustrate our thinking. We would like both to touch upon some general features of this inter- and intrapsychic dynamic, and to draw attention to Ferenczi's pioneering work in this sphere, as well as to that of those who followed in his footsteps not always acknowledging his theoretical legacy. Concerning the duration, fixity, and pervasiveness with which this typical (for us) constellation of "enactment" (Jacobs, 1986, 1991; McLaughlin, 1987, 1991; Ogden, 2001; Renik, 1993, 1997) takes place in the analytic relation, experience teaches us that – in the treatment of children and adults alike – the temporal dimension of role-reversal usually assumes two contrasting forms: it can be episodic, or it can be systematically repeated and structural – or to use a theatrical metaphor for these forms, the "one-off show" or the "two-hundredth Broadway rerun."

Generally speaking, the more persistent and rigid the fixity and duration of the scripts are, the greater the primary psychic disorder is at its roots (think of the psychotics who accept neither that the show is over nor that there are prescribed "correct ways" for playing it; more often than not they call for an encore, and another one, in endless, grueling, repeated performances). Yet we must not forget that rough, episodic, and limited acting can also signal an area of severe suffering that should be taken into serious consideration; this occurs, for example, with adolescents, but not only with them. Having said this, the protracted repetition of the same show can be linked, on the one hand, to a possible deficit in understanding on the analyst's part, while, on the other, it frequently corresponds to the patient's profound need to investigate closely and concretely how the mind of the other can bear being treated this way, as it becomes a container of vicissitudes that the patient had experienced but until then had been unable to speak about or think about.[3] This especially occurs when we are facing patients whose life histories are marked by preverbal traumatic events that have created such extensive damage to the structuring of the ego that their dramatic nature can no longer be "dramatized" so that catastrophic terror has taken the place of anxiety.

Apart from the extreme situations we have just outlined in which the ego and the symbolization process are evidently compromised, in infantile life and in child psychoanalysis role-reversal and dissociation of the self can be an almost natural event.[4] Through playing and dramatizing, the child often tends to actively play out what he has passively endured, and to use similar relational strategies as a common part of his way of communicating his physiological identifications (A. Freud, 1937, 1970). Irrespective of this, even the child analytic playroom – normally an ideal gym and laboratory for studying these phenomena – can sometimes turn into a place where we become spectators of and actors in obscure and disturbing role-reversals that have entirely lost their gamelike guise, paralleling what often occurs in the adult analytic room. These are precisely the situations in which the analyst, through his taxing work of decoding and interpreting the dissociated feelings and roles, has to provide – and give life to – those parental functions and those aspects of the infantile self that have been omitted and are lacking in the patient's history. In other words, in these cases the analyst will have to be simultaneously the suffering and inadequate parent the patient has had, and a parent different from the one fate provided him with; moreover, the analyst will have to be both the child the patient has been, and the child who is able to feel, to react, and in all senses to make himself heard: the very child the patient has never been or known in his childhood and adolescence.[5]

Now, before introducing a few patients who acted on this level, we would like to single out some of the historical roots of this theoretical-clinical view that we intend to highlight here. In so doing, we must first of all mention Ferenczi, who, from the very beginning of psychoanalysis, perceived and denounced a certain phobia of us analysts toward feelings, and, in particular, to identifying with the suffering child and his vulnerability. A phobia, by the way, that might also have led analysts to avoid what Ferenczi has called the "terrorism of suffering." This might well be what has prevented us from fully recognizing the importance of role-reversal in our work, and thus in turn may explain the scarcity of contributions in our literature about this topic (Ferenczi, 1930, 1932, 1988). This phobia might even have prevented this dynamic from occurring in the analytic relationship, compelling us instead to reproduce the behavior of that missing and depriving parent who is oftentimes the source of the patient's psychic pain, with his improper behavior dictated both by a "too much" or a "too little" of drives at work, and more simply due to the failure to assist and be witness to the traumatic experiences of the child or patient (Benjamin, 2011; Borgogno, 1999, 2011).

Irrespective of this, and to return to Ferenczi, we would like to recall first his surprising capacity, present early in his analytic career, to grasp and recognize how often the analyst finds himself experiencing in his own skin the way in which the patient (adult or child) felt treated by grown-ups, both in the past and in the present (Ferenczi, 1912). And secondly, we note the demanding working-through he did toward the end of his life – see the RN case (Ferenczi, 1932, 1988)[6] – of his own difficulties in identifying with the inadequate parent and, even more, with the child "intruded upon" and "deprived" by the aggressive and inappropriate adult. Although such difficulties did not lead him to formulate a proper theory based on role-reversal, they did permit him, even at such an early date, to illustrate how the intrapsychic can be relived within the interpsychic, and to understand that this was the royal road for recognizing and transforming past traumatic and traumatizing events.

With regard to the authors who subsequently delved into and explored this clinical-theoretical breach opened by Ferenczi, beside naming Deutsch (1926), Racker (1968), Searles (1959, 1978–1979) and Levenson (1972, 1983) for their general contributions to the processes of identification, we will mention those who in the course of our experience have most helped us to express the thoughts we have put forward here. Among these are, first, Paula Heimann (1965, 1975), for having underlined the fact that, when trauma is present in the patient's history, the analyst "unconsciously introjects the patient," who at this point acts internally on the analyst "on the basis of an identification with a rejecting, intrusive maternal figure, and repeats their personal experiences by role-reversing" (1965, p. 230). Then Masud Khan (1974), for his detailed case study of Peter, in which he skillfully outlined the fate of role-reversal in analysis and the need for the analyst to experience this situation through the acceptance of the loss of his own subjectivity in order to return, in a second moment, to the patient with a working-through of the painful pathogenic emotional states that the patient, due to a prevailing archaic affectivity, could not express or communicate in shared words. Pearl King (1951/1953/2004, 1962, 1978) also worked throughout her whole life in analytic explorations of this typical affective response of the analyst to the patient's communications, put forward since her first published paper that dealt with the psychic withdrawal of Philip, a boy aged 4 who was coping with the death of his little brother aged 2 and with his mother's depression–withdrawal and with whom he was mainly identified in the session while King had to personify his infantile self in his place. We also recognize Joseph Sandler (1976a, 1976b), for the importance he gave to the "actualizing" of the transference and countertransference processes, and for his penetrating notes about "role-resonance" and the complex system of unconscious communications, both issued and received, operating within the analytic couple in each partner's attempt to impose on the other a specific intrapsychic role-relationship. We also include Peter Giovacchini (1989), for his keenly sensitive description of the re-creation of the infantile traumatic environment in the transference-countertransference interaction with patients who suffer from primitive mental disorders. Among more recent authors, we mention René Roussillon (1991, 2011), who theorized, following Didier Anzieu's concept of "paradoxical transference" (1975), the transference *par détournement*, differentiating it from the more classic one *par déplacement*. And lastly, we add Philip Bromberg (1998, 2006) for his illuminating papers on the dissociative processes that he considers to be both a fundamental function of the ego (in maintaining personal continuity, coherence, and integrity of the sense of self, and for permitting personality growth), and also (in the wake of Ferenczi [1932, 1988], who conceived of the "autotomy" of personality and identification with the aggressor) a global defense of the human mind to avoid traumatic dissolution and fragmentation through hypnotic annulment. Annulment, specifically, not only of the awareness of the trauma and the potentially threatening memories and feelings connected to it, but even – in order to preserve sanity – of the very existence of that self which, however, remains in the mind in a nearly dead state.[7]

Working within the role-reversal area

We will now present some patients of ours who have inspired our thoughts: Mara, Alberto, Teddy, and Sandro. We will try to condense some aspects of their analytic history and the complex working-through of the role-reversal dynamics that characterized their treatments to just a few brushstrokes.[8]

Mara

Let us begin with Mara, a schizoid university student, mute and affectively inert, who came into a four-session weekly analysis following a terrible fall from a horse that had fractured her pelvis and kept her immobilized in bed for over six months, halting her life and projects. When Mara requested analysis, owing to a number of concomitant analogous accidents that had afflicted other members of her family and friends, she perceived her fall both as an imminent catastrophic change and as a sort of structural ("bone") breakdown of her family. She described this conjunction of events in the intake interviews thus: "A shadow or a black hole has invaded me and my family's life."

Almost immediately confronted with absolute silence on Mara's part – a silence that would last almost four years and was accompanied by moans and groans related to vague, tormenting, and painful bodily sensations, although marked sporadically by contrast with illuminating dreams that, in the communicative desert that marked the analytic exchange, seemed to be mirages rather than harbingers of any future subjectivity, given that nothing changed in the analytic scene – the analyst found himself obliged to "literally interpret" a character from the dream that Mara brought to the first session. A character that was not able to express himself and who, against his will, had to repeatedly attend to another character's hara-kiri and agony. This second character was perhaps Japanese, although also of uncertain identity and incapable of any verbal expression. Here is the dream that introduced Mara's analysis:

> A Japanese person of uncertain identity was committing hara-kiri in front of me in a sort of cloister and wanted me to see it. So I started to run, but this person followed me and periodically caught up with me, arch after arch, collapsing on the floor with all his intestines pouring out. I was horrified and disgusted.

Behaving herself almost exclusively in this way (that is, totally emptying out all her "insides-intestines"), Mara progressively led the analyst to embody an unwelcome and incompetent Mara-child (but also a "wise baby") who had no sense of agency on her parents or any effect on their withdrawn and enigmatic state of mind, and who – as a person foreign to their original language and psychic culture – believed herself to be unable to invite them to relate and talk to her because, simultaneously, she could not even be alive since existence for these parents meant disturbance and the threat of further loss, death, and suffering. Mara's mother, for example, wished not to have been born herself, and had not wanted her daughter to be born or to be alive, owing to the calamities, torments, mourning, and all the repeated abandonment inevitably caused by living.

For all these reasons, in this recurrent and static atmosphere, time after time the analyst had to put on – while certainly quite unaware of this at first – one by one the feelings the child Mara had for having a depressed, hypochondriac, fragile, and at the same time cumbersome mother, and a tired, withdrawn father, preoccupied by the exhausting job of scraping a living: two parents both suffering from a mysterious pain that was not talked about at home. Later in the analysis, it emerged that this shared pain sprang from the fact that in their families – both the mother's and the father's – the fathers had died at the birth of their children (especially when these children were unwelcomed and born late in life), thus leaving the mothers destitute widows, unable to make ends meet and provide for their children.

Only at a certain point, after having helped Mara integrate many strands of her history and himself risking analytic hara-kiri, could the analyst forcefully reclaim his inalienable right to exist and enable, with this new expressive opportunity, the patient's "rebirth." This occurred during the fifth year of analysis, when Mara, after a sort of analytic honeymoon in which she had emerged from her muteness and regularly participated verbally in the sessions, had once again suddenly plunged back into a state of dark, deafening silence from which there seemed no way out.

In this circumstance the analyst – feeling completely unable to bring Mara back to any form of dialogue, and after recalling a film by Bergman titled *The Serpent's Egg* (1977) about a mother who kills her baby because he won't stop crying and then commits suicide by throwing herself out of the window – exploded in a series of "rumbling interpretations." He began telling her with passion and pain (with brief pauses between words, as though he were thinking aloud in front of her) that the situation into which they had currently fallen seemed necessarily to end in a reciprocal fatal resignation, and so in a laying down of their weapons, killing both her as the patient and himself as her analyst. Then he went on to say that if he was doing something wrong, she had to help him and to give him a hand, and that if she continued to identify with her mother who, she knew, hated life, while he was the her-child who had to carry on trying to change her mother and help her to recover, he had to admit that this really was not possible in reality, since the analysis and her analyst were limited and could only help to her to give up this unhealthy behavior through understanding it, showing her how this dramatic struggle was inside herself and had to be resolved there.

A visibly moved Mara continued with these words:

> If you discover that you have an effect on other people, you are real, you exist: therefore, others also exist for you and are real. This is what you give me. It's not an indistinct or irritating noise that you don't know precisely what it is or where it's coming from. It's not a groan that torments you because you can't fight it or do anything to stop it; nor is it an echo that reiterates. It's something that comes rumbling from inside, which is alive and not dead at all, something that makes you feel reborn.

And she added that nobody had ever paid attention to her, either to her illness or to her withdrawal and silence, in childhood or adolescence. At home they had not noticed it or, if they had, they never talked about it: she was the model daughter who had no problems and was exactly what her parents wanted. She did not feel capable of arousing any feelings in other people apart from irritation and hassle, of which, however, she had never felt herself to be the source.

To sum up this analysis, which lasted more than ten years, it can be said that during it the analyst, according to the moment, had to be both the "Mara-child that she had been" and the "Mara-child that she was not allowed to be" (that is, a child capable of feeling, reacting, and also making herself noticed; the very child that the patient had never been able to be or know in her childhood and adolescence). Furthermore, the analyst had to be Mara's mother and father, that is the suffering and inadequate parents that she had had, and also, at the same time, a type of parent different from the ones that fate had provided her with.

Alberto

We come now to Alberto, a brilliant 33-year-old designer, who came to analysis because of a deep dissatisfaction with his relationships with other people and especially with women. At the time, he felt dominated by a sensation of persistent estrangement from reality that he experienced as a painful feeling of never being completely emotionally engaged in relationships, which always seemed to him of little account compared to his desires and phantasies.

Ever since he was a boy, Alberto had felt a strong sense of injustice because he felt that others, in interpersonal relationships, "took liberties" that he could not allow himself, and also demanded from him attitudes and performances that, in order to be done, brought him to the limit of exasperation, which he showed only by angry silences and opposition. In short, whatever investment he made – from friendships to sentimental relationships, from work to hobbies – was lived on a seesaw between expectations of a perfect and effortless performance and a constant effort that left him exhausted. Alberto succeeded in "setting things right" only by redrafting and in some way reshaping his inner reality; in this way he soothed the wounds inflicted by reality and worked off the anger and disappointment, painfully isolating himself as he incessantly brooded over everything. But he felt excessively absorbed by this latter activity – a background buzzing of schizoid stamp – experiencing it as both

301

ensnaring and as a guilty marker of his inadequacy in being able to live in the present and be authentic.

Alberto was the fourth of five brothers in a Catholic, middle-class family. His father was the headmaster of a school and his mother a housewife. The premature death of his father – an austere, rigid man – when Alberto was 10 years old dramatically changed family life, making it rather sad and melancholic, due also to the economic sacrifices to be made. However, even before then Alberto did not remember, in the family, any great attention to his childhood needs. This lack of parental thought capable of recognizing and giving feedback regarding each child's subjectivity and originality reappeared, subsequently becoming relevant again in analysis, through various dreams in which Alberto found himself living in anonymous colleges and eating in overcrowded dining halls where it was difficult to find a place at a table or a bed to sleep in.

Alongside all this, Alberto also felt there was a sort of rupture in his life between adulthood and the golden age of the child, in which he had felt more spontaneous, open, and vital. At times – in the sessions – he recalled with delight the summers spent in the countryside playing with his friends and his first adolescent experiences. After that it was as though something oppressive and gloomy had enveloped his life.

The first dream he described in analysis was a sign of the paranoid atmosphere that was soon to be established in the sessions: "I was locked up inside a medieval fortress and enemies were arriving outside. I had to defend myself but I only had some very old contraptions."

For a long period the analysis was permeated by this threatening sensation, despite Alberto's commitment to come regularly in order "to communicate and speak about himself." The image that emerged then was that of an analysis seen as a "purge" or "enema." Alberto could come only if he thought of it as a medicine "he had to take in order to feel better tomorrow," but he felt it to be a painful intrusion into his private spaces, and a forced production of verbal contents. On the other hand, though, silence was impossible; it generated an unbearable state of discomfort in him, so that for months the sessions were invaded by words after a preliminary "I've got nothing to say today." The super-egoic character and fear of merciless criticism were very evident; often in the dreams of that period he was operated on his stomach, cut open, and his guts examined.

While it was relatively easy to trace such a persecution in the transference back to the disturbing ghosts of a demanding and intrusive father-headmaster and a suffering mother (both of whom Alberto experienced as voraciously hungry for a communicative relational performance from him), it proved a much more arduous task to find a meaning for the patient's polite but continuous affirmations (contradicted by the regularity with which he arrived at his appointments) that he never wanted to come to the sessions, and that he was there exclusively to please the analyst and that perhaps, in the end, analysis was not really the right thing for him.

In fact, all this required the analyst both to become more aware of how much Alberto had been affected by his relationship with his mother (a parsimonious woman both in emotions and dynamism, who, as a widow, never expressed anything but duty and sacrifice in raising and looking after her five children), and to be the one to start opposing the stagnant atmosphere veined with nihilism and with threats of interruption that was bogging down the sessions and that posed the risk of making the analysis itself fail.

A turning point occurred in the treatment when the analyst made his patient notice that paradoxically – contrary to what his internal mother, with whom he was identified, maintained (that is, that Alberto was not at all interested in what was emerging from the analysis) – he continued to do his very best to recreate "his home atmosphere" so that "somebody" could finally understand what it had meant to be perpetually exposed to resignation and lack of desire. Alberto paled and began to cry quietly. Finally, he said:

> I want to let myself go, to be myself. In some part I feel that I could do it but I am terribly afraid that there is nothing but "duty" and emptiness. Something was missing in my life. I'm a battery that has never been charged! So the problem is not about adding water or replacing an element but about charging it!

In this analysis, which lasted seven years with four sessions a week, understanding and interpreting the role-reversal that was taking place in the sessions required from the analyst a careful and progressive working-through of his countertransference. At first, indeed, the analyst almost felt compassion because Alberto perceived him as a threatening and persecutory object connected with his parental imago. As time went by, however, the analyst passed from feeling perplexed and disconcerted, and, later, unpleasantly irritated, due to Alberto's subtle disdain and constant aloofness, to experiencing a deep sense of failure connected with his feeling useless and refused. To sum up, at an advanced stage of the analysis, these very signals were decoded as an indication of the presence of a role-reversal in which the analyst's identification with the dissociated infantile part of the patient corresponded unavoidably with Alberto's identification with a nihilistic, barely alive, and narcissistic mother.

Teddy

While Mara basically asked her analyst to stay alive in an atmosphere of agony and death, managing to think of it and consequently to slowly give it a convincing explanation, and Alberto asked his analyst to prove that a part of the self can survive feeling worthy of authentically existing and enjoying life despite having been exposed to the shadow of a deadly and humiliating object, in Teddy's case the analyst was asked to give voice to the dangerous and impossible situation of precarious equilibrium in which Teddy found himself – a situation where, in the end, even the best acrobats and tightrope-walkers would certainly have fallen, seriously injuring themselves physically and psychically. In the encounter with Teddy, as occurred in the previous cases, every infantile emotion of fear, impotence, despair, anger, and guilt had to be kept alive in the analyst's affective reception-participation in the relational vicissitudes experienced in the session, so that the tragic family situation that the boy was denouncing with his bizarre and risky behavior could emerge.

In brief, for the greater part of a short consultation motivated by a sudden failure in school and by maladjusted behavior, the deft and perspicacious "tightrope-walker," aged 12, whom we will call Teddy, after having depicted himself in a drawing as a "daring motorboat racer who had to dodge an incautious fluttering duck and a dangerous barracuda disguised as a torpedo-lifesaver-buoy," mimed in the twenty sessions the analyst had with him the adventures of this mad motorboat in a thousand different acrobatic poses. This induced intense feelings of terror and impotence in the analyst, as well as bewilderment, guilt, anger, and despair (the feelings of the small child), for the damage that such manic activity could have caused to the boy's physical integrity.

What was Teddy trying to avoid with his extreme and unmanageable behavior? What was the "freak wave" he was trying to escape? What was the substance of the storms he staged in the sessions? What might the consequences be of this nail-biting game? These were the issues the analyst was called on to experience in his own skin before succeeding in being able to bring the seriously critical and terrifying family context into sight, of which Teddy was an impotent and terrorized spectator and in which even the most skilful tightrope-walker would in the end be inescapably harmed. But this could be done only after a fair number of sessions and after the analyst had himself put on the garments – every time that he intervened signaling the presence of something terrible that must have suddenly terrified Teddy – of the "fluttering duck," the "treacherous lifesaver-buoy-barracuda," and also the "freak wave" that had at all costs to be avoided and pushed aside.

In the foreground in this family context was an exasperated father who returned home drunk, beating his wife, and threatening everyone to death, unable to accept that his marriage was over. The impossibility of the parents' separating connected explosively in Teddy with his similar intense anxieties about losing both the actual house he lived in and his child's body, which was rapidly changing and sending him numerous messages that he did not yet know how to decode. Teddy, having found a witness of what was happening not only in his body but also at home, was reassured by the fact that someone was able to deal with all this (in a later drawing he made, a "trustworthy lifesaver" – the analyst – appeared as a policeman on that turbulent and stormy sea). He then quit rather rapidly his antisocial and impulsive manifestations, as well as his provocative stupidity, and regained his good work at school, finally asking for his parents to be helped.

Sandro

Sandro was a 7-year-old boy who came to analysis because he was too terrified to go to school. Every morning he would be in tears when he had to leave his mother, and on the rare occasions he managed to enter the classroom he was totally inhibited and silent until it was time to go home. During the long years of treatment, along with other scenarios, he repeatedly played out a monotonous and repetitive game, in which he accompanied his analyst in the depths of winter to a "football ground." The analyst had to play the part of a child learning to play football. In this way Sandro was able to make his analyst live out all the fears and frustrations of feeling he was a "zero" facing a whole team of number "ones": severe coaches, demanding champions, and arrogant opponents, who despised his petty performances.

In this child analysis, the playing out and decoding of the role-reversal took place at various levels. While one part (the more symbolic one) developed through the analyst taking upon himself, in full awareness, the role of "junior," or baby, of the hated football team – a junior who could finally give form and voice to an infantile dimension that had remained until then completely frozen and dissociated – another substantial and more primitive part lay in the analyst physically becoming the repository of mysterious sensations of cold, boredom, and sadness that assailed him during and after the sessions. These sensations emerged gradually, indicating the presence of a seriously "frozen ego" in Sandro (concealed with difficulty by precarious manic defenses), resulting from his mother's subtle but deeply rooted melancholic disinvestment from him after she experienced profound death anxieties and a proliferation of phantasies about her son being irreparably brain-damaged following a dystocic and premature birth. To defend herself, she had literally made herself become a "block of ice" since she was too young and too psychically unprepared to cope with the possibility of her son's death. Furthermore, she was not supported by her husband, who, equally fragile and immature, disparagingly dismissed any fear, owing to the fact that he had had to deny and ignore his own weakness very early on in his own childhood.

Conclusions

Today – stronger and better equipped in our devotion to the psychoanalytic method – we believe that an authentic "talking cure" (Breuer and Freud, 1892–1895) is not possible without some "interacting cure," since action is sometimes a matrix for fertile thought in a fruitful working-through and psychic transformation. In the end, it takes a lot of groundwork, of a humble nature, to reach a mutative interpretation: above all, we must be willing to momentarily abandon our own safe role of the interpreting analyst to take on – as "interpreters" – the roles the patient asks us to play.

In brief, it is necessary at least for a short time – as Grotstein (2007) states following Bion – "to become the patient" in order to attain a really convincing understanding and verbalization of what is happening in the session.

In our opinion, grounded in what we have said earlier, one of the most valuable legacies left by Freud (1914) could be rewritten today in the following new sequence: "experiencing (making ourselves 'interpreters'), repeating, working and re-working-through, and remembering," with a strong emphasis on "experiencing (making ourselves 'interpreters')" and "repeating" as basic conditions for "working and re-working-through" and "remembering" – or, better, "thinking."

Notes

1   We utilize the term "dissociation" following Ferenczi and the British Independents in the use of this term.
2   When the phenomenon of role-reversal is discussed among colleagues, it is often rapidly dismissed as being something obvious, already known, and almost totally overlapping with the mechanism of projective identification. The same fate befell, in part, the concept of *enactment* (McLaughlin and Johan, 1992). On the contrary, we think that role-reversal is a much more complex phenomenon than projective identification because it is a particular kind of transference-countertransference relationship that involves: (1) transference repetition and acting out; (2) unconscious identification with an inadequate object; (3) the accompanying dissociation of the emotions linked to the suffering infantile self; and (4) the projective identification. For these reasons we prefer to speak about role-reversal as a form of "identification with the aggressor" in which the "victim" eliminates his own subjectivity and, in order to survive, becomes exactly like what his aggressor wants him to be. In brief, for us it is important to work, in analysis, on the characteristics of the introjected objects of the patient (rather than on his projective mechanisms), and on the subsequent identifications that produce, in many ways, a concurrent alienation, dissociation, and loss of one's subjectivity (see in this regard: Bollas, 1987, 1989; Borgogno, 2011; Frankel, 2002; Heimann, 1975; Sodré, 2004).
3   In his *Clinical Diary* (1988), Ferenczi describes a patient who asks the analyst to show him that he knows how to live with the type of pain he has experienced. In the case he refers to, Ferenczi intuits that his epileptic patient's insistent requests that he become Julius Caesar were, in fact, indicating something that his patient had been offering him – that he

307

concretely "take within himself" his patient's epileptic suffering in order to understand what he was experiencing. (The pronunciation of Caesar in English, recalling the words, "seize her = seizure" was interpreted by Ferenczi precisely in this sense.) Besides, this is exactly what Bion emphasizes, many years later, in *Cogitations* (1992, p. 286) when he points out that many patients, rather than having a need for an interpretation, need to keep on verifying for a long time whether the analyst can truly know the catastrophic suffering that pervades them and consequently see how he faces and deals with it.

4   Classic examples of this are all those situations in which the child becomes with the analyst a harsh teacher who scolds and mistreats a hopeless student; an assertive, bossy father who is absent-minded concerning the child's affective needs and wishes to play; or, on the contrary, an affectionate mother who cuddles her baby; the leader of the wolf pack teaching the little cub how to find its bearings in the forest, and so on.

5   The subject who in part is deprived of his own self is not aware of what he is really missing, in the same way that his parents – when he was a child – were not aware of what they were depriving the child of, nor of what was missing in their inappropriate caring for the child's needs and requests. At worst, these patients, despite feeling an intense uneasiness (though its source may be unclear to them), do not know that they have been deprived: they can discover this in analysis, when they obtain, through experiencing it, a psychic environment different from the one they grew up in, recovering at the same time within themselves those resources they had never imagined they had.

6   It was precisely with RN – his name for Elizabeth Severn – that Ferenczi came to realize that the patient was unconsciously identified with her abusing and depriving parents, and that he had been turned into the little girl that the patient had dissociated from herself. Ferenczi at first could not undertake the role RN asked him to assume, as he himself was not able to bear and contain the painful experience related to being in a relationship with parents that terrified their children with the "terrorism of suffering" (Ferenczi, 1930, 1932, 1988), since he had already directly experienced it in his own childhood with his mother.

7   There are, nevertheless, other authors who have explored the transference-countertransference dynamics linked to role-reversal: Fonagy (1991); Fonagy and Target (2001); and Modell (1990), for example.

8   For more on Mara and Teddy, see Borgogno (1999, 2004, 2011), and Bonomi and Borgogno (2006). For more on Alberto and Sandro, see Vigna-Taglianti (1999, 2002).

Bibliography

Anzieu, D. (1975) Le transfert paradoxal. De la communication paradoxale à la reaction thérapeutique negative. *Nouvelle Revue de Psychanalyse*, 12: 49–72.

Balint, E. (1963) On being empty of oneself. *International Journal of Psychoanalysis*, 44: 470–480.

Balint, M. (1952) *Primary Love and Psycho-Analytic Technique.* London: Maresfield, 1985.

Balint, M. (1968) *The Basic Fault: Therapeutic Aspects of Regression.* London: Tavistock.

Benjamin, J. (2011) The Analyst as Aggressor. Paper presented at the IPTAR Psychological Enslavement Conference, 29 January 29, 2011, New York City.

Beres, D. (1957) Communication in psychoanalysis and in the creative process: A parallel. *Journal of the American Psychoanalytic Association*, 5: 408–423.

Bergman, I. (1977) *The Serpent's Egg.* Germany: Rialto Film; USA: Dino de Laurentiis Corporation (original title: *Das Schlangenei*).

Bion, W. R. (1992) *Cogitations* (F. Bion, ed.). London: Karnac Books.

Boesky, D. (1982) Acting out: A reconsideration of the concept. *International Journal of Psychoanalysis*, 63: 39–55.

Bokanowski, T. (2005) Variations on the concept of traumatism: Traumatism, traumatic, trauma. *International Journal of Psychoanalysis*, 86: 251–265.

Bollas, C. (1987) *The Shadow of the Object: Psychoanalysis of the Unthought Known.* London: Free Association.

Bollas, C. (1989) *The Forces of Destiny: Psychoanalysis and Human Idiom.* London: Free Association.

Bonomi, C. and Borgogno, F. (2006) The broken symbol: The fear of the mind of the other in the symbolic history of the individual. *International Forum of Psychoanalysis*, 15: 169–177.

Borgogno, F. (1999) *Psicoanalisi come percorso.* Turin: Bollati Boringhieri. English edition: *Psychoanalysis as a Journey.* London: Open Gate Press, 2007.

Borgogno, F. (2004) On the patient's becoming an individual: the importance of the analyst's personal response to a deprived patient and her dreams. *Psychoanalytic Dialogues*, 14 (4): 475–502.

Borgogno, F. (2007) Ferenczi and Winnicott: Searching for a "missing link" (of the soul). *American Journal of Psychoanalysis*, 67: 221–234.

Borgogno, F. (2011) *"La signorina che faceva hara-kiri" e altri saggi.* Turin: Bollati Boringhieri. English edition: *The Young Woman Who Committed Hara-Kiri and Other Clinical-Historical Essays.* London: Karnac, 2013.

Botella, C. and Botella, S. (2005) *The Work of Psychic Figurability: Mental States without Representation* (trans A. Weller, M. Zerbib). Hove, East Sussex; New York: Brunner-Routledge.

Brenman-Pick, I. (1985) Working-through in the countertransference, *International Journal of Psychoanalysis*, 66: 157–166.

Breuer, J. and Freud, S. (1892–1895) *Studies on Hysteria*. In *The Standard Edition of the Complete Psychological Works of Sigmund Freud*, J. Strachey (ed., trans.), vol. 2: 19–305. London: Hogarth Press.

Britton, R. (1998) *Belief and Imagination*. London: Routledge.

Bromberg, P. M. (1998) *Standing in the Spaces: Essays on Clinical Process, Trauma, and Dissociation*. Hillsdale, NJ: The Analytic Press.

Bromberg, P. M. (2006) *Awakening the Dreamer: Clinical Journeys*. Hillsdale, NJ: The Analytic Press.

Deutsch, H. (1926) Occult processes occurring during psychoanalysis. In G. Devereux (ed.), *Psychoanalysis and the Occult* (pp. 143–146). New York: International Universities Press, 1953.

Feldman, M. (2009) *Doubt, Conviction and the Analytic Process*. London: Routledge.

Ferenczi, S. (1912) On transitory symptom-constructions during the analysis. In *First Contributions to Psychoanalysis* (pp. 193–212). London: Karnac.

Ferenczi, S. (1930) The principles of relaxation and neocatharsis. In M. Balint (ed.) and E. Mosbacher (trans.), *Final Contributions to the Problems and Methods of Psycho-Analysis* (pp. 108–125). London: Hogarth, 1955. Reprinted London: Karnac, 1994.

Ferenczi, S. (1932) Confusion of tongues between adults and the child. In M. Balint (ed.) and E. Mosbacher (trans.), *Final Contributions to the Problems and Methods of Psycho-Analysis* (pp. 156–167). London: Hogarth, 1955. Reprinted London: Karnac, 1994.

Ferenczi, S. (1955) Notes and fragments. In M. Balint (ed.) and E. Mosbacher (trans.), *Final Contributions to the Problems and Methods of Psycho-Analysis* (pp. 216–279). London: Hogarth; New York: Basic Books, 1955. Reprinted London: Karnac, 1994.

Ferenczi, S. (1988) *The Clinical Diary*, J. Dupont (ed.), M. Balint and N. Zarday Jackson (trans.). Cambridge, MA: Harvard University Press.

Fonagy, P. (1991) Thinking about thinking: Some clinical and theoretical considerations in the treatment of a borderline patient. *International Journal of Psychoanalysis*, 72: 639–656.

Fonagy, P. and Target, M. (2001) *Attaccamento e funzione riflessiva* (Attachment and Reflexive Function). Milan: R. Cortina.

Frankel, J. (2002) Exploring Ferenczi's concept of identification with the aggressor: Its role in trauma, everyday life, and the therapeutic relationship. *Psychoanalytic Dialogues*, 12(1): 101–139.

Freud, A. (1937) *The Ego and the Mechanisms of Defence*. London: Hogarth Press, London.

Freud, A. (1970) Child analysis as a subspeciality of psychoanalysis. In *The Writings of Anna Freud*, vol. 7 (pp. 204–219). New York: International Universities Press, 1971.

Freud, S. (1912) *The Dynamics of Transference. The Standard Edition of the Complete Psychological Works of Sigmund Freud*, J. Strachey (ed., trans.), vol. 12: 99–108. London: Hogarth Press.

Freud, S. (1914) Remembering, repeating and working-through. SE 12: 147–156.

Freud, S. (1937) *Constructions in Analysis*. SE 23: 255–269.

Giovacchini, P. L. (1989) *Countertransference Triumphs and Catastrophes.* Northvale, NJ: Jason Aronson.

Greenacre, P. (1968) The psychoanalytic process, transference, and acting out. *International Journal of Psychoanalysis*, 49: 211–218.

Grotstein, J. S. (2007) *A Beam of Intense Darkness: Wilfred Bion's Legacy to Psychoanalysis.* London: Karnac.

Heimann, P. (1965) Comment on Dr Kernberg's paper on "Structural derivatives on object relationships." In M. Tonnesmann (ed.), *Children and Children-No-Longer: Collected Papers 1942–80/Paula Heimann* (pp. 218–230). London: Routledge, 1989.

Heimann, P. (1975) From "cumulative trauma" to the privacy of the self: A critical review of M. Masud R. Khan's book. *International Journal of Psychoanalysis*, 56: 475–476.

Jacobs, T. (1986) On countertransference enactments. *Journal of the American Psychoanalytic Association*, 34: 289–307.

Jacobs, T. (1991) *The Use of the Self.* Madison, CT: International Universities Press.

Joseph, B. (1989) *Psychic Equilibrium and Psychic Change.* London: Routledge.

Khan, M. M. R. (1974) *The Privacy of the Self.* London: Hogarth Press.

King, P. (1951/1953/2004) Change: the psychoanalysis of a four-year-old boy and its follow-up. In P. King, *Time Present and Time Past* (pp. 15–40), London: Karnac, 2005.

King, P. (1962) The curative factors in psychoanalysis. In P. King, *Time Present and Time Past* (pp. 53–58), London: Karnac 2005.

King, P. (1978) The affective response of the analyst to the patient's communication. In P. King, *Time Present and Time Past* (pp. 88–97). London: Karnac, 2005.

Klein, M. (1929) Personification in the play of children. *International Journal of Psychoanalysis*, 10: 193–204.

Lagache, D. (1952). Le problème du transfert. In D. Lagache, *Oeuvres III, 1952—1956.* Paris: Presses Universitaires de France, 1980.

Levenson, E. (1972) *The Fallacy of Understanding.* New York: Basic Books.

Levenson, E. (1983) *The Ambiguity of Change: An Inquiry into the Nature of Psychoanalytic Reality.* New York: Basic Books.

McLaughlin, J. T. (1987) The play of transference: Some reflections on enactment. *Journal of the American Psychoanalytic Association*, 35: 557–582.

McLaughlin, J. T. (1991) Clinical and theoretical aspects of enactment. *Journal of the American Psychoanalytic Association*, 39: 595–614.

McLaughlin, J. T. and Johan, M. (1992) Enactments in psychoanalysis. *Journal of the American Psychoanalytic Association*, 40: 827–841.

Modell, A. H. (1990) *Other Times, Other Realities: Toward a Theory of Psychoanalytic Treatment*. Cambridge, MA: Harvard University Press.

Ogden, T. H. (2001) *Conversations at the Frontier of Dreaming*. Northvale, NJ: Jason Aronson.

O'Shaughnessy, E. (1992) Enclaves and excursions. *International Journal of Psychoanalysis*, 73: 603–611.

Racker, H. (1968) *Transference and Counter-transference*. New York: International Universities Press.

Renik, O. (1993) Analytic interaction: Conceptualizing technique in light of the analyst's irreducible subjectivity. *Psychoanalytic Quarterly*, 62: 553–571.

Renik, O. (1997) Conscious and unconscious use of the self. *Psychoanalytic Inquiry*, 17: 5–12.

Roussillon, R. (1991) *Paradoxes et situations limites de la psychanalyse*. Paris: Presses Universitaires de France.

Roussillon, R. (2011) *Primitive Anxiety and Symbolization*. London: Karnac.

Sandler, J. (1976a) Actualization and object relationships. *Journal of the Philadelphia Association for Psychoanalysis*, 2: 59–70.

Sandler, J. (1976b) Countertransference and role-responsiveness. *International Review of Psychoanalysis*, 3: 43–47.

Searles, H. F. (1959) The effort to drive the other person crazy: An element in the aetiology and psychotherapy of schizophrenia. In *Collected Papers on Schizophrenia and Related Subjects* (pp. 254–284). London: Hogarth Press and the Institute of Psychoanalysis, London, 1965.

Searles, H. F. (1978–1979) Concerning transference and countertransference. *International Journal of Psychoanalytic Psychotherapy*, 7: 165–188.

Sodré, I. (2004) Who's who? Notes on pathological identifications. In E. Hargreaves and A. Varchevker (eds.), *In Pursuit of Psychic Change* (pp. 53–59). Hove, East Sussex: Brunner-Routledge, 2004.

Steiner, J. (1993) *Psychic Retreats: Pathological Organizations in Psychotic, Neurotic and Borderline Patients*. London: Routledge.

Vigna-Taglianti, M. (1999) Interpret-agiti o interpret-azioni? (Interpretations as acting-in and interpretations as transformative actions). *Quaderni di Psicoterapia Infantile*, 39: 167–183.

Vigna-Taglianti, M. (2002) Transfert regressivo e transfert persecutorio: trasformazioni del Sé e funzioni analitiche (Regressive transference and persecutory transference: Transformations of the self and analytic functions). In F. Borgogno (ed.), *Ferenczi oggi* (Ferenczi Today). Turin: Bollati Boringhieri 2004.

312

Winnicott, D. W. (1963). Fear of breakdown. In C. Winnicott, R. Sheperd, M. Davis (eds.), *Psycho-Analytic Explorations* (pp. 87–95). London: Karnac, 1989.

Winnicott, D. W. (1967a) Mirror-role of mother and family in child development. In *Playing and Reality* (pp. 111–118). London: Tavistock, 1971.

Winnicott, D. W. (1967b) Postscript: D. W. W. on D. W. W. C. Winnicott, R. Sheperd, M. Davis (eds.), *Psycho-Analytic Explorations* (pp. 569–582). London: Karnac, 1989.

PSYCHOANALYSIS AND THE INFLUENCING MACHINE

Psychoanalysis as the influencing machine

Adrienne Harris

This paper sits in the long shadow cast by two supremely important psychoanalytic essays, each of which – Sam Gerson's "When the Third Is Dead" (2009) and Viktor Tausk's "On the Origin of the 'Influencing Machine' in Schizophrenia" (1933) – lies in the shadow of war and destructiveness on an overwhelming scale. While I have been working on the theoretical and clinical dimensions of these papers for a quite a long time, I again learned, in this last reworking, how melancholy and despair so dominate these projects. So I am writing now in an uncertain relation to the question of how and whether we can, collectively or individually, quell ghosts, repel the machine, or weather the marks of history. I will draw on a clinical case haunted by ghosts and technologies recruited to tumult and disequilibrium in which analyst and analysand were captured in the mesh of various machines.

I am interested in how the issues raised by Gerson's and Tausk's work enter and shape our understanding of transference and countertransference phenomena. I might use Cooper's (2010) phrase and think of "disturbances in the field." In particular, I want to be able to talk about the strange mingling of spectral presences, arising from analyst and analysand, when history, as it must, troubles the clinical waters.

First, I want to take up Sam Gerson's paper. "When the Third Is Dead" seems to me to touch on some of the most important ideas in our field: the necessity of witnessing, but also the question of what makes a witness not a voyeur. How does the analyst witness without shaming? What are the transference and countertransference consequences in the absence of cultural and collective resonance in response to what has been or is occurring still? Without the receptivity of meaningful witness there can only be despair, Gerson argued. How often is witnessing retraumatizing, for either party?

In the spirit of Gerson's particular plea to attend to witnessing, I inaugurated a supervision group.[1] With some sense of uncanny surprise, we began a series of clinical examinations in which we found ourselves in encounters with problems of witnessing, and engaged in questions of what is housed in absence. Most surprisingly, we found ourselves in the presence of ghosts, bidden and unbidden. We came to feel appalled, intrigued, grossed out, and even, on occasion, eager to encounter these spectral intruders, ghosts of patient and of analyst. We felt these presences, thought about them, but often our appreciation came in the forms of unbidden images, sensations, and temptations to action.

In tracking the present absence of ghosts and various forms of hauntings within psychoanalytic treatments, we are tracking the power of hidden and often shame-laden histories to enter and shape the clinical work, transferentially and countertransferentially. Ghosts, we have discovered, have been the transitional spaces in which we have been exploring the legacy of violence (actual and psychic), phobic hatreds, migrations, and many other ways of configuring loss as these appear in the lives, minds, and bodies of contemporary patients and their analysts.

Ghosts, sightings, séances, attempting to reach and speak to the dead, appear very powerfully in Western culture in the wake of loss of life on a mass scale. The Civil War, in the United States, particularly in the South (see Faust, 2008), and World War I in Europe, saw an astonishing outbreak of spiritism. Visions of the dead and sightings of religious figures haunted battlefields and postwar settings. We might remember that in the early prewar years Freud sent Ferenczi up and down various Hungarian mountains hunting strange folk who could bend spoons (see the Freud-Ferenczi correspondence in Falzelder and Brabant, 1996; Meszaros, 1985). We are in the complex domains of unconscious communication. But words like uncanny and haunted are required, the words and language of object relations and internal objects too orderly for the clinical experiences I will be describing.

315

Ghosts haunt analyst and analysand, participating in impasses, in uncanny experiences in the countertransference and in the transference. While the more traditional spiritual practices involving hauntings seek to expel ghosts and demons, psychoanalysis rather more often seeks to have them readmitted. Theorists have thought of these phenomena differently. There is the concept of intergenerational transmission of trauma (Coates and Moore, 1997; Davoine, 2010; Davoine and Gaudilliere, 2004; Fonagy et al., 2003), the telescoping of generations (Faimberg, 2004), the attention to witnessing and Thirdness (Benjamin, 1988, 2004; Gerson, 2009), and to encrypted identifications (Abraham and Torok, 1994) or radioactive identifications (Gampel, 2000; Puget, 2006). Across different theoretical traditions, each of these writers is trying to be mindful of the residue of trauma held unconsciously and repackaged – often over several generations. And each of these theorists struggles to capture the mix of uncanniness and drivenness that characterizes intersubjective clinical processes, drenched in history and in unconscious communications. It is important to see that each of these writers draws on but goes beyond the notion of introjects, internal object worlds, and similar terms.

Sometimes the ghostliness seems embodied in spectral presences, in figures actually dead or missing. Fascinating psychic processes underlie the deeply committed attempts patients make to keep the dead alive, close down space, or alternatively to keep it open and ready for habitation. Killing and saving seem often too close to each other. Rey (1988) has an intriguing way of thinking about this: the task of the analysand is to have the analyst cure the damaged objects he or she brings to the work. And, as I have argued (Harris, 2009), in clinical impasses we often see how the analyst similarly arrives in the work to cure old injuries, bury the undead, undertake the final repair of history. When psychoanalysts imagine and conjure up "history," what is meant? Here I think of the release and potential peace of the settling of personal history. But this term also conjures up more collective historical conversations. Here is where Gerson's work is so helpful, in his attunement to the potency of contained witnessing, witnessing that allows reflection and linkage, witnessing that is not retraumatizing.

This task of the repair of internal objects, laced into our countertransferences, is the source and wellspring of powerful sublimations and transformations into work ethics and skill. But there remains, in anyone conducting this work, the residue of uneasy spirits and unfixed figures. Part of the shared task of analytic work is the transformation of melancholy into mourning, an always partially incomplete task. Ghosts remain in various forms, and to reprise the brilliant insight of Abraham and Torok (1994), in their idea of encrypted identifications, sometimes the secrets passed remain unknown to bearer or receiver.

Despite these cautionary notes, there is the triumph when narrative enters treatment, when fragments and chaos are ordered through naming and genealogy. This has been Davoine's (2010) perspective, seeing the long hand of history. It takes a half-century, she felt, to process a war. Unprocessed historical trauma, in her view, was a prime engine of psychotic functioning. So there is, in the permanent tasks of mourning, both triumph and despair, and this must be parsed and held by analyst for the patient and for him- or herself.

If there is one danger in talk of ghosts, it might be the danger of melodrama. Michel Sebek, an analyst living in Prague, told me (personal communication, 2009) he thought that a ghost might be a friendly, manageable figure in a historical context in which trauma – tsunami-like – threatens engulfment of the known world. He was saying this in the context of the gulag, by which – in Sebek's culture – no family is untouched. A ghost, often in the form of psychotic delusions, could be a relief from history or at least its transitional container. This idea is hugely represented in Tausk's paper.

I have come to think of ghosts, rather than simply a part of intergenerational internalized object worlds, as spectral and uncanny presences of absence in the oddest aspects of clinical cases: tucked into the frame, seeping and leaking into mood and tempo and environment, bodily and material.

I am aware that in linking Gerson and Tausk I have taken on some highly polarized constructs: the spectral, wispy, enigmatic element of the ghost, and the hard wired, reified particularity of the machine. Both are deeply part of the conscious and unconscious phenomena that are interesting me here. Perhaps one way to see the link is to think of these processes – spectral absence on one hand and huge overwhelming apparatus of control on the other – as two sides of one process, two different but related efforts to manage the overwhelming intrusion and infusion of historic and lethal forces into individual psyches.

To turn now to "On the Origin of the 'Influencing Machine' in Schizophrenia," I would say that it is part of the genius of Tausk's essay that he so animates and renders uncanny, and horrifying, the nuts and bolts of modernity. "On the Origin of the 'Influencing Machine' in Schizophrenia" is a paper written in 1919, the year Tausk killed himself, a victim both of the influencing machines of war and of psychoanalytic politics. The paper was not translated and published in English until 1933, when Dorian Feigenbaum, another World War I veteran, put it in the *Psychoanalytic Quarterly*.

My interest in Tausk is part of a personal and now decade-long fascination with a set of psychoanalytic figures converging around the First World War: Ferenczi (1928), Feigenbaum, Bion, and Tausk. I am convinced that their experience of that war, either as working psychiatrist (Ferenczi and Tausk) or as soldier (Bion) altered forever the way they talked and thought about mind, about embodiment, about body ego, about treatment, and about psychopathology. Freudian theory developed an ambivalent relation to trauma as part of the etiology of psychic dysfunction. But these psychoanalytic figures were unequivocal in placing trauma center stage. One can see, also, that the experience of treating veterans of that war and coming to understand shellshock was transformative of the work of treatment, in particular, leading to a deeper understanding of the eerie mixture of transference and countertransference in analytic dyads.

Tausk's paper is much less well known than it should be, at least in North America. In looking more closely into this paper, I want to pay attention to the question of machines and the question of influence, two elements in the paper's title, set off in quotation marks by the author. So I want to introduce a short historical note about machines. Tausk's paper came at a high point (1919) in what we can think of as the machine age in the Western world. Herbert Sussman, a Victorianist and cultural theorist, explores the implications of mechanization in a new book: *Victorian Technology: Invention, Innovation, and the Rise of the Victorian Machine* (2009). There, he argues that it is the machine that is the defining character of the Victorian world. In the century up to Tausk's paper, there are huge movements in the mechanization of transportation, of work, and of warfare. Sussman's thesis is that these fast-evolving and overwhelmingly fast apparatuses transformed consciousness and subjectivity as they transformed cultures, economics, and production. When industrial machinery was first produced and used, people spoke of the machine as driving work, of machines as almost animated beings powerfully commandeering and controlling the

318

human worker. Rabinbach (1990), writing of the evolution of these cultural and social processes into the early twentieth century, notes the mechanization of the worker, particularly the body, tested and streamlined and organized into synchrony with the machinery of the factory. Tausk's "influencing machine" carries the pathologies of the state and the society as well as the individual, in a muddle of historical force and psychic dynamisms.

Sussman recounts the occasion of the operation of the first railway train in England, during which one of the visiting dignitaries in attendance at this gala event stepped into the tracks and became the first railroad fatality. People were simply so unfamiliar with the speed of machinery. Note how momentous and oddly uncanny machinery was. How unfathomable and overwhelming, how excessive the speed of machines actually was for the human actor. Machines ran time. Think of the clock as an early machine. When clocks get a second hand (during industrialization), human relations to time, machines, and labor are forever altered. Work is no longer seasonal, or weather or light driven, but mechanized. And rationalized.

As the nineteenth century unspooled, machinery became the stuff of delusional symptoms. Fantastical delusions of machines were standard stuff in the writings about madmen in Bedlam, for example.[2] We can think of the influencing machine in many ways, as I will be suggesting, but at the outset I want you to think of this delusion as both social and intrapsychic. This is also a way of thinking about interpellation, to use another political concept (Althusser, 1971; Guralnik, 2011; Žižek, 1989) the call from the state, the other, the now very big Other that instantiates you into being. I am also, through this essay, thinking of the intersubjectivity of psychotic states. And of the intersect or interpenetration of madness and rationalized subjectivities.

Any patient, or any person, lives in a complex relation to state machinery. It renders us intelligible and captive. Complex freedoms and indentured loyalties attend on our encounter with the micro and macro machinery of culture, subculture, and organs of state or economic life. I think you will hear all this in the patient's material I will be discussing. Is she delusional, prescient, representing the unspeakability of trauma, trying to gain control, manage omnipotence, unearth the truth? Answer: all of the above.

The other term in Tausk's title I want us to attend to is "Influence," and to connect this concept, as Tausk develops it, to the question of covert operations, mind control, mimesis, and doubling (see Stein, 2010, on mind control). The aspect of the delusion that specifies influence may stand for excess itself, for the various processes, internal and personal, that overwhelm the subject and in so doing constitute him or her. We can draw on Stein's (2008) work on sexuality here, and on her particular use of Laplanche (1999). And also we can see how Tausk is trying to speak about fragmentation in the face of overwhelming trauma. The influencing machine in this sense stands for all manner of excess, with the delusion or distortion perhaps a frantic attempt at containment.

It is also worth noting that in the term "influencing" Tausk may be activating crucial and incendiary ideas about transference and countertransference, intersubjectivity, and the interpenetration of self and other, ideas that continue to dominate our psychoanalytic thinking about treatment.

Tausk begins the essay with the statement that this phenomenon of psychotic delusions of control from external machinery is rare. He has only one case, he says. But interestingly, as he progresses and describes the symptoms and their implications, everything begins to be spoken of in the plural.

> The patients are able to give only vague hints of its construction. It consists of boxes, cranks, levers, wheels, buttons, wires, batteries, and the like. Patients endeavor to discover the construction of the apparatus by means of their technical knowledge, and it appears that with the progressive popularization of the sciences, all the forces known to technology are utilized to explain the functioning of the apparatus.
>
> (Tausk, 1933, p. 521)

One person has expanded into multitudes. After his first apologetic remark that he is only dealing with one very rare variant, patients are always described in the plural. I think he begins in a diffident tone and then, perhaps outside his own awareness, a host of others (soldiers, I would say) burst into the discourse. As with Bion and Ferenczi, the war looms as the ultimate influencing machine.

Tausk wants to move from the generic to the specific. He notes that the psychiatry of his day dealt in generality, and in this essay he has the explicit agenda to move the psychoanalytic forms of inquiry with their specificity of meaning into this more usually psychiatric attention to psychosis and primitive mental states. It is thus an early and important attempt to give a dynamic explanation for psychotic states which, he clearly thought, had become delusions embodied and externalized as aspects of mechanization.

The Machine's character: It is mystical. It is odd and enigmatic and at the same time full of everyday simple details: levers, buttons, and gadgets in a system of mystery and confusion.

What does the machine do?

It makes people see things.
It controls what one thinks and feels.
It persecutes the body and mind, simultaneously draining and flooding.
It manages all of sexuality, all of the motoric life of the person.
In every domain of functioning, machine trumps human, combining strange brittle parts with fluids and stinking ghastly substances.

These symptoms begin in muddle and uncertainty. The machine resolves everything. But the person remains in a state of inner estrangement. The influencing machine is a solution, a delusion that resolves and organizes terrible uncertainty.

Tausk has many interesting speculations on the influencing machine as symptom of psychotic process. He considers it in relation to the unconscious, to problems in development, and in relation to identification.

He has some proto ideas about identification with the aggressor in this regard, seeing the construction of the symptom as an externalization, a creation of an evil and ruinous figure/machine, which the individual then identifies with. Again, I see the impact of trauma work on Tausk (and Ferenczi, as well) in seeing the intersubjective aspects of mental functioning, the enmeshment and co-construction of individual and world.[3]

Tausk finds the processes of projection and self-estrangement in the genesis of the Influencing Machine. The creation of a machine, run by enemies, is a kind of projective identification in which the projections have become "not me" but then "sort of" me.

In some cases it may be stated with certainty, and in others with strong probability, that the sense of persecution originates from the sensations of change accompanied by a sense of estrangement. These feelings of persecution are ascribed to a foreign, personal interference, "suggestion", or "telepathic influence". In other

321

cases, the ideas of persecution or influence may be seen entering into the construction of an influencing apparatus. It is necessary to assume, therefore, that the influencing apparatus represents the terminal stage in the evolution of the symptom, which started with simple sensations of change.

(Tausk, 1933, p. 523)

He notices the mix of uncertainty–obscurity on one hand and the highly specific creation of machinery on the other. The mind is in ruins and the mind is in overdrive, an apt description of my patient. Drawing on the crucial ideas of libido theory, Tausk links the creation of the machine as a reaction to sexualities – normative or not. The machine is a kind of giant genital: bisexual, penetrating, enigmatic.

Tausk has some ideas about this that are both very classically Freudian and very object relational, seeing the problematic in this delusion as emerging from periods of infant or child enmeshment. He notes the psychotic use of omnipotence alongside regression. The machine merges into awareness from early preverbal primitive states. The mind is an exceedingly complex place for Tausk. And the body too. The influencing machine is constructed out of the fantasy of one's body, and of its organs. The machine screens the inside of the patient's mind and body, suggesting a fascinating precursor to x-ray machines and to machine invasions inside the body carapace.

The influencing machine, Tausk says, is an attempt at "self-cure," a way to forestall anxiety. One of the most interesting and I would say innovative elements in the essay is his use of splitting and projection to think with complexity about the difference between object finding and object choosing (think of Winnicott [1969] on the use of an object). The psychotic mechanism emerges from a state or developmental position in which the child has not yet fully located his own body. So externality and internality are not yet worked out, to use more modern, perhaps Loewaldian language. He struggles with making distinctions between what he calls innate and acquired narcissism. And he seems to be reaching for an idea that one might locate oneself via projection. He continues with this idea to another, namely that the production of the influencing machine symptom, estranged organs, and "psychic inventories" (his term) may become part of a communication, a representation. Tausk does not explore this idea, but we might think of the therapeutic implications of thinking of a symptom as a kind of signifier. This kind of thinking presages the idea of projective identification as a communication.

All this fascinating theorization is written down in 1919 by a very fragile man, living in a complex world, both professionally and socially. And he writes this essay in the wake of the chaos and fragmenting minds and bodies of the war in which he was healer, heroic rescuer, and victim. It is also impossible not to wonder how much these very unusual and speculative ideas about psychosis influenced subsequent generations of psychoanalysts working in the area of deep disturbance. One sees evocations and elaborations of many of these ideas in Bion, Rosenfeld, and others.

Clinical case: Emily and the computer as a site for contamination

Emily is brilliant, lovely, and in acute struggles about many matters, personal, intellectual and social. In the beginning of treatment, she cycled madly between entitlement and self-loathing. Her dissociative but often oddly hypomanic style could crash into deep sadness if she had just a nanosecond of reflection. At one level she lived a twentysomething life set amid cell phones, Skype, Facebook, and late-night partying. At another level, she was in free fall. Only her work and school-based projects really anchored her and these, interestingly, she has always done with nonmechanical and hand-crafted tools. No electronics enter and influence the work that she feels defines her and could save her.

I found that rethinking Emily's history in the light of Tausk's essay made me mindful of her developmental struggles, the mix of precocity and strangely fused and annealed[4] identifications in her early relationships, the mixture of invasion and absence or misuse in many crucial relational dynamics. Through Tausk's text I am also very mindful of the potent way high levels of disturbance invaded Emily's organic being and the mechanical extensions that came to dominate her.

In the three years of treatment there have been a number of advances. About these advances and gains, I felt always a mix of relief and worry. What really could be counted on? In my repeated query, I feel my countertransference as an identification with Emily's own sense of other people's unsteady presence. Emily took up school again, with many mixed motives and results, alternately, curious, related, chaotic, and disdainful. Almost reluctantly, she found herself liking the structure, even spending a semester on the Dean's list, but also often alienated and adrift. She was slowly trying to tolerate genuinely succeeding, wary of the machinery of acceptance and its excitements. Grandiosity was giving way to genuine integration of strengths, yet she also maintained a strangely blind eye to envies – her own and others. Friendships and relationships were tumultuous and filled with conflict.

Where was I in this? I am sometimes confused and sometimes clear. Emily had a bond with me that was genuine, but also it was frayed, often lived as a kind of performance, and often put to the test. In truth, I must be and have been loved and feared, hated, and manipulated. I am the new object with whom she can sometimes have a "reverie," something she knows to be a difficult achievement. Of course, I am also an old object, well meaning but swamped by the swirling traumas of her childhood. My reliability, even at a kind of animal, simple level, doglike even, gave some structure. But my words or my ideas were not always of use or internalizable.

What did happen when she was little? Where is truth, accusation, envious destruction, and grievance? She needs, she longs for a mechanism for revelation, accountability, reconciliation perhaps. The goal is to produce a scene in which witnesses and testimony will appear and finally she will know the truth. But which truth? I see Emily's struggle in this regard as a complex multi-temporal experience in which witnessing is sought for ambiguous and underrepresented or misrepresented experiences, sometimes in more than one generation. Drawing on Gerson's account of witnessing to aid in the creating of presence and memory, I see Emily as carrying unwitnessable experience, both in her own early history and in the parts of her family history when historical trauma dominated individual lives and then, as Davoine and Gerson write, that trauma was psychotically disavowed.

Still within this complex relational matrix, things moved. Emily's cutting stopped, became unimaginable, interestingly. Drug use and alcohol stopped and started and mostly stopped. Certain rhythms arose in the treatment: insight flashing in then an almost stuporous, languorous, depressive state falls over her. Her words are wonderful, defensive, jewel-like, weapon-like. But knowing or feeling something authentic is alarming and saddening. Dissociation coming and going like waves in sessions. Slow, slow progress.

324

But the scene that opens initially via a cell phone is familiar and more ominous. Uncanny. There have been many contrivances and crises orchestrated over several decades in which Emily will try and get her parents to unite to save her so that in the union, something will be repaired and magically restored, through her heroic efforts. But even more crucially, in this crafted scene of reunion, something will be finally learned. Was there abuse in her childhood? Was there neglect and hatred under the many excesses of her household? Where is truth, accusation, envious destruction, grievance? She needs, longs for a mechanism for revelation, accountability, reconciliation perhaps. The goal is to produce a scene in which witnesses and testimony will appear and finally she will know the truth. But which truth? And why does this never work?

Yet the terrifying influencing machine that heaves into view catches both me and Emily's psychiatrist, with whom I am closely at work, really off guard. Enigma turns into horror and obsession. Our shared surprise remains one of my dilemmas. How had I been rendered the unknowing witness? How had I become one of Gerson's failing witnesses? What had blinded me? What identifications of mine or Emily's was I caught up in?

What now emerged, first in fuzzy and somewhat confused form, and then clearer and clearer, with more definition and passion, was Emily's sharp conviction that someone had invaded her apartment, that she might have, yes, really she had been drugged and assaulted, evidence was in the machinery and on a screen.

Emily, now the determined detective, was amassing evidence, a file, many files, hundreds of pages of notation, strips of computer code holding the key to everything. Emily imagines that the perps are some shadowy figures mostly available to her, or torturing her, via Facebook. As Facebook becomes the object of paranoia, fears of hacking and altering skyrocket, and we enter the world of double agents, mimesis, mind control. The hacking is intended, Emily feels, to make her crazy and in that regard, as Tausk's many examples of influencing machine indicate, the machine succeeds. As the machine takes over, the ghost and machine co-mingle in one terrible episode where surveillance tapes running while she sleeps record a door opening and enigmatic shadows. Sent off for analyses, the tapes show nothing. Ghostly forms are stand-ins, doubles, absences. Identity is fragmenting in much the way Tausk describes. Helpers could be agents or dangerous. Interestingly, I was not overtly a target of

325

paranoia, not an agent of the machine, but often I was functioning as an indifferent or helpless witness.

I certainly came to feel that Emily and I were tied together at the mercy of the influencing machine of madness and delusion. Something was washing over her and us that no one could get a purchase on. Sometimes in a session we could reach the quieter places of reverie. But only momentarily. The high technology of medicine seemed similarly awash, and mostly drugs seemed like stopgap, inadequate measures. The influencing machines had both produced and eaten meaning. I begin to fear Emily, fearing my phones, her madness. How can I fight this machinery? How have I contributed to it?

As these scenes and demands escalated I felt caught in a repetition. I could not calm or settle Emily's desperation to know. Addressing the meaning I found in her passionate system was sometimes regulating but sometimes again cast me as the indifferent disengaged adult. Within my countertransference I have an intense experience, which I sometimes can convey to her, of being swept away, by history, by madness, by incomprehensibility. The Internet machine is infinite in its information base. One cannot get to the bottom. I interpret to her that with the Internet as she has cast it, there is no bottom, only the endless availability of danger, secret doubling, and attacks.

As I worked with Emily, over months, I realized that, even as I had been deeply engaged with Emily's care and survival, which seemed very much at stake, I had, at the same time, been very consumed by a novel I was reading. Whenever I thought about Emily – and she was deeply, if anxiously, held in my mind, which may have been helpful and certainly would have been part of the unconscious communication, alongside my despair and frustration – I also thought of this novel. It is a novel by the British writer, Sarah Waters (2009). Called *The Little Stranger*, it is the story of a young man who as a very little child enters a great English house, steals something from the décor of the house, grows up, becomes a doctor, and returns to the village of his childhood, drawn back by memories of and fascination with the great house and its inhabitants. He is the narrator, a man with no first name. He is only called Dr Faraday and, as the novel unfolds, he comes back to know and draw close to the inhabitants of the great house. As he does so, slowly all the members of this family die, including a dog. Slowly, the impassive voice of the narrator turns subtly into the oddly dissociated voice of the serial killer.

Why am I living in this novel? Thinking of Ogden's (2004) notion of the instructive reverie, I begin to pay attention to where my mind is drifting. I find myself searching the Internet (and I begin to feel like Emily) trying to see why no one but me thinks the novel's narrator is a serial killer. I know the murderer. Why is everyone else in the dark? I am becoming Emily.

But, more ominously, I worry and I think that I am the doctor Faraday, the little stranger, the analyst entering the great family house and everything is killed off. Faraday, who discovered electrical current, an icy murder machine. Am I a doctor who murders and cannot heal? Am I an envious one voyeuristically engaged in a world of celebrity and fascination?

There is one more element in this story that I know had become part of my countertransference worry. This worry is captured in the reverie about Dr Faraday. For a long while, there had been an aspect of Emily's history that had tugged at me, and when clinical material began to focus on tattoos and cutting, I begin to speak about intergenerational transmission. I see this as another site of machinery, of influencing machines invading the psyche from another generation. But as you can also see, I am also worrying about the influencing machinery of psychoanalysis, in particular from the side of the countertransference. Suggestion, as invasion, arises consciously and unconsciously from the analyst's side. I cannot quite shake the idea that I am the electrifying doctor Faraday. Or, perhaps more benignly, I fear that I am cast in the analytic frame not as witness but voyeur.

In thinking of Emily's desperate struggle to maintain life and meaning (even as she put everything at risk), I see her struggle through Gerson's and Tausk's filters. Around key and chronic events in her history and her childhood, Thirdness[5] was decidedly absent, replaced by perverse disavowal, literal absence, and staggering failures in mirroring and containing.

And of course there is the bidirectional impact of the patient on the doctors, with whom she felt alternately enraged with and desperate to nest in. It took months to quell and work on the experience of breakdown. Murderous rage in the patient was projected out into the state and its machinery. Emily came to know this from time to time. And still the influencing machine of technology, information, and family exerted its terrible pulls on Emily's mind. The influencing machines are both prescient and psychotic, part of the avant-garde and part of mania. And, inevitably,

327

doctors and analyst became a frightening and not always useful part of the state apparatus.

In regard to the ultimate difficulty in establishing Thirdness with Emily, I have had many thoughts. Was the focus on history premature, too much my issue and history, unmanageable for her? Are we also in the terrain of the dead mother, of a preoccupation with a figure (mother or father) lost to the present, rooted in the past and unfixable, but also un-leavable? As Rey (1988) suggests, either killing or saving the lost objects seems at once too close and too in conflict. The repair of internal objects, Rey felt, was part of the unconscious projects in all patients and in Emily, this need for the repair of others was often in conflict with her own needs.

Conclusion

Ghosts and machines continue their haunting. Recently, no doubt in the context of working on this paper, I dreamed that I was having a session with Emily and her mother and that I had found a colleague to take care of the mother. A remnant of my ghosts and Emily's.

Art and cultural historians chart the movement of the uncanny on through the concluding decades of the nineteenth century. The uncanny moves from the landscape to the machine (the factory, the war machine, the computer) and thence into the family, and finally penetrates into the heart of the individual, the unconscious. Tausk sends it back from the collapsing, traumatized mind of the individual out into the culture, the state, the machinery housing otherness. Relationally, we see the movement in both directions.

Attentive to Gerson's cautionary tale in regard to witnessing, I see Emily's crushing encounter with the machine as linked to the strange occlusions in her family of ghostly presences, operating in histories that remain invisible to her. I think this is one of the meanings of her determination, often very catastrophically expressed, to know the truth, to find out. This is the longing for the moral but also epistemological Third, making ghosts into ancestors. The absence of historical reality in her life and narrative leaves madness in its wake. And to link Gerson and Tausk in another way, Gerson is looking at the collapse of witnessing in the shadow of the terrible machinery of the Holocaust.

I present a treatment swamped and invaded by frightening distortions that remain imperfectly managed. There is also my battle with the machine, the battle of the analyst with the influencing machine of the family system engulfing the patient. But also I consider that I am part of the psychoanalytic influencing machine, joined up with the pharmaceutical machines, mechanizing minds and symptoms.

As I suggested at the beginning of this essay, Tausk was himself caught and undone in the potent influencing machine of psychoanalysis. The environment of competition and anxiety about conformity and originality haunted Tausk in the writing and presenting of this essay (Roazen, 1969). But I want to push this idea further – to see psychoanalysis as an aspect of state management, as a powerful institution both generative of and projection-ready for destructive and creative fantasies. Psychoanalysis, as theory of mind, of development, and of pathology, functions as an influencing machine, and as practitioners we live in a complex relation to its power and its machinery. We are more accustomed to thinking of the obvious links among pharmacology, corporate machinery, and social control.

What Tausk and Gerson's work adds, for me, to the relational attention to co-construction and intersubjectivity, is the dimension of history, of the powerful constituting force of history and apparatuses, both tiny and gigantic. And in thinking of multiplicity, I find the attention to ghostly figures, presences defined by absence, to be illuminating in considering both subjectivities within clinical dyads, caught in such deeply dangerous and dire circumstances.

It is these concerns about influencing machines as aspects of normal work and life that led me earlier in this chapter to propose the influencing machine as that aspect of interpellation by which individuals are constituted through an encounter with state machinery. Laplanche (1999) considers this in relation to sexuality as excess transcribed into psyche. Others (Guralnik, 2011; Guralnik and Simeon, 2010) chart the complex site of this interpellation as freedom and subjugation. Emily lives in this contradiction, avoiding becoming a functioning member of the machine and losing much in that project. Transference and countertransference workings, in this context, are lived out in ethical complexities. Freedom and regulation are matters of endless negotiation; the influencing machine the moment where paranoia takes over from the processes of social and self-regulation. But, as I reflect on Emily's terrible struggles and my own less endangered struggles to help her, I feel caught in an irresolvable conflict. Her fantasies of the influencing machines reflect a deep conscious and unconscious knowledge that she is swamped by history and by her life circumstances. I remain unsure which of us is Dr Faraday and which his victim. The sites of victim, witness, and perpetrator circulate without relief.

And finally, I would say of the deadly machinery of history that it is grandiose and a form of omnipotence to imagine mastering it. I indict my grandiosity in a determination to fight the machinery of madness and of family history, a grandiosity that I have argued underlies many analysts' ghost-driven projects of work and cure (Harris, 2009). Emily will perhaps always be threatened with vulnerability. Sometimes I fear that she seems to have ceded a victory to her traumatic and historic family origins. Or is she on her way through them to some new safer space? Certainly there has been significant relief in the experience of collective witnessing in a trauma group. Is there a hope for reprieve, or have I written and lived in a cautionary tale of ghosts and machines, phenomena of enormous power? Answer: All of the above.

Notes

1   I thank the members of that group: Galit Atlas-Koch, Michael Feldman, Heather Ferguson, Arthur Fox, Margery Kalb, and Susan Klebanoff.
2   The writings of an early doctor, John Haslam, reported the "ravings" of John Tilly Matthews, who believed a machine called an Air Loom controlled his mind and body and was part of a plot to overthrow the government. In the 1800s to say nothing of today, a paranoid reaction to the machinery of labor and war and commerce seems often prescient, not insane.
3   In writing of a patient's dream, Tausk describes a process of self-estrangement that we would surely term dissociative (cf. Bromberg). He does not have the terminology but he has the clinical observation: a woman describing a trauma in which she sees herself hovering near the ceiling, suspended above a frightening scene in which she is being injured.
4   I use this term in the sense Farhi (2010) employs it, to describe a relation not exactly of merger but of some hard-soldered link that resists differentiation.
5   Thirdness is a complex term, used in a variety of ways to describe experiences emergent from dyads. The appearance of or absence of Thirdness relates to containing experiences in large historical contexts or more intimate ones. Healthy or malignant, Thirdness is an alternative to dyadic life, holding a place for otherness, for history and for culture.

Bibliography

Abraham, N. and Torok, M. (1994) *The Shell and the Kernel*. Chicago, IL: University of Chicago Press.

Althusser, L. (1971) Ideology and ideological state apparatuses. In L. Althusser (ed.), *Lenin and Philosophy and other Essays* (pp. 127–170). New York: Monthly Review Press, 2001.

Benjamin, J. (1988) *The Bonds of Love: Psychoanalysis, Feminism, and the Problem of Domination*. New York: Pantheon.

Benjamin, J. (2004) Beyond doer and done to: An intersubjective view of thirdness. *Psychoanalytic Quarterly*, 73: 5–46.

Coates, S. W. and Moore, M. S. (1997) The complexity of early trauma: Representation and transformation. *Psychoanalytic Inquiry*, 17: 286–311.

Cooper, S. (2010) *Disturbances in the Field*. New York: Taylor & Francis.

Davoine, F. (2010) Casus belli. In A. Harris and S. Botticelli (eds.), *First Do No Harm* (pp. 201–222). New York: Taylor & Francis.

Davoine, F. and Gaudilliere, J. M. (2004) *History Beyond Trauma*. New York: Other Press.

Faimberg, H. (2004) *The Telescoping of Generations: Listening to the Narcissistic Links between Generations*. London: Karnac.

Falzeder, E. and Brabant, E. (1996) *The Correspondence of Sigmund Freud and Sándor Ferenczi, vol. 2, 1914–1919*. Cambridge, MA: The Belknap Press of Harvard University Press.

Farhi, N. (2010) The hands of the living God: "Finding the familiar in the unfamiliar." *Psychoanalytic Dialogues*, 20: 478–503.

Faust, D. G. (2008) *This Republic of Suffering: Death and the American Civil War*. New York: Knopf.

Ferenczi, S. (1928), Two types of war neurosis. In *Further Contributions to the Theory and Practice of Psychoanalysis* (pp. 124–141). New York: Brunner-Mazell, 1980.

Fonagy, P., Gergely, G., Jurist, E., Target, M. (2003), *Attachment, Mentalization, and the Regulation of the Self*. New York: Other Press.

Gampel, Y. (2000) Reflections on the prevalence of the uncanny in social violence. In A. C. G. M. Robben and M. M. Suarez-Orozco (eds.), *Cultures Under Siege: Collective Violence and Trauma* (pp. 48–69). Cambridge, UK: Cambridge University Press.

Gerson, S. (2009) When the third is dead: Memory, mourning, and witnessing in the aftermath of the Holocaust. *International Journal of Psychoanalysis*, 90: 1341–1357.

Guralnik, O. (2011) Interpellating grace. In M. Dimen (ed.), *With Culture in Mind: Psychoanalytic Stories* (pp. 123–128). New York: Taylor & Francis.

331

Guralnik, O. and Simeon, D. (2010) Depersonalization: Standing in the spaces between recognition and interpellation. *Psychoanalytic Dialogues*, 20: 400–416.

Harris, A. (2009) You must remember this. *Psychoanalytic Dialogues*, 19(1): 2–21.

Laplanche, J. (1999) *Essays on Otherness*. London: Routledge.

Meszaros, J. (1985) Ferenczi's pre-analytic world. In Aron, L. and Harris, A. (eds.), *The Legacy of Sándor Ferenczi* (pp. 41–52). Hillsdale, NJ: The Analytic Press, 1993.

Ogden, T. (2004) The analytic third: Implications for psychoanalytic theory and technique. *Psychoanalytic Quarterly*, 73: 167–196.

Puget, J. (2006) The use of the past and the present in the clinical setting. *International Journal of Psychoanalysis*, 87: 1691–1707.

Rabinbach, A. (1990) *The Human Motor: Energy, Fatigue, and the Origins of Modernity*. New York: Basic Books.

Rey, J. H. (1988) That which patients bring to analysis. *International Journal of Psychoanalysis*, 69: 457–470.

Roazen, P. (1969) *Brother Animal: The story of Freud and Tausk*. New York: Knopf. Reprint New York: New York University Press, 1986.

Stein, R. (2008) The otherness of sexuality: Excess. *Journal of the American Psychoanalytic Association*, 56: 43–71.

Stein, R. (2010) Notes on mind control. In A. Harris and S. Botticelli (eds.), *First Do No Harm* (pp. 251–278). New York: Taylor & Francis.

Sussman, H. (2009) *Victorian Technology: Invention, Innovation, and the Rise of the Victorian Machine*. New York: Praeger.

Tausk, V. (1933) On the origin of the 'influencing machine' in schizophrenia. *Psychoanalytic Quarterly*, 2: 519–556. Original paper written 1919.

Waters, S. (2009) *The Little Stranger*. New York: Riverhead Books.

Winnicott, D. W. (1969) The use of an object. *International Journal of Psychoanalysis*, 50: 711–716.

Žižek, S. (1989) *The Sublime Object of Ideology*. London: Verso.

TRANSFERENCE
AND COUNTERTRANSFERENCE
WITH SOMATIC PATIENTS

Marilia Aisenstein

The question of the transference-countertransference in psychoanalytic treatments of patients suffering from somatic illnesses is both a crucial and difficult one. Thirty years ago, it was customary to read in the literature of the Paris School of Psychosomatics (École psychosomatique de Paris) that these patients did not form a "real transference." This was an affirmation that had taken on the status of a dogma and has never convinced me.

On the other hand, the countertransference, when faced with the disorganization of soma, was finally studied by Pierre Marty in a fundamental text published in 1952 in the *Revue française de psychanalyse*. This text was republished in 2010 by the *International Journal of Psychoanalysis* with an introduction by Claude Smadja and myself, and a remarkable commentary by Richard Gottlieb.

In this text entitled "The Narcissistic Difficulties Presented to the Observer by the Psychosomatic Problem," Pierre Marty (2010) from the outset adopts a perspective that is radically different from the existing psychosomatic models at the time. He sets out his hypothesis of an erasure of psychic work underpinned by a degradation of the libido, which henceforth regresses toward the somatic.

"Psychosomatics," he writes, "is not merely a hyphenated compound word or concept; it is the study of an evolution centred on a long moment of which the limits are indefinite." Its study is centered on psychosomatic investigation and on Freudian metapsychology. It introduces new parameters: that of the countertransference, "the narcissistic difficulties of the observer," and that of the process, "a long moment of which the limits are indefinite" (p. 344).

While this text is founded on psychosomatic investigation, it nonetheless tackles the philosophical and epistemological question in more detail than the clinical issues. It presents Marty's thoughts on the countertransference of the psychosomatician faced with somatic illness as a process involving the destruction of the body. He shows that certain particularities of the mental functioning of the patient suffering from an organic illness have the effect of modifying the countertransference of the psychoanalyst–psychosomatician.

A twofold identificatory process develops in the latter: on the one hand, he experiences personally, through identification with his patient, the fragmentation of his body and the alteration of his image; and, on the other, he is subjected to a movement of identification on the patient's part that attacks the quality of the psychoanalyst as object, and thus undermines his sense of alterity or otherness. What Marty describes is a form of primary narcissistic identification in which the subject projects himself, partly or completely, into the object, implying a psychical confusion with the object. This mechanism, defined here as a "difficulty" in the encounter with the somatizing patient, seems to me, in view of the self-destructive behavior of the latter, to be similar to projective identification. These complex and varied identificatory movements contribute to increasing the narcissistic difficulties of the psychoanalyst–psychosomatician faced with psychosomatic facts and the ill patient.

In our introduction to the text for the *IJPA*, we pointed out that although the French translation of Klein's 1955 "On Identification" only appeared in 1958, Melanie Klein had been invited in 1950 to the Paris Society by its then president, Sacha Nacht, and it is fair to assume that Marty was present at this meeting. Though it dates back 60 years, this article remains amazingly modern and is one of the only texts to address so clearly the specific difficulties of the analyst's countertransference when faced with the sick body and with the vital danger that we sometimes encounter with these patients.

Transference and countertransference are indissociable; I would even go as far as to contend, like others, among them Jacques Lacan, that it is one and the same phenomenon.

Nevertheless, I shall begin by speaking about the counter-transference, which does not mean, however, that I attribute any form of precession to the countertransference as Michel Neyraut (1974) has proposed in France.

Freud and the countertransference

In the German language, "countertransference" is written *Gegenübertragung* – the prefix *gegen* means both "counter" (opposed) and also "against" ("very close to"), as in "I was leaning against you"; the same double meaning of the word also exists in French with *contre*, but this is not the case in English; and I think this is a pity because the *counter of the transference* does not only signify opposition or reaction, but also *being very close to* the transference, a reflection of the transference. Rather than being a repercussion of the transference, what was called countertransference may be considered as a co-transference. Lacan expresses this very clearly in his *Seminar XI*:

> The countertransference is a phenomenon in which subject and psycho-analyst are both included. To divide it in terms of transference and countertransference—however bold, however confident what is said on this theme may be—is never more than a way of avoiding the essence of the matter.
>
> (Lacan, 1979, p. 231)

The term "countertransference" comes from Freud himself, without it being clear which of the two meanings of *gegen* in German he is referring to. It was in a letter of June 1909 written to Jung about the Sabina Spielrein affair that the word "countertransference" appeared for the first time in his writings, between inverted commas. The affair was very embarrassing, which led him to think that it was really necessary to reflect on and write about the "countertransference," although this was something he never actually did. Originating in these circumstances, the notion of countertransference was marked from the outset by a certain ambivalence. Freud recognized the importance of it, as well as its dangerous character, but did not speak much about it and preferred only to mention it in meetings with his closest followers. Established discourse saw the countertransference as a technical difficulty of psychoanalysis that had to be recognized and "mastered."

It seems to me, however, that the text of 1914, "Observations on Transference-Love," could resemble the essay on countertransference that Freud never wrote. He ends by saying:

> The psychoanalyst knows that he is working with highly explosive forces and that he needs to proceed with as much caution and conscientiousness as a chemist. But when have chemists ever been forbidden, because of the danger, from handling explosive substances, which are indispensable, on account of their effect? ... No, in medical practice there will always be room for the '*ferrum*' and the '*ignis*' side by side ... we shall never be able to do without a strictly regular, undiluted psycho-analysis which is not afraid to handle the most dangerous mental impulses and to obtain mastery over them for the benefit of the patient.
>
> (Freud, 1914, pp. 170–171)

I would like to propose the idea here that though Freud never "officially" produced articles on the phenomenon of the countertransference, the latter never ceased to be a matter of concern to him, but under the cover of his interest, also very ambivalent, in what he called *thought-transference, thought-transmission*, or telepathy.

It is very interesting to note that it was also in June 1909, when Freud first referred to the countertransference, that he was preparing a trip to New York on which he had invited Ferenczi to accompany him. The trip was planned for the end of the summer, and was an opportunity for these two men, who shared a common interest in the psychical phenomena underlying the transmission of thought, to deepen their relations.

The correspondence of Freud and Ferenczi (1992) refers to *experiments carried out by Ferenczi and supervised by Freud*. Ferenczi consulted a soothsayeress in Berlin, Frau Seidler, and then a medium in Budapest, Frau Jelinek. The *consultations* with these two women were conducted with great seriousness and in a spirit of neutral "scientific" research. In order to sift out truth from falsehood Freud and Ferenczi set traps for the soothsayeresses (letters 72–75, August 11, 1909–October 11 1909; and 84–86, November 10–21, 1909). Though the letters of the two men are not solely devoted to thought-transmission or telepathy, the latter nonetheless takes up a large part of them right up until the end of 1909.

I do not want to go into this correspondence in detail here but, at any rate, Freud and Ferenczi came to the firm conclusion that wishes or unconscious formations active in the interlocutor could be reflected in the clairvoyant's mind in a state of passivity. *Thought transference definitely exists*: "If this cannot be proved, then one has to believe it—then it is not a ψ phenomenon, but rather a purely somatic one, certainly a novelty of the first rank. In the meantime, let us keep absolute silence about it" (Letter 75, October 11, 1909).

Freud had the feeling that he had put his finger on phenomena that were essential to understanding the analytic process, but also seemed disappointed at not being able to explain the mechanisms further (Granoff and Rey, 1983; Rolland, 2009).

Two elements emphasized by Freud seem important to me, even though he did not draw their consequences at the time: first, he describes a process of *formal regression* in the soothsayer, close to that of the dream, which goes from word-presentation to thing-presentation. Secondly, he insists on the *somatic quality of the phenomenon*.

All of this received no further mention for several years. We cannot, of course, overlook the context of the times: Freud sought to impose psychoanalysis as a scientific discipline, and he was afraid of being reproached for associating himself with magic and occultism. Some of his disciples, and particularly Jones, dissuaded him from pursuing this path.

It was necessary to wait until 1915 when, in part VI of "The Unconscious," "Communication Between the Two Systems," he writes:

> It is a very remarkable thing that the unconscious of one human being can react upon that of another, without passing through the conscious. This deserves closer investigation, especially with a view to finding out whether preconscious activity can be excluded as playing a part in it; but, descriptively speaking, the fact is incontestable.
>
> (Freud, 1915, p. 194)

In this same text, an earlier section, "Unconscious Emotions" (pp. 177–179) develops the idea that "to suppress the development of affect is the true aim of repression and ... its work is incomplete if this aim is not achieved" (p. 178). Freud explains that there are no unconscious affects:

> there are no unconscious affects as there are unconscious ideas. But there may very well be in the system *Ucs.* affective structures

337

which, like others, become conscious. The whole difference arises from the fact that ideas are cathexes—basically of memory-traces—whilst affects and emotions correspond to processes of discharge, the final manifestations of which are perceived as feelings.

(Freud, 1915, p. 178)

In a footnote a page later, he points out that: "Affectivity manifests itself essentially in motor (secretory and vasomotor) discharge resulting in an (internal) alteration of the subject's own body, without reference to the external world; motility, in actions designed to effect changes in the external world" (p. 179).

Freud's insistence on the bodily dimension of affect seems important to me not only as a psychosomatician, but also because it emphasizes the extent to which the actual presence of the bodies of the two protagonists in the treatment is essential in general, but especially with regard to the analysis of the countertransference.

The question of *thought-transference*, which is connected with that of *unconscious perception* (I shall speak about the latter further on) never ceased, in my view, to interest Freud, since he returned to it in 1922 with "Psychoanalysis and Telepathy," in 1922 with "Dreams and Telepathy," and finally, in 1933, in the thirtieth lecture of the *New Introductory Lectures*, "Dreams and Occultism." From these three articles, it appears that Freud had overcome his dread of tainting psychoanalysis with what is unscientific. He asserts that thought-transference can occur between two minds:

In my opinion it shows no great confidence in science if one does not think it capable of assimilating and working over whatever may perhaps turn out to be true in the assertions of occultists. And particularly so far as thought-transference is concerned, it seems actually to favour the extension of the scientific (or as our opponents say, the mechanistic) mode of thought to the mental phenomena which are so hard to lay hold of. The telepathic process is supposed to consist in a mental act in one person instigating the same mental act in another person. What lies between those two mental acts may easily be a physical process into which the mental one is transformed at one end and which is transformed back once more into the same mental one at the other end.

(Freud, 1933, p. 55)

It seems to me that if, after 1909, the countertransference is still not specifically referred to in Freud's writings, through his correspondence with Ferenczi, his article of 1915 on the "Unconscious," and his papers on telepathy, he laid down the bases of what, after D. W. Winnicott, Heinrich Racker, Paula Heimann, Margaret Little, Lucia Tower, and others, we today call "countertransference" – not as an artifact of the transference and an obstacle to be overcome by the psychoanalyst, but as a precious tool of the analytic process and an instrument of therapeutic action. I would say today that it is still the definition that Heimann (1950) gave of it in her Zurich paper in 1949 that remains the closest to my own.

My hypothesis is that if this is true in all analyses, it is even truer with "difficult patients" and, in particular, with "psychosomatic" patients.

Transference–countertransference in the field of psychosomatics

After "The Ego and the Id" (1923), Freud replaces the unconscious with the "id," which introduces important changes. The second topography gives an anthropomorphic view of an ego without limits, whose defensive operations are for the most part unconscious, at grips with the "id," described as a chaos full of energy coming from the drives, without organization or general willing, and open at its extremity on the somatic side. The subject is an unknown and unconscious psychic id, on the surface of which an ego is formed that is the portion of the id modified by influences from the external world – in other words, sensory perceptions from outside. While the unconscious of the first topography remains in the register of pleasure, the id, on the other hand, consists of contradictory instinctual impulses, including those of destruction and chaos. Now this change of orientation toward the economic implies a promotion of affect, which is a new feature in Freud's thought.

This modification of the accent, which is shifted from representation to affect, has considerable clinical implications. Indeed with certain patients, including but not exclusively somatic patients, the entire work of analysis will now be centered on gaining access to affects and on their metabolization. In analyses of psychoneuroses, the guiding thread that allows us to gain access to unconscious material is that of free association. In analytic work with non-neurotic patients, actual neuroses, borderline cases, and somatic patients, we are frequently faced with a lack of associativity. The patient's discourse is not, or is no longer, "alive"; psychic functioning can prove to be "mechanical" (*opératoire*) (Aisenstein, 2006, 2008; Aisenstein and Smadja, 2010) and affects are apparently absent. Psychic energy is not elaborated and manifests itself more through acts or, as I maintain, through soma. Neither resistances, nor offshoots of the repressed, nor compromise formations can be detected; it is as if there were no conflict between opposing psychic forces. Often, the only guiding thread is anxiety, or anxiety-affect as Freud calls it. An affect of unpleasure, anxiety is a flight from the libido of which it is at once an outcome and an alteration. I cannot enter here into the complex question of the relations between anxiety and the agencies, but will just say that the locus of anxiety, as well as of affect, is the preconscious, and, in Freud's thought after 1923, the ego. A rudiment of unconscious affect seeking to break though may thus appear, transformed into anxiety. The work of analytic therapy and the transference-countertransference interplay can qualify it and give it the status of real affect.

Clinical vignettes

Two brief clinical vignettes seem to me to illustrate this type of work.[1]

Mr A, a seriously hypertensive patient, whose mode of "mechanical" functioning was unmistakable and exemplary, was in the habit of telling me the facts and events of the week in chronological order. Affects and anxiety had never appeared in his discourse. After two years of work that was very trying for me, he arrived for his session one morning, sat down, looked at me, and then remained silent. He contorted himself like a terrified child. I asked him what was going on: "I'm afraid," he told me; so I asked: "Afraid, here, now? ... you are afraid of me?" "Yes," the patient replied; I feel that "you aren't the same, you are angry." Now that very morning I had woken up suddenly from a nightmare in which I had been in a mad state of anger. This furious anger, barely contained and poorly elaborated on awakening, had just been set aside. It was only from that point on that his recollections of feeling terrified as a child, abandoned to a psychotic and sadistic mother, began to come back to him.

Ms B is a young single woman, aged 40, without children; she suffers from extremely serious asthma, an illness that prevents her from working. Her psychic organization is typically borderline, but she functions for long periods in a mechanical mode (*mode opératoire*).

For months now she has needed to maintain constant eye contact with me, and launches either into factual descriptions of her life or into furious diatribes against the weather, the government, the social security, doctors, and so on.

One day, after complaining about her allergist, the secretary, and my silence, she began to describe at length a new and violent intercostal pain she had been having since the weekend: she had been diagnosed with a cracked rib due to her coughing fits and to strong doses of corticoids.

I then thought about a dear friend who had died from an embolism; she had not seen a doctor about the pain she was having, assuming – she herself was a doctor – that it must be a broken rib. I was overcome by powerful emotions of sadness. A few seconds later, my patient was fidgeting, breathing noisily, and started to have an asthma attack. She got up, as if to leave, and shouted at me: "There, it's all your fault … you've abandoned me."

I asked her to sit down again and then spoke to her at some length.

I said to her that she was right, I had been thinking about someone else whom she had made me think of, but that we needed to think together about her intolerance at not being able to control another person's mind completely.

At that point, the patient was able to breathe more normally and I proposed a construction to her, saying that it was probable that she was making me experience something from which she must have suffered in the distant past, namely, the feeling that her own mind was being invaded and controlled … She cried for the first time.

From the moment a third party and history was introduced, analytic work could begin.

In both cases, these are patients whose discourse is actual and factual. For both of them, there was a rare moment in which affect-anxiety appeared. These turned out to be fruitful moments in both these treatments, but it will be worth our while to examine the conditions under which they appeared.

In these two short examples, affect-anxiety could be qualified and then became the object of a construction or interpretation thanks to the transference-countertransference work. I am referring here to a broad understanding of the countertransference that includes the mental functioning and emotional state of the psychoanalyst in the session. But above all these clinical fragments show that there is transference, even if it is not a classical transference that can be interpreted as in a transference neurosis. Now, some of our patients who suffer from a somatic illness and who come for a consultation at the Institute of Psychosomatics, arrive "on prescription." They say that they are not interested in "psychical issues," nor in introspection; but, generally speaking, they continue to come, often for years. For a long time, I found this submission to the rule very enigmatic. The classical explanation, to the effect that they continue their treatment because, for them, it is "nonconflictual" has never convinced me. *I believe that they come and continue to do so because there exists within the human mind a "transference compulsion."* Small children fall in love with a doll, or a toy truck – now these are already transferences. The classical transference is the most developed form, but it includes transference onto language, and into language, and the first form of transference, namely, from the somatic to the psychic (I will explain this later with the help of an example). I would like to recall here the definition of the drive in "Instincts and Their Vicissitudes":

> an instinct appears to us as a concept on the frontier between the mental and the somatic, as the psychical representative of the stimuli originating from within the organism and reaching the mind, as a measure of the demand made upon the mind for work in consequence of its connection with the body.
>
> (Freud, 1915, pp. 121–122)

With respect to the transference, Freud adopted two successive theories. The first covers the period from 1895 (*Studies on Hysteria*) to 1920 ("Beyond the Pleasure Principle"); and the second, the period from 1920 up to the end of his work. The first has often been referred to as the "libidinal theory of the transference," a term I find somewhat outdated but which he explained clearly in 1912 in "The Dynamics of Transference." The motor of the transference is the constantly repeated need for instinctual satisfactions, and this occurs within the framework of the pleasure–unpleasure principle. The second was, in my opinion, present in germ as early as 1914 when he named it the compulsion to repeat, but it only took shape after 1920; it sees the transference as a fundamental tendency to repeat that is "beyond the pleasure principle." In the chapter of his book devoted to the transference, Maurice Bouvet writes:

> As the traumatic situation, or the experience responsible for the complex, has entailed unbearable tension, it can only be under the sign of the quest for pleasure that the subject transfers, but in conformity with an innate tendency to repetition.
>
> (Bouvet, 2007, p. 227)

These two conceptions of the transference do not contradict each other and can coexist; however, they have imposed themselves on the basis of different clinical experiences, since the clinical failures were what led Freud to rethink the opposition between the instinctual drives, topographical issues, anxiety, and masochism. There was one conviction, though, that Freud never revised at any point from 1895 to 1938: A "strange" phenomenon, the transference is the most powerful motive of the treatment: *the decisive part of the work depends on it. This striking phenomenon, a manifestation of the unconscious, is also the only tool for gaining access to it.* We may wonder, and some have done so,[2] why Freud never discussed this idea and what his reasons were for never calling it into question.

The short answer I would give today, but which perhaps needs to be nuanced, is as follows:

First period. All the clinical cases and the theoretical elaborations that Freud makes of them have as their reference or matrix the psychoneuroses of defense, which he was also to call the "transference neuroses," the principal model for which is hysteria. The work of analysis aims essentially at gaining access to latent material via mechanisms such as displacement and condensation. We are in the domain of representation and under the aegis of the pleasure principle.

The transference, a process whereby instinctual impulses and unconscious wishes are actualized on the object, is "classical"; it involves displacements of affect from one representation to another, then from one object to another. Transference manifestations are symbolic equivalents of unconscious desire and phantasies. The ideal model would be: the transferences organize themselves, the clinical neurosis becomes a transference neurosis, which leads to the elucidation of the infantile neurosis.

Second period. Freud is faced with clinical material in which negative narcissism, destructivity, action, and discharge were the predominant features; the transference is no longer "libidinal" and under the aegis of the pleasure–unpleasure principle, but under the aegis of pure repetition compulsion. So what is its texture? It is a compulsion, an appetite for the object that condenses a tendency to inertia with regulatory mechanisms designed to relieve instinctual tensions by breaking them down into smaller quantities. This type of transference *functions to my mind on the model of traumatic dreams*; it remains blind repetition for a long time, the sense of which will unfold later in the treatment.

I wonder if this type of transference should not be examined and taken into account at different levels or strata – transference of the somatic to the psychic, transference into language and then on to language (the fundamental rule requires somato-psychic experience to be transferred into words) – so that a transference can finally appear with displacements from one object to another, which will actualize the subject's history and thus permit real regression.

Now affect, a drive representative par excellence, is the only access to the id; but, first and foremost, it is the means for linking up these strata.

From what I understand by "levels or strata" of the transference, I am going to try to offer a clinical illustration by giving a detailed account of a session that took place in the fourth year of a patient's analysis.

Account of a session

Miss C had come for a consultation at the Paris Institute of Psychosomatics after a referral from her doctors. When she was 32, she had suffered from breast cancer; during the 18 months that followed her treatment, involving a mastectomy and chemotherapy, she had suffered two strokes. Miss C was a young, sportive-looking, fair-haired woman; she was 34 when she began face-to-face psychoanalytic therapy with me. She told me that she had come to see me "because she trusted her doctors, but she didn't believe in it; she felt she didn't have any problems, any anxieties, or depression." She said she didn't dwell on herself too much; she "didn't like thinking and preferred action." In fact, she was a professional sportswoman, and had no social or erotic life. She didn't try to make friends because she quickly felt "invaded" by the presence of other people. Her very ascetic life revolved around her training sessions, which exhausted her, though she had no complaints about that.

In view of her fear of intrusion, I proposed just one session a week to her to begin with.

Miss C accepted my proposal and did not manifest any scepticism, reticence, or mistrust. For a long time her discourse was very factual, without affect, and mechanical in style, but she soon seemed to enjoy coming, did not miss any sessions, and, of her own accord, asked for a second session. At the end of the first year, she was surprised that she was now dreaming so much. Her first dream was of *a snowy, white landscape; everything was still and icy, but the snow was not cold.* I pointed out that there was no one in the dream. Yes, it's "like a still life" she replied. I suggested that this dream might be understood as a picture of her emotional life: immobile, iced up. I added: but it isn't cold ... or hot? The patient was moved and said: "You know, when I was about 12, I lost the hot and the cold." As I was surprised by this unusual formulation, she explained that shortly after she had had her first periods, she had stopped being able to sense temperatures; she didn't burn herself with boiling water, didn't feel cold in winter, and so on. "It was like that."

I suggested to her that it was as if she had been *anaesthetized*. In the sessions that followed, I learned that before "the loss of the hot and the cold," her father had died accidentally. She now began to recall her childhood. Her mother was a hard and violent woman who used to "scream and hit her the whole time" (five years later I learned that the mother had virtually become a nymphomaniac, receiving her various lovers while locking her daughter in the kitchen).

Miss C had not forgotten anything, but she never thought about it. It was all "frozen, anaesthetized." It was not repression that was involved but rather a drastic suppression that was aimed at warding off affect, and it explained the "struggle against thinking," the discharge into action, and the exhausting physical exercise. From a psychosomatic point of view, the sequence that I have qualified as "somatic disorganization" (a cancer and two strokes) had followed a bad fracture that had immobilized her and deprived her of sport for more than six months, thereby barring all the usual paths of discharge.

A second period of analytic work also began with a dream. It was after the summer vacation, in the third year of the treatment, when she was coming three times a week, face-to-face.

At the beginning of the session she told me this dream:

Patient: *"I dreamt that I was falling asleep; I was fighting against an invasive and dangerous sleepiness; I succumbed, and a black veil was*

345

going to cover my head; I was afraid, and felt my brain was imprisoned as if in a net, it was going to be numb forever. Was it my stroke? Was it death? I struggled to wake up during the dream. Then I woke up for real.

"I was all clammy, and my heart was beating fast; I turned the light on, went to the toilet, and then drank some water ... strangely that calmed me down."

Analyst: "Because you could see that you were still alive, physically and psychically."

P: *"Oh, I have forgotten a bit of the dream: I managed to wake up, perhaps, because a man I didn't know entered the room and held out his hand to me; it was reassuring."*

A: As for me, I thought: a man she doesn't know; the opposite of a woman she knows, but who is absent because she's on vacation ...

I was caught up in network of associations: her strokes, the fear that aroused in me, the constant state of alert that I felt myself to be in with this patient, *Le voile noir* (The Black Veil), the title of a novel by Anny Dupérey;[3] and a very old Greek film in which Clytemnestra had Agamemnon entangled in a big cloth net while he was asleep in his bath, so she could kill him. I thought about the patient's first dream (the still life), which had seemed to me to depict her psychic functioning. I was struck by the idea: "it's the murder of a psyche."

After I had told her that she was alive, she recalled the fragment "a man I didn't know entered the room holding out his hand to me ... it was reassuring." In her short childhood nightmares, which always woke her up with a start, there was a disturbing unknown male figure.

This was why I was interested in the reversal: an unknown man and not a familiar woman. I found myself thinking again about the Greek film and the murderous expression of Clytemnestra, who ordered her lover, Aegisthus, to put the net around Agamemnon. In the whirlwind of my emotions, Clytemnestra seemed like my patient's mother. I told myself that I hated this woman and that I was afraid for my patient. I felt guilty about my vacation – and what if, instead of a dream, she had had another stroke? I thought about her father who had died in an accident; he was absent and had left her to this soul-murdering mother ... She spoke to me so little about her father that I could not imagine his face. The man in the dream *reminded me that she had no man in her life or in her head. That distressed me* ... Did I have sexuality enough in my mind with her?

At this point I noticed that Miss C was crying silently. Tears were running down her face. She said:

P: *"These strokes ... the idea of having a scar in the brain. It hurt so much. Just six months after the end of the chemotherapy, it was too much. I don't like to think about it."* She talked to me for the second time about her first stroke, but her narrative was very different now, it was full of affect.

A: She was in the process of recovering from her breast cancer. Now she was woken up by an invasive pain in the head, *"not a headache, but an unimaginable pain."* She wanted to get up but felt dizzy. She was transported to hospital. The diagnosis always remained vague except that the presence of a scar from recent bleeding was confirmed. She did not know, she didn't want to think about it, but *"it was worse than two cancers ... "*

I felt very weak, as if I were going to faint, and I thought that although she often played down her illnesses, she must have in her (which she was transmitting to me) an "experience of slipping away from life," of fainting, closely linked to the "anaesthesia" of affects but also to her experience of anaesthesias during her operations, repeated by the strokes.

I was in complete disarray and said to her: "A scar from bleeding in the brain makes me think of the blood of your first periods ... it was just after that there was an anaesthesia of hot and cold sensations ... and you are so afraid of the sleep induced by anaesthesia ... "

Miss C had understood very well; she sobbed and said to me: "*And all this time I thought that there was nothing going on in my head.*"

I have related the session of the dream of "the black veil" to show at what point we were in the process, but the session I want to report in detail occurred roughly a year later, toward the beginning of the fifth year.

With this session I would like to try to illustrate clinically what I mean by "levels or strata" of the transference.

The patient was still being followed by two hospital medical teams of neurologists and cardiologists. She had been advised to see a specialist in cardiac arrhythmias whom she did not know.

She told me in a light tone of voice that Professor R had asked her if she had had paroxysmal tachycardia for a long time. She had replied, "*Yes, since adolescence; how did you know that?*"

A: Totally shocked and fuming with anger inwardly, I said to her: *"Are you telling me that you've had paroxysmal tachycardia since adolescence and that you've been hiding it from me as well as your doctors?"*

P: *"Yes,"* Miss C replied, *"but I wasn't able to put it into words for myself ... at first I didn't hide it, and then, after, I didn't want to share this thing."*

I was shocked in view of the serious health risk that she was running like this, and I asked her to explain things more clearly.

I understood that when she had her first bouts of tachycardia she hadn't given it any thought. She simply experienced them and "liked it." Later, when she was questioned by her doctors, she suspected that she should've have spoken about it, but feared that they would be taken away from her.

Interested by her admission that she "liked it," I noticed that my own heart was beating faster, which I saw as being linked to my anger. I felt she had deceived me: she had hidden from me, even from me, the pleasure that she derived from a symptom that was reminiscent of the state of being in love.

I put this to her in the following way:

A: *"While for months you have been telling me that there is no man or woman in your life who makes your heart throb, you have been enjoying paroxysmal heart beats all by yourself? You are in love without addressing it to anyone ..."*

Dumbfounded, Miss C looked at me and burst out laughing: *"I would never have thought about it like that."* She seemed cheerful and it was only after a very long silence that, taking up the material again, I completed my interpretation by suggesting to her that she was now well over her "anaesthesia" and was hiding her heartbeats from me because they were perhaps addressed to me.

This session marked a turning-point in this fascinating treatment which lasted 8 years.

The strata of the transference:

I simply want to say that interpreting the transference is only possible here after a work of decomposition.

She can feel things in her body, but has no words. Then she has the words and can transform "this thing" into word- and thing-presentations.

It is only after the transposition into language that the space of polysemy (tachycardia / her heart beating with love) can open up; but the object to whom she can address these words is still lacking. Yet the displacement that defines the transference requires an object to make itself available.

Unconscious perception

Freud never explicitly elaborated a theory of unconscious perception; nevertheless, it exists in his work and underpins his theory of dreams. Without it, the whole of chapter VII of *The Interpretation of Dreams* would be strictly incomprehensible (Bollas, 2007, pp. 33–68). Consequently, it seems to me that part of the analyst's unconscious and preconscious countertransference consists of "counter-perceptions" to the aspects of his patient's transference that he knows least well. Similarly, some patients react violently to the slightest sign of emotion in the analyst. Here I fully agree with Lacan when he says that whatever name we give to the countertransference, it is the other side of the transference. The transference thus includes the subject and the psychoanalyst in a continuous unconscious flow.

Very recently, while I was worried about one of my relations, a female patient, who is psychotic but also suffers from insulin-dependent diabetes and from severe asthma, said to me at the beginning of a session: "A great sense of sadness came over me as soon as I came into the room; it's to do with illness and death ... I can't think about anything else." As I kept silent, she began to talk about the long illness of her grandfather, whom she had not spoken about before. It seemed obvious to me that she had noticed something that concerned me and that this was inevitably going to orient the material. I think it is necessary to accept that this will be the case, but that one should definitely not respond.

These phenomena that concern unconscious perception are situated at the heart of the countertransference and exist in every analysis. They are very discreet in classical analyses, where the process of putting things into words and the play of representations are favored by associations, but become very important in the technique of "more difficult" treatments. And this is because the transference is "libidinal," and also "beyond the pleasure principle"; but, above all, because the conversion of the psychic apparatus toward language, containing infinite metaphorical possibilities, cannot be taken for granted.

I think that with these borderline patients, whose psychic organization is not characterized by an oedipal achievement indicative of neurotic and elaborative capacities, receptivity to the unconscious of the other, and of the analyst, as if to the cathected object, is increased. This riddle of the sensibility of certain patients to the analyst's unconscious-preconscious system has tormented me for a long time. Pierre Marty remarked on it: "Be careful, their unconscious does not emit, but it receives," he used to say in supervisions. How is this clinical phenomenon to be understood?

In 1915, in "The Unconscious," section VI, Freud explains that the preconscious protects itself against the pressure of ideas (or presentations) by a countercathexis nourished by precisely that energy that is withdrawn from the ideas. In the two short examples related above of Mr A and Ms B, we witness a sudden movement of acting out in one, and a surge of anxiety in the other, in relation to an affective state of the analyst. In other words, there is unconscious perception in them of an affect in me. I would say that with Miss C there is an unconscious circulation consisting of perceptions between the two of us. But if the repressed idea or presentation remains in the unconscious as a real formation, the unconscious affect is just a "rudiment," charged with energy, which seeks to break through the barrier of the preconscious. In the same section, Freud studies the "communications between the two systems." Each passage from one system to another involves a change in the cathexis. This does not suffice, however, to explain the constant nature of primal repression. It is thus necessary to make the hypothesis of a process that makes the latter endure. Here Freud proposes the idea that the preconscious protects itself against the pressure of ideas thanks to countercathexis, which draws its energy from the source of the ideas. It is my contention that, in certain patients, this countercathexis is so drastic that it paralyzes the preconscious and isolates the unconscious. However, these same patients cathect the outside world, and they compulsively cathect the object–analyst. But here, in this first stage of intersubjective relations, this drastic countercathexis concerns the internal world, the endopsychic. On the other hand it has no effect on what originates in the cathected external object. If this notion of *unconscious perception*, which is of cardinal importance for me, is accepted, it could explain the hypersensitivity of these patients, and their acute perception of the other.

Conclusion

The return that I have made to Freud's texts concerning "thought-transference" is not to be attributed to some sort of idolatry that drives me to return systematically to Freud. On the other hand, I have always been intrigued by Freud's passionate and ambivalent interest in these questions, brought together in his work under the title of "telepathy." The latter raises the difficult question of "unconscious communication" that is at the heart of the modern view of countertransference as conceived of by its precursors, that is, essentially, Winnicott, Racker, and Paula Heimann. Unconscious perception, which I have spoken about a lot, has already been discussed with great subtlety by Christopher Bollas, and seems to me to be central in clinical practice with psychosomatic patients.

This is what I have tried to illustrate through the clinical examples of Mr A, Ms B, and Miss C. My practical experience with these patients, but also with borderline or psychotic patients, has taught me not to be afraid of my own emotional storms or somatic signs, and to try and make use of them, with them, and for them. This is not always without its dangers. Pierre Marty had already pointed out the inherent difficulties in this type of "narcissistic" identification with our ill patients, and with thoughts about bodily destruction: this can even lead to a physical malaise or a vacillating sense of identity in the analyst. But if they do not become the object of denial or rationalization, these very difficulties can be vehicles of meaning.

Far from being only an instrument in the process, the countertransference, or rather, what I would call today the "co-transference," is at the center of this "co-creation" by two psyches that constitutes a psychoanalytic treatment. I believe this to be true for all patients, but perhaps even more so for patients suffering from somatic illnesses.

Translated from the French by Andrew Weller.

Notes

1   These vignettes were published in "Les exigences de la représentation," *Revue française de psychanalyse*, December 2010, 73: 1367–1392.
2   See Sander M. Abend, "Freud: Transference and Therapeutic Action," *Psychoanalytic Quarterly*, 78(3): 871–892, 2009, with a discussion by Marilia Aisenstein.

3   Anny Dupérey is a well-known actress in France, who wrote a best seller
     about her amnesia of more than 20 years of an infantile trauma in which
     both her parents and her siblings died in a fire at their family home.

Bibliography

Aisenstein, M. (2006) The indissociable unity of psyche and soma.
    International Journal of Psychoanalysis, 87: 667–680.
Aisenstein, M. (2008) Beyond the dualism of psyche and soma. *Journal of the
    Academy of Psychoanalysis and Dynamic Psychiatry*, 36: 103–123.
Aisenstein, M. and Smadja, C. (2010) Conceptual framework from the Paris
    Psychosomatic School. *International Journal of Psychoanalysis*, 91: 621–640.
Bollas, C. (2007) *The Freudian Moment*. London: Karnac.
Bouvet, M. (2007) *La cure psychanalytique classique*. Paris: Presses Universitaires
    de France.
Freud, S. (1912) The dynamics of transference. *The Standard Edition of the
    Complete Psychological Works of Sigmund Freud*, J. Strachey (ed., trans.).
    London: Hogarth, vol. 12: 97–108.
Freud, S. (1914) Observations on transference-love. *SE* 12: 157–171.
Freud, S. (1915) The unconscious. *SE* 14: 159–209.
Freud, S. (1922) Dreams and telepathy. *SE* 18: 175–193.
Freud, S. (1922) Psychoanalysis and telepathy. *SE* 18: 175–193.
Freud, S. (1923) The ego and the id. *SE* 19: 12–66.
Freud, S. (1933) Dreams and occultism. In *New Introductory Lectures*. *SE* 22:
    31–57.
Freud, S. and Ferenczi, S. (1992) Letters 72–75, August 11–October 11,
    1909; letters 84–86, November 19–21, 1909. In E. Brabant, E. Falzeder,
    and P. Giamperi-Deutsch (eds.), P. T. Hoffer (trans.), *The Correspondence
    of Sigmund Freud and Sándor Ferenzci, vol. 1, 1908–1914*. Cambridge,
    MA: The Belknap Press of Harvard University Press.
Granoff, W. and Rey, J. M. (1983) *L'occulte objet de la pensée freudienne* (The
    occult object of Freudian thought). Paris: Presses Universitaires de France.
Heimann, P. (1950) On countertransference. *International Journal of.
    Psychoanalysis*, 31: 81–84.
Klein, M. (1955) On identification. In M. Klein, P. Heimann, S. Isaacs, and
    R. Money-Kyrle (eds.), *New Directions in Psycho-Analysis* (pp. 176–235).
    London: Tavistock; New York: Basic Books, 1955.
Lacan, J. (1979) *Seminar XI. The Four Fundamental Concepts of Psycho-
    Analysis*, J-A. Miller (ed.), A. Sheridan, (trans.). London: Hogarth Press
    and Institute of Psychoanalysis, 1977. In French: Lacan, J. (1973) *Le
    Séminaire de Jacques Lacan, Livre XI, 'Les quatre concepts fondamentaux de la
    psychanalyse.'* Paris: Seuil.

Marty, P. (2010) The narcissistic difficulties presented to the observer by the psychosomatic problem. *International Journal of Psychoanalysis*, 91(2): 343–370.

Neyraut, M. (1974) *Le transfert* (Transference). Paris: Presses Universitaires de France.

Rolland, J. C. (2009) Clinique et contretransfert (Clinical work and countertransference), *Libres Cahiers pour la Psychanalyse*, 20 (Autumn 2009): 167–183.

Index

acting out 45
actualization 187–8, 297
aerial view (of analysis) 132–3, 277
affectivity 337–8
aggressive feelings, within analytic
    relationship 18–26, 31–2, 71, 72,
    78
analysis: analytic dialogue 46–7,
    278–9; analytic history 225–6;
    end of (case histories) 113–19,
    265–7; presence of ghosts
    315–17; problems of reporting
    216; of symbolization 291
analysts: actualization 187–8;
    alienation of 277–8; blind spots
    6–7, 239, 252, 281, 284–5;
    demands of child analysis 9,
    189–93; dissociation 282–3;
    emotional demands upon 291–2;
    emotional response to patient
    236–8, 273–6; emotional
    responses, reviewed 90, 93–4,
    99; erotic feelings 31–2, 80, 81;
    filiation of 12–13, 50–1; as
    good/bad/new object 273–8,
    283–6, 324; habituation to
    transference 281–3; identification
    and somatic illnesses 222, 334;
    influence of own gender 33–4;

influence of the personal in
    countertransference 11–12, 52,
    341–2, 351; interpretation of
    analytic material 22–3, 142–3,
    144; interpretations beyond
    transference 134–42, 293–4,
    307; listening positions 64–5;
    maternal containing function 9,
    11, 160–2, 168–9; negativization
    77; objectivity/subjectivity 73–4;
    physical appearance (case history)
    261–5; prioritization of
    technique 280–1; psychic
    functioning 51–3; psychic
    presence 54–6; role 150–1,
    152–3, 169–71; transference to
    the patient 56–7; unmetabolized
    past 169–71; unmetabolized
    present external reality 6–7,
    170–1; see also analytic
    relationship
analytic attitude 145
analytic relationship: aggressive
    feelings 18–26, 31–2, 71, 72, 78;
    covenant between 203, 211–12;
    empathic identification 80, 83;
    here-and-now transference
    128–30, 143–4, 240; importance
    of 31, 46; interactive aspect 47,

95–7, 151, 198–200; intuitive communication 2–3, 4, 6, 236–8, 256–67; transference-countertransference unity 270–1
analytic third 74, 77, 203, 212, 217
annafreudian technique 183
anxiety-affect 340–2
attachment, positive 182–4
attention, suspended 82–4

Balint, A. and Balint, M. 95
Balint, Michael 54
Baranger, W. and Baranger M. 75–6
Bion, Wilfred: aim of analysis 127, 142, 198; on caesura 7, 215; containing function 13–14; on correct procedure 169; countertransference 10–11, 89; on Freud 200; infant development 205; theory of transformation 220; on thought 168; time in Los Angeles 206–7; on transference 127, 216–20
blind spots 6–7, 239, 252 n., 284–5, 2814
Borensztejn, C. 75–6
Bouvet, Maurice 343
breast-feeding 47
breasts: dependency (misconception) 106; relationship with 34, 205–8
Brenman-Pick, I. 97
Bromberg, Philip 297–8

Cabral, Alberto C. 73, 76, 77
caesura: and emotional turbulence model 224–32; use of term 223–4
Caper, R. 277
case histories, reviewed: Little Hans 97–101; Rat Man, the 92–7; Wolf Man, the 90–1

castration anxiety 26, 32
cathexes, of object 8, 30, 197, 338
child analysis: analyst's countertransference 190; challenges (case vignette) 192–3; demands on analyst 189–90; distinction play/enactment 187–9; infantile experiences 180–1; relationships with real parents 190–1; role-reversal 295–6; technical challenges (boundaries) 191–3
children: container-contained relations 186–7; intergenerational trauma 152–69, 171–3; play technique 181–2, 189–90, 295; projective identification 5, 183, 186–7; squiggle game (Winnicott) 154–60, 162–3, 164–5, 166–7, 169–70; three case vignettes 177–80; transference 182–6
Choisy, Maryse 59–61, 62–3
Chused, J. F. 183
communication: preverbal 3–4, 7, 240; telepathy 2–3, 335–9, 351; through phantasy enactment 188; unconscious to unconscious 82–3, 336–9; *see also* nonverbal communication
complementary countertransference 75, 80
complementary identification 53–4, 57–8, 64, 65
concepts: impact of new concept on existing interpretations 59–65; missing 57–8, 64, 65
concordant countertransference 75, 79–81
concordant identification 53, 80–1
conflict 33–4, 46–7
conscious affective manifestation 71

container-contained function: analyst for patient 160–2, 209–10; case history 244–5; of countertransference 11, 13–14, 210, 211; infant development 186–7, 199–200, 201, 203, 207–8; maternal containing function 11, 160–2, 168–9,

counter-resistance (of analysts) 6–7, 12, 53–4, 121; *see also* transference-countertransference surround

countertransference: actualization 187–8; as analyst's psychical activity 51–3; characteristics 89, 252; in child analysis 189–90, 247–8; in clinical practice (case histories) 2, 76–8, 81–2; containing function 11, 13–14, 210, 211; as exorcism 199–200, 201; impact of somatic illness 334; link with content of transference 19–22; nature of interpretation 101–2; negative 10, 19; as an obstacle 73; as positive force 10, 237–8, 339; a religious analogy 202–3; and self-analysis 55, 70, 71, 76, 78, 82, 252; surround 12; as technical instrument 9–10, 11, 18, 19–22, 72–3; transference-countertransference surround 12–13, 269–73; as transformation 107; unconscious aspect 71

countertransference position: analyst's psychic position 54–6, 72–3; containing function 56; defined 50, 51–3; Freud and Abraham Kardiner 61–2; Freud and Maryse Choisy 59–61, 62–3; impact as new concept 59–65; relation to listening position 51–3, 64–5

countertransference reactions: as guide for analytic treatment 19–22, 24–7; as indicators of "moving on" 23–4, 72; intensity of 23

Davoine, F. 317
death, as misconception 107
depressive position (infant) 199, 200, 203, 205, 208, 211
Dodds, E. R. 204
Dora (case study) 32
Duncan, Dennis 78–9

elaborative moments 77
emotional turbulence 217, 223–32
emotions 7, 198, 200, 212; *see also* aggressive feelings; guilt
empathy: analyst for patient 80, 279–80; as distinct from countertransference 11; importance of 23; subverbal 83
enactment: actualization 187–8; case history 244–5; child analysis 187–9; and countertransference 10, 77, 83, 89, 239; as distinct from projective counter-identification 75–6, 239; early transference 45; Freud's actions reviewed 91, 94–5, 99–101; nonverbal communication 261–5; object relationships 276–7; phantasy 188; as role reversal 291–2; through misconceptions 112, 120–1
erotic feelings (of analyst) 31–2, 80, 81
Etchegoyen, R. Horacio 71, 75, 79
evacuation 77, 186, 218
exorcism, transference as 199–200, 201, 202
extrasensorial communication 3, 335–9, 351

fantasies *see* phantasies
Feldman, M. 276–7, 281
female sexuality 32–3
Ferenczi, S. 292, 296, 336–7
field theory 75–6
filiation of analyst 12–13, 50–1
Freud, Anna 182, 183
Freud, Sigmund: Abraham
    Kardiner (testimony) 61–2;
    analyst's resistance 54–5; "blind
    spots" 6–7; on child
    psychoanalysis 181–2; concept of
    countertransference 10, 335–6;
    concept of transference 3, 30–2,
    46, 236, 342–4; female sexuality
    32–3; hysteric conversions 4;
    importance of culture 52; lack of
    religious instinct 200; Little Hans
    13, 32, 97–101, 180, 193;
    Maryse Choisy (testimony)
    59–61; neurotic responses 55–6;
    psychoanalytic technique 76;
    Rat Man, the 92–7, 102, 180;
    self-analysis 70–1; systems *Ucs.*
    and *Cs.* 210, 337–8; technical
    limitations (theoretical
    standpoint) 13, 32, 58–9;
    telepathy 335–9, 351; three
    masters of the ego 9; uncanny
    217; *unheimlich* 171; Wolf Man,
    the 90–1, 102, 180

Gedankenübertragung 3
Gegenübertragung 335
Gerson, Sam 314–17
ghosts (within analysis) 315–17
Gill, Merton 272
Giovacchini, Peter 297
Girard, René 202–3
Glover, Edward 64
Grinberg, L. 74–5
guilt: breast, relationship with
    207–8; expression though

dreams 206–7; infant-object
    relationship 198–9; within
    Oedipus complex 204–5

hallucinosis 8, 222–3
Heimann, Paula 55, 72, 237, 297
here-and-now transference 128–30,
    143–4, 240
hidden order: concept 196–7;
    "human sacrifice" 197, 198;
    within infant development
    207–8; Oedipus complex 204–5
Høglend, Per *et al* (2008, 2010)
    143
homosexuality: Freud's failure to
    interpret 32; transference and
    analyst's gender (case history)
    34–45
"human sacrifice" 197, 198, 201,
    204–5, 208

identification: complementary
    identification 53–4, 57–8, 64,
    65; concordant identification 53,
    80–1; *see also* projective
    identification
identity, transforming (case history)
    248–51
illusional moments 77
infant development: case example
    205–7; developmental stages
    207–8, 211–12, 240; dissociation
    of suffering to analyst 203–4,
    292–3, 294–6, 298–306; hidden
    orders within 198–9; and
    influencing machine 322; objects
    as victims 198, 207–8; paranoid-
    schizoid, depressive positions
    205; separation of conflict from
    transference 33–4, 46;
    transference of infantile neurosis
    45–6, 180–1, 182–4, 197,
    202–3, 209, 212, 343

influencing machine 318–28
intergenerational past: case history
153–69; influencing machine
327; within Oedipus complex
204–5; transmission 152–3,
171–3; and trauma 5–6, 315–17
interpellation 319, 329
interpretations: analyst-centered
122; as habituated 281–3;
patient-centered 121; responses
to 101–2; transference 142–3,
272; working within alternative
interpretations 162–6, 169–70
interventions: additional to here-
and-now transference 129–30,
132, 143–5, 162–6, 169–70; case
history, use of alternative
interventions 134–42; merits of
pedestrian interventions 131–4
intuitive reception 2, 10–11, 79

Jones, Ernest 32–3
Joseph, Betty 4, 188

K relationships 7, 143–5, 220–1
Kardiner, Abraham 61–2
Khan, Masud 297
King, Pearl 297
Klein, Melanie: infant development
47, 205; play technique 181–2;
projective identification 182–3,
186, 199, 237; unconscious
fantasy 222; use of
countertransference 239
Kleinian analysis 240, 270–1

Lacan, Jacques 32, 54–5, 79, 335
Laplanche, J. and Pontalis, J. B. 83
Lévi-Strauss, Claude 202
libido theory: Freud's development
of (Little Hans) 97–101; in
influencing machine 322;
libidinal bonds (case histories)

21–2, 24–5, 28 n.5; and pleasure
principle 242–4, 249
listening positions: aerial view (of
analysis) 132–3, 277; and
countertransference position
64–5; de-centered 51–3; and
psychic presence of analyst 54
Little, M. 96
Little Hans 13, 32, 97–101, 180,
193
loss and separation, use of
misconceptions 107, 108–20,
122

manic defenses 20–2
Mark of Cain 211
Marty, Pierre 333–4
maternal transference 33–4
mechanization 318–19; *see also*
influencing machine
Meltzer, D. 183–4, 199, 205
memory 150
misconceptions: background to
106–8; case history 109–11;
identifying 121–3; use for loss
and separation anxieties 107,
108–9, 111–20, 122
missing concepts: complementary
identification 57–8, 65;
countertransference as 88–9,
101–2
Money-Kyrle, R. 96, 106–7,
121–2, 123
Morales, E. 201
mothers: maternal breast 206–7;
maternal containing function 9,
11, 160–2, 168–9; maternal
transference 33–4, 37;
relationship with (case history)
301–4; as vessels for suffering
199, 200, 203, 208–9, 211–12

narcissistic pathologies 77, 83

narcissistic resistance 52, 60, 62–3
negative capabilities 56
negative transference: analytic
relationship 10, 283–4; child
analysis 182–3; as exorcism
198–200, 201; Freud's
interpretation 31, 93–4;
importance in interpretation
45–6; maternal (case history) 37
negativization 77
neuroses: from analysts' psyche 52;
and countertransference position
55–6, 57; modes of attention 83;
transference of infantile 45–6,
180–1, 182–4, 197, 202–3, 209,
212, 343
nonverbal communication: case
histories 2–3, 257–67;
codification 4, 5;
countertransference 336–9;
enactment 261–5; intersubjective
"ventriloquist" 210; role of 4, 5,
256–7, 267

O transformations 7, 216, 219–21
object: aggressive object relations
186; analyst as good/bad/new
object 273–8, 281, 283–6, 324;
countertransference and the
patient 23–4, 79, 80, 210; within
the influencing machine 322;
internalized object relations
270–1; psychic presence and
suitability of object 54;
psychoanalytic (Bion) 218–19;
and transference interpretation
143
object relational approaches 128
objectivation 145
obsessional patients 92
Oedipus complex 32–3, 57, 204–5,
242–3
Oelsner, R. 186–7

paranoid-schizoid, depressive
positions 205
paraverbal conflict 3–4, 45
parents: analyst in role of 295–6,
298–305; parental transference
33–4; sexual intercourse as
misconception 106–7; *see also*
mothers
pedestrian interventions 131–4
penis envy 32, 34
phantasies: enactment 188, 239,
244; external phantasy objects
277; masturbatory phantasies
(case history) 249–50; patient
projection 211, 222, 238, 291
play technique 181–2, 189–90, 295
positive attachment 182–3
prenatal psyche 7
preverbal trauma 290–1, 295
prey-predator instincts 201, 207–8
projective counter-identification
74–5, 121, 187
projective identification: analyst's
role 160–1; case histories 241–6;
child analysis 5, 183, 186–7;
compared to role-reversal 307
n.2; containing function (infants)
199, 208–9; directed object
relationship 276–7; and
enactment 75–6, 239; paranoid-
schizoid position 200; somatizing
patients 222, 334; and
subjectivity 74
projective transformations 222
psychic reality: acknowledging 106,
284–5; compulsion to transfer
8–9; transmission intergenerational
trauma 152–69, 171–3
psychoanalysis: aim of 106–7, 123,
127, 144–6; analyst and
transference process 273–6; child
psychoanalysis 180–1; as
influencing machine 328–9;

interactive aspect 95–7; and
memory 150; trauma in 318
psychoanalytic field 218–19
psychosomatics: case history 344–9;
projective identification 222,
334; transference-
countertransference 339–40
psychotic misrepresentation: case
histories 108–19; use of
mechanisms 119–20

Racker, Heinrich: complementary
identification 53;
countertransference as a tool 9–10,
11, 72–3, 237; countertransference
position 50; filiation, of analysts
(Argentina) 50–1; impact external
realities 169–70; types of
countertransference 75
Rat Man, the 92–7, 102, 180
Reik, T. 71, 82, 83
religious instincts 200–1
resistance: of analyst 274; narcissistic
52; overcoming 23–4; and training
analysis 54–5; transference as 8
reverie 186–7
rigid-motion transformations 222
role-reversal: analyst as traumatic
parent 291–2; case histories
298–306; child analysis 295–6;
compared to projective
identification 307 n.2;
dissociation infantile self 294–6;
enactment 291–2; history of
concept 296–8; patient/analyst 8
Roussillon, René 297

sadomasochism 208
Sandler, J. 187, 297
Sebek, Michel 317
second degree dilemmas 122
self-analysis 55, 70, 71, 76, 78, 82,
252

separation anxiety (case history)
108–19
social violence, impact on analysis
151–3, 171–2
somatic illness: case history 344–9;
lack of associativity 339–40;
transference in 333–4
spectral model 221
spiritism 315, 336–7
squiggle game (Winnicott) 154–60,
162–3, 164–5, 166–7, 169–70
Steiner, J. 240
subjectivity 74, 145, 219
supervision (of analyst): and analytic
relationship 12, 14, 52; case
history 240–52; inception 252
n.4; nonverbal communication
to patient (case history) 257–61;
presence of ghosts 315
suspended attention 82–4
Sussman, Herbert 318–19
symbolization (historical past) 78,
290–1, 293–4
systems *Ucs.* and *Cs.* 210, 337–8
Szpilka, Jaime 77

Tausk, Viktor 317–23
technique: idealization of 130–2;
influence on transference
interpretation 13–15; play
technique 181–2, 189–90, 295;
prioritization by analyst 280–1;
and transference interpretation
128–30
telepathy 2–3, 335–9, 351
temporality 221–3, 232 n.3, 294–5
theoretical positions: and
countertransference position 52;
effects on practice 78–9; and
missing concepts 57–8
thirdness 328, 330 n.5
thought transference 335–9
training analysis 52, 55, 236

transference: actualization 187–8;
alternative interpretations (case
history) 134–42, 162–6, 169–70;
analyst's habituation to 281–3;
case histories, reviewed 90,
92–3, 97–8; in children 182–6;
as compulsion 8–9, 342;
conceptions 4–5; creation of 7;
early transference 19, 45; Freud's
concept of 3, 30–2, 342–4;
interpretations 14, 142–3;
non-emergence of 291;
psychotic anxiety (case history)
109–11; a religious analogy
202–3; self to object 210; strata,
psychosomatic analysis (case
history) 344–9; through
countertransference position
51–2, 53; *see also* negative
transference
transference-countertransference: as
a hidden order 196–7;
highlighting significance of 272;
in psychosomatics 339–40; as
suffering 212; unity of 270–1
transference-countertransference
surround 12–13, 269–73; *see also*
counter-resistance (of analysts)

transformations (Bion) 216, 220–3
transgenerational trauma *see*
intergenerational past
trauma: impact on psychoanalysis
318; intergenerational past 5–6,
151–3, 171–3, 315–17; and
spiritism 315

Übertragung 3
uncanny 32, 171, 217, 315–16,
317–18, 328
unconscious: actualization 187–8;
Bion's theory of 218;
communication 82–3, 336–9;
countertransference as 71
unconscious knowledge 63–4
unconscious perception 349–51
unknown: containing anxiety of
56; emergence of 63, 223, 225;
transformation of 7, 216
unmetabolized past 5–6, 151–3,
171–3
Urtubey, Luisa de 71, 76

Winnicott, D.W. 73, 75, 95–6,
106–7, 142–3
witnessing 315, 324–5, 328
Wolf Man, the 90–1, 102, 180